THE EVOLUTION OF KEATS'S POETRY

VOLUME II

LONDON : HUMPHREY MILFORD

OXFORD UNIVERSITY PRESS

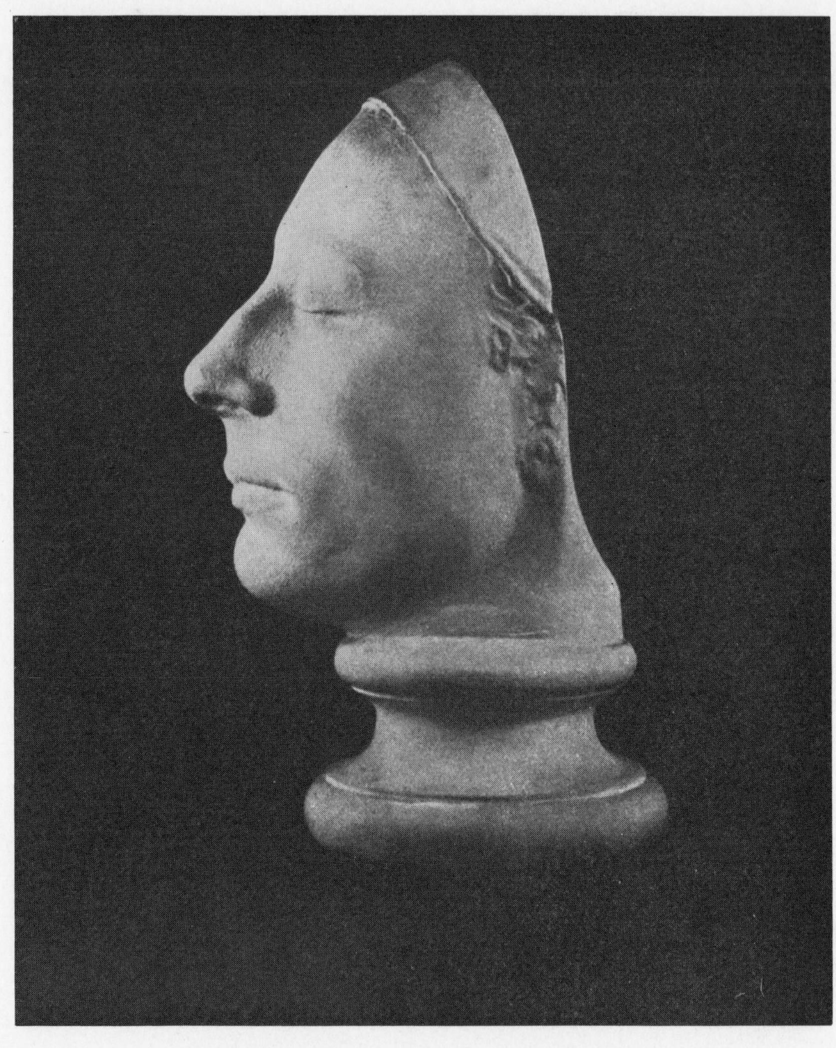

THE LIFE–MASK OF KEATS, PROBABLY MADE BY
BENJAMIN ROBERT HAYDON

Reproduced from a copy by permission of the Harvard College Library

THE EVOLUTION OF KEATS'S POETRY

BY

CLAUDE LEE FINNEY

VOLUME II

CAMBRIDGE, MASSACHUSETTS
HARVARD UNIVERSITY PRESS
1936

PRINTED AT THE HARVARD UNIVERSITY PRESS

CAMBRIDGE, MASS., U. S. A.

CONTENTS

Volume II

LIST OF ILLUSTRATIONS

Volume II

THE EVOLUTION OF KEATS'S POETRY

CHAPTER V

INTRODUCTION TO *THE FALL OF HYPERION*

I

BEFORE setting out on their pedestrian tour through the north of England into Scotland, Keats and Brown accompanied George and Georgiana Keats to Liverpool. The boat party took the coach from London on Monday, June 22, stopped for dinner at Redbourne, where they met Henry Stephens, and arrived in Liverpool on Tuesday evening. Without waiting for George and Georgiana Keats to embark on their boat, Keats and Brown left Liverpool Wednesday morning, taking a coach to Lancaster, where they intended to begin their tour.

On April 24, when Keats accepted Wordsworth's humanitarianism, he planned to retire from the world and study literature and philosophy. He thought, at first, of giving up his tour with Brown; but he decided that he could acquire as much knowledge by this tour as by studying Greek and reading Homer at home among his books. He could walk through the country, as Wordsworth had done, studying simple villagers and meditating upon ways of increasing their happiness. In the course of the tour, we shall find, he manifested a philanthropic interest in the peasants whom he observed. He could also absorb impressions of lakes, waterfalls, and mountains, which he had never seen, in the most beautiful country of England and Scotland. In July, when he was in the middle of his tour, he wrote Bailey:

> I should not have consented to myself these four Months tramping in the highlands but that I thought it would give me more experience, rub off more Prejudice, use [me] to more hardship, identify finer scenes[,] load me with grander Mountains, and strengthen more my reach in Poetry, than would stopping at home among Books, even though I should reach Homer.

The only books which Keats took with him on his tour were the three minute volumes of Cary's translation of Dante's *Divina Commedia*. Brown took a volume of Milton's poems. From *The Divine Comedy*, which Bailey persuaded him to read, Keats drew the idea of casting the humanitarian version of "Hyperion" into the form of a dream or vision.

On Thursday morning, June 25, Keats and Brown left Lancaster on the first stage of their pedestrian tour. On Friday they approached Windermere, the heart of Wordsworth's country. At a turn in the road, before they descended to the hamlet of Bowness, Brown [1] said, they caught their first sight of the lake. "How can I believe in that?" Keats exclaimed. "Surely it cannot be!" A little later when he saw the farther extremity of the lake, he thought it "more and more wonderfully beautiful." He had never seen lakes and mountains before, and he was unprepared for the impression which they made upon him.

I cannot describe [the Lake and Mountains of Winander, Keats wrote his brother Tom on June 26] — they surpass my expectation — beautiful water — shores and islands green to the marge — mountains all round up to the clouds. . . . I have an amazing partiality for mountains in the clouds [he added]. There is nothing in Devon like this, and Brown says there is nothing in Wales to be compared to it. . . .

The two views we have had of it [the lake] are of the most noble tenderness — they can never fade away — they make one forget the divisions of life; age, youth, poverty and riches; and refine one's sensual vision into a sort of north star which can never cease to be open lidded and stedfast over the wonders of the great Power.

Friday afternoon Keats and Brown walked from Bowness to Ambleside along the border of the lake. Saturday morning, before breakfast, they went to see the Ambleside waterfall —"the first waterfall I ever saw," Keats wrote his brother George.

We, I may say, fortunately, missed the direct path [he wrote his brother Tom], and after wandering a little, found it out by the noise — for, mark you, it is buried in trees, in the bottom of the valley — the stream itself is interesting throughout with "mazy error over pendant shades." Milton meant a smooth river — this is buffetting all the way on a rocky bed ever various — but the waterfall itself, which I came suddenly upon, gave me a pleasant twinge. First we stood a little below the head about half way down the first fall, buried deep in trees, and saw it streaming down two more descents to the depth of near fifty feet — then we went on a jut of rock nearly level with the tsecond [*sic*] fall-head, where the first fall was above us, and the third below our feet still — at the same time we saw that the water was divided by a sort of cataract island on whose other side burst out a glorious stream — then the thunder and the freshness. At the same time the different falls have as different characters; the first darting down the slate-rock like an arrow; the second spreading out like a fan — the third dashed into a mist — and the one on the other side of the rock a sort of mixture of all these. We afterwards moved away a space, and saw nearly the whole more mild, streaming silverly through the trees.

[1] Charles Brown, "Walks in the North during the Summer of 1818," *The Plymouth and Devonport Weekly Journal*, beginning with the issue of October 1, 1840 and stopping with the fourth installment.

In this description we see Keats in the process of identifying finer scenes in his mind, loading his mind with grander mountains, and strengthening more his reach in poetry. He had read descriptions and he had seen paintings of mountains and waterfalls, but he could not imagine their identity, their individual character, until he stood before them and received sensations directly from them.

> What astonishes me more than any thing [he said] is the tone, the coloring, the slate, the stone, the moss, the rock-weed; or, if I may so say, the intellect, the countenance of such places. The space, the magnitude of mountains and waterfalls are well imagined before one sees them; but this countenance or intellectual tone must surpass every imagination and defy any remembrance.

Contrasting the impression which mountains made upon him with that which they made upon Hazlitt, he said:

> I cannot think with Hazlitt that these scenes make man appear little. I never forgot my stature so completely — I live in the eye; and my imagination, surpassed, is at rest.

After this stirring experience of natural beauty, he restated that theory of the function of the poet which he had expressed in the second book of *Endymion*.

> I shall learn poetry here [he said] and shall henceforth write more than ever, for the abstract endeavor of being able to add a mite to that mass of beauty which is harvested from these grand materials, by the finest spirits, and put into etherial existence for the relish of one's fellows.

This description which I have quoted in part is the most elaborate description in Keats's letters. He made a distinction between his poetry and his prose, reserving description for his poetry.

> Let any of my friends see my letters [he wrote Tom] — they may not be interested in descriptions — descriptions are bad at all times — I did not intend to give you any; but how can I help it?

Keats looked forward to a short visit with Wordsworth as the climax of his tour of the lake country. He was forever alternating, we have seen, in his opinion of Wordsworth. When he arrived in Lancaster he found himself in the midst of a spirited contest between the Tories and the Whigs. Lord Brougham, the friend of Leigh Hunt, was challenging the supremacy of the tories in Westmorland. At Bowness, where he had dinner on June 26, Keats heard that Wordsworth was canvassing for the Lowthers, the leading Tory family of the county.

I enquired of the waiter for Wordsworth [Keats wrote his brother Tom] — he said he knew him, and that he had been here a few days ago, canvassing for the Lowthers. What think you of that — Wordsworth versus Brougham!! Sad — sad — sad — and yet the family has been his friend always. What can we say? We are now about seven miles from Rydale, and expect to see him to-morrow. You shall hear all about our visit.

Keats was irritated also by the conspicuous position of Wordsworth's house. After hearing that Wordsworth was canvassing for the Tory party, he was in a mood to find fault with him.

Lord Wordsworth [he wrote his brother Tom], instead of being in retirement, has himself and his house full in the thick of fashionable visitors quite convenient to be pointed at all the summer long.

On June 27, after he had seen the Ambleside waterfall, he called upon Wordsworth.

He was not at home [he wrote his brother George] nor was any Member of his family. I was much disappointed. I wrote a note for him and stuck it up over what I knew must be Miss Wordsworth's Portrait and set forth again. . . .

This letter which Keats addressed to his brother George at Liverpool was returned to him, for it arrived there after George's ship had departed. In the section of the letter dated June 27, Keats composed an *ex tempore* acrostic of Georgiana Augusta Keats's name —"on my word," he said, "the first and most likely the last [acrostic] I ever shall do." And in the section dated June 28, he composed another *ex tempore* poem *Sweet sweet is the greeting of eyes.* He copied the acrostic again in the letter which he wrote his brother George in September 1819. "I would not copy it," he said, "if I thought it would ever be seen by any but yourselves." He intended, he said in the former letter, "to be immortal in the best points and let all his Sins and peccadillos die away." The original letter containing these poems is in the Lowell Collection in the Harvard College Library.

After leaving Rydal Mount, Keats and Brown passed into Cumberland, visiting Thirlswater, Helvellyn, Derwent Water, and the Falls of Lodore.

The approach to Derwent Water [he wrote his brother Tom] surpassed Winandermere — it is richly wooded, and shut in with rich-toned Mountains.

The friends made a complete circuit of Derwent Water, a distance of ten miles, and saw the falls of Lodore on their way.

I had an easy climb among the streams, about the fragments of Rocks, and should have got I think to the summit, but unfortunately I was damped by slipping one leg into a squashy hole. There is no great body of water, but the accompaniment is delightful; for it oozes out from a cleft in perpendicular Rocks, all fledged with ash and other beautiful trees. It is a strange thing how they got there.

On the morning of June 29, Keats and Brown climbed to the top of Mount Skiddaw.

It promised all along to be fair, and we had fagged and tugged nearly to the top [Keats wrote his brother Tom], when, at half-past six, there came a Mist upon us, and shut out the view. We did not, however, lose anything by it: we were high enough without mist to see the coast of Scotland — the Irish Sea — the hills beyond Lancaster — and nearly all the large ones of Cumberland and Westmoreland, particularly Helvellyn and Scawfell. It grew colder and colder as we ascended, and we were glad, at about three parts of the way, to taste a little rum which the Guide brought with him, mixed, mind ye, with Mountain water. I took two glasses going and one returning. It is about six miles from where I am writing to the top. So we have walked ten miles before Breakfast to-day. We went up with two others, very good sort of fellows. All felt, on arising into the cold air, that same elevation which a cold bath gives one — I felt as if I were going to a Tournament.

On June 30 Keats and Brown walked from Mount Skiddaw to Ireby, the oldest market town in Cumberland; and on June 31 they walked from Ireby to Wigton and from Wigton to Carlisle. Having absorbed scenery, Keats became interested in people, and he studied the peasants whom he met from the angle of his new humanitarian philosophy. At Ireby he was greatly amused by a country dancing-school, in which the dancers "kickit and jumpit with mettle extraordinary, and whiskit, and friskit, and toed it, and go'd it, and twirl'd it, and whirl'd it, and stamped it, and sweated it, tattooing the floor like mad."

I was extremely gratified [he wrote his brother Tom] to think that, if I had pleasures they knew nothing of, they had also some into which I could not possibly enter. I hope I shall not return without having got the Highland fling. There was as fine a row of boys and girls as you ever saw; some beautiful faces, and one exquisite mouth. I never felt so near the glory of Patriotism, the glory of making by any means a country happier. This is what I like better than scenery. I fear our continued moving from place to place will prevent our becoming learned in village affairs: we are mere creatures of Rivers, Lakes, and Mountains.

On Wednesday, July 1, Keats and Brown entered Scotland, travelling by coach, for the first time on this tour, from Carlisle to Dumfries. At this point Keats's high spirits suffered a sudden depression, for he was completely exhausted in body and in mind. Within the last six days he had tramped 114 miles, walking around lakes, clambering about waterfalls, and climbing up mountains, his sensuous and mental faculties in a state of continuous excitement. After he had eaten dinner in Dumfries, he visited Burns's tomb and composed a sonnet.

> You will see by this sonnet that I am at Dumfries [he wrote to Tom]. We have dined in Scotland. Burns's tomb is in the Churchyard corner, not very much to my taste, though on a scale large enough to show they wanted to honour him. M[rs] Burns lives in this place; most likely we shall see her to-morrow. This sonnet I have written in a strange mood, half-asleep. I know not how it is, the Clouds, the Sky, the Houses, all seem anti-Grecian and anti-Charlemagnish.

The letter to his brother Tom containing this sonnet is known only in the imperfect transcript made by John Jeffrey for Lord Houghton.

> The Town, the churchyard, and the setting sun,
> The Clouds, the trees, the rounded hills all seem,
> Though beautiful, cold — strange — as in a dream,
> I dreamed long ago, now new begun.
> The short-liv'd, paly Summer is but won
> From Winter's ague, for one hour's gleam;
> Though sapphire-warm, their stars do never beam:
> All is cold Beauty; pain is never done:
> For who has mind to relish, Minos-wise,
> The Real of Beauty, free from that dead hue
> Sickly imagination and sick pride
> [Cast?] wan upon it! Burns! with honour due
> I have oft honour'd thee. Great shadow, hide
> Thy face; I sin against thy native skies.

Keats expressed in this sonnet a mood somewhat similar to that which Coleridge had expressed in *Dejection: an Ode*. He could see beauty in nature around him but he could not feel joy in it, for there was no joy in his soul. His imagination was not waning, like Coleridge's; but it was sickly, he said, casting a dead hue upon the beauty which he saw. As in the *Epistle to Reynolds*, he accused his imagination of intensifying his consciousness of the disagreeables of life:

> All is cold Beauty; pain is never done:
> For who has mind to relish, Minos-wise,
> The Real of Beauty, free from that dead hue
> Sickly imagination and sick pride
> [Cast?] wan upon it!

The phraseology of these verses, as de Sélincourt suggested, is reminiscent of Hamlet's soliloquy *To be or not to be* —

> Thus conscience does make cowards of us all;
> And thus the *native hue* of resolution
> Is *sicklied* o'er with the *pale cast* of thought. . . .

On Thursday morning, July 2, Keats and Brown visited the ruins of Lincluden College; and in the afternoon, after Keats's coat had been repaired, they walked to the village of Dalbeattie. Keats recovered his spirits in some measure after the delay in Dumfries. On July 3, before breakfast, they walked from Dalbeattie to Auchencairn, passing through the country of Meg Merrilies.

> For the most part [Brown wrote in his journal], our track lay through cornfields, or skirting small forests. I chatted half the way about Guy Mannering, for it happened that Keats had not then read that novel, and I enjoyed the recollection of the events as I described them in their own scenes. There was a little spot, close to our pathway, where, without a shadow of a doubt, old Meg Merrilies had often boiled her kettle, and, haply cooked a chicken. It was among fragments of rock, and brambles, and broom, and most tastefully ornamented with profusion of honeysuckle, wild roses and fox-glove, all in the very blush and fulness of blossom.[2]

At Auchencairn, while they were writing letters after breakfast, Brown discovered that Keats was composing a ballad about Meg Merrilies into his letter to his sister Fanny. Keats protested that the ballad was "a trifle"; but he copied it afterwards into a letter to his brother Tom and also into a letter to Dilke. He wrote his brother Tom:

> We are now in Meg Merrilies' country, and have, this morning, passed through some parts exactly suited to her. Kirk[c]udbright County is very beautiful, very wild, with craggy hills, somewhat in the Westmoreland fashion. We have come down from Dumfries to the seacost part of it. The following song you will have from Dilke, but perhaps you would like it here.

Two autograph manuscripts of the ballad have survived. The letter to Fanny Keats into which Keats composed the ballad is in the Pierpont Morgan Library; and the letter to Tom Keats into which Keats copied the ballad is, Miss Lowell [3] discovered, in the possession of James Freeman Clarke of Boston, Massachusetts, to whose grandfather George Keats gave it.

This ballad represents Keats's closest approach to the spirit and style of the mediaeval folk ballad. It is the only poem in which he was influenced, although indirectly, by Sir Walter Scott. In his literary group it was the fashion to scorn Scott's poems. He had read some of Scott's novels with discrimination, however; for, in a letter to his brothers on January 5, 1818, he observed:

> You ask me what degrees there are between Scott's Novels and those of Smollett. They appear to me to be quite distinct in every particular — more especially in their aim — Scott endeavours to throw so interesting and romantic a colouring into common and low Characters as to give them a touch of the

[2] *Ibid.* Quoted by Amy Lowell, Vol. II, p. 36.

[3] Amy Lowell, Vol. II, pp. 37–38.

Sublime — Smollett on the contrary pulls down and levels what with other Men would continue Romance. The Grand parts of Scott are within the reach of more Minds that [than] the finest humours in Humphrey Clincker. . . .

On Friday, July 3, after they had breakfast in Auchencairn, Keats and Brown walked to Kirkcudbright:

— since I scribbled the Song [(Meg Merrilies) Keats wrote his sister Fanny] we have walked through a beautiful Country to Kirk[c]udbright — at which place I will write you a song about myself —

There was a naughty Boy, etc.

My dear Fanny I am ashamed of writing you such stuff, nor would I if it were not for being tired after my day's walking, and ready to tumble into bed so fatigued that when I am asleep you might sew my nose to my great toe and trundle me round the town like a Hoop without waking me. . . .

Keats and Brown passed Saturday, July 4, in Kirkcudbright. "The country is very rich," Keats wrote his brother Tom, "very fine, and with a little of Devon." On Sunday, July 5, they walked through Newton Stewart and stopped for the night in Glenluce. On Monday, July 6, they set out for Stanraer, "in a burning sun, and had gone about six miles," Keats wrote Tom, "when the Mail overtook us: we got up, were at Port Patrick in a jiffey. . . ." That same day they took the daily packet from Port Patrick, Scotland, to Donaghadee, Ireland. They desired to visit the Giant's Causeway, and walked as far as Belfast; but, finding the distance greater than they had thought, they returned to Donaghadee. They passed altogether two nights and two days in Ireland.

Keats observed Irish peasants with the Messianic passion of the humanitarian; but, seeing their abject poverty, he despaired of their improvement.

On our walk in Ireland [he wrote his brother Tom], we had too much opportunity to see the worse than nakedness, the rags, the dirt and misery of the poor common Irish. A Scotch cottage, though in that sometimes the smoke has no exit but at the door, is a palace to an Irish one. We could observe that impetuosity in Man and Woman. We had the pleasure of finding our way through a Peat-bog, three miles long at least — dreary, flat, dank, black, and spongy — here and there were poor dirty Creatures, and a few strong men cutting or carting Peat. We heard on passing into Belfast through a most wretched suburb, that most disgusting of all noises, worse than the Bagpipes — the laugh of a monkey — the chatter of women — the scream of a Macaw — I mean the sound of the Shuttle. What a tremendous difficulty is the improvement of such people. I cannot conceive how a mind "*with child*" of philanthropy could grasp at its possibility — with me it is absolute despair.

Humanitarianism contributed, in one respect at least, to Keats's artistic development; it caused him to study men and women. The following passage reveals that he had an unexpected faculty for realistic description.

> On our return from Belfast [he wrote his brother Tom on July 9] we met a sedan — the Duchess of Dunghill. It is no laughing matter though. Imagine the worst dog-kennel you ever saw, placed upon two poles from a mouldy fencing. In such a wretched thing sat a squalid old woman, squat like an ape half-starved, from a scarcity of biscuit in its passage from Madagascar to the Cape, with a pipe in her mouth, and looking out with a round-eyed, skinny-lidded inanity; with a sort of horizontal idiotic movement of her head — squat and lean she sat, and puffed out the smoke, while two ragged, tattered girls carried her along. What a thing would be a history of her life and sensations. . . .

Keats made a conventional contrast between Irishmen and Scotsmen in the letter which he wrote his brother Tom on July 11. What he said of Irishmen, indeed, applies to Southern Irishmen, who are Celts, rather than to the Ulster Scots whom he saw in Ireland.

Keats saw much more deeply into Scottish character than into Irish. He was rather irritated by the self-complacency of the Scotsman, who, he said, "has made up his Mind with himself in a sort of snail shell wisdom." In the letter which he wrote his brother Tom on July 7, he discussed with penetrating insight the effect of the Scottish Kirk upon the character and the happiness of the Scottish people. He decided that the Kirk had done the Scottish people good by making them thrifty, but that it had done them harm by suppressing their natural instincts.

> These Kirk-men have done Scotland good. They have made men, women; old men, young men; old women, young women; boys, girls; and all infants careful — so that they are formed into regular Phalanges of savers and gainers. Such a thrifty army cannot fail to enrich their Country, and give it a greater appearance of Comfort than that of their [this?] poor rash [Irish] neighbourhood. These Kirk-men have done Scotland harm; they have banished puns, and laughing, and kissing, etc. (except in cases where the very danger and crime must make it very gustful). . . .

Burns's dissipation was provoked, he thought, by the restrictions which the Scottish Kirk imposed upon the natural instincts of the people.

> Burns — poor unfortunate fellow, his disposition was Southern — how sad it is when a luxurious imagination is obliged, in self-defence, to deaden its delicacy in vulgarity and in things attainable, that it may not have leisure to go mad after things which are not.

After speaking of Burns he continued:

> I have not sufficient reasoning faculty to settle the doctrine of thrift, as it is consistent with the dignity of human Society — with the happiness of Cottagers. All I can do is by plump contrasts; were the fingers made to squeeze a guinea or a

white hand? — were the lips made to hold a pen or a kiss? and yet in Cities man is shut out from his fellows if he is poor — the cottager must be very dirty, and very wretched, if she be not thrifty — the present state of society demands this, and this convinces me that the world is very young, and in a very ignorant state. We live in a barbarous age — I would sooner be a wild deer, than a girl under the dominion of the Kirk; and I would sooner be a wild hog, than be the occasion of a poor Creature's penance before those execrable elders.

Keats and Brown returned from Donaghadee, Ireland, to Port Patrick, Scotland, on Wednesday, July 8. They left Port Patrick on July 9, walked to Stanraer for breakfast, and stopped in Ballantrae for the night. That evening Keats composed a song in Scottish dialect and the next morning copied it into a letter to his brother Tom.

> The reason for my writing these lines [he said] was that Brown wanted to impose a Galloway song upon Dilke — but it won't do. The subject I got from meeting a wedding just as we came down into this place. . . .

H. B. Forman published the letter to Tom on July 10, containing this song, from the original manuscript which was in Haydon's Journal. The dialect of the song may not be authentic Scottish, but the spirit and the rhythm remind me of those of Burns's songs.

On Friday, July 10, Keats and Brown walked to Girvan, thirteen miles north of Ballantrae, and stopped there for the night in "comfortable quarters." Keats composed his sonnet *To Ailsa Rock* that evening, it seems, and copied it into his letter to his brother Tom.

> This is the only Sonnet of any worth I have of late written [he said] — I hope you will like it.

The letter to Tom Keats, containing the sonnet *To Ailsa Rock* together with the Galloway song, was published by H. B. Forman, we have seen, from the original manuscript which was in Haydon's Journal. The sonnet, which is rather heavy, is not nearly so vivid as Keats's prose description of Ailsa Rock. He caught his first sight of it on July 9 while he was walking from Cairn to Ballantrae. His "Road lay half way up the sides of a green mountainous shore, full of clefts of verdure and eternally varying — sometimes up sometimes down, and over little Bridges going across green chasms of moss, rock and trees — winding about every where." When he climbed to the top of the mountains he saw Ailsa Rock standing fifteen miles from the shore and rearing its head 940 feet above the sea.

> The effect of Ailsa with the peculiar perspective of the Sea in connection with the ground we stood on, and the misty rain then falling gave me a complete Idea of a deluge. Ailsa struck me very suddenly — really I was a little alarmed.

As he walked from Ballantrae to Girvan on the morning of July 10, Ailsa Rock towered beside him the whole way.

On Saturday, July 11, Keats and Brown walked from Girvan to Kirkoswald for breakfast and to Maybole for dinner. That afternoon, as they approached Ayr, the village in which Burns was born and reared, Keats was filled with high expectation.

> I am approaching Burns's Cottage very fast [he wrote Reynolds]. . . . One of the pleasantest means of annulling self is approaching such a shrine as the Cottage of Burns — we need not think of his misery — that is all gone — bad luck to it — I shall look upon it hereafter with unmixed pleasure as I do upon my Stratford on Avon day with Bailey.

Late in the afternoon, when he turned a corner in the road, he saw suddenly the full panorama of Burns's country.

> We were talking on different and indifferent things [he wrote Reynolds], when on a sudden we turned a corner upon the immediate Country of Ayr — the Sight was as rich as possible. I had no Conception that the native place of Burns was so beautiful — the Idea I had was more desolate, his "rigs of Barley" seemed always to me but a few strips of Green on a cold hill — O prejudice! it was rich as Devon — I endeavour'd to drink in the Prospect, that I might spin it out to you as the Silkworm makes silk from Mulber[r]y leaves — I cannot recollect it. Besides all the Beauty, there were the Mountains of Arran Isle, black and huge over the Sea. We came down upon every thing suddenly — there were in our way the "bonny Doon," with the Brig that Tam O'Shanter crossed, Kirk Alloway, Burns's Cottage, and then the Brigs of Ayr.

When he saw the black mountains of Arran, Keats wrote his brother Tom, he said to himself, "How is it they did not beckon Burns to some grand attempt at Epic[?]."

> The bonny Doon is the sweetest river I ever saw [he wrote his brother] — overhung with fine trees as far as we could see — We stood some time on the Brig across it, over which Tam o'Shanter fled — we took a pinch of snuff on the Key stone — then we proceeded to the "auld Kirk Alloway." As we were looking at it a Farmer pointed the spots where Mungo's Mither hang'd hersel' and "drunken Charlie brake's neck's bane." Then we proceeded to the Cottage he was born in — there was a board to that effect by the door side — it had the same effect as the same sort of memorial at Stratford on Avon.

The mood of exalted reverence in which Keats entered Burns's cottage was dashed by the keeper, a drunken blackguard, who told anecdotes of Burns's dissipation. Keats's reaction was bitter, for he was tired and irritable, having walked twenty-six miles that day.

> We went to the Cottage and took some Whiskey [he wrote Reynolds]. I wrote a sonnet for the mere sake of writing some lines under the Roof — they are so bad I cannot transcribe them. The Man at the Cottage was a great Bore with his Anecdotes — I hate the Rascal — his Life consists in fuz, fuzzy, fuzziest. He drinks glasses five for the Quarter and twelve for the hour — he

is a mahogany faced old Jackass who knew Burns. He ought to have been kicked for having spoken to him. He calls himself "a curious old Bitch" — but he is a flat old Dog — I sho^{d} like to employ Caliph Vatheck to kick him. O the flummery of a birth place! Cant! Cant! Cant! It is enough to give a spirit the guts-ache. Many a true word they say is spoken in jest — this may be because his Gab hindered my sublimity. The flat dog made me write a flat sonnet.

Keats revealed to Reynolds his keen insight into the relation of immediate experience, recollection of experience by ordinary men, and expression of experience by great poets.

I cannot write about scenery and visitings — Fancy is indeed less than a present palpable reality, but it is greater than remembrance — you would lift your eyes from Homer only to see close before you the real Isle of Tenedos — you would rather read Homer afterwards than remember yourself. One song of Burns's is of more worth to you than all I could think for a whole year in his native country.

His Misery [Keats added] is a dead weight upon the nimbleness of one's quill — I tried to forget it — to drink Toddy without any Care — to write a merry Sonnet — it wont do — he talked with Bitches — he drank with blackguards, he was miserable. We can see horribly clear in the works of such a Man his whole life, as if we were God's spies.

After visiting Burns's cottage, Keats wrote his brother Tom, "we walked into Ayr Town and before we went to Tea saw the new Brig and the Auld Brig and Wallace tower." He wrote his brother, as he had written Reynolds, that the sonnet which he composed in Burns's cottage was "so bad" he would not copy it, and he wrote Bailey on July 22 that it was "so wretched" he had destroyed it. Brown preserved a copy, it is probable; for Lord Houghton, to whom Brown gave his records of Keats, published it in 1848. D. G. Rossetti wrote H. B. Forman that the sonnet, "for all Keats says about it himself, is a fine thing." It does not reveal Keats's reactions in Burns's cottage so vividly, however, as the passages which I have quoted from his letters.

This mortal body of a thousand days
  Now fills, O Burns, a space in thine own room,
Where thou didst dream alone on budded bays,
  Happy and thoughtless of thy day of doom!
My pulse is warm with thine own Barley-bree,
  My head is light with pledging a great soul,
My eyes are wandering, and I cannot see,
  Fancy is dead and drunken at its goal;
Yet can I stamp my foot upon thy floor,
  Yet can I ope thy window-sash to find
The meadow thou hast tramped o'er and o'er,—
  Yet can I think of thee till thought is blind,—
Yet can I gulp a bumper to thy name,—
O smile among the shades, for this is fame!

On July 12 and 13 Keats and Brown walked to Glasgow by way of Kilmarnock and Kingswells. When they entered the city their queer appearance aroused considerable attention. Brown, writing Mr. Dilke senior, described himself as an odd figure, with a thick stick in his hand, a knapsack on his back, spectacles on his nose, a white hat, a tartan coat and trowsers, and a Highland plaid thrown over his shoulders. Keats wore a fur cap and a plaid and bore a knapsack on his shoulders.

We enter'd Glasgow last Evening [Keats wrote his brother Tom on July 14] under the most oppressive Stare a body could feel. When we had crossed the Bridge Brown look'd back and said its whole pop[ulation] had turned [out] to wonder at us — we came on till a drunken Man came up to me — I put him off with my Arm — he returned all up in Arms saying aloud that, "he had seen all foreigners bu-u-ut he never saw the like o' me." I was obliged to mention the word Officer and Police before he would desist.

On July 14, it seems, Keats and Brown set out for Loch Lomond. They walked along the banks of the Clyde to Dumbarton, turned north, and arrived at Tarbet on the north shore of the lake on the evening of July 15. A steamboat on Loch Lomond and barouches on the road beside the lake dashed Keats's romantic spirits.

— the Evening was beautiful nothing could surpass our fortune in the weather [he wrote his brother Tom] — yet was I worldly enough to wish for a fleet of chivalry Barges with Trumpets and Banners just to die away before me into that blue place among the mountains . . . [after drawing a sketch of the blue place among the mountains, he continued:] — the Water was a fine Blue silverd and the Mountains a dark purple the Sun setting aslant behind them — meantime the head of ben Lomond was covered with a rich Pink Cloud. . . .

Keats and Brown did not ascend Ben Lomond, for the hire of a guide was very high and a half day of rest was quite acceptable to them. On July 17, at four o'clock in the morning, they set out for Loch Fyne; and, after walking fifteen miles and passing through two "tremendous Glens," they stopped for breakfast at "Cairn-something" on the shore of the lake.

When we came through Glencroe [Keats wrote his brother Tom] it was early in the morning and we were pleased with the noise of Shepherds Sheep and dogs in the misty heights close above us — we saw none of them for some time, till two came in sight creeping among the Craggs like Emmets, yet their voices came quite plainly to us. . . .

After having breakfast in Cairndow, Keats took a bath in Loch Fyne, was stung by the gadflies, and composed a doggerel ballad.

I have just been bathing in Loch fine [he wrote his brother Tom] a saltwater Lake opposite the Window — quite pat and fresh but for the cursed Gad flies — damn 'em they have been at me ever since I left the Swan and two necks.

All gentle folks who owe a grudge, etc.

That afternoon Keats and Brown walked to Inverary, passing by the Duke of Argyle's Castle, where they heard a band playing.

> I must say I enjoyed t[w]o or three common tunes [Keats wrote his brother Tom] — but nothing could stifle the horrors of a solo on the Bag-pipe — I thought the Beast would never have done. . . .

That evening at Inverary, while Brown was nursing sore feet, Keats attended a performance of Kotzebue's *The Stranger*.

> On entering Inverary [he wrote Tom] we saw a Play Bill — Brown was knock'd up from new shoes — so I went to the Barn alone where I saw the Stranger accmpanied by a Bagpipe. There they went on about "interesting creaters" and "human nater" till the Curtain fell and then Came the Bag pipe. When M[rs] Haller fainted down went the Curtain and out came the Bag-pipe — at the heartrending, shoemending reconciliation the Piper blew amain. I never read or saw this play before; not the Bag pipe, nor the wretched players themselves were little in comparison with it — thank heaven it has been scoffed at lately almost to a fashion.

Keats, like Wordsworth, Coleridge, Hazlitt, Hunt, and other literary men, scoffed at the sentimental, melodramatic German tragedies which were popular on the English stage in this period.

The next morning Keats composed into the letter which he was writing to his brother Tom a satiric sonnet on the play and the bagpipe (*Of late two dainties were before me plac'd*). The letter to Tom Keats, containing this sonnet together with the ballad on the gadfly, is in the Dilke Collection in the Hampstead Public Library.

Keats and Brown stopped in Inverary through Saturday, July 18. "I think we are the luckiest fellows in Christendom," Keats wrote his brother Tom after he had copied the sonnet, "— Brown could not proce[e]d this morning on account of his feet and lo there is thunder and rain." Writing Bailey on July 18, Keats made an analysis of his own temperament. He had written Bailey a very morbidly pessimistic letter on June 10, we remember; and Bailey, becoming very much wrought up over Keats's state of mind, endeavored to console him. Keats replied:

> And here Bailey I will say a few words written in a sane and sober Mind, a very scarce thing with me, for they may hereafter save you a great deal of trouble about me, which you do not deserve, and for which I ought to be bastinadoed. I carry all matters to an extreme — so that when I have any little vexation it grows in five Minutes into a theme for Sophocles — then and in that temper if I write to any friend I have so little self-possession that I give him matter for grieving at the very time perhaps when I am laughing at a Pun. Your last letter made me blush for the pain I had given you — I know my own disposition so well that I am certain of writing many times hereafter in the same strain to you — now you know how far to believe in them — you must allow for imagination. I know I shall not be able to help it.

We who study Keats's poetry should bear his warning in mind. He lived life intensely, exaggerating insignificant matters either into boisterous comedy or into passionate tragedy and swinging from the extreme of joy to the extreme of grief. The faculties of feeling intensely and of thinking intensely were essential faculties of his genius. The grief which he had poured out in his letter to Bailey on June 10, however, was a real one, a grief over the illness of his brother Tom and the emigration of his brother George to America. It had been assuaged somewhat by his excursion into Scotland; but in less than a month, we shall see, the fatal relapse of his brother Tom made it more intense than ever before.

Keats and Brown set out from Inverary on the afternoon of Saturday, July 18 and walked to Loch Awe.

> The approach to Loch Awe was very solemn towards nightfall [Keats wrote his brother Tom] — the first glance was a streak of water deep in the Bases of large black Mountains. — We had come along a complete mountain road, where if one listened there was not a sound but that of Mountain Streams.

On Sunday, July 19 Keats and Brown walked twenty miles by the side of Loch Awe —"every ten steps creating a new and beautiful picture." Writing his brother on July 20, Keats said:

> Yesterday our walk was of this description — the near Hills were not very lofty but many of their steeps beautifully wooded — the distant Mountains in the Hebrides very grand[,] the Saltwater Lakes coming up between Crags and Islands fulltide and scarcely ruffled — sometimes appearing as one large Lake, sometimes as th[r]ee distinct ones in different directions. At one point we saw afar off a rocky opening into the main Sea — We have also seen an Eagle or two. They move about without the least motion of Wings when in an indolent fit. — I am for the first time in a country where a foreign Language is spoken — they gabble away Gaelic at a vast rate. . . .

Keats and Brown stopped that night at an inn "between Loch Craignish and the sea just opposite Long Island"— a place which Colvin identified as Kilmelfort, with the island of Luing in sight, to the east of Scarba Sound. The next morning, July 20, they were detained by rain. Keats described this inn (the first comfortable one he had stopped at for several days) with vivid detail.

On the "flapped mahogany" table in this inn, Miss Lowell conjectured, Keats composed his *Lines written in the Highlands after a Visit to Burns's Country*. The eagle and possibly other details which he saw on July 19 appear in this poem and prove that he did not compose it before the evening of July 19. He copied the poem at the end of the letter to Bailey which he began on July 18 and finished on July 22.

> One of the pleasantest bouts we have had [he wrote Bailey on July 22] was our walk to Burns's Cottage, over the Doon and past Kirk Alloway — I had determined to write a Sonnet in the Cottage. I did but lauk it was so wretched I destroyed it — however in a few days afterwards I wrote some lines cousin-german to the Circumstance which I will transcribe or rather cross scribe in the front of this [letter].

The autograph letter to Bailey containing this poem is in the Lowell Collection in the Harvard College Library. An autograph manuscript of the poem (apparently the first draft) is in the Houghton Collection in Lord Crewe's possession. There are transcripts of the poem in Keats's copy of *Endymion*, George Keats's Book of Autographs and Transcripts, Woodhouse's Scrap-book, and Woodhouse's Book of Transcripts.

Keats expressed in the poem a composite impression of his whole excursion through the north of England and into the Highlands of Scotland; and one familiar with his itinerary might identify the various descriptive details. He celebrated his visit in Burns's cottage as the climax of his excursion —

> To find a Bard's low Cradle-place about the silent north.

The theme of the poem, representing Keats's reflection upon his excursion into the picturesque parts of England and Scotland, is human rather than romantic. The man, Keats said, who sees places renowned in history and poetry is lifted out of himself, he forgets the cares of life; but, after a short reprieve, he is glad to return to the world of human affections.

> Scanty the hour and few the steps beyond the Bourn of Care,
> Beyond the sweet and bitter world — beyond it unaware;
> Scanty the hour and few the steps because a longer stay
> Would bar return and make a Man forget his mortal way.
> O horrible! to lose the sight of well remember'd face,
> Of Brother's eyes, of Sister's Brow, constant to every place;
> Filling the Air as on we move with Portraiture intense
> More warm than those heroic tints that fill a Painter's sense,
> When Shapes of old come striding by, and visages of old,
> Locks shining black, hair scanty grey and passions manifold.
> No, No that horror cannot be — for at the Cable's length
> Man feels the gentle Anchor pull and gladdens in its strength —
> One hour half ideot he stands by mossy waterfall,
> But in the very next he reads his Soul's memorial:
> He reads it on the Mountain's height where chance he may sit down
> Upon rough marble diadem, that Hill's eternal crown.
> Yet be the Anchor e'er so fast, room is there for a prayer
> That Man may never loose his Mind on Mountains bleak and bare;
> That he may stray league after league some great Berthplace to find
> And keep his vision clear from speck, his inward sight unblind —

In this poem, as in his *Hymn to Pan* and his *Epistle to Reynolds*, he recalled the word "bourn" from Hamlet's soliloquy *To be or not to be*. Whenever he felt melancholy, he remembered Hamlet's brooding phrases. He composed the poem in the septenaries of Elizabethan poets and was influenced doubtless by the septenaries of Chapman's translation of Homer's *Iliad*.

In the afternoon of July 20 Keats and Brown walked fifteen miles in a soaking rain to Oban, where they had intended to take the regular excursion boat to the Isle of Staffa. They found that it would cost them seven guineas, for the excursion was fashionable, and they decided to set out for Fort William. One of the guides, however, offered to conduct them to Staffa by a cheaper but more arduous route. On July 22 they crossed from Oban to the Island of Kerrera by a ferry and from the Island of Kerrera to the Island of Mull by another ferry, and they stopped for the night at a wretched shepherd's hut in the middle of the island.

> The road through the Island, or rather the track [Keats wrote his brother Tom on July 23] is the most dreary you can think of — between dreary Mountains — over bog and rock and river with our Breeches tucked up and our Stockings in hand. About eight oClock we arrived at a Shepherd's Hut into which we could scarcely get for the Smoke through a door lower than my Shoulders. We found our way into a little compartment with the rafters and turf thatch blackened with smoke — the earth floor full of Hills and Dales.

Brown described their walk across the Island of Mull as

> Thirty-seven miles of jumping and flinging over great stones along no path at all, up the steep and down the steep, and wading through rivulets up to the knees, and crossing a bog, a mile long, up to the ankles.

In the wretched shepherd's hut Keats completed his letter to Bailey and copied into it his *Lines written in the Highlands after a Visit to Burns's Country*. The next morning, July 23, Keats and Brown walked six miles to Dun an cullen (Derrynaculen?) for breakfast. Here Keats began a letter to his brother Tom and finished it on July 26 after he had returned to Oban.

Keats and Brown crossed from the Island of Mull to the Island of Iona (or Icolmkill) by a ferry, it is probable; and they spent some time viewing the antiquities of this historic island. They hired a boat to take them to the Island of Staffa, the object of their journey.

Keats described for his brother Tom the picturesque topography of the Island of Staffa, the island of basaltic pillars, with Fingal's Cave hollowed out of the gigantic pillars.

> I am puzzled how to give you an Idea of Staffa. It can only be represented by a first rate drawing. One may compare the surface of the Island to a roof —

this roof is supported by grand pillars of basalt standing together as thick as honeycombs. The finest thing is Fingal's Cave — it is entirely a hollowing out of Basalt Pillars. Suppose now the Giants who rebelled against Jove had taken a whole Mass of black Columns and bound them together like bunches of matches — and then with immense Axes had made a cavern in the body of these columns — of course the roof and floor must be composed of the broken ends of the Columns — such is fingal's Cave except that the Sea has done the work of excavations and is continually dashing there — so that we walk along the sides of the cave on the pillars which are left as if for convenient Stairs — the roof is arched somewhat gothic wise and the length of some of the entire side pillars is 50 feet. About the island you might seat an army of Men each on a pillar. The length of the Cave is 120 feet and from its extremity the view into the sea through the large Arch at the entrance [is very grand] — the colour of the colum[n]s is a sort of black with a lurking gloom of purple therein. For solemnity and grandeur it far surpasses the finest Cathedrall. At the extremity of the Cave there is a small perforation into another cave, at which the waters meeting and buffeting each other there is sometimes produced a report as of a cannon heard as far as Iona which must be 12 Miles. As we approached in the boat there was such a fine swell of the sea that the pillars appeared rising immediately out of the crystal — But it is impossible to describe it.

Not Alad[d] in magian
Ever such a work began.
Not the Wizard of the Dee
Ever such a dream could see
Not St. John in Patmos isle
In the passion of his toil
When he saw the churches seven
Golden-aisled built up in heaven
Gazed at such a rugged wonder.
As I stood its roofing under
Lo! I saw one sleeping there
On the marble cold and bare
While the surges washed his feet
And his garments white did beat
Drench'd about the sombre rocks,
On his neck his well-grown locks
Lifted dry above the Main
Were upon the curl again.
What is this and what art thou?
Whisper'd I and touch'd his brow.
What art thou and what is this?
Whisper'd I and strove to kiss
The Spirit's hand to wake ~~him up~~ his eyes.
Up he started in a trice.
I am Lycidas said he
Fam'd in funeral Minstrelsy.
This was architected thus
By the great Oceanus
Here his mighty waters play
Hollow Organs all the day

Here by turns his dolphins all
Finny palmers great and small
Come to pay devotion due —
Each a mouth of pea[r]ls must strew.
~~Many a mortal comes to see~~
~~This Cathedrall of the S~~
Many a Mortal of these days
Dares to pass our sacred ways
Dares to touch audaciously
This Cathedrall of the Sea.
I have been the Pontif priest
Where the Waters never rest
Where a fledgy sea bird choir
Soars for ever — holy fire
I have hid from Mortal Man.
~~Old~~ Proteus is my Sacristan.
But the stupid eye of Mortal
Hath pass'd beyond the Rocky portal
So for ever will I leave
Such a taint and soon unweave
All the magic of the place.
'Tis now free to stupid face
To cutters and to fashion boats
To cravats and to Petticoats.
The great Sea shall war it down
For its fame shall not be blown
At every farthing quadrille dance.
So saying with a Spirit glance
He dived —

Keats composed this poem directly, I believe, into his letter to his brother Tom on July 26 after he had returned to Oban. This letter, which he began on July 23 and finished on July 26, is in the Marquess of Crewe's Collection. Keats began the poem with imaginative seriousness, but he brought it to an end with a trivial satire on the fashionable tourists who visited Fingal's Cave. He copied a revised version of the poem into the letter which he wrote his brother George in September 1819. He omitted verses 7 and 8, which he adapted into *The Eve of St. Mark*, and the last thirteen verses, in which he had satirized fashionable tourists. This letter to George Keats is now in the Pierpont Morgan Library. There is another revised version of the poem in William Sharp's *Life and Letters of Joseph Severn*, printed from a transcript which Brown sent to Severn. Brown's version omits verses 39 and 40 and the last eight verses. There is a transcript in Woodhouse's Commonplace Book and another in his Book of Transcripts. When Keats copied the poem for his brother George, he entitled it "Incipit Poema Lyrica de Staffa tractans"; and Woodhouse entitled his transcripts "Lines on visiting Staffa."

Keats composed the poem in the heptasyllabic metre with which he had been experimenting since the beginning of 1818. The introduction of Lycidas into the poem shows that his imagination was playing with Milton's poetic creations. On July 18 he wrote Bailey: "When I see you the first thing I shall do will be to read that about Milton and Ceres and Proserpine" (*Paradise Lost*, IV. vv. 268–272). He was thinking about the plot of his *Hyperion* also, for in his prose description of Fingal's Cave he referred to the "Giants who rebelled against Jove."

Keats and Brown remained for four or five days in Oban, since Keats was suffering from a sore throat caused by exposure in wading through bogs on the Island of Mull. On August 1 they walked to Fort William, and on August 2 they climbed Ben Nevis, the highest peak in the British Isles. On August 3 Keats wrote his brother Tom a long account of his ascent of the mountain, copied a sonnet which he said he had composed on the top, and, to amuse Tom, composed an *ex tempore* dialogue between Mrs. Cameron and Ben Nevis. He said that Mrs. Cameron, who was fifty years of age and the fattest woman in Invernessshire, had climbed Ben Nevis several years ago. "True she had her servants," he observed, "but then she had herself."

In the sonnet which he composed on Ben Nevis on August 2, Keats expressed agnostic reflections on the futility of man's endeavor to solve the problems of his source and his destiny. He was speculating about knowledge, which, he had learned from Wordsworth's humanitarian philosophy, would bring about the happiness of men by expelling evil from human nature and human society. He doubted, however, that man, a poor witless elf, would ever acquire that knowledge.

Read me a lesson, Muse, and speak it loud
  Upon the top of Nevis, blind in mist!
I look into the chasms, and a shroud
  Vaprous doth hide them, — just so much I wist
Mankind do know of hell; I look o'erhead,
  And there is sullen mist, — even so much
Mankind can tell of heaven; mist is spread
  Before the earth, beneath me, — even such,
Even so vague is man's sight of himself!
  Here are the craggy stones beneath my feet, —
Thus much I know that, a poor witless elf,
  I tread on them, — that all my eye doth meet
Is mist and crag, not only on this height,
But in the world of thought and mental might!

H. B. Forman published the letter to Tom Keats containing this sonnet from the autograph manuscript which was in Haydon's Journal.

From Fort William Keats and Brown walked to Inverness, where they were compelled to stop again because of Keats's sore throat. "My Sore throat is not quite well," Keats wrote his brother Tom, "and I intend stopping here a few days." Keats and Brown visited the ruins of Beauly Abbey, found some skulls which they presumed to be skulls of ancient monks, and composed, in imitation of Burns's style, a satiric poem on the life of the monks. Keats's part in the collaboration consists of stanzas 2, 8, and 10 and the first two verses of stanza 1. Images in stanza 8 of this poem, like those in verses 7 and 8 of the *Lines on visiting Staffa*, foreshadow images in *The Fall of Hyperion, a Dream* and *The Eve of St. Mark*.

Keats and Brown had intended to walk from Inverness down the eastern coast of Scotland to Edinburgh, visit Bailey, who had a curacy near Carlisle in Cumberland, and return to Hampstead. They had walked 642 miles, Brown computed, over rough country in all sorts of weather, climbing mountains, wading through bogs, sleeping in peasants' huts, and eating coarse food. Keats became too ill in Inverness to proceed farther. He consulted a physician, who advised him to abandon his excursion and to return to London by boat. On August 7 Brown wrote Mr. Dilke of Chichester:

> We came out to endure, and to be gratified with scenery, and lo! we have not been disappointed either way. As for the Oat-cakes, I was once in despair about them. I was not only too dainty, but they absolutely made me sick. With a little gulping, I can manage them now. Mr Keats however is too unwell for fatigue and privation. I am waiting here to see him off in the Smack for London. He caught a violent cold in the Island of Mull, which, far from leaving him, has become worse, and the Physician here thinks him too thin and fevered to proceed on our journey. It is a cruel disappointment. We have been as happy as possible together.

In the meantime Keats's brother Tom had suffered a relapse. On August 16 Mrs. Dilke wrote her father-in-law, Mr. Dilke of Chichester:

> John Keats' brother is extremely ill, and the doctor begged that his brother might be sent for. Dilke accordingly wrote off to him, which was a very unpleasant task. However, from the journal received from Brown last Friday, he says Keats has been so long ill with his sore throat, that he is obliged to give up. I am rather glad of it, as he will not receive the letter, which might have frightened him very much, as he is extremely fond of his brother. How poor Brown will get on alone I know not, as he loses a cheerful, good-tempered, clever companion.

Keats arrived in London, by his own dating, on Monday, August 17. He wrote his sister from Hampstead on August 18:

> I did not intend to have returned to London so soon but have a bad sore throat from a cold I caught in the island of Mull: therefore I thought it best to get home as soon as possible and went on board the Smack from Cromarty. We had a nine days passage and were landed at London Bridge yesterday.

Keats was very careless about dates, however, and he may have arrived in London on August 19; for Mrs. Dilke wrote from Hampstead on August 19:

> John Keats arrived here last night, as brown and as shabby as you can imagine; scarcely any shoes left, his jacket all torn at the back, a fur cap, a great plaid, and his knapsack. I cannot tell what he looked like.

The Scottish excursion shortened Keats's life, it is probable, by several years. The hardships which he underwent on this walking tour weakened his constitution and lessened his resistance to tuberculosis. The sore throat which he contracted in the Island of Mull was his third warning of the insidious attack of this disease. The first warning was his illness in October 1817, after he returned from his visit with Bailey in Oxford; and the second was his illness in June 1818, on the eve of his Scottish excursion. In these first two illnesses he suffered, it is probable, from a sore throat; for in both cases he was confined to his room and he was afraid, he said, to expose himself to the night air.

2

On his return to Hampstead, Keats was compelled to face the greatest ills of his life up to this time — his own illness, the fatal relapse of his brother Tom, and the malignant attacks of the reviewers upon *Endymion*. For five or six weeks he was confined closely in Hampstead, treating his own sore throat and nursing his dying brother. He feared that he himself might have consumption, I presume, for he took another course of mercury. He was vexed also by Abbey's reluctance to permit Fanny Keats to visit her dying brother. In the midst of this adversity, much of which was unexpected, he was deprived of the sympathy and assistance of his closest friends. His brother George was in America; Brown was still tramping through Scotland; Haydon was visiting his sister in Bridgewater; Severn was ill with "a Typhous fever"; Dilke went to Brighton to recuperate from an illness; and Reynolds went to Exeter to visit his fiancée. Keats found in William Haslam, however, a friend upon whom he could rely. "His behaviour to Tom during my absence and since my return," Keats wrote his brother George, "has endeared him to me for ever." By the beginning of October, Keats had recovered somewhat from his sore throat, and his friends had returned to London. He called upon few friends except the Dilkes and the Reynoldses, however, for he could not leave his brother, who was morbidly depressed by the prospect of death. He wrote his brother George in the middle of October: "I have been but once to Haydon's, onece [*sic*] to Hunt's, once to Rice's, once to Hessey's. I have not seen Taylor, I have not been to the Theatre."

The infamous reviews of *Endymion* in *Blackwood's Edinburgh Magazine* for August and in *The Quarterly Review* for April appeared in September. The reviewers attacked Keats as a disciple of Leigh Hunt in politics and in poetry. Reviewers in this period were venomously partizan, judging literary works by political and religious rather than by aesthetic principles. Leigh Hunt, as editor of *The Examiner*, had made powerful enemies by attacking the tyranny of the Tory party and the bigotry of Christian sects. He provoked personal attacks, he admitted in after years, by *The Feast of the Poets*, in which he ridiculed contemporary poets such as William Gifford, Walter Scott, Wordsworth, Coleridge, Southey, and others. "It drew upon my head," he said, "all the personal hostility which had hitherto been held in suspense by the vaguer daring of *The Examiner*." When he published his *Story of Rimini* at the beginning of 1816, his enemies launched their attacks against him. John Wilson Croker, a Tory and a neo-classicist, slashed the poem in *The Quarterly Review*, a Tory periodical published by John Murray and edited by William Gifford. Croker, angered by Hunt's censure of the school of Pope, condemned the poem for its licenses in versification and licenses and vulgarities in diction. Hazlitt, who was a member of Hunt's coterie, praised the poem in *The Edinburgh Review*, a Whig periodical published by Archibald Constable and edited by Francis Jeffrey.

In April 1817 William Blackwood, a Tory bookseller of Edinburgh, established *The Edinburgh Monthly Magazine* to oppose the periodicals of the Whig bookseller Archibald Constable. After six months, since the magazine was not a success, he changed its name to *Blackwood's Edinburgh Magazine*, dismissed his incompetent editors, took charge of it himself, and employed John Wilson and John Gibson Lockhart as his assistants. Wilson and Lockhart were not belated neo-classicists like Gifford and Croker. Wilson had visited Wordsworth's group in the lake country, and Lockhart had frequented Goethe's circle in Weimar. They were irresponsible and inconsistent in their reviews, but for the most part they praised Wordsworth, Scott, Southey, Byron, and Moore.

Blackwood, Wilson, and Lockhart promoted their reorganized magazine by unscrupulous means, attacking their political and literary opponents with savage invective and indecent ridicule. In the first number of the reorganized magazine, published in October 1817, they began the notorious series of articles "On the Cockney School of Poetry." As a motto for the series, they chose with diabolical cunning some silly verses which Cornelius Webb, a disciple of Hunt's, had composed —

> Our talk shall be (a theme we never tire on)
> Of Chaucer, Spenser, Shakespeare, Milton, Byron,
> (Our England's Dante) — Wordsworth — HUNT, and KEATS,
> The Muses' son of promise; and of what feats
> He yet may do.

Wilson and Lockhart collaborated, it is probable, in writing these articles, which they signed "Z." In a letter to Leigh Hunt, in the magazine for January 1818, Z summed up his accusations against Hunt:

> The charges which I have brought against your literary life and conversation are these: 1. The want and the pretence of scholarship; 2. A vulgar style of writing; 3. A want of respect for the Christian religion; 4. A contempt for kingly power, and an indecent mode of attacking the government of your country; 5. Extravagant admiration of yourself, the Round Table, and your own poems; 6. Affectation; 7. A partiality for indecent subjects, and an immoral manner of writing concerning the crime of incest, in your poem of Rimini; 8. I have asserted, that you are a poet vastly inferior to Wordsworth, Byron, and Moore!

Z developed these charges in terms of personal scurrility. In his first article (October 1817) he said:

> Mr Hunt cannot utter a dedication, or even a note, without betraying the *Shibboleth* of low birth and low habits. He is the ideal of the Cockney Poet. He raves perpetually about "green fields," "jaunty streams," and "o'er-arching leafiness," exactly as a Cheapside shop-keeper does about the beauties of his box on the Camberwell road. . . . He would fain be always tripping and waltzing, and is sorry that he cannot be allowed to walk about in the morning with yellow breeches and flesh-coloured silk-stockings. He sticks an artificial rosebud into his button hole in the midst of winter. He wears no neckcloth, and cuts his hair in imitation of the Prints of Petrarch. In his verses he is always desirous of being airy, graceful, easy, courtly, and ITALIAN. . . .

This passage, however, is comparatively mild. In the climax of his invective Z said:

> The extreme moral depravity of the Cockney School is another thing which is for ever thrusting itself upon the public attention, and convincing every man of sense who looks into their productions, that they who sport such sentiments

can never be great poets. How could any man of high original genius ever stoop publicly, at the present day, to dip his fingers in the least of those glittering and rancid obscenities which float on the surface of Mr Hunt's *Hippocrene*? His poetry is that of a man who has kept company with kept-mistresses. He talks indelicately like a tea-sipping milliner girl. Some excuse for him there might have been, had he been hurried away by imagination or passion. But with him indecency is a disease, as he speaks unclean things from perfect inanition. The very concubine of so impure a wretch as Leigh Hunt would be to be pitied, but alas! for the wife of such a husband! For him there is no charm in simple seduction; and he gloats over it only when accompanied with adultery and incest.

Keats had reacted against Hunt's poetic style six months before this review was published. In his correspondence with Haydon, we have seen, he had referred to Hunt's personal character in terms very little milder than those of Blackwood's reviewers. But there is a great deal of difference, as Sir Sidney Colvin observed, between the ethics of private correspondence and the ethics of a periodical. In a letter to Bailey postmarked November 5, 1817, Keats expressed his reactions to the article "On the Cockney School of Poetry":

There has been a flaming attack upon Hunt in the Endinburgh [*sic*] Magazine. I never read any thing so virulent — accusing him of the greatest Crimes dep[r]eciating his Wife his Poetry — his Habits — his company, his Conversation — These Philip[p]ics are to come out in Numbers — call'd "the Cockney School of Poetry." There has been but one Number published — that on Hunt to which they have prefixed a Motto from one Cornelius Webb Poetaster — who unfortunately was of our Party occasionally at Hampstead and took it into his head to write the following — something about — "we'll talk on Wordsworth Byron — a theme we never tire on[''] and so forth till he comes to Hunt and Keats. In the Motto they have put Hunt and Keats in large Letters — I have no doubt that the second Number was intended for me: but have hopes of its non appearance from the following advertisement in last Sunday's Examiner. "To Z. The writer of the Article signed Z in Blackwood's Ed[i]nburgh magazine for October 1817 is invited to send his address to the printer of the Examiner, in order that Justice may be executed of [on] the proper person" I dont mind the thing much — but if he should go to such lengths with me as he has done with Hunt I must infal[l]ibly call him to an account — if he be a human being and appears in Squares and Theatres where we might possibly meet. I dont relish his abuse[.]

In public letters and articles in the magazine, Z defended his incognito with righteous indignation, posing as a divine fury avenging outraged morality; but in private, as Miss Lowell observed, he conducted himself like a mischievous monkey. He wrote a private letter to Leigh Hunt, saying that he was John Graham Dalyell of Edinburgh; and Hunt,[4] suspecting a hoax, wrote a letter to Dalyell, in-

[4] Edmund Blunden, *Leigh Hunt, A Biography*.

quiring whether he were a real person. Dalyell was a staunch Whig who detested Blackwood's coterie. Raging with indignation, he showed Hunt's letter to a friend, exclaiming, "Oh, the villany of these fellows!" Hunt could have prosecuted Blackwood for libel; but when Z refused to divulge his identity he resolved to ignore the articles, and he kept this decision to the end. He said afterwards that it was not he but his brother, John Hunt, who had challenged Z (in the advertisement to which Keats referred) to send his address to the printer of *The Examiner*.

Keats's friends took steps to conciliate the Tory reviewers. On November 21, 1817 Keats wrote Bailey from Burford Bridge: "I should have been here a day sooner but the Reynoldses persuaded me to stop in Town to meet your friend Christie." Bailey and Reynolds did not know at this time that Christie's friend, Lockhart, was the author of the article "On the Cockney School of Poetry" in the October number of *Blackwood's Edinburgh Magazine*; but they knew that Christie had influence in the literary coteries of Edinburgh. Sir Sidney Colvin discovered that in January 1818 Christie wrote Lockhart that he had met Keats and that he had been favorably impressed by him. Lockhart replied:

> What you say of Keates is pleasing, and if you like to write a little review of him, in admonition to leave his ways, etc., and in praise of his natural genius, I shall be greatly obliged to you.

This correspondence between Christie and Lockhart about Keats gives credence to Lord Houghton's statement, on Brown's authority, that, while Keats was tramping through Scotland in the summer of 1818,

> Some mutual friend . . . forwarded him an invitation from Messrs. Blackwood, injudiciously adding the suggestion, that it would be very advisable for him to visit the Modern Athens, and endeavour to conciliate his literary enemies in that quarter. The sensibility and moral dignity of Keats were outraged by this proposal: it may be imagined what answer he returned, and also that this circumstance may not have been unconnected with the article on him which appeared in the August number of the *Edinburgh Magazine*. . . .

In the summer of 1818, after *Endymion* had been published, Taylor, the publisher, sought to conciliate the Tory reviewers. Leigh Hunt said (in *Lord Byron and Some of his Contemporaries*) that Taylor called upon Gifford, the editor of *The Quarterly Review*, and that Gifford gave his visitor very plainly to understand that he would attack *Endymion*. Taylor met Blackwood also in London in the summer of 1818; for Bailey wrote Taylor from Scotland on October 5:

> I was introduced to Blackwood who told me he had seen you, and that he was sorry on his return to find the attack on Keats. I told him it was "*infamous.*" He did not like to be told so — but no matter for that.
>
> [Woodhouse's Scrap-book.]

On June 10, twelve days before Keats set out on his excursion with Brown, he wrote Bailey:

> With respect to domestic Literature — the Endinburgh [*sic*] Magazine in another blow up against Hunt calls me "the amiable Mister Keats" and I have more than a Laurel from the Quarterly Reviewers for they have smothered me in "Foliage."

There was a covert allusion to Keats in the review of Hunt's *Foliage* in *The Quarterly Review* for June 1818.

In the latter part of July, Bailey met Lockhart in the home of Bishop Gleig in Scotland. He wrote three accounts of this meeting — the first in a letter to Taylor on August 29, 1818; the second in a memorandum in 1821 for Taylor's projected memoir of Keats; and the third in a letter to Lord Houghton on May 7, 1849, thirty-one years afterwards. The first and the second are preserved in transcripts in Woodhouse's Scrap-book in the Pierpont Morgan Library, and the third is in the Houghton Collection in the Marquess of Crewe's possession. In the letter to Taylor on August 29, 1818, Bailey said:

> I have something to tell you respecting Endymion: but it must be *in your ear*: That is, I do not wish it to be repeated to Keats, it being my determination to do him all the good I can without creating mischief. I fear Endymion will be dreadfully cut up in the Edinburgh Magazine (Blackwood's) I met a man in Scotland who is concerned in that publication, & who abused poor Keats in a way that, although it was at the Bishop's table, I could hardly keep my tongue. I said that I supposed he would be attacked in Blackwood's. He replied "not by *me*;" which would convey the insinuation he would by some one *else*. The objections, he stated, were frivolous, in the extreme. They chiefly respected the *rhymes*. But I feel convinced *now* the Poem will not sell; & I *fear* his future writings will not. In Scotland he is very much despised from what I could collect. In the Edinburgh Magazine I can get an article inserted; and I will certainly write one in his defence if he be grossly attacked. As a *man of genius* I know Keats is defensible. . . .

I stop this quotation at the beginning of a passage which I have quoted in an earlier connection. Bailey himself censured immoral elements in *Endymion*, referring to the nympholeptic dream in the second book and the principle of love in the fourth book.

Bailey wrote the second account of his meeting with Lockhart for Taylor's projected memoir of Keats, which was to be printed with an edition of his poems. He wrote Taylor on April 28, 1821:

I think his [Keats's] unhappy life might be a means of exposing the nefarious spirit of that most odious publication of Blackwood's. . . . Were such an exposure intended I can have no objection that the communication I have related to you between Lockhart & myself should be stated anonymously, not so that I shall be referred to by L— or any other person who on his behalf may answer it. In which case, I should state it to the Biographer in my language, or not, as it suited his Biography.

Bailey desired to expose Lockhart's unscrupulous conduct, but he was reluctant to draw the enmity of Blackwood's coterie upon himself. He related his meeting with Lockhart, therefore, without mentioning names.

In the month of July, 1818, a friend of poor Keats met with one of the supposed editors of Blackwood's Edin. Magazine in Scotland. It was not doubted at that time that he was a principal conductor of this Miscellany. He may have since relinquished this office as the public disavowal of it on a late unhappy occasion must force us to conclude.

Keats's Endymion had just been published. It was acrimoniously criticized by the writer in Blackwood's, and as warmly defended by the friend of the unhappy Poet, who was classed among those authors which were designated by the writer Z in Blackwood's Mag.: the "Cockney School of Poetry." He was in short supposed by this gentleman to be under the patronage of Leigh Hunt.

The friend of Keats deprecated the idea that because the young Poet had been in the first instance introduced to public notice by Leigh Hunt, he was to be considered as under the *patronage* of that gentleman, & to have borrowed from him his Style of Poetry. Mr. Hunt, he knew, had not seen, much less corrected Endymion prior to its publication.

He moreover explained that Keats was of a respectable family; & though he & his brothers & sister were orphans, they were left with a small but independent Patrimony. He had been brought up to the profession of medicine which he had abandoned for the pursuit of Literature.

The critic in, if not the conductor, of Blackwood's magazine, declared that he sh[d] not attack Keats.

It cannot be supposed therefore that he did make that violent, cruel, and ungentlemanly attack contained in the article no. IV of the "Cockney School of Poetry," signed Z, which appeared in the August following. This was the first direct attack on this amiable and unhappy young man. After the above avowal the gentleman alluded to could not forfeit his title to veracity as to be the writer of this article. Nor is it for an instant supposed that he was.

But some particulars of that article must nevertheless lay him under suspicion that he furnished materials to one of his coadjutors with a view to the nefarious purpose of making that shameless attack, so full of contempt and scorn that no one who professes himself a Xtian [Christian] can avow himself the author of it without subjecting himself to the aversion of all good men. And until this suspicion is removed, he must appear as an accesory to the perversion of facts, xxxxx which were in themselves honorable to Keats, to the wicked purpose of sinking a respectable, unoffending, & amiable man into the lowest contempt. Witness the following passages. —

Bailey's memory was tenacious and exact and his reminiscences of Keats are always trustworthy. The third account of his meeting with Lockhart, which he wrote for Lord Houghton thirty-one years afterwards, is consistent with the two contemporary accounts which I have quoted above. I shall quote this third account, however, for it adds a few details and it states more definitely Lockhart's declaration that he would not employ the facts which Bailey gave him in an attack upon Keats.

It was about this time, the latter part of July, 1818, that I paid my first visit to Scotland, to my friend Gleig, (afterwards my brother-in-law), at his father's, the late Venerable Bishop Gleig, the Primus or Premier Bishop of the Scottish Episcopal Church, too well known in the literary and scientific world to need further mention. Here I met a Gentleman, then and since well known as one of the principal contributors to Blackwood's Magazine, which was then a novel publication, got up avowedly in opposition to the Edinburgh Review, & the Whig party in politics, — and the discredit of Mr. (now Lord) Jeffrey — not even redeemed by his honorable, though too late, advocacy of poor Keats — the unrelenting antagonist of Mr. Wordsworth. . . . I had always been (at least from the year 1813) through good & through evil report, one among the few unflinching admirers of Mr. Wordsworth's poetry, now almost universally appreciated, but upon which as much (& yet more) foolish ridicule was poured, as upon Keats. On this ground, therefore, we [that is, Bailey and Lockhart] met as friends and allies; regarding Keats and the proscribed Endymion, we were as uncompromising antagonists.

The war had already begun, in Blackwood, under the head of "Cockney School of Poetry." . . .

Not only Keats & his friends, but the reading public in general, were prepared for what was to follow, to "make them sport." I took occasion, therefore, seriously to expostulate with this Gentleman regarding Keats; that he was a young man, to whom Mr. Hunt had shewn kindness which called forth gratitude in so young & warm a bosom, — but that he himself mingled in no party politics, & as I could confidently say, from his own lips, saw the weakness of his friend, & the impolicy of having his name mixed up with so decidedly a party-man as Mr. Hunt. I gave him an outline of Keats' history — that he had been brought up as a surgeon and apothecary; & though not highly, that he was respectably educated. Insisted, if I rightly remember, on the injustice & cruelty of thus condemning & crushing a young man who, from feelings most honorable to human nature, adhered personally to the man who had befriended him when he was friendless, & needed a kindly eye & a helping hand. But I distinctly remember saying something to this effect, "Now do not avail yourself of my information, which I give you in this friendly manner, to attack him in your next number of Blackwood." His answer, too, I well remember, was to the effect *that he certainly should not do so*."

This conversation took place at the latter end of July; & in the following month of August, came out that *in*famous article, ending with "Go back to your gallipots, Johnny!"

I make no further comment than that the coincidence was so extraordinary that, until cleared up — and it never has been cleared up to this day, now nearly 31 years agone — my inevitable conclusion was, that my communications had been taken advantage of.

Bailey delivered Keats into the hands of his enemies by supplying them with those personal facts which they had to have in order to ridicule him. For thirty-one years it rankled in Bailey's mind that, as he expressed it, his confidence had been abused to the injury of a beloved friend. Lockhart wrote the article, we must believe, or he imparted to Wilson those facts which he had learned from Bailey. It is very unlikely that the reviewer obtained these facts from another source, for Keats was so reticent about his early life that only his most intimate friends knew anything about it. Lockhart's part in the article is revealed also by the references to German literature.

The article on Keats in *Blackwood's Edinburgh Magazine* for August, the fourth article "On the Cockney School of Poetry," consists almost entirely of personal criticism. It is less foul in its personal ridicule, however, than the preceding articles on Hunt.

> Of all the manias of this mad age [Z began], the most incurable, as well as the most common, seems to be no other than the *Metromanie*.

After alluding to the prevalence of this mania among farm laborers, footmen, and unmarried ladies, Z came to the sad case of Keats, the apothecary's apprentice.

> This young man appears to have received from Nature talents of an excellent, perhaps even of a superior order — talents which, devoted to the purposes of any useful profession, must have rendered him a respectable, if not an eminent citizen. His friends, we understand, destined him to the career of medicine, and he was bound apprentice some years ago to a worthy apothecary in town. But all has been undone by a sudden attack of the malady to which we have alluded. Whether Mr John had been sent home with a diuretic or composing draught to some patient far gone in the poetical mania, we have not heard. This much is certain, that he has caught the infection, and that thoroughly. For some time we were in hopes, that he might get off with a violent fit or two; but of late the symptoms are terrible. The phrenzy of the "Poems" was bad enough in its way; but it did not alarm us *half* so *seriously* as the calm, settled, imperturbable drivelling idiocy of "Endymion."

In the second paragraph of the review Z disclosed the cause of his attack upon Keats.

> The readers of the Examiner newspaper were informed, some time ago, by a solemn paragraph, in Mr Hunt's best style, of the appearance of two new stars of glorious magnitude and splendour in the poetical horizon of the land of Cockaigne. One of these turned out, by and by, to be no other than Mr John Keats. This precocious adulation confirmed the wavering apprentice in his desire to quit the gallipots, and at the same time excited in his too susceptible

mind a fatal admiration for the character and talents of the most worthless and affected of all the versifiers of our time.

Z quoted and ridiculed Keats's sonnets on Hunt's leaving prison and on Wordsworth, Haydon, and Hunt as the three great spirits now sojourning on earth. He waxed indignant that Keats should dare to join together the names of Wordsworth, the purest and noblest of living poets, and Hunt, the meanest and filthiest of cockney poetasters. He quoted passages from *Sleep and Poetry* and censured Keats's presumption in condemning Pope and his folly in praising Hunt. He quoted also some "pruriant and vulgar lines" from Keats's *Hadst thou liv'd in days of old* and said that they were "evidently meant for some young lady east of Temple-bar." He called attention to Keats's cockney rhymes by italicizing "thorns/fawns," "higher/Thalia," and "ear/Cytherea."

Passing from the *Poems* to *Endymion*, Z continued:

The old story of the Moon falling in love with a shepherd, so prettily told by a Roman Classic, and so exquisitely enlarged and adorned by one of the most elegant of German poets, has been seized upon by Mr John Keats, to be done with as might seem good unto the sickly fancy of one who never read a single line either of Ovid or of Wieland. . . . His Endymion is not a Greek shepherd, loved by a Grecian goddess; he is merely a young Cockney rhymester, dreaming a phantastic dream at the full of the moon. . . . [The poem] has just as much to do with Greece as it has with "old Tartary the fierce." . . .

Z quoted a series of "amorous scenes" from *Endymion*, including the nympholeptic dream in the second book which Bailey had feared he would attack. He did not censure the moral principles of *Endymion* nearly so much, however, as he had censured those of Hunt's *Story of Rimini*.

Z was reminded by a passage at the beginning of the third book of *Endymion* that Keats was a radical in politics.

We had almost forgot to mention, that Keats belongs to the Cockney School of Politics, as well as the Cockney School of Poetry. It is fit that he who holds Rimini to be the first poem, should believe the Examiner to be the first politician of the day. We admire consistency, even in folly. Hear how their bantling has already learned to lisp sedition.

In the last paragraph of the review Z advised Keats to go back to the apothecary's shop.

And now, good-morrow to "the Muses' son of Promise"; as for "the feats he yet may do," as we do not pretend to say, like himself, "Muse of my native land am I inspired," we shall adhere to the safe old rule of *pauca verba*. We venture to make one small prophecy, that his bookseller will not a second time venture £50 upon any thing he can write. It is a better and a wiser thing to be a starved apothecary than a starved poet; so back to the shop, Mr John, back to "plasters, pills, and ointment boxes," etc. But, for Heaven's sake, young Sangrado, be a little more sparing of extenuatives and soporifics in your practice than you have been in your poetry.

In September also appeared Croker's review of *Endymion* in the April number of *The Quarterly Review*. Croker's criticism is less personal and more literary than Lockhart's. He judged *Endymion* rigidly by the principles of neo-classicism, pointing out all its defects in form and ignoring all its beauties of the imagination.

Reviewers have been sometimes accused [Croker began] of not reading the works which they affected to criticise. On the present occasion we shall anticipate the author's complaint, and honestly confess that we have not read his work. Not that we have been wanting in our duty — far from it — indeed, we have made efforts almost as superhuman as the story itself appears to be, to get through it; but with the fullest stretch of our perseverance, we are forced to confess that we have not been able to struggle beyond the first of the four books of which this Poetic Romance consists.

Croker, like Lockhart, attacked Keats as a disciple of Leigh Hunt.

This author is a copyist of Mr. Hunt; but he is more unintelligible, almost as rugged, twice as diffuse, and ten times more tiresome and absurd than his prototype, who, though he impudently presumed to seat himself in the chair of criticism, and to measure his own poetry by his own standard, yet generally had a meaning. But Mr. Keats had advanced no dogmas which he was bound to support by examples; his nonsense therefore is quite gratuitous; he writes it for its own sake, and, being bitten by Mr. Leigh Hunt's insane criticism, more than rivals the insanity of his poetry.

After ridiculing the preface to *Endymion*, Croker quoted and condemned defects in versification and diction.

Of the story we have been able to make out but little; it seems to be mythological, and probably relates to the loves of Diana and Endymion; but of this, as the scope of the work has altogether escaped us, we cannot speak with any degree of certainty; and must therefore content ourselves with giving some instances of its diction and versification: — and here again we are perplexed and puzzled. — At first it appeared to us, that Mr. Keats had been amusing himself and wearying his readers with an immeasurable game at *bouts-rimés*; but, if we recollect rightly, it is an indispensable condition at this play, that the rhymes when filled up shall have a meaning. . . . He seems to us to write a line at random, and then he follows not the thought excited by this line, but that suggested by the *rhyme* with which it concludes. There is hardly a complete couplet inclosing a complete idea in the whole book. He wanders from one subject to another, from the association, not of ideas but of sounds, and the work is composed of hemistichs which, it is quite evident, have forced themselves upon the author by the mere force of the catchwords on which they turn.

We now present them [our readers] with some of the new words with which, in imitation of Mr. Leigh Hunt, he adorns our language. We are told that "turtles *passion* their voices," (p. 15); that "an arbour was *nested*," (p. 23); and a lady's locks "*gordian'd* up," (p. 32); and to supply the place of the nouns thus verbalized Mr. Keats, with great fecundity, spawns new ones; such as "men-slugs and human *serpentry*," (p. 41); the "*honey-feel* of bliss," (p. 45); "wives prepare *needments*," (p. 13) — and so forth. Then he has formed new verbs by the process of cutting off their natural tails, the adverbs, and affixing them to their foreheads; thus, "the wine out-sparkled," (p. 10); the "multitude up-followed," (p. 11); and "night up-took," (p. 29). "The wind up-blows," (p. 32); and the "hours are down-sunken," (p. 36). But if he sinks some adverbs in the verbs he compensates the language with adverbs and adjectives which he separates from the parent stock. Thus, a lady "whispers *pantingly* and close," makes "*hushing* signs," and steers her skiff into a "*ripply* cove," (p. 23); a shower falls "*refreshfully*," (45); and a vulture has a "*spreaded* tail," (p. 44).

Croker concluded his review with a challenge to the readers of the romance:

But enough of Mr. Leigh Hunt and his simple neophyte. — If any one should be bold enough to purchase this "Poetic Romance," and so much more patient, than ourselves, as to get beyond the first book, and so much more fortunate as to find a meaning, we entreat him to make us acquainted with his success; we shall then return to the task which we now abandon in despair, and endeavour to make all due amends to Mr. Keats and to our readers.

In September also appeared an attack upon *Endymion* in the June number of the *British Critic*, a periodical "conducted by persons of the established church, and on the orthodox principles of that respectable body." The Anglican reviewer was more malignant than Lockhart and Croker, the Tory reviewers. He combined, indeed, Lockhart's method of ridicule with Croker's method of censuring the faults and ignoring the virtues. He summarized the poem, quoting and ridiculing every phrase which, if taken out of its context, could be ridiculed. For example —

. . . it seems that one evening when the sun had done driving "his snorting four," "there blossom'd suddenly a magic bed of sacred ditamy,"(Qu. dimity?) and he looked up to the "lidless-eyed train of planets," where he saw "a completed form of all completeness," "with gordian'd locks and pearl round ears," and kissed all these till he fell into a "stupid sleep," from which he was roused by "a gentle creep," (N. B. Mr. Tiffin is the ablest bug-destroyer of our days,) to look at some "upturn'd gills of dying fish."

Bailey, believing that Lockhart had betrayed the confidences of their private conversation, was very much wrought up over the review in *Blackwood's Edinburgh Magazine*. He wrote an article in defense of Keats and sent it to Blackwood, but Blackwood refused to print it. "They attack people," he wrote Taylor on October 5, "but do not leave their columns open to defence." He wrote an article in censure of the principles of reviewing in *Blackwood's Edinburgh Magazine* and sent it to Constable's *Scotts and Edinburgh Magazine*; but Constable, reluctant to be drawn into the controversy, returned it "without a word."

Keats's friends in England ignored the review of *Endymion* in *Blackwood's Edinburgh Magazine*; but they answered the article in *The Quarterly Review*, for they feared that the reviewer's pretense of condemning the poem on the basis of its poetic defects would destroy Keats's reputation as a poet and prevent the sale of copies of the poem. A correspondent in *The Morning Chronicle* for October 3 protested against the injustice which the *Quarterly* reviewer had done to Keats.

Sir, Although I am aware that literary squabbles are of too uninteresting and interminable a nature for your Journal, yet there are occasions when acts of malice and gross injustice towards an author may be properly brought before the public through such a medium. — Allow me, then, without further preface, to refer you to an article in the last Number of The Quarterly Review, professing to be a Critique on "The Poems of John Keats." Of John Keats I know nothing; from his Preface I collect that he is very young — no doubt a heinous sin; and I have been informed that he has incurred the additional guilt of an acquaintance with Mr. Leigh Hunt. That this latter Gentleman and the Editor of The Quarterly Review have long been at war, must be known to every one in the least acquainted with the literary gossip of the day. Mr. L. Hunt, it appears, has thought highly of the poetical talents of Mr. Keats; hence Mr. K. is doomed to feel the merciless tomahawk of the Reviewers, termed Quarterly, I presume from the modus operandi. From a perusal of the criticism, I was led to the work itself. I would, Sir, that your limits would permit a few extracts from this poem. I dare appeal to the taste and judgment of your readers, that beauties of the highest order may be found in almost every page — that there are also many, very many passages indicating haste and carelessness, I will not deny; I will go further, and assert that a real friend of the author would have dissuaded him from an immediate publication.

Had the genius of Lord Byron sunk under the discouraging sneers of an Edinburgh Review the nineteenth century would scarcely yet have been termed the Augustan aera of Poetry. Let Mr. Keats too persevere — he has talents of [no] common stamp; this is the hastily written tribute of a stranger, who ventures to predict that Mr. K. is capable of producing a poem that shall challenge the admiration of every reader of true taste and feeling; nay if he will give up his acquaintance with Mr. Leigh Hunt, and apostatise in his friendships, his principles and his politics (if he have any), he may even command the approbation of the Quarterly Review.

I have not heard to whom public opinion has assigned this exquisite morceau of critical acumen. If the Translator of Juvenal [William Gifford] be its author, I would refer him to the manly and pathetic narrative prefixed to that translation, to the touching history of genius oppressed by and struggling with innumerable difficulties, yet finally triumphing under patronage and encouragement. If the Biographer of Kirke White [Robert Southey] have done Mr. Keats this cruel wrong, let him remember his own just and feeling expostulation with the Monthly Reviewer, who "sat down to blast the hopes of a boy, who had confessed to him all his hopes and all his difficulties." If the "Admiralty Scribe" [John Wilson Croker] (for he too is a Reviewer) be the critic, let him compare the "Battle of Talavera" with "Endymion."

I am, Sir, Your obedient servant,

J. S.

A correspondent in *The Morning Chronicle* for October 8 made a similar protest.

Sir, — The spirited and feeling remonstrance of your correspondent J. S. against the cruelty and injustice of the Quarterly Review, has most ably anticipated the few remarks which I had intended to address to you on the subject. But your well known liberality in giving admission to every thing calculated to do justice to oppressed and injured merit, induces me to trespass further on your valuable columns, by a few extracts from Mr. Keat's Poem. As the Reviewer professes to have read only the first book, I have confined my quotations to that part of the Poem; and I leave your readers to judge whether the Critic who could pass over such beauties as these lines contain, and condemn the whole Poem as "consisting of the most incongruous ideas in the most uncouth language," is very implicitely to be relied on.

I am, Sir, Your obedient servant,

R. B.

Temple, Oct. 3rd 1818.

By pointing out the political causes of the attack upon Keats, by showing the cruelty and injustice of the attack, by referring readers to the poem itself, and by quoting extracts from the poem, J. S. and R. B. did all that they could possibly do to counteract the influence of the *Quarterly* reviewer. The identities of these correspondents have never been established. J. S. may have been John Scott or James Smith. I should like to believe that J. S. was John Scott, who was killed in a duel with Lockhart's friend, J. H. Christie, in January 1821, a week before Keats's death. Scott, the editor of *The London Magazine*, published by Taylor and Hessey, was drawn into the duel by denouncing Lockhart as the author of the articles signed "Z" in *Blackwood's Edinburgh Magazine*. Keats had met Scott in 1817, when Scott was editor of *The Champion*; and Tom Keats had met him in Paris in September 1817 and had given him a notebook containing transcripts of some of Keats's poems. The approval of Leigh Hunt in J. S.'s article and the flattering allusion to Byron indicate, however, that J. S. was not Scott, who had quarrelled with Leigh Hunt over the question of Byron's separation from Lady Byron. They indicate, on the other hand, that J. S. was James Smith, who, like his brother Horace Smith, was an intimate friend of Leigh

Hunt's. We cannot be sure, however, that J. S. was James Smith; for Keats, who knew Smith, never discovered, it seems, the identity of J. S. The identity of R. B., who wrote the other article in defense of Keats in *The Morning Chronicle*, is not known at all. There is a transcript of his article in Woodhouse's Scrap-book, in which his signature is copied "B. B." instead of "R. B.", with "aily" written in pencil after the second "B," making the signature "B. B. (aily)." R. B. was not Benjamin Bailey, however, for Bailey, who wrote several letters to Taylor in September and October relating his efforts in behalf of Keats, did not mention the article in *The Morning Chronicle*.

Reynolds, who was visiting in Exeter, published an article in defense of Keats in *The Alfred, West of England Journal and General Advertiser* for October 6; and Leigh Hunt reprinted this article in *The Examiner* for October 11. Reynolds, having a sympathetic understanding of Keats's mind, answered the *Quarterly* reviewer as Keats himself might have done. After condemning the cruelty and injustice of the reviewer in attacking Keats as a political disciple of Leigh Hunt, Reynolds defined the impersonal and objective character of Keats's poetic genius, comparing him to "our older poets" and contrasting him with contemporary poets. His definition of the objectivity of Keats's poetry, which I have quoted in an earlier connection, might be a paraphrase of the letter which Keats wrote him on February 3, 1818, eight months before. In conclusion he said:

> Two things have struck us on the perusal of this singular poem [*Endymion*]. The first is, that Mr. Keats excels, in what Milton excelled — the power of putting a spirit of life and novelty into the Heathen Mythology. The second is, that in the structure of his verse, and the sinewy quality of his thoughts, Mr. Keats greatly resembles old Chapman, the nervous translator of Homer. His mind has "thews and limbs like to its ancestors." Mr. Gifford, who knows something of the old dramatists, ought to have paused before he sanctioned the abuse of a spirit kindred with them. If he could not feel, he ought to know better.

Reynolds returned to London from Exeter in the early part of October and called on Keats in Hampstead on Tuesday, October 13, two days after his article in defense of Keats had been reprinted by Leigh Hunt in *The Examiner*. He read *The Pot of Basil*, which Keats had composed in Teignmouth, advised Keats to revise those parts of the romance which the reviewers might attack, suggested the alteration of one word, and urged him to publish the poem as an answer to the reviewers. He took the manuscript home with him for a more careful perusal, and the next morning he wrote Keats:

My Dear Keats.

I was most delighted at seeing you yesterday, — for I hardly knew how I was to meet with you, situated as you are, and confined as I am. I wish I could have stayed longer with you. As to the Poem I am of all things anxious that you should publish it, for its completeness will be a full answer to all the ignorant malevolence of cold lying Scotchmen and stupid Englishmen. The overweening struggle to *oppress* you only shows the world that so much of Endeavour cannot be directed to Nothing. Men do not set their muscles, and strain their sinews to break a straw. I am confident, Keats, that the Pot of Basil hath that simplicity and quiet pathos, which are of sure sovereignty over all hearts. I must say that it would delight me to have you prove yourself to the world, what we know you to be; — to have you annul the Quarterly Review, by the best of all answers.

When I see you I will give you the Poem, and pray look over it with that eye to the *littleness* which the world are so fond of excepting to (though I confess with that word altered which I mentioned I see nothing that can be cavilled at) — And let us have the Tale put forth, now that an interest is aroused. One or two of your Sonnets you might print, I am sure — And I know that I may suggest to you, which — because you can decide as you like after[ward. You] will remember that we were [to] pu[t out] together. I give over all intention and you ought to be alone. I can never write anything now — my mind is taken the other way; — But I shall set my heart on having you, high, as you ought to be. Do *you* get Fame — and I shall have it in being your affectionate and steady friend. There is no one I am more interested in — and there is no one that I have more pleasure in communicating my own happiness to. You will gratify me much by letting me have, whenever you have leisure, copies of what you write;— for *more than myself* have a sincere interest in you. When shall I see you — & when shall I go with you to Severn's[?]

Your ever affectionate

Wed^{n} Morn. J. H. Reynolds[5]

[Postmarked October 14.]

Keats, deeply appreciative of Reynolds' generous encouragement, referred to it in the journal letter which he wrote his brother George in October 1818.

Reynolds has returned from a six weeks enjoyment in Devonshire, he is well and persuades me to publish my pot of Basil as an answer to the attacks made on me in Blackwood's Magazine and the Quarterly Review.

Richard Woodhouse, the friend of Taylor, publisher of *Endymion*, was the most whole-hearted defender of Keats. He encouraged Keats himself, as we shall see, maintained Taylor's faith in him, and defended the poet on all occasions. He wrote a letter in defense of Keats to his cousin, Mary Frogley of Hounslow, shortly after the attack of the Tory reviewers upon *Endymion*. He had obtained copies of Keats's juvenile poems, we remember, from Miss Frogley, who had been a member of George Felton Mathew's coterie in 1815.

[5] Amy Lowell, Vol. II, pp. 105–106. M. B. Forman, Vol. I, pp. 249–250.

My dear Mary,

I returned from Hounslow late last night, & your mother desired me to forward to you the enclosed letter. I brought Endymion back, thinking you might like to have it in Town whilst with your friends.

You were so flattering as to say the other day, you wished I had been in a company where you were, to defend Keats. — In all places, & at all times, & before all persons, I would express, and as far as I am able, support my high opinion of his poetical merits — Such a genius, I verily believe, has not appeared since Shakespeare & Milton: and I may assert without fear of contradiction from any one competent to judge, that if his Endymion be compared with Shakespeare's earliest work (his Venus & Adonis) written about the same age, Keats's poem will be found to contain more beauties, more poetry (and that of a higher order) less conceit & bad taste and in a word much more promise of excellence than are to be found in Shakespeare's work — This is a deliberate opinion; nor is it merely my own. The Justice of which, however, can only be demonstrated to another upon a full review of the parts & of the whole of each work. I sh^{d} not shrink from the task of doing it to one whose candour I was acquainted with, and whose Judgment I respected.

But in our common conversation upon his merits, we should always bear in mind that his fame may be more hurt by indiscriminate praise than by wholesale censure. I would at once admit that he has great faults — enough indeed to sink another writer. But they are more than counterbalanced by his beauties; and this is the proper mode of appreciating an original genius. His faults will wear away — his fire will be chastened and then eyes will do homage to his brilliancy. But genius is wayward, trembling, easily daunted. And shall we not excuse the errors, the luxuriances of youth? Are we to expect that poets are to be given to the world, as our first parents were, in a state of maturity? Are they to have no season of childhood; are they to have no room to try their wings before the steadiness & strength of their flight are to be finally judged of? So says Mr. Gifford of the Quarterly — But the world meted out a far different measure to his youthful infirmities, — though he forgets it — So said the Edinburgh Review of Ld Byron — So said the Monthly of Kirke White — So said Horace Walpole of Chatterton. And how are such critics now execrated for their cruel injustice. I see the daily papers teem with remonstrances against Gifford's arbitrary decision. An appeal to the Country is lodged against it. Perhaps this age, — certainly posterity, — will judge rightly — However the decision be, the competence of a poet to write, and of a critic to judge of poetry are involved in the dispute, and one reputation must suffer deeply. Had I any literary reputation I would stake it on the result. You know the side I should espouse. As it is, — I can only prophesy. And now, while Keats is unknown, unheeded, despised of one of our archcritics, neglected by the rest — in the teeth of the world, and in the face of "these anxious days," I express my conviction, that Keats during his life (if it please God to spare him to the usual age of man, and the critics not to drive him from the free air of the Poetic heaven before his wings are full fledged,) will rank on a level with the best of the last or of the present generation; and after his death will take his place at their head. —

But, while I think thus, I would make persons respect my judgment by the discrimination of my praise, and by the freedom of my censure where his writings are open to it. These are the Elements of true criticism — It is easy, like Momus, to find fault with the clattering of the slippers worn by the Goddess of beauty; but "the serious Gods" found better employment in admiration of her unapproachable loveliness. — A Poet ought to write for Posterity. But a critic should do so too. — Those of our times write for the hour. Their thoughts & judgments are fashionable garbs, such as they imagine a skin-wise world would like to array itself in at second hand. — How is the great Johnson

Fallen, fallen, fallen, fallen,
Fallen from his high Estate

by the malice, the injustice, & envy of his criticisms in that "Monument of his Mortality, the lives of the Poets," and by his deadness to exalted and excellent in Poetry.

Adieu, my dear Mary; — I have mounted so far into the clouds that I am, like Endymion,

—"Become loth & fearful to alight
From such high soaring;"

but when he did, it was to pay his respects to a divinity. In this too I follow his example, kissing your poor *one* hand, and craving kind remembrances to the divine ones around you.

I am yours, Rich[d] Woodhouse
Friday Even[g] —

[From a transcript in Woodhouse's Scrap-book.]

From the fall of 1818 to the end of Keats's life, Woodhouse was untiring in his efforts to assist him in every possible way. Even Reynolds, one of the most intimate and most loyal of Keats's friends, admitted that Woodhouse was the champion of Keats's poetry. He wrote Woodhouse from Esher on April 6, 1820:

I was so vexed last evening to hear his Endymion so abused by some ladies who drank tea here and Mr. Neville how much I wished for you to point out some of the countless beauties with which it abounds, but I think even your rhetoric would have been useless so prejudiced did they seem against the whole of his writings even that beautiful and grand Sonnet to the "sea" failed to interest them after that I gave them up as *lost muttons*. . . .

[From a transcript in Woodhouse's Scrap-book.]

We have no record of Keats's first reactions to the savage attacks of the Tory reviewers of *Endymion*; but we have a record of his reactions to the earlier attacks upon Hunt. He wrote Bailey on November 5, 1817, we remember, that he did not "relish" the abuse of Blackwood's reviewer. "If he should go to such lengths with me as he has done with Hunt," he said, "I must infal[l]ibly call him to an account — if he be a human being and appears in Squares and Theatres where we might possibly meet." When he was ridiculed in *Blackwood's Edinburgh Magazine* in September 1818, his first impulse doubtless was to seek out the reviewer and chastise him in a personal encounter. He was restrained, however, by circumstances, the chief of which were his own illness and the fatal relapse of his brother Tom. He resolved therefore to ignore the "abuse" of the Tory reviewers.

About the middle of September 1818, Keats, Hazlitt, Woodhouse, and probably others dined with Hessey. The August number of *Blackwood's Edinburgh Magazine*, containing the scurrilous review of *Endymion* and an equally scurrilous article upon Hazlitt ("Hazlitt Cross-questioned"), had appeared but the April number of *The Quarterly Review* had not yet been published. The guests at the dinner party conversed with one another in an atmosphere of restraint and suspense, none venturing to mention the attacks upon Keats and Hazlitt in *Blackwood's Edinburgh Magazine.*

I suppose you will have heard [Keats wrote Dilke on September 21] that Hazlitt has on foot a prosecution against Blackwood. I dined with him a few days since at Hessey's — there was not a word said about [it], though I understand he is excessively vexed.

Woodhouse revealed Keats's conversation at Hessey's dinner party in a letter which he wrote Keats on October 21, a month later. Keats declared that there was now nothing original to be written in poetry, that its riches were already exhausted, and that he should, consequently, write no more. Woodhouse believed that Keats's statements were provoked by the ridicule of his poetry by Blackwood's reviewer. Keats's answer to Woodhouse's letter of encouragement, we shall see later, represents a significant change in his philosophy of poetry.

Hessey, like Woodhouse, feared that Keats would lose his confidence in his poetry; and, in the first part of October, he sent Keats the copies of *The Morning Chronicle* in which J. S. and R. B. answered the *Quarterly* reviewer's attack upon *Endymion.* Keats wrote Hessey on October 9:

My dear Hessey,

You are very good in sending me the letters from the Chronicle — and I am very bad in not acknowledging such a kindness sooner — pray forgive me. It has so chanced that I have had that paper every day — I have seen today's. I cannot but feel indebted to those Gentlemen who have taken my part. As for the rest, I begin to get a little acquainted with my own strength and weakness. — Praise or blame has but a momentary effect on the man whose love of beauty in the abstract makes him a severe critic on his own Works. My own domestic criticism has given me pain without comparison beyond what Blackwood or the Quarterly could possibly inflict — and also when I feel I am right, no external praise can give me such a glow as my own solitary reperception and ratification of what is fine. J. S. is perfectly right in regard to the slip-shod Endymion. That it is so is no fault of mine. — No! — though it may sound a little paradoxical. It is as good as I had power to make it — by myself. Had I been nervous about its being a perfect piece, and with that view asked advice, and trembled over every page, it would not have been written; for it is not in my nature to fumble — I will write independantly. — I have written independently *without Judgment*. I may write independently, and *with Judgment* hereafter. The Genius of Poetry must work out its own salvation in a man: It cannot be matured by law and precept, but by sensation and watchfulness in itself. That which is creative must create itself. In Endymion, I leaped headlong into the Sea, and thereby have become better acquainted with the Soundings, the quicksands, and the rocks, than if I had stayed upon the green shore, and piped a silly pipe, and took tea and comfortable advice. — I was never afraid of failure; for I would sooner fail than not be among the greatest. But I am nigh getting into a rant. So, with remembrances to Taylor and Woodhouse etc. I am

Yours very sincerely

John Keats.

This famous letter deserves all of the praise which Keats's biographers and critics have bestowed upon it. It is the classic answer of a great poet to the fault-findings of small reviewers. It is also of great significance in a study of the evolution of Keats's poetry.

Keats composed *Endymion* independently. He rejected Leigh Hunt's system of poetry in April 1817, studied Shakespeare's plays, and developed an independent system of poetry. He composed *Endymion* and developed his new system of poetry at the same time. He was not able to discard at once the diction and the versification which he had learned from Hunt. His philosophy of poetry developed so rapidly that, before he had completed the third book of *Endymion*, he was dissatisfied with what he had composed. He perceived the defects in the style of the poem but he was unwilling to revise them. He regarded the poem as a discipline by which he strengthened his poetic faculties and perfected his poetic style; and he was eager to have done with it and begin a new poem.

Keats showed poor judgment in publishing *Endymion* without thorough revision. Since he perceived the defects of the poem, he ought either to have revised them or not to have published the poem. He had to publish the poem, however; for he had already received partial payment for it from his publishers. He took the easiest way out of the matter: he published the poem with a very slight revision. He did not take the trouble, for instance, to copy the first draft of the first book. The reviewers of *Endymion* taught him a painful but valuable lesson. He composed his poems thereafter not only independently but also with judgment. The manuscripts of the poems which he published in his third and last volume, such as that of *The Eve of St. Agnes*, show the most careful and painstaking revision.

The sane and manly character of Keats's reactions to the scurrilous reviews of *Endymion* stands out clearly in the letter which he wrote his brother George in October 1818.

> There have been two Letters in my defence in the Chronicle and one in the Examiner, coppied from the Alfred Exeter paper and written by Reynolds. I don't know who wrote those in the Chronicle — this is a mere matter of the moment — I think I shall be among the English Poets after my death. Even as a Matter of present interest the attempt to crush me in the ~~Chro~~ Quarterly has only brought me more into notice and it is a common expression among book men "I wonder the Quarterly should cut its own throat."
>
> It does me not the least harm in Society to make me appear little and rediculous [*sic*]: I know when a Man is superior to me and give him all due respect — he will be the last to laugh at me and as for the rest I feel that I make an impression upon them which insures me personal respect while I am in sight whatever they may say when my back is turned.

3

The fall of 1818 has been the most difficult period for critics of Keats's poetry to analyze and to interpret. Keats did not compose any poetry at all for a month after he returned to Hampstead from Scotland. About September 21 he translated one of Ronsard's sonnets and he composed, I believe, an introduction to a projected humanitarian and Wordsworthian version of "Hyperion." In the latter part of October a crisis occurred in his poetic evolution — his rejection of Wordsworth's humanitarianism and his resumption of the humanism of Shakespeare and Milton. And at the end of October (or possibly at the middle of December after the death of his brother Tom), he began the humanistic and Miltonic *Hyperion*.

To understand this crisis in Keats's poetic evolution, we must analyze those elements of his experience in which and by which it was engendered. In the first place, he was exhausted and ill when he returned to Hampstead on August 17; and, although his sore throat left him for a while, it returned and persisted to the second week in October. This sore throat was a serious attack of laryngeal tuberculosis, although neither he nor his physician, Dr. Sawrey, recognized it as such. In the second place, when he returned to Hampstead he found that Tom had suffered a relapse and was indeed sinking through the final stage of pulmonary tuberculosis. His brother, who had an exquisite love of life, faced death with rebellious despair and clung to him with pathetic dependence. His constant attendance at the bedside of his brother not only distressed him with pity and grief but it also destroyed any slight chance which he may have had to recover from tuberculosis. In the third place, the malignant reviews of *Endymion* were published in the Tory periodicals in the latter part of September. These reviews were a minor affliction in comparison with the slow and painful death of his brother. In the fourth place, a rising tide of sexual feelings, stimulated doubtless by tuberculosis, entered into the turmoil of his mind in this period.

Keats's life and poetry before the fall of 1818 were singularly unaffected by personal experience in love. The circumstances of his boyhood — the disruption of his home by the death of his father in 1804 and his residence in the Clarke School from 1803 to the midsummer of 1811 — removed him almost altogether from association with women. The only women with whom he was intimately associated in his early youth were, as far as there is record, his mother, who was ill and despondent, his aged grandmother, and his very young sister. He formed his ideal of women from the gentle, clinging, ethereal ladies of romantic poetry. The first young women with whom he had social intercourse were Ann and Caroline Mathew, whom he met on his visits with his brother George in London in 1814 and 1815. He met Georgiana Augusta Wylie in the summer of 1816 and Jane and Marianne Reynolds in the fall of 1816. He admired Miss Wylie, the fiancée of his brother George, but he was disappointed in general with the young women of London. He complained that the women whom he knew were "flippant, vain, inconstant, childish, proud, and full of fancies" and compared them unfavorably to the "meek, and kind, and tender" ladies of romance. He was never quite able to outgrow his artificial, chivalric ideal of women. He did not like to regard women as flesh-and-blood human beings. He desired women to be devoid of human foibles and vices, and at the same time he had a low opinion of their imagination and intellect. He confessed, in August 1820, that he had "a tendency to class women in [his] books with roses and sweetmeats."

A second force which influenced Keats's relations with women was his painful consciousness of his abnormally short stature. His feeling of physical inferiority revealed itself for the first time, we have seen, in the sonnet *Had I a man's fair form*, which he composed in the spring of 1816. It appeared also, we shall see, in the letter which he wrote Bailey in July 1818; and it was one of the basic causes of his jealousy of Miss Brawne in the last years of his life.

The masculine and academic environment of Keats's boyhood, combined with the feeling of physical inferiority, delayed and complicated the period of his adolescence or sexual awakening. The rapid and premature development of his imaginative and intellectual faculties may have been, as Miss Lowell suggested, another cause of his belated adolescence. The normal boy experiences this sexual awakening in his sixteenth year, but Keats was nearly twenty-two years of age when he experienced it. The first woman who aroused his sexual feelings was a lady with whom he had a mild flirtation in Hastings in May 1817, after he had composed the first book of *Endymion*. The effect of this excitation shows itself in the second book of *Endymion*, which he composed in Hampstead in the summer of 1817. The nympholeptic dream in the second book, which distorts the neo-Platonic theme of the romance, is a vivid representation of the turmoil of sexual feelings through which he was passing.

An uneasy sex-consciousness, combined with a boyish conception of women as delicate, ethereal beings who lack imagination and intellect, manifested itself in Keats's relations with young women as well as in his poetry. The letters which he wrote the Misses Reynolds in the fall of 1817 and the Misses Jeffrey in the late spring and early summer of 1818 are full of trivial and self-conscious banter. He was displeased with the Misses Reynolds in January 1818 because they disapproved of his brother George's plan to marry Miss Wylie and to emigrate with her to the backwoods of America; and in the late spring of 1818, just before the marriage of his brother to Miss Wylie, he very nearly stopped visiting them. Bailey, who was a suitor of Marianne Reynolds', protested and Keats replied from Scotland on July 18. He made a frank and complete analysis of his attitude toward women in general.

> I am certain I have not a right feeling towards Women — at this moment I am striving to be just to them but I cannot — Is it because they fall so far beneath my Boyish imagination? When I was a Schoolboy I thought a fair Woman a pure Goddess, my mind was a soft nest in which some one of them slept, though she knew it not — I have no right to expect more than their reality. I thought them ethereal above Men — I find them perhaps equal — great by comparison is very small. Insult may be inflicted in more ways than by Word or action — one who is tender of being insulted does not like to think an insult against another. I do not like to think insults in a Lady's Company — I commit a Crime with her which absence would have not known. Is it not extraordinary? When among Men I have no evil thoughts, no malice, no spleen — I feel free to speak or to be silent — I can listen and from every one I can learn— my hands are in my pockets[—] I am free from all suspicion and comfortable. When I am among Women I have evil thoughts, malice, spleen — I cannot speak or be silent — I am full of suspicions and therefore listen to nothing — I am in a hurry to be gone — You must be charitable and put all this perversity to my being disappointed since Boyhood. Yet with such feelings I am happier alone among Crowds of men, by myself or with a friend or two. With all this trust me Bailey I have not the least idea that Men of different feelings and inclinations are more short-sighted than myself. I never rejoiced more than at

my Brother's Marriage and shall do so at that of any of my friends. I must absolutely get over this — but how? The only way is to find the root of evil, and so cure it "with backward mutters of dissevering Power"— that is a difficult thing; for an obstinate Prejudice can seldom be produced but from a gordian complication of feelings, which must take time to unravell and care to keep unravelled. I could say a good deal about this but I will leave it in hopes of better and more worthy dispositions — and also content that I am wronging no one, for after all I do think better of Womankind than to suppose they care whether Mister John Keats five feet high likes them or not. You appear'd to wish to avoid any words on this subject — don't think it a bore my dear fellow — it shall be my Amen.

Keats understood and described clearly the morbid sexual feelings which women stimulated in him but, as he confessed, he did not know the causes of these morbid feelings. Because of his ignorance and inexperience, his sexual desires, instead of being sublimated into an ideal of love, were perverted into an antagonism to women. "I must absolutely get over this," he said, "— but how? The only way is to find the root of evil, and so cure it 'with backward mutters of dissevering Power'— that is a difficult thing; for an obstinate Prejudice can seldom be produced but from a gordian complication of feelings, which must take time to unravell and care to keep unravelled." He studied the problem of his feelings and tried to solve it. At the end of July 1818 he wrote his brother Tom:

With respect to Women I think I shall be able to conquer my passions hereafter better than I have yet done.

In the middle of September, after he had returned to Hampstead from Scotland, Keats called upon the Misses Reynolds and met their cousin, Miss Jane Cox, whose imperial beauty stirred him deeply. He described his reactions to Miss Cox in a letter which he wrote his brother George in the first part of October.

The Miss Reynoldses are very kind to me — but they have lately displeased me much and in this way. Now I am coming the Richardson. On my return the first day I called they were in a sort of taking or bustle about a Cousin of theirs who having fallen out with her Grandpapa in a serious manner was invited by M^rs^ R to take Asylum in her house. She is an east indian and ought to be her Grandfather's Heir. At the time I called Mrs R. was in conference with her up stairs and the young Ladies were warm in her praises down stairs, calling her genteel, interesting and a thousand other pretty things to which I gave no heed, not being partial to 9 days wonders. Now all is completely changed — they hate her; and from what I hear she is not without faults — of a real kind: but she has othe[r]s which are more apt to make women of inferior charms hate her. She is not a Cleopatra, but she is at least a Charmian. She has a rich eastern look; she has fine eyes and fine manners. When she comes into a room she makes an impression the same as the Beauty of a Leopardess. She is too fine and too con[s]cious of her self to repulse any Man who may address her — from habit she thinks that nothing *particular*. I always find myself more at ease with such a woman; the picture before me always gives me a life and animation which I cannot possibly feel with anything inferior. I am at such times too much occupied in admiring to be awkward or on a tremble. I forget myself entirely because I live in her. You will by this time think I am in love with her; so before I go any further I will tell you I am not — she kept me awake one Night as a tune of Mozart's might do. I speak of the thing as a passtime and an amuzement than which I can feel none deeper than a conversation with an imperial woman the very "yes" and "no" of whose Lips is to me a Banquet. I dont cry to take the moon home with me in my Pocket not [nor] do I fret to leave her behind me. I like her and her like because one has no *sensations* — what we both are is taken for granted. You will suppose I have by this had much talk with her — no such thing — there are the Miss Reynoldses on the look out. They think I dont admire her because I did not stare at her. They call her a flirt to me. What a want of knowledge! She walks across a room in such a manner that a Man is drawn towards her with a magnetic Power. This they call flirting! they do not know things. They do not know what a Woman is. I believe tho' she has faults — the same as Charmian and Cleopatra might have had. Yet she is a fine thing speaking in a worldly way....

Miss Cox was one of the few young women with whom Keats felt at ease. She had sufficient beauty, poise, and tact, as Miss Lowell observed, to dissolve his self-consciousness into an admiration for herself. For two or three days she haunted his imagination, keeping him awake at night. He did not fall in love with her — circumstances were not favorable — but she contributed to his amorous experience and prepared him for falling in love with Miss Brawne.

The amorous feelings which Miss Cox aroused in him, his grief for his brother Tom, and Ronsard's sonnets, which Woodhouse had lent him a few days before — these three forces, reacting upon one another in his mind, impelled him to seek relief in poetic composition. He regarded love as "a new strange and threatening sorrow." He felt, so perverted were his feelings, that admiration for Miss Cox was treason to his passion for poetry, to his affection for his brothers and sister, and above all to his devotion to his brother Tom. Constant attendance at the bedside of his dying brother strained his powers of endurance; but the composition of poetry, which would give him momentary relief, seemed to him to be a crime. He wrote Dilke on September 21:

I wish I could say Tom was any better. His identity presses upon me so all day that I am obliged to go out — and although I intended to have given some time to study alone I am obliged to write, and plunge into abstract images to ease myself of his countenance his voice and feebleness — so that I live now in a continual fever — it must be poisonous to life although I feel well. Imagine "the hateful siege of contraries"— if I think of fame[,] of poetry it seems a crime to me, and yet I must do so or suffer. I am sorry to give you pain — I am almost resolv'd to burn this — but I really have not self possession and magnanimity enough to manage the thing otherwise — after all it may be a nervousness proceeding from the Mercury.

The abstract images — or some of them — into which Keats plunged to ease himself of the countenance, the voice, and the feebleness of his dying brother were a translation of the second sonnet of Ronsard's *Les Amours de Cassandre*. At the end of his letter to Dilke he said:

The following is a translation of a Line of Ronsard —

'Love poured her Beauty into my warm veins'—

You have passed your Romance and I never gave into it or else I think this line a feast for one of your Lovers.

Keats wrote a letter to Reynolds on the same day; and to Reynolds, who was romantically in love, he confessed the influence of his admiration for a lady upon his composition of the sonnet. He did not mention her name, however, for she was Reynolds' cousin. He congratulated Reynolds on his happiness in love, but his own bitter unhappiness gave his congratulations a pessimistic twist.

My dear Reynolds,

Believe me I have rather rejoiced in your happiness than fretted at your silence. Indeed I am grieved on your account that I am not at the same time happy. But I conjure you to think at present of nothing but pleasure — "Gather the rose, etc." — gorge the honey of life. I pity you as much that it cannot last for ever, as I do myself now drinking bitters. Give yourself up to it— you cannot help it — and I have a consolation in thinking so. I never was in love — yet the voice and shape of a Woman has haunted me these two days — at such a time, when the relief, the feverous relief of Poetry seems a much less crime. This morning Poetry has conquered — I have relapsed into those abstractions which are my only life — I feel escaped from a new strange and threatening sorrow — and I am thankful for it. There is an awful warmth about my heart like a load of Immortality.

While he was distressed by the illness of his brother and haunted by the beauty of Miss Cox, Keats remembered Ronsard's description of the beauty of Cassandra; and, composing a free and creative translation of Ronsard's sonnet, he escaped from the turmoil of his feelings.

Poor Tom — that woman — and Poetry were ringing changes in my senses. Now I am in comparison happy — I am sensible this will distress you — you must forgive me. . . . Here is a free translation of a Sonnet of Ronsard, which I think will please you — I have the loan of his works — they have great Beauties.

Keats translated only the first twelve verses of Ronsard's sonnet. After copying the translation for Reynolds, he said:

> I had not the original by me when I wrote it, and did not recollect the purport of the last lines.

The autograph letter to Reynolds containing the translation has not been discovered. There is a transcript of it, however, in Woodhouse's Book of Transcripts of Keats's Letters, which is in the Marquess of Crewe's Collection. There are transcripts of the sonnet also in Woodhouse's Scrap-book and in his Book of Transcripts of Keats's Poems. There is an autograph of the sonnet, representing an earlier version, in the copy of Shakespeare's *Poetical Works* which Reynolds gave to Keats and which is now in the Dilke Collection in Hampstead. Underneath Keats's draft of the sonnet Woodhouse wrote the following note:

> This is a translation from one of Ronsard's sonnets (a book I lent Keats) — It begins
>
> Nature ornant Cassandre qui devoit
> De ses forcer les plus rebelles.
>
> I believe I have the translation complete at home.
>
> R. W.

Woodhouse's transcripts, however, also lack the last two verses.

4

Most critics believe that Keats began the composition of one of the two versions of the "Fall of Hyperion" in September 1818, but they do not agree upon the particular version which he began to compose. The "abstract images" into which Keats was obliged to plunge on September 21 to relieve himself from the countenance, the voice, and the feebleness of his dying brother and from the haunting beauty of Miss Cox refer, as we have seen, to his translation of Ronsard's sonnet. They may (but do not necessarily) refer also to a version of the "Fall of Hyperion." Abstract images, in Keats's terminology, mean poetic images as distinguished from sensations or direct impressions from which they are abstracted. It is probable, however, that, having been wrought up into the mood for poetic composition by translating Ronsard's sonnet, Keats began a version of the "Fall of Hyperion," a subject upon which he had been meditating for months. This probability is supported (if not proved to be a fact) by an allusion to persons of the poem in a letter which he wrote Woodhouse on October 27. At Hessey's dinner party, which occurred a few days before September 21, he told Woodhouse that he would not compose any more poetry. Woodhouse wrote him a letter of encouragement on October 21, and he replied on October 27.

> Where is the Wonder that I should say I would write no more? Might I not at that very instant have been cogitating on the Characters of Saturn and Ops?

The proof that he began a version of the "Fall of Hyperion" at this time is based, however, upon internal evidence which we shall consider presently.

The two versions of the "Fall of Hyperion" present the most difficult problems both in dating and in interpretation in the whole course of Keats's poetry. He published *Hyperion* in his *Poems* of 1820. An autograph manuscript, possessed in turn by Leigh Hunt, Thornton Hunt, and Miss Bird, was acquired by the British Museum in 1904 and published in photographic facsimile by de Sélincourt in 1905. There are also transcripts in Woodhouse's Commonplace Book and Book of Transcripts. Keats did not publish *The Fall of Hyperion, a Dream.* After his death the autograph manuscript passed into the possession of Brown, who permitted Woodhouse to transcribe it. Brown gave Lord Houghton a transcript which was made by two of Woodhouse's clerks but, it seems, kept the autograph manuscript, which is now either destroyed or lost. Lord Houghton published the poem in 1856 and in 1867. In October 1904 the Marquess of Crewe, the son of Lord Houghton, found the transcript, which had been mislaid for years, and de Sélincourt printed it in 1905. In 1914 the Marquess of Crewe acquired Woodhouse's Book of Transcripts, which contains Woodhouse's transcript of the poem. In the absence of the autograph manuscript, Woodhouse's transcript is the authoritative text of the poem.

Critical opinion of the relative dates of composition of these two incomplete versions has swayed to and fro. In 1848 Lord Houghton referred to *The Fall of Hyperion, a Dream* as a recast of *Hyperion*; in 1856 he expressed doubt whether it was a first draft or a recast; and in 1867 he decided that it was a first draft. In 1887 Sir Sidney Colvin [6] argued that *The Fall of Hyperion, a Dream* was a reconstruction of *Hyperion*. He based his argument upon evidence of style and upon a statement in Brown's memoir of Keats that "in the evening [November and December 1819] he was deeply engaged in remodeling the fragment of *Hyperion* into the form of a vision." Colvin, together with de Sélincourt, believed that Keats began *Hyperion* in September and October 1818, while he was taking care of his dying brother in Well Walk, and that he completed it in its present form

[6] Sir Sidney Colvin, *Keats* (EML Series), pp. 187, 232.

from the middle of December to the middle of January, while he was living with Brown in Wentworth Place after the death of his brother. They believed also that he composed *The Fall of Hyperion, a Dream* in November and December 1819. In 1924 Miss Lowell[7] argued that Keats composed the introduction to *The Fall of Hyperion, a Dream* in the fall of 1818, beginning it about September 21; that he composed *Hyperion* in the period from December 1818 to April 1819; and that in September 1819 he fused these two separate versions into the extant form of *The Fall of Hyperion, a Dream.* She based her argument chiefly upon quotations from *The Fall of Hyperion, a Dream* in an unpublished letter which Keats wrote to Woodhouse on September 21, 1819. When Miss Lowell published this letter to Woodhouse, Colvin and de Sélincourt[8] modified their dating of *The Fall of Hyperion, a Dream,* arguing that Keats reconstructed *Hyperion* into the form of a vision in September 1819. The opinion of J. M. Murry,[9] the chief opponent of Miss Lowell's dating, differs only in details from that of Colvin and de Sélincourt.

The body of *The Fall of Hyperion, a Dream* (Canto I, vv. 294–468, and Canto II, vv. 1–61) is undoubtedly, as Colvin proved, a reconstruction of the first book of *Hyperion.* The question is whether Keats composed a draft of the introduction to *The Fall of Hyperion, a Dream* before he began *Hyperion.* Statements of Keats, Brown, and Woodhouse, which have been arrayed plausibly in support of both sides of the question, are inconclusive. The question can only be decided, I believe, by a study of the style and philosophy of the introductory part of the poem in relation to the evolution of Keats's philosophy of poetry. His philosophy was continually changing, sometimes developing and progressing, sometimes alternating backward and forward; but we can trace, by means of his letters, each movement in the progress and in the alternation of his ideas. Every one of his poems, we find, reflects invariably the ideas which he held on the day or days on which he composed it.

Keats brooded upon the subject of the "Fall of Hyperion" for about a year before he began to compose it into the form of a poem. In this period there were three changes in his philosophy of poetry and consequently three changes in his intuition of the poem. In September 1817, while he was visiting Bailey in Oxford and composing the third book of *Endymion*, he chose the "Fall of Hyperion"

[7] Amy Lowell, Vol. II, pp. 339 *et seq.*

[8] Ernest de Sélincourt, pp. 484 *et seq.*; and letter to *The Manchester Guardian* for September 22, 1922.

[9] J. M. Murry, *Keats and Shakespeare*, pp. 242 *et seq.*

as the subject of his next long poem. Taking Spenser and Shakespeare as his poetic masters but not understanding Shakespeare very well, he believed that the function of poetry was the subjective expression of ideal or essential beauty in a sensuous, diffuse, and romantic style. He intuited the "Fall of Hyperion" therefore as a romance like *Endymion*. He wrote Haydon on October 28 that he had finished the third book of *Endymion*, that he was tired of the poem, and that he had "a new romance" in his eye "for next summer." In the third and fourth books of *Endymion*, we have seen, he alluded to some of the chief persons of the story of the "Fall of Hyperion."

In September 1817 Keats began to study Wordsworth's humanitarianism and to distrust his philosophy of beauty; but at the end of November he wrote Bailey that he could not accept Wordsworth's philosophy. In November and December he discovered the intensity and the objectivity of Shakespeare's plays. In December he discovered the conciseness, the intensity, and the sublimity of Milton's *Paradise Lost* and rejected Spenser's style as sentimental and diffuse. He developed his philosophy of negative capability out of the neo-Platonic philosophy of beauty, the conciseness and sublimity of Milton's *Paradise Lost*, and the intensity and objectivity of Shakespeare's plays. The neo-Platonic philosophy of beauty, which he had learned from Spenser, he found also in Shakespeare and Milton.

In January 1818 Keats changed his intuition of the "Fall of Hyperion" to conform to his new philosophy of negative capability. He wrote Haydon on January 23 that he intended to compose the "Fall of Hyperion" in a "naked and grecian Manner" instead of in the "deep and sentimental" style of *Endymion*. He added that "the march of passion and endeavour" in the "Fall of Hyperion" will be undeviating, and that the great contrast between the two poems will lie in the characters of the heroes: that Endymion, being mortal, is led on, like Buonaparte, by circumstance whereas Apollo, being a foreseeing god, will shape his actions like one. In other words, he decided to compose a Miltonic epic instead of a Spenserian romance.

On April 24, 1818, as we have seen, Keats rejected his philosophy of negative capability and accepted a humanitarian philosophy of poetry which he developed out of Wordsworth's *Excursion*; but on October 27, for reasons which we shall study in detail, he resumed his philosophy of negative capability. From this time to the end of his life, we shall see, he became more and more sceptical of humanitarian principles. The period from April 24 to the end of October 1818 is, therefore, the only period in his life in which he professed humanitarianism. In this period, to judge by his action in the preceding periods, he changed his intuition of the "Fall of Hyperion" from that of a Miltonic and humanistic epic to that of a Wordsworthian and humanitarian vision. In this period also, I am convinced, he composed a draft of an introduction to a humanitarian version of the poem. I base my conviction upon the fact that the introductory part of *The Fall of Hyperion, a Dream* is humanitarian and Wordsworthian in philosophy and natural and Wordsworthian in style.

We must overrun chronology to show the relation between the two versions of the "Fall of Hyperion." At the end of October 1818, after Keats had resumed his philosophy of negative capability, he began the Miltonic and humanistic *Hyperion* and completed it in its present form in April 1819, when he gave the manuscript to Woodhouse. In September 1819 he became dissatisfied with Milton's artificial style and made a futile attempt to fuse the Miltonic and Wordsworthian versions of the poem into a third version, *The Fall of Hyperion, a Dream*. He was unable to complete the poem, however, because consumption was beginning to sap his vitality, because he no longer believed in humanitarianism, and because he could not remove the style of Milton from the Miltonic version without destroying the beauty of the verse. As a result of this incomplete fusion, *The Fall of Hyperion, a Dream* has an introduction which is Wordsworthian and humanitarian and a body which is Miltonic and humanistic.

We can conjecture the approximate (possibly the exact) date on which Keats began the humanitarian version of the "Fall of Hyperion." He did not begin this version in May 1818, the beginning of his humanitarian period, for he was strongly resolved at this time to acquire knowledge by reading and travelling before he composed another long poem. He did not begin the poem in June, July, and August, for his energies in these months were consumed by the marriage and emigration of his brother George and by his own excursion into Scotland. After he returned to Hampstead on August 17, his composition of poetry was stopped for a month by his own illness and that of his brother Tom. On September 21, we have seen, he was "obliged to plunge into abstract images" to relieve himself from the pressing identity of his dying brother and from the haunting beauty of Miss Cox. After he resumed poetic composition by translating Ronsard's sonnet, he began, I believe, the humanitarian version of the "Fall of Hyperion." Ronsard and this version of the poem were associated in some way in his mind. For on September 21, 1819, exactly a year later, he began a sonnet "in the french of Ronsard" while he was attempting to fuse the humanitarian and humanistic versions of the "Fall of Hyperion." Another bit of evidence that he was working on a version of the "Fall of Hyperion" in September and October 1818 is contained, as we have seen, in his letter to Woodhouse on October 27. "Might I not at that very instant [the dinner party at Hessey's a few days before September 21] have been cogitating," he asked, "on the Characters of Saturn and Ops?"

The original draft of the introduction to the humanitarian version of the "Fall of Hyperion" has not survived. In September 1819, however, Keats prefixed a revised version of this introduction to a revised body of the humanistic *Hyperion*. He made very few alterations in the original introduction, it is probable. He did not change the humanitarian symbolism of the original introduction; for, to have changed this symbolism, he would have had to rewrite the whole introduction, and he did not have sufficient vitality at this time to attempt the labor of rewriting. He contented himself, therefore, with the insertion of a passage of 24 verses (Canto I, vv. 187–210), in which he expressed a humanistic answer to the humanitarian theme of the introduction. J. M. Murry differs with me in my interpretation of the reconstructed poem, but he agrees that the thought of this passage is contradictory to the thought of the introduction in which it is embedded. This passage, which was omitted by Lord Houghton in his editions of the poem, was unknown to editors and critics until the discovery of Woodhouse's transcript in 1904. Woodhouse cancelled the passage with a pencil mark and added a marginal note to the first verse:

> Keats seems to have intended to erase this and the next twenty-one lines.

Keats did not, of course, intend to erase this passage. It was a crude first draft which he had inserted into the more finished verses of the original introduction. He never had the vitality to revise it, and he left in it four verses which occur a few lines later in the introduction. Since this passage represents a later stage of Keats's philosophy of poetry, I shall omit it from the following interpretation of the introduction.

Keats based the theme of this introduction upon that natural and rational humanitarianism which he developed with Bailey's assistance out of Wordsworth's *Excursion*. In April 1818, we remember, he distrusted his philosophy of negative capability and in particular the principle of the imagination as the faculty which apprehends truth and beauty. He longed for a rational principle by means of which he could control and reconcile his imaginative intuitions (or sensations, as he termed them). At the end of April he accepted the humanitarian principles of universal benevolence or philanthropy, the perfectibility of human nature, and the progress of society by means of education. He believed that knowledge and reason, the faculty of knowledge, would enable him to reconcile his painful imaginative intuitions and to assist the progress of humanity to a state of happiness. "An extensive knowledge," he wrote Reynolds on May 3, "is needful to thinking people — it takes away the heat and fever; and helps, by widening speculation, to ease the Burden of the Mystery." "I find that I can have no enjoyment in the World but continual drinking of Knowledge," he wrote Taylor on April 24, "— I find there is no worthy pursuit but the idea of doing some good for the world." He decided that Wordsworth was a greater philosopher than Milton because he saw more deeply into the human heart and strove more intensely to alleviate human ignorance, poverty, and misery. He thought, however, that Wordsworth's deeper insight into the human heart was due to a "grand march of intellect" rather than to superior intellectual faculties.

Keats cast the materials of *The Fall of Hyperion, a Dream* into the form of a dream or vision, the idea for which he derived from Dante's *Divine Comedy.* Bailey had induced him to study Dante; and the only books which he took with him on his Scottish excursion were the three minute volumes of an edition of Cary's translation of *The Divine Comedy.*

Keats began the introduction with reflections upon the dreams by which poets have interpreted the problems of human existence.

> Fanatics have their dreams, wherewith they weave
> A paradise for a Sect; the Savage too
> From forth the loftiest fashion of his Sleep
> Guesses at Heaven; pity these have not
> Trac'd upon vellum or wild indian leaf
> The shadows of melodious utterance.
> But bare of laurel they live, dream and die;
> For Poesy alone can tell her dreams,
> With the fine spell of words alone can save
> Imagination from the Sable chain
> And dumb enchantment — Who alive can say,
> "Thou art no Poet — may'st not tell thy dreams?"
> Since every Man whose Soul is not a clod
> Hath visions, and would speak, if he had lov'd,
> And been well nurtured in his mother tongue.
> Whether the dream now purposed to rehearse
> Be Poets or Fanatics will be known
> When this warm scribe my hand is in the Grave.[10]

[10] This and the following passages are quoted from Ernest de Sélincourt's *Hyperion, A Facsimile of Keats's Autograph Manuscript. With a Transliteration of the Manuscript of The Fall of Hyperion, a Dream.*

We can trace the sources of these reflections in *The Excursion*. The idea that "every Man whose Soul is not a clod Hath visions, and would speak, if he had lov'd, And been well nurtured in his mother tongue" was suggested by a passage in the first book of *The Excursion* (vv. 77 *et seq.*), in which Wordsworth described the Wanderer as an untaught and inarticulate poet and observed:

> Oh! many are the Poets that are sown
> By Nature; men endowed with highest gifts,
> The vision and the faculty divine;
> Yet wanting the accomplishment of verse,
> . . . through lack
> Of culture and the inspiring aid of books . . .
> All but a scattered few, live out their time. . . .
> And go to the grave, unthought of.

The idea that "the Savage too From forth the loftiest fashion of his Sleep Guesses at Heaven" may have been suggested by more than one passage of *The Excursion*. In the fourth book (vv. 631 *et seq.*) Wordsworth, speculating about the mysteries of human existence, explained the origins of primitive religions. Keats employed this theory, we remember, in two earlier poems: *I stood tip-toe upon a little hill* and *Endymion*. In the third book (vv. 232 *et seq.*) Wordsworth referred to the "dreams" by which primitive men, such as American Indians, explained the mystery of whence men come and whither they go; and, in defense of the "dreams" which poets have expressed, he said:

> . . . if smiles
> Of scornful pity be the just reward
> Of Poesy thus courteously employed
> In framing models to improve the scheme
> Of Man's existence, and recast the world,
> Why should not grave Philosophy be styled,
> Herself, a dreamer of a kindred stock,
> A dreamer yet more spiritless and dull?

The distinction which Keats drew later in his humanitarian introduction between true or humanitarian poets and idle or visionary poets was suggested to him by this and other passages in *The Excursion*. In the first book (vv. 634 *et seq.*) the Wanderer, after relating the story of Margaret to Wordsworth, observed that a power friendly to virtue may be found always in mournful thoughts —

> . . . were't not so,
> I am a dreamer among men, indeed
> An idle dreamer!

Keats derived the symbolism of the first half of the introduction from the stages of man's development which Wordsworth defined in *Tintern Abbey* — childhood, the age of sensation; youth, the age of feeling; and maturity, the age of thought. In the letter which he wrote Reynolds on May 3, 1818, Keats translated these stages of man's development into an allegory of human life.

> I compare human life to a large Mansion of Many Apartments, two of which I can only describe, the doors of the rest being as yet shut upon me. The first we step into we call the infant or thoughtless Chamber, in which we remain as long as we do not think. We remain there a long while, and notwithstanding the doors of the second Chamber remain wide open, showing a bright appearance, we care not to hasten to it; but are at length imperceptibly impelled by the awakening of the thinking principle within us — we no sooner get into the second Chamber, which I shall call the Chamber of Maiden-Thought, than we become intoxicated with the light and the atmosphere, we see nothing but pleasant wonders, and think of delaying there for ever in delight. However among the effects this breathing is father of is that tremendous one of sharpening one's vision into the heart and nature of Man — of convincing one's nerves that the world is full of Misery and Heartbreak, Pain, Sickness and oppression— whereby this Chamber of Maiden Thought becomes gradually darken'd and at the same time on all sides of it many doors are set open — but all dark — all leading to dark passages.

On May 3, 1818, when Keats wrote this letter to Reynolds, he believed that he and Reynolds were on the point of passing out of this Chamber of Maiden-Thought.

> We see not the ballance of good and evil [he told Reynolds]. We are in a Mist. *We* are now in that state — We feel the "burden of the Mystery." To this point was Wordsworth come, as far as I can conceive when he wrote "Tintern Abbey" and it seems to me that his Genius is explorative of those dark Passages. Now if we live, and go on thinking, we too shall explore them. He is a Genius and superior [to] us, in so far as he can, more than we, make discoveries, and shed a light in them.

In the latter part of September 1818, when Keats composed the introduction to the humanitarian "Fall of Hyperion," he was exploring the third chamber of human life and looking forward into the fourth chamber. He dropped the allegory of human life as a mansion of many apartments, however, and invented a new symbolism. He introduced his symbolism of the stages of man's development with the second stage, omitting the first stage as unnecessary to his purpose. The second stage, as he described it, is the stage of sensuous and thoughtless enjoyment of nature; the third is the stage of visionary sympathy with human misery; and the fourth is the stage of active endeavor to alleviate the sufferings of humanity. In his conversation with Moneta at the end of the introduction, he defined three types of poets—the thoughtless, the visionary, and the humanitarian—corresponding to these three stages of man's development.

In the following passage Keats described his entrance into the thoughtless stage and his passage from this stage into that of visionary sympathy with human misery.

> Methought I stood where trees of every clime,
> Palm, Myrtle, Oak, and Sycamore, and Beech,
> With Plantane, and Spice blossoms, made a screen;
> In neighbourhood of fountains (by the noise
> Soft-showering in mine ears), and, (by the touch
> Of scent,) not far from roses. Turning round,
> I saw an arbour with a drooping roof
> Of trellis vines, and bells, and larger blooms,
> Like floral-censers, swinging light in air;
> Before its wreathed doorway, on a mound
> Of Moss, was spread a feast of summer fruits,
> Which nearer seen, seem'd refuse of a Meal
> By angel tasted or our Mother Eve;
> For empty shells were scatter'd on the grass,
> And grape-stalks but half bare, and remnants more,
> Sweet smelling, whose pure kinds I could not know.
> Still was more plenty than the fabled horn
> Thrice emptied could pour forth, at banqueting
> For proserpine return'd to her own fields,
> Where the white heifers low. And appetite
> More yearning than on Earth I ever felt
> Growing within, I ate deliciously;
> And, after not long, thirsted, for thereby
> Stood a cool vessel of transparent juice,
> Sipp'd by the wander'd bee, the which I took,
> And, pledging all the Mortals of the World,
> And all the dead whose names are in our lips,
> Drank. That full draught is parent of my theme.
> No Asian poppy nor Elixir fine
> Of the soon-fading jealous Caliphat;
> No poison gender'd in close Monkish Cell,
> To thin the scarlet conclave of old Men,
> Could so have rapt unwilling life away.
> Among the fragrant husks and berries crush'd,
> Upon the grass I struggled hard against
> The domineering potion; but in vain:
> The cloudy swoon came on, and down I sunk,
> Like a Silenus on an antique vase.

The forest with "trees of every clime" reminds us of a forest of fairyland in *The Faerie Queene*. The chief source of the feast of summer fruits, as Keats himself suggested by his allusion to the "Meal By angel tasted or our Mother Eve," was the feast which Eve prepared for the Archangel Raphael in the fifth book of *Paradise Lost.* A comparative analysis of the sources of the feast in this introduction with those of the feast which Keats described four or five months later in *The Eve of St. Agnes* would be an interesting study in the progressive transmutation of poetic matter in his mind.

Keats believed, following Wordsworth, that each stage of man's development grows out of the preceding stage. He wrote Reynolds on May 3, 1818 that one is impelled imperceptibly out of the Infant or Thoughtless Chamber into the Chamber of Maiden-Thought by the awakening of the thinking principle within him. In the passage which I have quoted from the introduction to the humanitarian "Fall of Hyperion," he symbolized his passage from the stage of thoughtless enjoyment of nature into the stage of visionary sympathy with human misery by the drinking of a "transparent juice" which cast him into a "cloudy swoon." He wrote Reynolds that "among the effects this breathing (this breathing the atmosphere of the Chamber of Maiden-Thought) is father of is that tremendous one of sharpening one's vision into the heart and nature of Man — of convincing one's nerves that the world is full of Misery etc." He remembered in particular, I believe, a passage in the fifth book of *The Excursion* (vv. 1207 *et seq.*) in which Wordsworth, explaining the development of man from youth, the age of feeling, into maturity, the age of thought, said that nature is infused with the spirit of love and that man, by communing with nature, absorbs this spirit and becomes compassionate and wise.

When Keats awoke from his "cloudy swoon" he was in the third stage of his development, the stage of visionary sympathy with human misery. He described this stage with vivid poetic symbols and afterwards, in a conversation with Moneta, explained the significance of the symbols.

> I looked around upon the carved sides
> Of an old Sanctuary with roof august,
> Builded so high, it seem'd that filmed clouds
> Might spread beneath, as o'er the Stars of heaven;
> So old the place was, I remembered none
> The like upon the Earth: what I had seen
> Of grey Cathedrals, buttress'd Walls, rent towers,
> The superannuations of sunk realms,
> Or nature's Rocks toil'd hard in waves and winds,
> Seem'd but the faulture of decrepit things
> To that eternal domed Monument. —
> Upon the Marble at my feet there lay
> Store of strange vessels, and large draperies,
> Which needs had been of dyed asbestos wove,

Or in that place the moth could not corrupt,
So white the linen, so, in some distinct
Ran imageries from a sombre loom.
All in a mingled heap confus'd there lay
Robes, golden tongs, censer and chafing dish,
Girdles, and chains, and holy Jewelries.

This sanctuary, as Keats tells us later, is a temple of Saturn. Details of this description of the sanctuary are closely connected with images which were impressed upon Keats's mind on his Scottish excursion. "Nature's Rocks toil'd hard in waves and winds" and "the silent massy range Of Columns north and south, ending in Mist" were suggested by Fingal's Cave (the cathedral of the sea) with its huge natural columns of black basalt. The bright, golden, mystic images of "Robes, golden tongs, censer and chafing dish, Girdles, and chains, and holy Jewelries" look backward to the poem on Fingal's Cave (July 26, 1818) and the stanzas on Skulls in Beauly Abbey (early August 1818) and forward to *The Eve of St. Mark* (February 1819).

After gazing at the "embossed roof" of the sanctuary and the "silent massy range Of Columns north and south," he looked eastward, where black gates were shut evermore against the sunrise of his youth; and then he turned to the west, to which he must travel, and he saw

An image, huge of feature as a cloud,
At level of whose feet an altar slept,
To be approached on either side by steps,
And marble balustrade, and patient travail
To count with toil the innumerable degrees.

When Keats approached the altar with sober pace, the veiled priestess who ministered there informed him that he would rot on the cold pavement unless he ascended the innumerable steps to the altar before the gummed leaves which burned thereon be consumed. He struggled toward the steps of the altar with prodigious toil. A palsied chill from the pavement numbed his limbs and threatened to stifle his heart.

I strove hard to escape
The numbness; strove to gain the lowest step.
Slow, heavy, deadly was my pace: the cold
Grew stifling, suffocating, at the heart;
And when I clasp'd my hands I felt them not.
One minute before death, my iced foot touch'd
The lowest stair; and as it touch'd, life seem'd
To pour in at the toes: I mounted up,
As once fair Angels on a ladder flew
From the green turf to Heaven. . . .

The symbolism of this passage may be interpreted as follows. A poet will perish for lack of nutriment unless he leaves his palace of art and acquires a knowledge of human beings and a sympathy for their sufferings. The veiled priestess, as we learn later, is Moneta, the Goddess of Memory, the faculty by which knowledge is preserved. The altar of humanitarianism at which she ministers can be reached only by a slow and laborious attainment of knowledge.

When Keats stood before the altar at the foot of the statue of Saturn, he drew from Moneta by means of questions the meaning of his visionary experience.

Keats —

Holy Power . . .
What am I that should so be saved from death?

Moneta —

. . . Thou hast felt
What 'tis to die and live again before
Thy fated hour, that thou hadst power to do so
Is thy own safety; thou hast dated on
Thy doom. . . .

None can usurp this height . . .
But those to whom the miseries of the World
Are misery, and will not let them rest.
All else who find a haven in the World,
Where they may thoughtless sleep away their days,
If by a chance into this fane they come,
Rot on the pavement where thou rotted'st half. —

Keats —

Are there not thousands in the World. . .
Who love their fellows even to the death,
Who feel the giant agony of the World,
And more, like slaves to poor humanity,
Labour for mortal good? I sure should see
Other men here; but I am here alone.

Moneta —

They whom thou spak'st of are no vision'ries
. . . They are no dreamers weak,
They seek no wonder but the human face;
No music but a happy-noted voice —
They come not here, they have no thought to come —

And thou art here, for thou art less than they —
What benefit canst thou, or all thy Tribe,
Do the great World? Thou art a dreaming thing;
A fever of thyself — think of the Earth;
What bliss even in hope is there for thee?
What haven? every creature hath its home;
Every sole man hath days of Joy and pain,

Whether his labours be sublime or low —
The pain alone; the joy alone; distinct:
Only the dreamer venoms all his days,
Bearing more woe than all his Sins deserve.

The Tory reviewers did not censure Keats so severely or so unjustly as he censured himself in this passage. He dismissed with bitter contempt the poetry which he had composed up to this time as either thoughtless or visionary. Thoughtless poets, he said, "thoughtless sleep away their days"; and, if by chance they come into the sanctuary of humanity, they rot for lack of nutriment. Visionary poets are sensitive souls who feel the misery of humanity; but, being weak dreamers, they are powerless to alleviate this misery. Humanitarian poets are active, courageous reformers who not only "feel the giant agony of the World" but also, "like slaves to poor humanity, Labour for mortal good." Keats, in his self-depreciation, classed himself as a dreamer. In the letter which he wrote Bailey in October 1817, when he was first considering Wordsworth's humanitarianism, he admitted that he could not measure up to the humanitarian standard.

I wish I had a heart always open to such sensations [sensations of human kindness] — but there is no altering a Man's nature and mine must be radically wrong for it will lie dormant a whole Month. This leads me to suppose that there are no Men thouroughly [*sic*] wicked, so as never to be self spiritualized into a kind of sublime Misery — but alas! 'tis but for an Hour — he is the only Man "who has kept watch on Man's Mortality" who has philantrophy [*sic*] enough to overcome the disposition [to] an indolent enjoyment of intellect — who is brave enough to volunteer for uncomfortable hours.

After Moneta had censured Keats as an idle dreamer, he said:

If it please,
Majestic shadow, tell me where I am,
Whose Altar this; for whom this Incense curls;
What Image this, whose face I cannot see,
For the broad marble knees; and who thou art,
Of accent feminine so courteous?

When Moneta answered, Keats knew by her voice that she shed long-treasured tears:

This temple, sad and lone,
Is all spar'd from the thunder of a War
Foughten long since by Giant Hierarchy
Against rebellion: this old Image here,
Whose carved features wrinkled as he fell,
Is Saturn's; I Moneta, left supreme
Sole Priestess of his desolation.

Keats, unable to make fit response to Moneta's lament, looked at the altar on which the flame was dying. Then Moneta spoke:

> The Sacrifice is done, but not the less,
> Will I be kind to thee for thy good will.
> My power, which to me is still a curse,
> Shall be to thee a wonder; for the Scenes
> Still swooning vivid through my globed brain,
> With an electral changing misery
> Thou shalt with these dull mortal eyes behold,
> Free from all pain, if wonder pain thee not.

Moneta, perceiving that the robes and veils which enveloped her frightened Keats, parted the veils.

> Then saw I a wan face,
> Not pined by human sorrows, but bright blanch'd
> By an immortal sickness which kills not;
> It works a constant change, which happy death
> Can put no end to; deathwards progressing
> To no death was that visage; it had past
> The lily, and the Snow; and beyond these
> I must not think now, though I saw that face —
> But for her eyes I should have fled away.
> They held me back, with a benignant light,
> Soft mitigated by divinest lids
> Half closed, and visionless entire they seem'd
> Of all external things — they saw me not,
> But in blank splendor beam'd like the mild moon,
> Who comforts those she sees not, who knows not
> What eyes are upwards cast.

This is probably the most vivid portrait in Keats's poetry. The first part of the description — the wan face bright blanched by an immortal sickness, etc.— was inspired by the pale, consumptive countenance of his dying brother. He plunged into the abstract images of poetry, he wrote Dilke on September 21, to ease himself of the countenance, the voice, and the feebleness of his dying brother. The pale countenance of his brother forced itself, however, into the very midst of his poetic images.

Moneta's wan face, reflecting the pale countenance of his brother Tom, brought to an end his composition of the humanitarian "Vision of the Fall of Hyperion." He composed this introduction to the poem, it is probable, between September 21 and October 24. By the middle of October he began to find that humanitarianism could not console him in the painful experience through which he was passing.

On October 24 he rejected humanitarianism, resumed his humanistic philosophy of negative capability, and, it is probable, began the humanistic and Miltonic *Hyperion.*

5

In the first part of October, while he was still working at the composition of the introduction to the humanitarian version of the "Fall of Hyperion," Keats walked frequently to Wentworth Place and talked with Dilke about different and indifferent matters — politics, metaphysics, the Bible, Shakespeare, Euclid, and the system of fagging in the great public schools. After he had reacted against Leigh Hunt in 1817 his politics were influenced by Dilke, who, as a disciple of William Godwin, believed in a slow but inevitable progress of social liberty, justice, and happiness by means of education. Keats derived this principle, which was the theme of his humanitarian version of the "Fall of Hyperion," from Dilke's conversation as well as from Wordworth's *Excursion.*

Keats described the state of politics in England and in Europe at the beginning of the journal letter which he wrote to his brother George in October. He distrusted the political leaders of contemporary England and looked back with longing to the Commonwealth of Cromwell and Milton. "The motives of our worst Men are interest and of our best Vanity," he said. "We have no Milton, no Algernon Sidney." He was still believing in the humanitarian principles of the perfectibility of human nature and the progress of society.

> Dilke, whom you know to be a Godwin perfectibil[it]y Man, pleases himself [he said] with the idea that America will be the country to take up the human intellect where england leaves off — I differ there with him greatly.

The humanity of the United States, he said, can never reach the sublime. Franklin and Washington cannot be compared to Milton and the two Sidneys — the one was a philosophical Quaker full of mean and thrifty maxims and the other sold the very charger which had taken him through his battles.

> — you must endeavour [he told his brother George] to infuse a little Spirit of another sort into the Settlement, always with great caution, for thereby you may do your descendants more good than you may imagine. If I had a prayer to make for any great good, next to Tom's recovery, it should be that one of your Children should be the first American Poet. I have a great mind to make a prophecy and they say prophecies work out their own fullfillment —
>
> 'Tis "the witching time of night"
> Orbed is the Moon and bright, etc.

This *ex tempore* prophecy has no intrinsic poetic merit. The quotation from *Hamlet* (III. ii. 406) in the first verse and the heptasyllabic metre indicate, however, that Keats was reverting to his Renaissance poetic masters.

In the first part of October 1818, while Keats was discussing the progress of political liberty with Dilke, he composed, it is probable, the Spenserian stanza in which he objected to the conservative political philosophy of the fifth book of *The Faerie Queene*. Lord Houghton published the stanza in 1848 in *The Life and Letters*, introducing it as follows:

The copy of "Spenser" which Keats had in daily use contains the following stanza, inserted at the close of canto ii. book v. His sympathies were very much on the side of the revolutionary "Gyant," who "undertook for to repair" the "realms and nations run awry," and to suppress "tyrants that make men subject to their law," "and lordings curbe that commons over-aw," while he grudged the legitimate victory, as he rejected the conservative philosophy, of the "righteous Artegal" and his comrade, the fierce defender of privilege and order. And he expressed, in this *ex post facto* prophecy, his conviction of the ultimate triumph of freedom and equality by the power of transmitted knowledge.

In after-time, a sage of mickle lore
Yclep'd Typographus, the Giant took,
And did refit his limbs as heretofore,
And made him read in many a learned book,
And into many a lively legend look;
Thereby in goodly themes so training him,
That all his brutishness he quite forsook,
When, meeting Artegal and Talus grim,
The one he struck stone-blind, the other's eyes wox dim.

It is possible that Lord Houghton transcribed this stanza from a copy of Spenser into which Keats had written it. It is possible also that a transcript of the stanza was given to him by Charles Brown. The copy of Spenser into which Keats composed it has been lost. There was an autograph of the stanza also in the copy of Spenser which Keats marked and gave to Fanny Brawne in May 1820. Into this book he copied the markings, annotations, and compositions which he had written in the copy which he had in daily use. He wrote Miss Brawne:

Tuesday af^{tn}.

My dearest Fanny,

For this Week past I have been employed in marking the most beautiful passages in Spenser, intending it for you, and comforting myself in being somehow occupied to give you however small a pleasure. It has lightened my time very much. I am much better. God bless you.

Your affectionate

J. Keats

Miss Brawne cherished her copy of Spenser for many years and finally lost it, together with other books, in Germany. Miss Lowell quoted the following passage from a letter which Miss Brawne wrote to a correspondent to whom she lent this copy:

> I have therefore sent you Spenser instead, which you will feel the more pleasure in reading as you will find the best part marked by one who I have heard called the best judge of poetry living — they were marked for me to read, and I need not say with what pleasure I did so.

CHAPTER VI

HYPERION, *EVE OF ST. AGNES*, ETC.

I

KEATS'S reaction against humanitarianism occurred sometime after the middle of October. It appeared in the section of the journal letter which he wrote to his brother George on October 24 and in the letter to Woodhouse of October 27. When he rejected humanitarianism he resumed the philosophy of negative capability which he had developed out of Shakespeare's plays.

On Saturday afternoon, October 24, Keats had an amorous adventure with the lady with whom he had had a mild flirtation on his vacation in Hastings in May 1817. He met her in a street which runs from Bedford Row to Lamb's Conduit Street and walked with her to a boarding school in Islington, which a friend of hers kept, and then to her home at 34 Gloucester Street, Queen's Square.

As I had warmed with her before and kissed her [he wrote his brother], I though[t] it would be living backwards not to do so again — she had a better taste: she perceived how much a thing of course it was and shrunk from it — not in a prudish way but in as I say a good taste. She continued to disappoint me in a way which made me feel more pleasure than a simple kiss could do. She said I should please her much more if I would only press her hand and go away. Whether she was in a different disposition when I saw her before — or whether I have in fancy wrong'd her I cannot tell.

A Shelleyan thought flashed into his mind and he said:

I expect to pass some pleasant hours with her now and then: in which I feel I shall be of service to her in matters of knowledge and taste: if I can I will.

Then, fearing that his brother George might think that this lady was stirring his sexual feelings, he added:

I have no libidinous thought about her — she and your George are the only women à peu près de mon age whom I would be content to know for their mind and friendship alone.

The story of his adventure with the lady whom he had met at Hastings led Keats into a discussion of marriage and poetry. His conception of love, marriage, and women is that of an adolescent boy. His conception of the negatively capable imagination, however, is profound and significant.

— I shall in a short time write you as far as I know how I intend to pass my Life — I cannot think of those things now Tom is so unwell and weak. Notwithstand[ing] your Happiness and your recommendation I hope I shall never marry. Though the most beautiful Creature were waiting for me at the end of a Journey or a Walk; though the carpet were of Silk, the Curtains of the morning Clouds; the chairs and Sofa stuffed with Cygnet's down; the food Manna, the Wine beyond Claret, the Window opening on Winander mere, I should not feel—or rather my Happiness would not be so fine, as my Solitude is sublime. Then instead of what I have described, there is a Sublimity to welcome me home. The roaring of the wind is my wife and the Stars through the window pane are my Children. The mighty abstract Idea I have of Beauty in all things stifles the more divided and minute domestic happiness — an amiable wife and sweet Children I contemplate as a part of that Beauty, but I must have a thousand of those beautiful particles to fill up my heart.

I feel more and more every day [he continued], as my imagination strengthens, that I do not live in this world alone but in a thousand worlds. No sooner am I alone than shapes of epic greatness are stationed around me, and serve my Spirit the office which is equivalent to a King's body guard — then "Tragedy with scepter'd pall, comes sweeping by." According to my state of mind I am with Achilles shouting in the Trenches, or with Theocritus in the Vales of Sicily. Or I throw my whole being into Troilus, and repeating those lines, "I wander, like a lost Soul upon the Stygian Banks staying for waftage," I melt into the air with a voluptuousness so delicate that I am content to be alone.

These things [he concluded] combined with the opinion I have of the generality of women — who appear to me as children to whom I would rather give a Sugar Plum than my time, form a barrier against Matrimony which I rejoice in.

We find in this passage a complete revolution in Keats's philosophy of poetry. He has swung again from Wordsworth to Shakespeare and Milton, from reason to imagination, from the principle of benevolence to the principle of beauty in all things, from subjectivity to objectivity, from the simple and the natural to the sublime.

Keats rejected humanitarianism because it did not solve the painful problems of his experience. A universal love of humanity did not comfort him for the absence of his brother George in the backwoods of America and the approaching death of his brother Tom. His love of humanity and his passion to do the world some good were diminished by the malignancy of the reviewers and the indifference of the public to *Endymion*. The evil which he saw in men and the tyranny which he observed in governments shattered his faith in the perfectibility of human nature and in the progress of society.

Keats resumed, in this crisis, the humanistic philosophy of negative capability which he had developed in December 1817 out of the poetry of Spenser, Shakespeare, and Milton. The imagination, the principle of negative capability, gave him a relief from unhappiness which reason, the principle of humanitarianism, could not give him. On September 21, we remember, he was obliged to plunge into the abstract images of poetry to relieve himself from the countenance, the voice, and the feebleness of his dying brother. By means of his imagination he could escape for a moment into the beautiful world of poetry. He reaffirmed, therefore, his faith in the principle of beauty in all things and in the imagination, which intuits images of beauty. He resolved to seek his happiness in intuiting beauty and in expressing it in the medium of poetry.

> The only thing that can ever affect me personally for more than one short passing day [he wrote his brother George], is any doubt about my powers for poetry — I seldom have any, and I look with hope to the nighing time when I shall have none. I am as happy as a Man can be — that is in myself I should be happy if Tom was well, and I knew you were passing pleasant days. Then I should be most enviable — with the yearning Passion I have for the beautiful, connected and made one with the ambition of my intellect.

Keats revealed inadvertently to his brother George the influence of the scurrilous reviews of *Endymion* in causing him to revert to his philosophy of negative capability.

> Think of my Pleasure in Solitude, in comparison of my commerce with the world — there I am a child — there they do not know me, not even my most intimate acquaintance — I give into their feelings as though I were refraining from irritating a little child. Some think me middling, others silly, others foolish — every one thinks he sees my weak side against my will, when in truth it is with my will — I am content to be thought all this because I have in my own breast so great a resource. This is one great reason why they like me so; because they can all show to advantage in a room, and eclipse from a certain tact one who is reckoned to be a good Poet. I hope I am not here playing tricks "to make the angels weep": I think not: for I have not the least contempt for my species, and though it may sound paradoxical, my greatest elevations of Soul leave me every time more humbled.

The scurrility and the malignancy of the Tory reviewers destroyed Keats's faith in the innate goodness of humanity, lessened his passion to make humanity happy, and drove him within himself to seek his own happiness in his elevations of soul in solitude. They impelled him also to resume his philosophy of negative capability as a defensive philosophy. Smarting under the ridicule of the reviewers, he suspected that all men — even his friends — despised him. "Some think me middling, others silly, others foolish," he said, "— every one thinks he sees my weak side against my will." His friends liked him, he thought, because they could eclipse him in social groups. He maintained his self-respect and his self-esteem by means of his philosophy of negative capability. He was not an egotistic or subjective poet, he said, who has an impressive, dominant personality; he was an objective poet like Shakespeare, a poet of negative capability who, having no personality himself, enters into and reflects the personalities of the men around him. He believed also that by means of the principles of negative capability he could compose poems which could not be ridiculed. Who could ridicule a poem which has neo-Platonic beauty, Miltonic sublimity, and Shakespearean objectivity?

We should err, however, if we should seek the source of Keats's philosophy of negative capability in an inferiority complex. He was sensitive and introspective, but he was also proud and objective, perceiving, with extraordinary clarity, his virtues and his defects. He was ashamed of his small stature and of his humble origins, but he was also magnanimous, knowing the high quality of his genius and asserting that he would be among the English poets after his death. He began to develop his philosophy of negative capability in the fall of 1817, a year before he was ridiculed by the reviewers of *Endymion*. The negatively capable qualities which he discovered in Shakespeare made him conscious of the negatively capable qualities of his own genius. He resumed his philosophy of negative capability primarily because it was the philosophy which most perfectly satisfied his whole personality.

Woodhouse drew from Keats the finest exposition of the objective principles of his philosophy of negative capability. On October 21, 1818 he wrote Keats:

> My Dear Keats,
>
> Whilst in the country, from whence I am but lately returned, I met with that malicious, but weak & silly article on Endymion in the last Quarterly Review. God help the Critic, whoever he be! He is as ignorant of the rudiments of his own craft as of the Essentials of true Poetry.

After discounting the effect of the review, Woodhouse continued:

> The appearance of this "critical morsel," however, determines me to address you on the subject of your late conversation at Hessey's, on which I have often since reflected, and never without a degree of pain — I may have misconceived you; but I understood you to say, you thought there was now nothing original to be written in poetry; that its riches were already exhausted, & all its beauties forestalled — & That you should, consequently, write no more. I cannot assent to your premises, and I most earnestly deprecate your conclusion. — For my part I believe most sincerely, that the wealth of poetry is unexhausted and inexhaustible —

After a long argument Woodhouse praised the high quality of Keats's genius, exhorted him to disregard malevolent reviewers, encouraged him to persevere with his composition of poetry, and concluded:

> The world, I hope & trust, is not quite so dead dull and ungrateful as you may have apprehended — or as a few malevolent spirits may have given you

reason to imagine. It contains, I know, many who have a warm "affection for the cause of stedfast Genius toiling gallantly," — many who, tho' personally unknown to you, look with the eye of hope & anticipation to your future course — but very few who in sincere wishes for your welfare, & passion for your fame, exceed, Dear Keats,

Yours most truly,

Rich[d] Woodhouse.

[Manuscript in the Harvard College Library.]

Woodhouse was the most unselfish, the most loyal, and the most generous of Keats's friends but not the most understanding. In taking seriously Keats's declaration that he would not compose more poetry, he did not understand the poet's innate tendency to swing from one extreme of feeling to the other. The only thing that could stop Keats from composing poetry was fatal illness.

Keats answered Woodhouse's letter on October 27, 1818.

My dear Woodhouse,

Your Letter gave me a great satisfaction; more on account of its friendliness, than any relish of that matter in it which is accounted so acceptable in the "genus irritabile." The best answer I can give you is in a clerk-like manner to make some observations on two principle points, which seem to point like indices into the midst of the whole pro and con, about genius, and views and atchievements and ambition and coetera.

Keats explained, in the first place, his philosophy of negative capability, making a distinction between egotistic poets, such as Wordsworth, and negatively capable poets, such as Shakespeare. He revealed a complete reaction against Wordsworth's type of poetry.

1st. As to the poetical Character itself (I mean that sort of which, if I am anything, I am a Member; that sort distinguished from the wordsworthian or egotistical sublime; which is a thing per se and stands alone) it is not itself — it has no self — it is every thing and nothing — It has no character — it enjoys light and shade; it lives in gusto, be it foul or fair, high or low, rich or poor, mean or elevated — It has as much delight in conceiving an Iago as an Imogen. What shocks the virtuous philosopher, delights the camelion Poet. It does no harm from its relish of the dark side of things any more than from its taste for the bright one; because they both end in speculation. A Poet is the most unpoetical of any thing in existence; because he has no Identity — he is continually in for and filling some other Body — The Sun, the Moon, the Sea and Men and Women who are creatures of impulse are poetical and have about them an unchangeable attribute — the poet has none; no identity — he is certainly the most unpoetical of all God's Creatures. If then he has no self, and if I am a Poet, where is the Wonder that I should say I would write no more? Might I not at that very instant have been cogitating on the Characters of Saturn and Ops? It is a wretched thing to confess; but is a very fact that not one word I ever utter can be taken for granted as an opinion growing out of my identical nature — how can it, when I have no nature? When I am in a room with People if I ever am free from speculating on creations of my own brain, then not myself goes home to myself: but the identity of every one in the room begins to to [so?] press upon me that I am in a very little time an[ni]hilated — not only among Men; it would be the same in a Nursery of children: I know not whether I make myself wholly understood: I hope enough so to let you see that no dependence is to be placed on what I said that day.

Keats declared, in the second place, that he was abandoning for the present his ambition of doing the world some good and that he would compose poems from his yearning passion for the beautiful. He did not express so frankly to Woodhouse as he had expressed to his brother George his loss of faith in humanity. In succeeding months, however, as his reaction against the humanitarian philosophy of poetry strengthened, he acquired a very empirical and a very realistic conception of human nature.

In the second place I will speak of my views, and of the life I purpose to myself. I am ambitious of doing the world some good: if I should be spared that may be the work of maturer years — in the interval I will assay to reach to as high a summit in Poetry as the nerve bestowed upon me will suffer. The faint conceptions I have of Poems to come brings the blood frequently into my forehead. All I hope is that I may not lose all interest in human affairs — that the solitary indifference I feel for applause even from the finest spirits, will not blunt any acuteness of vision I may have. I do not think it will. I feel assured I should write from the mere yearning and fondness I have for the Beautiful even if my night's labours should be burnt every morning, and no eye ever shine upon them. But even now I am perhaps not speaking from myself: but from some character in whose soul I now live. I am sure however that this next sentence is from myself. I feel your anxiety, good opinion and friendliness in the highest degree, and am

Your's most sincerely

John Keats

In November 1817, when Keats first developed his philosophy of negative capability, he drew a distinction between men of power, who have dominant identities or individualities and whose intellects, being subject to their wills, shape and color their conceptions of the world in accordance with their practical desires, and men of genius, who have no identities or individualities and whose intellects, being free, reflect the world as in a mirror. In December 1817 he drew a distinction between an egotistic poet such as Coleridge who "would let go by a fine isolated verisimilitude caught from the Penetralium of mystery, from being incapable of remaining content with half-knowledge" and a negatively capable poet such as Shakespeare who "is capable of being in uncertainties, mysteries, doubts, without any irritable reaching after fact and reason." He drew a distinction likewise between the reason, the faculty by which the egotistic poet constructs an absolute and comprehensive system of philosophy out of his imaginative intuitions or apprehensions, and the imagination, the faculty by which the negatively capable poet intuits truth in isolated particles. He believed that the negatively capable poet is content with the isolated particles of truth which his imagination intuits because the intense beauty in these intuitions overcomes every other consideration, or rather obliterates all consideration.

In October 1818, when Keats resumed his philosophy of negative capability, he made two changes in it. He introduced, in the first place, the romantic element of escape. He had learned from experience that the intense beauty with which his imagination intuited painful truth did not obliterate the painfulness. He sought to escape from the painful facts of life, therefore, by taking refuge in the ideal world of poetry. He found a few months later, however, that his romantic escape was temporary and inadequate. In the second place, he introduced into his philosophy of negative capability the principle of knowledge which he had developed in his humanitarian period. He had learned that his reason could not construct, by means of knowledge, a satisfactory system of philosophy. He believed, however, that his imagination could make use of knowledge in the creation of beautiful ideal worlds.

We have already observed that Keats's philosophy of negative capability, an interpretation of Shakespeare's humanism in the light of English empiricism, was inspired by Hazlitt's critical and philosophical essays. We should note in this connection Hazlitt's influence upon Keats's distinction between the egotistic poet such as Wordsworth and the negatively capable poet such as Shakespeare. Hazlitt said that Cellini, Rousseau, and Wordsworth were the three greatest egotists that he knew. In his essay *On Mr. Wordsworth's "Excursion,"* which he reprinted in *The Round Table,* he observed:

> An intense intellectual egotism swallows up every thing. Even the dialogues introduced in the present volume are soliloquies of the same character, taking different views of the subject. The recluse, the pastor, and the pedlar, are three persons in one poet. . . . The power of his mind preys upon itself. It is as if there were nothing but himself and the universe. He lives in the busy solitude of his own heart; in the deep silence of thought. . . .
>
> He does not present the reader with a lively succession of images or incidents, but paints the outgoings of his own heart, the shapings of his own fancy. He may be said to create his own materials; his thoughts are his real subject. . . . He sees all things in himself. . . . He only sympathizes with those simple forms of feeling, which mingle at once with his own identity, or with the stream of general humanity. . . .

Hazlitt said that Shakespeare had "no personal character"; that, by means of observation and imagination, he could see life through the minds of other men; and that he represented, with understanding and with justice, both the good and the evil, the noble and the base, etc. In *The Examiner* for June 11, 1815, Hazlitt wrote a review of a production of Milton's *Comus* at Covent Garden.

> The genius of Milton [he said] was essentially undramatic; he saw all objects from his own point of view, and with certain exclusive preferences. Shakespeare, on the contrary, had no personal character, and no moral principle, except that of good nature. He took no part in the scene he describes, but gave fair play to all his characters, and left virtue and vice, folly and wisdom, right and wrong, to fight it out between themselves, just as they do on their "old fighting stage," — the world.

In an essay *On Posthumous Fame* in *The Round Table*, Hazlitt said that Shakespeare "was almost entirely a man of genius," "that in him this faculty bore sway over every other."

> He seemed scarcely to have an individual existence of his own, but to borrow that of others at will, and to pass successively through "every variety of untried being," — to be now *Hamlet*, now *Othello*, now *Lear*, now *Falstaff*, now *Ariel*.

In an essay on *Schlegel on the Drama* in *The Edinburgh Review* for February 1816, Hazlitt explained the "wonderful variety and perfect individuality" of Shakespeare's characters as follows:

> The poet appears, for the time, to identify himself with the character he wishes to represent, and to pass from one to the other, like the same soul successively animating different bodies. By an art like that of the ventriloquist, he throws his imagination out of himself, and makes every word appear to proceed from the mouth of the person in whose name it is spoken. . . . His characters are real beings of flesh and blood: they speak like men, not like authors. One might suppose that he had stood by at the time, and overheard all that passed.

Hazlitt repeated this passage in the *Lectures on the English Poets* which Keats heard him deliver in February 1818.

The interpretation of Shakespeare's dramatic genius which Keats learned from Hazlitt stands in direct antithesis to that which Coleridge taught in his lectures on Shakespeare. Hazlitt, who was an empiricist, explained the variety and individuality of Shakespeare's characters by the theory that Shakespeare observed men and entered imaginatively into their minds. Coleridge, who was a transcendentalist, said that Shakespeare created his various and individual characters out of the human character which existed in its potentiality in his own mind. In his *Lectures on Shakespeare* Coleridge said:

One character belongs to all true poets, that they write from a principle within, not originating in anything without. . .

[Shakespeare could] paint truly, and according to the colouring of nature, a vast number of personages by the simple force of meditation: he had only to imitate certain parts of his own character, or to exaggerate such as existed in possibility, and they were at once true to nature, and fragments of the divine mind that drew them. . . .

The truth is, Shakespeare's characters are all *genera* entirely individualized; the results of meditation, of which observation supplied the drapery and colours necessary to combine them with each other. . . .

The character of the Nurse [in *Romeo and Juliet*] is the nearest of any thing in Shakespeare to a direct borrowing from mere observation.

When Keats resumed his philosophy of negative capability, he resumed also his earlier humanistic and Miltonic intuition of the "Fall of Hyperion." If he began the composition of *Hyperion* at the end of October, his nursing his dying brother prevented him from progressing very far with it. Poetic composition gave him a momentary relief from painful reality; but, in the last weeks of his brother Tom's life, he could not compose. After the middle of October he wrote his brother George that he intended to compose a prose tale —

which I must begin [he said] on account of the activity of my Mind; of its inability to remain at rest. It must be prose and not very exciting. I must do this because in the way I am at present situated I have too many interruptions to a train of feeling to be able to write Poetry.

At the end of October he wrote George and Georgiana that Tom was so nervous that he could not speak to him of them.

— indeed it is the care I have had to keep his Mind aloof from feelings too acute [he said] that has made this Letter so short a one — I did not like to write before him a Letter he knew was to reach your hands — I cannot even now ask him for any Message — his heart speaks to you. Be as happy as you can. Think of me and for my sake be cheerful.

In November Tom grew so much worse that Keats could neither compose the prose tale (he never composed it) nor continue the journal letter to George. On December 1 Brown wrote Woodhouse, by Keats's request, that Tom had died that morning at 8 o'clock. After Keats had watched his brother breathe his last breath, he fled to Brown for sympathy and assistance.

I was awakened in my bed by a pressure on my hand [Brown said in his memoir of the poet]. It was Keats, who came to tell me that his brother was no more. I said nothing, and we both remained silent for a while, my hand fast locked in his. At length, my thoughts returning from the dead to the living, I said, —

"Have nothing more to do with those lodgings, — and alone too! Had you not better live with me?" He paused, pressed my hand warmly, and replied, — "I think it would be better." From that moment he was my inmate.

Keats's friends rallied to his assistance in this catastrophe. Haslam undertook the difficult task of writing George Keats that Tom was dead; and Brown, we have seen, persuaded Keats to leave the lodgings in Well Walk where Tom had died and to live with him in his half of Wentworth Place, the other half of which was the residence of the Dilkes. Keats wrote his brother George about the middle of December:

My friends have been exceedingly kind to me every one of them — Brown detained me at his House. . . . With Dilke and Brown I am quite thick — with Brown indeed I am going to domesticate, that is, we shall keep house together. I shall have the front parlour and he the back one, by which I shall avoid the noise of Bentley's Children — and be the better able to go on with my Studies — which have been greatly interrupted lately, so that I have not the shadow of an idea of a book in my head, and my pen seems to have grown too gouty for verse.

The first two weeks after his brother's death, Keats's friends endeavored to divert his brooding grief by keeping him going from one place to another. "Within the last week I have been every where," he wrote his brother George about the middle of December, "— and I will tell you as nearly as possible how all go on." He attended a prizefight between Randall and Turner; he saw Kean in *Brutus*, a tragedy written by Howard Payne; he called on Hazlitt; Haydon called on him and related Lieutenant Hoppner's adventures on a voyage with Sir John Ross into the North Polar regions; he went to a party at Novello's, where he saw Hunt, Hazlitt, Lamb, and others; he called on Mrs. Wylie, Georgiana Keats's mother; and he went to a supper given by Redhall, who ranged bottles of wine up the kitchen and cellar stairs.

In the meantime Keats fell in love with Fanny Brawne, who more than anyone else distracted him from his grief and gave him a new and absorbing interest in life. Frances, or Fanny, Brawne was the daughter of Mrs. Samuel Brawne, a widow of independent means. She had a brother, Samuel, and a sister, Margaret, who were very much younger. Keats met Miss Brawne for the first time, I believe, either in November or in December 1818. Dilke, in his annotated copy of Lord Houghton's *Life, Letters and Literary Remains of John Keats*, said:

[Keats] met Miss Brawne for the first time at my house. Brown let his house when he and Keats went to Scotland to Mrs. Brawne, a stranger to all of us. As the house adjoined mine in a large garden, we almost necessarily became acquainted. When Brown returned, the Brawnes took another house at the top of Downshire Hill; but we kept up our acquaintance and no doubt Keats, who was daily with me, met her soon after his return from Teignmouth ["Teignmouth" is an error for "Scotland"].

In his memoir of Keats, Dilke related Tom Keats's death and said:

John now agreed to live with Brown, paying for his board. Here he became very intimate with the Brawnes who resided in the adjoining cottage, & fell in love with Fanny Brawne.

Keats's reactions to Jane Cox on September 21 and to the lady of Hastings on October 24 show, we have seen, that his amorous feelings were active and passionate although perverted with sex-antagonism. He was in the mood to fall in love, and, when he met Fanny Brawne, he fell in love with her at first sight.

I have, believe me, not been an age in letting you take possession of me [he wrote Miss Brawne on July 25, 1819]; the very first week I knew you I wrote myself your vassal; but burnt the Letter as the very next time I saw you I thought you manifested some dislike to me. If you should ever feel for Man at the first sight what I did for you, I am lost.

Keats's first mention of Fanny Brawne occurs in the journal letter which he wrote his brother in the latter half of December 1818. He endeavored to conceal his love for her from everyone, but he was so absorbed with thoughts of her that he could not keep her out of his letter to his brother.

M[rs] Brawne who took Brown's house for the Summer [he said], still resides in Hampstead — she is a very nice woman — and her daughter senior is I think beautiful and elegant, graceful, silly, fashionable and strange — we have a little tiff now and then — and she behaves a little better, or I must have sheered off....

Shall I give you Miss Brawn[e]? [he said a little later]. She is about my height — with a fine style of countenance of the lengthen'd sort — she wants sentiment in every feature — she manages to make her hair look well — her nostrills are fine — though a little painful — her mouth is bad and good — her Profil[e] is better than her full-face which indeed is not full but pale and thin without showing any bone. Her shape is very graceful and so are her movements — her Arms are good, her hands badish — her feet tolerable — she is not seventeen — but she is ignorant — monstrous in her behaviour[,] flying out in all directions, calling people such names — that I was forced lately to make use of the term *Minx* — this is I think no[t] from any innate vice but from a penchant she has for acting stylishly. I am however tired of such style and shall decline any more of it.

She had a friend to visit her lately [he continued] — you have known plenty such — her face is raw as if she was standing out in a frost — her lips raw and seem always ready for a Pullet — she plays the Music without one sensation but the feel of the ivory at her fingers. She is a downright Miss without one set off. We hated her and smoked her and baited her, and I think drove her away. Miss B — thinks her a Paragon of fashion, and says she is the only woman she would change persons with. What a stupe — She is superior as a Rose to a Dandelion. When we went to bed Brown observed as he put out the Taper what a very ugly old woman that Miss Robinson would make — at which I must have groan'd aloud for I'm sure ten minutes.

Keats drew a vivid and, I believe, a true sketch of Fanny Brawne. Like most girls of seventeen years, she was interested in social rather than in intellectual matters. She craved admiration and she endeavored to obtain it by affecting those airs and wiles which were fashionable in her period. Her greatest ambition was to be deemed stylish. Beneath her fashionable affectations she had an imperious will. In her maturity, as Miss Lowell showed, she manifested moderately literary and intellectual qualities, but in her girlhood these qualities were latent and undeveloped.

Keats loved Fanny Brawne for her physical beauty and feminine graces rather than for her mind and character. He was astonishingly mature in many respects but in love he was adolescent. He demanded intellectual qualities in his friends but not in the girl he loved. He longed to love a Juliet rather than an Imogen and to be a Romeo to be worthy of her. In July 1819, when Miss Brawne objected to his passionate praise of her beauty, he replied:

Why may I not speak of your Beauty, since without that I could never have lov'd you? — I cannot conceive any beginning of such love as I have for you but Beauty. There may be a sort of love for which, without the least sneer at it, I have the highest respect and can admire it in others: but it has not the richness, the bloom, the full form, the enchantment of love after my own heart.

He desired to be loved for himself rather than for his poetry.

I believe you have liked me for my own sake [he wrote Miss Brawne] and for nothing else. I have met with women whom I really think would like to be married to a Poem and to be given away by a Novel.

Keats had a prejudice against literary women as well as against women who had a sentimental admiration for men of letters. About the middle of December, shortly after he had fallen in love with Fanny Brawne, he declined an introduction to Jane and Anna Maria Porter, authors of popular romantic novels. One of the Misses Porter borrowed a copy of *Endymion* from Henry Neville, who had borrowed it from Mary Frogley, who had in turn borrowed it from Woodhouse. On December 10 Woodhouse sent Keats a letter in which Miss Porter, writing to Neville, praised *Endymion* and expressed a desire to meet the poet. Keats wrote Woodhouse on December 18:

My dear Woodhouse

I am greatly obliged to you. I must needs feel flattered by making an impression on a set of Ladies — I should be content to do so in meretricious romance verse if they alone and not Men were to judge. I should like very much to know those Ladies — tho' look here Woodhouse — I have a new leaf to turn over — I must work — I must read — I must write — I am unable to afford time for new acquaintances — I am scarcely able to do my duty to those I have. Leave the matter to chance. But do not forget to give my Remb[rs] to you[r] Cousin [Mary Frogley].

Yours most sincerely

John Keats

Keats related the matter to his brother George, copied a part of Miss Porter's letter to Neville, and observed:

Now I feel more obliged than flattered by this — so obliged that I will not at present give you an extravaganza of a Lady Romancer. I will be introduced to them if it be merely for the pleasure of writing to you about it — I shall certainly see a new race of People. I shall more certainly have no time for them.

Keats regarded literature as the domain of men. Lady romancers — indeed lady authors of any kind — seemed to him to be a strange and unnatural variety of human beings. It was his ambition also to compose poems which would please men rather than women. Romance, sentimentality, and affectation were becoming increasingly repugnant to him. He was beginning the composition of *Hyperion*, and he was in the elevated mood of the Miltonic epic.

Keats's reaction against sentimentality is one of the most significant phases of the growth of his mind in this period. He had steadily outgrown sentimentality after his rejection of Hunt's poetic style in March 1817; but he had reverted to sentimentality in *The Pot of Basil*, which he composed in the spring of 1818. The ridicule of his poetry in the Tory journals in September 1818, more than anything else, I believe, killed every germ of sentimentality that persisted in his mind. In the journal letter which he wrote his brother George in the latter part of December 1818, he referred to Hunt with the scorn of a Tory reviewer:

Hunt keeps on in his old way — I am completely tired of it all. He has lately publish'd a Pocket-Book called the literary Pocket-Book — full of the most sickening stuff you can imagine. . . .

The Night we went to Novello's [he said] there was a complete set to of Mozart and punning. I was so completely tired of it that if I were to follow my own inclinations I should never meet any one of that set again, not even Hunt who is certainly a pleasant fellow in the main when you are with him — but in reallity he is vain, egotistical, and disgusting in matters of taste and in morals. He understands many a beautiful thing; but then, instead of giving other minds credit for the same degree of perception as he himself professes — he begins an explanation in such a curious manner that our taste and self-love is offended continually. Hunt does one harm by making fine things petty and beautiful things hateful. Through him I am indifferent to Mozart, I care not for white Busts — and many a glorious thing when associated with him becomes a nothing. This distorts one's mind — make[s] one's thoughts bizarre — perplexes one in the standard of Beauty.

He wrote for his brother a satiric comedy on the vanity and the affectation in Hunt's coterie. At the end of the satire Gattie asks Hunt when his *Literary Pocket-Book* will come out, and Hunt replies:

"What is this abso[r]bs me quite?" O we are spinning on a little, we shall floridize soon I hope. Such a thing was very much wanting — people think of nothing but money getting — now for me I am rather inclined to the liberal side of things. I am reckoned lax in my christian principles etc. etc. etc. etc.

Another incident in this period illustrates Keats's repugnance to sentimentality. He wrote his brother George that an anonymous admirer from Teignmouth had sent him through Taylor and Hessey, his publishers, a £25 note and a sentimental sonnet in defense of his genius. He copied the sonnet, which begins —

Star of high promise! — not to this dark age
Do thy mild light and loveliness belong. . . .

and concludes —

And there is one whose hand will never scant
From his poor store of fruits all *thou* canst want.

I could not copy [it] for any in the world but you [he told his brother George] — who know that I scout "mild light and loveliness" or any such nonsense in myself.

And referring to the £25 note he said:

If I had refused it I should have behaved in a very bragadochio dunderheaded manner — and yet the present galls me a little, and I do not know whether I shall not return it if I ever meet with the donor, after whom to no purpose have I written.

It has never been suggested, I believe, that this Teignmouth admirer may have been one of the Misses Jeffrey of Teignmouth, who were very kind to Keats when he was taking care of his brother Tom there in the spring of 1818. One of them, according to Teignmouth tradition, fell in love with Keats; and in 1830, after she had become Mrs. I. S. Prowse, she published a volume of poems, in several of which she referred to Keats in the sentimental style of the anonymous sonnet.

Woodhouse was a persistent collector of everything related to Keats, but he was too tactful to ask Keats for a copy of this anonymous sonnet. In a letter to Taylor, a copy of which is in his Scrapbook, he said:

Do you think you could manage to procure me a copy of the Sonnet you were talking of last night — as it is "a thought" complimentary, Keats may not be disposed, out of his excessive modesty, to give copies, and I would not wish to make an unpleasant application to him, but the circumstance is an interesting one, and I sho[d] like to add that to my collection of "Keatsiana"— Do try — Perhaps Reynolds will get one for himself, & it may be done easily through that channel.

A copy of this sonnet does not appear, however, in Woodhouse's books of transcripts.

At the end of December 1818 Keats analyzed and evaluated the development of his mind. He explained to his brother George his outgrowth of sentimental poets; his understanding of the supreme greatness of Shakespeare; his appreciation of the "heroic simplicity and unaffected grandeur" of Raphael's cartoons; the power of his imagination to re-create and to live the life of the past; and his faith in the principle that beauty is truth.

You are very little more removed from general association than I am [he wrote his brother] — recollect that no Man can live but in one society at a time — his enjoyment in the different states of human society must depend upon the Powers of his Mind — that is you can imagine a roman triumph or an olympic game as well as I can. We with our bodily eyes see but the fashion and Manners of one country for one age — and then we die. Now to me manners and customs long since passed whether among the Babylonians or the Bactrians are as real, or eveven [*sic*] more real than those among which I now live. My thoughts have turned lately this way. The more we know the more inadequacy we discover in the world to satisfy us — this is an old observation; but I have made up my Mind never to take any thing for granted — but even to examine the truth of the commonest proverbs. This however is true —M[rs] Tighe and Beattie once delighted me — now I see through them and can find nothing in them or weakness, and yet how many they still delight! Perhaps a superior being may look upon Shakespeare in the same light — is it possible? No — This same inadequacy is discovered (forgive me little George — you know I don't mean to put you in the mess) in Women with few exceptions — the Dress Maker, the blue Stocking and the most charming sentimentalist differ but in a Slight degree and are equally smokeable. But I'll go no further — I may be speaking sacrilegiously — and on my word I have thought so little that I have not one opinion upon any thing except in matters of taste — I never can feel certain of any truth but from a clear perception of its Beauty — and I find myself very young minded even in that perceptive power — which I hope will encrease. A year ago I could not understand in the slightest degree Raphael's cartoons — now I begin to read them a little — and how did I learn to do so? By seeing something done in quite an opposite spirit — I mean a picture of

Guido's in which all the Saints, instead of that heroic simplicity and unaffected grandeur which they inherit from Raphael, had each of them both in countenance and gesture all the canting, solemn[,] melodramatic mawkishness of Mackenzie's father Nicholas.

2

Keats resumed his composition of poetry on December 17. His brother Tom was buried on December 7, and for the next week and a half, we have seen, his friends strove to divert his grief by calling upon him, having him call upon them, inviting him to parties, and taking him to the theatre. On Thursday, December 17, the first quiet day he had passed for more than a week, he wrote his brother George:

Bentley [the postman from whom he had rented lodgings in Well Walk] . . . has just brought me a cloathe's basket of Books. Brown has gone to town to day to take his Nephews who are on a visit her[e] to see the Lions. I am passing a Quiet day — which I have not done a long while — and if I do continue so, I feel I must again begin with my poetry — for if I am not in action mind or Body I am in pain — and from that I suffer greatly by going into parties where from the rules of society and a natural pride I am obliged to smother my Spirit and look like an Idiot — because I feel my impulses given way to would too much amaze them — I live under an everlasting restraint — never relieved except when I am composing — so I will write away.

The next day, Friday, he continued the letter to his brother:

Friday. — I think you knew before you left England that my next subject would be "the fall of Hyperion." I went on a little with it last night, but it will take some time to get into the vein again. I will not give you any extracts, because I wish the whole to make an impression. I have however a few Poems which you will like and I will copy out on the next sheet.

These poems (*Fancy*, *Bards of Passion and of Mirth*, and *I had a dove*), which Keats copied two weeks later at the end of this December journal letter to his brother George, were composed evidently before Friday, December 17, the day on which he promised to copy them for his brother. It is improbable that he composed them in the week and a half preceding December 17; for he wrote his brother George on December 17 that he had been everywhere the past week, that he was passing the first quiet day for a long while, and that he "must again begin with" his poetry, implying clearly that his composition of poetry had been interrupted for some time. It is improbable that he composed the poems between December 1, the day on which his brother Tom died, and December 7, the day on which he was buried. It is improbable also that he composed them in the latter part of November; for "the last days of poor Tom," he said, "were of the most distressing nature." We must set back the date of the composition of the poems, I believe, to the first part of November or to the latter part of October.

Keats's first statement in regard to the composition of *Hyperion* needs little explanation. "I think you knew before you left England," he told his brother George, "that my next subject would be 'the fall of Hyperion.'" He began to meditate upon this subject, we remember, as early as September 1817. He employed the titles "Hyperion" and "The Fall of Hyperion" to designate without distinction both the Wordsworthian and humanitarian dream and the Miltonic and humanistic epic. In this case, he meant the Miltonic and humanistic *Hyperion*; for, in the first place, his philosophy in this period was the humanistic philosophy of negative capability and, in the second place, Brown, relating the first weeks of Keats's residence with him in Wentworth Place, said: "It was then he wrote *Hyperion*."

Keats's second statement presents a problem which is difficult but not essential. "I went on a little with it last night, but it will take some time to get into the vein again. I will not give you any extracts, because I wish the whole to make an impression." This statement proves that he had already composed a part of a version of the "Fall of Hyperion" and that last night, December 17, he resumed the composition. It is my opinion that he began the Miltonic and humanistic *Hyperion* on or after October 24, when he resumed his philosophy of negative capability, and that he worked on it until he was stopped by the last distressful days of his brother Tom. He began *Hyperion*, I believe, in the same period in which he composed *Fancy* and *Bards of Passion and of Mirth*. The manuscripts of these three poems were probably in the basket of books which Bentley brought him from Well Walk on December 17. When he unpacked the books he got out the manuscripts and that night he resumed work on the manuscript of *Hyperion*. It is possible, however, that his statement refers to the fragment of the humanitarian dream, which he composed in the latter part of September, and that he began instead of resumed the composition of *Hyperion* on December 17. The two versions were one and the same poem to him instead of two different poems.

Keats worked steadily on *Hyperion* throughout the two last weeks of December 1818 and the two first weeks of January 1819. Three other references to the poem occur in the journal letter to his brother.

Just now I took out my poem to go on with it [he wrote on December 22] — but the thought of my writing so little to you came upon me and I could not get on.

I will insert any little pieces I may write [he wrote on December 24] — though I will not give any extracts from my large poem which is scarce began.

And on January 2, 1819 he wrote:

I have no thought pervading me so constantly and frequently as that of you — my Poem cannot frequently drive it away — you will retard it much more that [than] you could by taking up my time if you were in England.

His work on *Hyperion* was interrupted in the latter part of January 1819 by the composition of *The Eve of St. Agnes* and in the first part of February by the composition of *The Eve of St. Mark*. About the middle of February he was beset with new problems, which I shall consider in the next chapter, and his inspiration to compose *Hyperion* — indeed, to compose any poem — waned. He wrote his brother on February 14 that he had composed *The Eve of St. Agnes* and *The Eve of St. Mark* and added:

I have not gone on with Hyperion, for to tell the truth I have not been in great cue for writing lately — I must wait for the spring to rouse me up a little.

Keats composed only a sonnet, it seems, from the middle of February to the middle of April. He could not compose poetry, for he could not solve the problems of his experience. He wrote Haydon on March 8:

You must be wondering where I am and what I am about! I am mostly at Hampstead, and about nothing; being in a sort of qui bono temper, not exactly on the road to an epic poem.

And Haydon, who approved of the epic style of *Hyperion*, replied on March 10:

At any rate finish your present great intention of a poem — it is as fine a subject as can be.

Keats solved the problems of his experience by the middle of April; and between April 15 and April 20 he composed, I believe, the fragment of the third book of *Hyperion* which reflects his new wisdom. He abandoned the composition of the poem at this point and gave the manuscript to Woodhouse, who copied it on April 20. Woodhouse wrote the following note at the end of his transcript of the poem in his Book of Transcripts:

The copy from which I took the above was the original & only copy. The alterations are noted in the margin — With the exception of them, it was completed and written down at once as it now stands. Copied 20 Ap! 1819 from J.K.'s manuscript written in 1818/9.

In his interleaved and annotated copy of *Endymion*, Woodhouse wrote a similar note under the date "April. 1819":

> K. lent me the fragment here alluded to for perusal. It contains 2 books & ½ — (ab^t 900 lines in all). He said he was dissatisfied with what he had done of it; and should not complete it. This is much to be regretted.

Woodhouse's transcript, like the autograph manuscript, contains 896 verses and the version printed in 1820 has 883 verses. Woodhouse had his transcript of Keats's autograph manuscript copied into his Commonplace Book by one of his clerks. This transcript in the Commonplace Book was, as H. B. Forman showed, the manuscript from which the poem was printed in 1820. The autograph manuscript, from which Woodhouse made his transcript, is now in the British Museum. The final revisions which Keats made before the poem was published in 1820 are inscribed on the margins of Woodhouse's transcripts.

Before we interpret *Hyperion* it is convenient for us to consider the lyric poems which Keats composed while he was beginning the composition of the epic. He wrote his brother on December 18, we remember, that he would not give him any extracts from *Hyperion* but that he had a few poems which he could copy out on the next sheet of the letter. On January 2 he copied three poems, *Fancy*, *Bards of Passion and of Mirth*, and *I had a dove*.

> Here are the Poems [he observed humorously] — they will explain themselves — as all ["piraems" or "poiaeems"?] should do without any comment —

After copying *Fancy* he said:

> I did not think this had been so long a Poem. I have another not so long — but as it will more conveniently be coppied on the other side I will just put down here some observations on Caleb Williams by Hazlitt. . . .

On the other side of the page he said:

> Now I will copy the other Poem — it is on the double immortality of Poets —

After copying *Bards of Passion and of Mirth* he continued:

> In my journal I intend to copy the poems I write the days they are written — there is just room I see in this page to copy a little thing I wrote off to some Music as it was playing —
>
> I had a dove and the sweet dove died, etc.

Fancy and *Bards of Passion and of Mirth* are evidently the poems which Keats had promised on December 18 to copy for his brother. *I had a dove* was copied, it seems, as an afterthought. There is a transcript of this song in Woodhouse's Book of Transcripts, dated

"1818" and inscribed "from C. B." (Charles Brown). Keats said that he composed this song "to some Music as it was playing." It was inspired doubtless by one of the melodies which, Charlotte Reynolds told H. B. Forman, she used to play to Keats for hours at a time. It may have been composed in the latter part of October and the first part of November or in the latter part of December. I am inclined to place it in the earlier period in which Keats was a more frequent visitor in the home of the Reynoldses.

A fourth lyric, *Hush, hush! tread softly!* belongs to this same period. It was composed, Charlotte Reynolds told H. B. Forman, to a Spanish air which she used to play to Keats. There is an autograph in Keats's copy of Hunt's *Literary Pocket-Book* and a transcript in his copy of *Endymion*, both of which are in the Dilke Collection in Hampstead. There is a transcript in Woodhouse's Book of Transcripts, dated "1818" and inscribed "from C. B." There is a transcript also in Woodhouse's Scrap-book.

A fifth lyric, *Where's the Poet?* belongs also to this period. There is a transcript in Woodhouse's Book of Transcripts, dated "1818" and inscribed "from C. B." There is a transcript also in George Keats's Book of Autographs and Transcripts, entitled "Fragment" and dated "1818."

A Fragment

Where's the Poet? show him! show him,
Muses nine! that I may know him.
'Tis the man who with a man
Is an equal, be he King,
Or poorest of the beggar-clan,
Or any other wondrous thing
A man may be 'twixt ape and Plato;
'Tis the man who with a bird,
Wren, or Eagle, finds his way to
All its instincts; he hath heard
The Lion's roaring, and can tell
What his horny throat expresseth,
And to him the Tiger's yell
Comes articulate and presseth
On his ear like mother-tongue.

. . . . .

The theme of this unrevised fragment is the essential principle of Keats's philosophy of negative capability. The poet, he believed, could not only enter imaginatively into the mind of a man but he could also find his way to the instincts of the beast and the bird. "If a sparrow come before my Window," he wrote Bailey on November 21, 1817, "I take part in its existence and pick about the Gravel."

His negatively capable imagination was supported by an extraordinarily keen organic sensibility. Woodhouse wrote a long, rambling commentary upon the letter which Keats wrote him on October 27, 1818, the letter in which Keats explained his philosophy of negative capability.

> He has affirmed [Woodhouse said] that he can conceive of a billiard Ball that it may have a sense of delight from its own roundness, smoothness & volubility & the rapidity of its motion. [Woodhouse's Scrap-book.]

The lyrics which Keats composed in the fall of 1818 are similar in theme, genre, and versification to those which he composed in the spring of 1818. They are less naïve, however, and more sophisticated in tone. The poetic tendencies of his humanitarian period seem to have been erased from his mind. When he resumed his philosophy of negative capability he not only began the Miltonic *Hyperion* but he also resumed his imitation of Elizabethan and Jacobean lyrics. He composed *Where's the Poet?*, *Fancy*, and *Bards of Passion and of Mirth* in the heptasyllabics of Jonson, Fletcher, and Browne.

The theme of *Fancy*, the pleasure which Keats took in a mingling together of things contrary by nature, is the same as that of *Welcome joy, and welcome sorrow* and *The Castle Builder*, two lyrics which he composed in the early part of 1818. He made a clear distinction between imagination and fancy. He believed, we have seen, that imagination was the faculty which intuits truth in the form of beauty, which enters sympathetically into the minds of men and beasts and birds, and which revives and lives the life of past ages. He believed that fancy, on the contrary, was a free, lawless faculty which, delighting in change and contrast, collects images of beauty from all parts of space and time and joins them together, however incompatible and contradictory they may be. His conception of fancy was influenced, Colvin suggested, by the definition of fancy in Fuller's *Holy State*, a definition which Lamb quoted in his *Specimens* from Fuller.

> Fancy. — It is the most boundless and restless faculty of the soul . . . it digs without spade, sails without ship, flies without wings, builds without charges, fights without bloodshed; in a moment striding from the centre to the circumference of the world; by a kind of omnipotency creating and annihilating things in an instant; and things divorced in Nature are married in Fancy as in a lawless place.

Keats copied an early version of *Fancy* on January 2 into the December journal letter to his brother, the original of which is in the Marquess of Crewe's Collection. There is a transcript, dated

"1818," in Keats's copy of *Endymion* and another in Woodhouse's Book of Transcripts, dated "1818" and inscribed "from C. B." When Keats published the poem in 1820 he made considerable changes in it, reducing the number of verses from 112 to 94. Some of the verses which he omitted from the printed version deny the theme of the poem that fancy delights in change, that every joy is spoilt by use, and that there is not a mistress but doth cloy. These verses express, as J. M. Murry suggested, the rapture of Keats's discovery of Miss Brawne.

> O the Ravishment — the Bliss!
> Fancy has her there she is —
> Never fulsome, ever new,
> There she steps! and tell me who
> Has a Mistress to [so] divine?
> Be the palate ne'er so fine
> She cannot sicken. . . .

Keats wrote the first draft of *Bards of Passion and of Mirth* in a volume of the plays of Ben Jonson and Beaumont and Fletcher on a blank page opposite *The Fair Maid of the Inn.* This volume is now in the Dilke Collection in Hampstead. Keats copied the poem on January 2 into the December journal letter to his brother; and he published it in his *Poems* of 1820. Woodhouse obtained it from Reynolds and copied it into his Commonplace Book and Book of Transcripts, dating it erroneously "from J. H. R. 26 Mar. 1819."

Keats expressed in this poem, as he explained to his brother, "the double immortality of Poets," who live both in their poems on earth and in the Elysian Fields in Heaven.

> Bards of Passion and of Mirth,
> Ye have left your souls on earth!
> Have ye souls in heaven too,
> Double-lived in regions new?

Hazlitt also expressed this idea in his *Lectures on the Literature of the Age of Elizabeth,* delivered at the Surrey Institution in 1820 and published in the same year. Discussing the premature deaths of Beaumont and Fletcher, Hazlitt said that "Poets however have a sort of privileged after-life, which does not fall to the common lot" and that they "leave the best part of what was theirs, their thoughts, their verse, what they most delighted and prided themselves in, behind them — imperishable, incorruptible, immortal!"

Keats created an original type of lyric poem in *Mermaid Tavern,* which he composed in February 1818, and in *Fancy* and *Bards of Passion and of Mirth,* which he composed in October or November

1818. He did not discover a proper name for this genre, but at one time he called it a rondeau and at another time an ode. He gave it a circular movement by repeating the opening verses at the end, and he gave it freedom by employing fluent, flexible heptasyllabic metre and by putting no arbitrary limit to the number of verses. He created it to take the place of the sonnet, whose resources he had exhausted and whose invariable form he felt was restrictive and confining. After he had copied *Fancy* and *Bards of Passion and of Mirth* into the journal letter to his brother, he said:

> These are specimens of a sort of rondeau which I think I shall become partial to — because you have one idea amplified with greater ease and more delight and freedom than in the sonnet.
>
> It is my intention [he continued] to wait a few years before I publish any minor poems — and then I hope to have a volume of some worth — and which those people will relish who cannot bear the burthen of a long poem.

3
Hyperion

Hyperion represents the climax of Keats's progressive efforts to re-create and to reanimate the life of ancient Greece, the Greece of the gods, the demi-gods, and the heroes. *Endymion*, the reviewer in *Blackwood's Edinburgh Magazine* could say, has no more to do with Greece than with old Tartary the fierce. *Endymion* revealed, however, Keats's ability to create myths; and the Hymn to Pan in the first book of this romance and the ode *To Maia*, composed on May 1, 1818, gave promise of his ability to revive the spirit of Greek religion and to express it in an elevated style.

Keats derived most of the mythological matter of *Hyperion* from English (chiefly Renaissance English) translations of Greek and Roman poems and histories. He was especially indebted to Chapman's translations of Homer's *Iliad*, *Odyssey*, and *Hymns* and Hesiod's *Georgics* (or *Works and Days*); Cooke's translation of Hesiod's *Works and Days* and *Theogony* (printed in Chalmer's *English Poets*, 1810); Sandys's translation of Ovid's *Metamorphosis*; and Booth's translation of Diodorus Siculus' *Historical Library*. He was indebted also to allusions to Greek myths in Renaissance poetry and in particular to those in Ronsard's ode *A Michel de l'Hospital*, Spenser's *Faerie Queene*, Shakespeare's plays, and Milton's *Paradise Lost*.

Keats drew much of the mythological matter, also, from classical dictionaries such as Lempriere's *Classical Dictionary*, Spence's *Polymetis*, and Tooke's *Pantheon*. At the beginning of 1819, while he was composing *Hyperion*, he purchased a copy of *Auctores Mythographi Latini* and signed and dated it "John Keats, 1819." This book contains treatises on Greek mythology by Hyginus, Fulgentius, Lactantius Placidus, and Albricus Philosophus. Keats borrowed this book probably from Taylor and Hessey, who were booksellers as well as publishers, several months before he purchased it; for he was indebted to it for material in both of his versions of the "Fall of Hyperion." After his death, when his books were divided among his friends, his copy of this book was given to Benjamin Bailey, who described it as follows:

> The book is characteristic of Keats, & shews that he read other and better books than Lempriere's Dictionary, on the Greek Mythology, as was sneeringly said of him by the vulgar, would-be critics of the day. — The book, — a fine old quarto, which now lies before me, with his name, — "John Keats, 1819," written at the top corner of the title page, — is "Auctores Mythographi Latini, Gajus Julius Hyginus, Fab. Planciad. Fulgentius, Lactantius Placidus, Albricus Philosophus. Lugd. Bat. Amstelaed. 1742." Fronting the title page is a curious engraving mingling together the higher Deities, and the torments of the Infernal Regions. It contains upwards of 900 pages, and is a very learned work. In the flyleaf I find this written memorandum by myself: — "This book formed part of the collection of the late John Keats, who died in Italy. He desired that his books should be distributed among his friends, and after his death this volume, with a print of Shakespeare, was sent me by Charles Brown Esqr. — July 1823." [Bailey's letter to Lord Houghton, May 7, 1849.]

Keats derived the basis of the mythological matter of *Hyperion* from Hesiod's *Theogony*, which he read in Cooke's translation. Hesiod interpreted the genesis of the gods by a principle of evolution, according to which successive generations of gods overcame and supplanted their predecessors. Chaos first came to be, Hesiod said, and next Earth and Erebus and Love. Earth bore Heaven, Hills, and Sea. And Heaven and Earth, mating together, produced Ocean, Coeus, Creüs, Hyperion, Japhet, Thea, Rhea, Themis, Mnemosyne, Phoebe, Tethys, and Saturn, the youngest and the most terrible. Afterwards Heaven and Earth produced a second brood — Brontes, Steropes, and Arges, who were called Cyclopes because each of them had a single orbed eye in the middle of his forehead. And finally Heaven and Earth produced a third brood — Cottus, Gyges, and Briareus, each of whom had fifty heads and a hundred arms. Heaven, hating Cottus, Gyges, and Briareus, confined them in a secret place in Earth; and Earth, groaning within, incited Saturn to mutilate Heaven. The blood which dripped from Heaven's members upon Earth produced the Giants and the Furies and the nymphs called Meliae; and the members, thrown into the sea, produced Venus. Hesiod said that Heaven called those sons whom he himself begot Titans — that is, Strainers — because they strained and did a presumptuous and evil deed in mutilating him. Hesiod did not give the names of the Giants who were produced by the blood which fell from Heaven's members upon Earth.

Saturn, the leader of the Titans, became the ruler of the universe after he had overthrown his father Heaven. Sea mated with Earth and begot Nereus, Thaumas, Phorcys, Ceto, and Eurybia; and Phorcys, uniting with Ceto, begot the Gorgons and others. Japhet and Clymene, daughter of Ocean and Tethys, produced Atlas, Prometheus, and others. Hyperion and Thea produced Sun, Moon, and Dawn. And Saturn and Rhea produced Vesta, Ceres, Juno, Pluto, Neptune, and Jupiter. Saturn, learning that he was destined to be overcome by his own son, swallowed each one of his children as soon as it was born. Rhea was filled with grief by the loss of her children; and, when she was bearing Jupiter, she besought and obtained the assistance of her parents Heaven and Earth. When Jupiter was born, Earth concealed him and Rhea gave Saturn a stone, wrapped in swaddling clothes, to swallow. After Jupiter grew to maturity, Earth tricked Saturn into vomiting up his children; and Jupiter led his brothers and sisters in a war against Saturn and the Titans. After the war had endured ten years without decision, Jupiter released Cottus, Gyges, and Briareus, whom Heaven had confined in Earth and whom Saturn had kept in this imprisonment. With their assistance Jupiter defeated the Titans and confined them in a place near the farthest bounds of Tartarus. Hesiod related the war between the Titans and the Olympians somewhat in detail. After Jupiter had overthrown the Titans, Earth, mating with Tartarus, bore Typhoeus, her youngest son, who had a hundred heads of a serpent growing from his shoulders. He began a fierce strife and frightened the gods, but Jupiter, leaping from Olympus, destroyed him with a thunderbolt in the glens of a mountain. In the remaining parts of the *Theogony*, Hesiod related the amours and listed the offspring of Jupiter.

The two other chief sources from which Keats learned the story of the genesis of the gods are Hyginus' *Fabulae* and Lempriere's *Classical Dictionary*. I quote the pertinent parts of Hyginus' genealogy of the gods:

> Ex Caligine, Chaos.
> Ex Chao & Caligine, Nox, Dies, Erebus, Aether.
> Ex Nocte & Erebo Fatum, . . . Porphyrion, etc.
> Ex Aethere & Die, Terra, Coelum, Mare.

Ex Aethere & Terra, Dolor, Dolus, Ira, Luctus, Mendacium, Jusjurandum, Ultio, Intemperantia, Altercatio, Oblivio, Socordia, Timor, Superbia, Ingestum, Pugna, Oceanus, Themis, Tartarus, Pontus, & Titanes, Briareus, Gyges, Steropes, Atlas, Hyperion, & Ptolus, Saturnus, Ops, Moneta, Dione, Furiae tres, id est, Alecto, Megaera, Tisiphone.

Ex Terra & Tartaro, Gigantes, Enceladus, Coemse, Lentesmophius, Astraeus, Pelorus, Pallas, Emphitus, Phorcus, Jenios, Agrus, Alemone, Ephialtes, Eurytus, Effra, Corydon, Pheomis, Theodamas, Otus, Typhon, Poliboetes, Meniphiaraus, Abseus, Colophomus, Iapetus.

Ex Nereo & Doride Nereides quinquaginta . . . Clymene, etc.

Ex Japeto & Clymene, Atlas, Epimetheus, Prometheus.

Ex Hyperione & Aethra, Sol, Luna, Aurora.

Ex Saturno & Ope, Vesta, Ceres, Juno, Jupiter, Pluto, Neptunus.

Ex Jove & Moneta, Musae.

Ex Jove & Clymene, Mnemosyne.

Hyginus' genealogy of the gods differs in many details from Hesiod's. He represented the Titans as sons of Aether and Terra and the Giants as sons of Tartarus and Terra. He enumerated many sons of Aether and Terra but he called only five of them — Briareus, Gyges, Steropes, Atlas, and Hyperion — Titans. And he differed from all other mythologists in representing Moneta, instead of Mnemosyne, as the daughter of Aether and Terra and the mother of the Muses.

Lempriere, a modern mythologist, derived his definitions of the gods from various and contradictory classical sources — from Homer, Hesiod, Apollodorus, Pausanias, Diodorus Siculus, Hyginus, Virgil, Ovid, and others. His account of Coelus (or Heaven) is a summary of Hesiod's story of this cosmic god. Under the word "Titanes" he said:

Titanes, a name given to the sons of Coelus and Terra. They were 45 in number, according to the Egyptians. Apollodorus mentions 13, Hyginus 6, and Hesiod 20, among whom are the Titanides. The most known of the Titans are Saturn, Hyperion, Oceanus, Japetus, Cottus, and Briareus, to whom Horace adds, Typhoeus, Mimas, Porphyrion, Rhoetus, and Enceladus, who are by other mythologists reckoned among the giants.

Defining the Titanides, who were the daughters of Coelus and Terra, he said:

The most celebrated were Tethys, Themis, Dione, Thea, Mnemosyne, Ops, Cybele, Vesta, Phoebe, and Rhea.

He said that the Giants were the sons of Coelus and Terra according to Hesiod, and the sons of Tartarus and Terra according to Hyginus. He observed that the Giants were "often ignorantly confounded" with the Titans. Following Lactantius, whose source was

Ennius, he said that the Titans warred against Saturn and the Giants against Jupiter. He himself confused the Giants with the Titans, however; for he included Cottus, Gyges, and Briareus among the Giants, although, as we saw above, he called Cottus and Briareus Titans. Other Giants whom he mentioned are Enceladus, Aloides, Porphyrion, Typhon, and Otus.

Keats based his list of Titans upon Hesiod's but derived the names of certain Titans from Hyginus, Lempriere, and other sources. His list includes Saturn and Ops, Hyperion and Thea, Oceanus and Tethys, Coeus, Gyges, Briareus, Typhon, Dolor, Porphyrion, Creüs, Iäpetus, Cottus, Enceladus, Atlas, Phorcus, Mnemosyne, Phoebe, Themis, Asia, Clymene, and Cybele (confused with Ops). He followed Chapman, Cooke, and other English poets and translators in the use of the Latin names of the gods. These Latin names are either native Latin words (Saturnus for Greek Κρόνος and Coelus for Greek Οὐρανός), representing the identification of Roman gods with Greek gods; or they are Greek derivatives (Hyperion for Greek Ὑπερίων and Coeus for Greek Κοῖος), representing the introduction of Greek gods into the Roman pantheon.

Some critics, referring to Lempriere's *Classical Dictionary*, have said that Keats confused the Giants with the Titans. His classical authorities distinguish between Titans and Giants, but they do not agree in their distinctions. Some primeval gods which are called Titans in Hesiod's list, for instance, are called Giants in Hyginus' list. Since classical authorities differed in regard to the number and the personnel of the Titans, Keats selected his Titans freely from various classical lists. Every Titan in his list, however, was called a Titan by at least one of his authorities.

Keats departed from most of his sources in representing Saturn as the "first-born" of Heaven and Earth (I. 323). He may have diverged from his sources deliberately, thinking it more fitting that the aged Saturn should be the oldest of the Titans; or he may have been influenced by Diodorus Siculus, who, relating the religious traditions of the Cretans, said that Saturn was the oldest of the Titans (Book V, Chapter IV).

Keats, following Lempriere, Hyginus, and Fulgentius, represented Ops as the wife of Saturn and the mother of Jupiter, Neptune, and Pluto. In the autograph manuscript of *Hyperion* (II. 3–4) he represented Cybele as the mother of the Titans —

And Saturn gain'd with Thea that sad place
the Titans
Where Cybele and ~~her~~ bruised ~~Children~~ mourn'd.

And at the end of the second book (v. 384) he said that "Saturn sat near the mother of the Gods"—that is, near Cybele. He derived this conception of Cybele, it is probable, from Diodorus Siculus' *Historical Library* (Book III, Chapter IV), Albricus' *De Deorum Imaginibus*, and Sandys's commentary upon the first book of Ovid's *Metamorphosis*. "Cybele mater deorum," Albricus said, "fuit dicta terra: quam & deos genuisse dixerunt veteres, & gigantes." And Sandys said that "Saturne is fained to be the sonne of Coelus, or Heaven, and Cybel, which is the Earth." Keats had already represented Terra, or Earth, as the cosmic mother of the Titans; and he did not desire, apparently, to identify Cybele with Terra. When he revised *Hyperion* he altered the verse which I quoted above, "Where Cybele and her bruised Children mourn'd," into "Where Cybele and the bruised Titans mourn'd." In September 1819, when he attempted to combine the humanitarian and humanistic versions of the "Fall of Hyperion," he identified Cybele with Ops, the wife of Saturn (I. 425). He derived this conception of Cybele from Lempriere, who defined Cybele as the "daughter of Coelus and Terra, and wife of Saturn." "She is supposed to be the same," Lempriere said, "as Ceres, Rhea, Ops, Vesta, etc."

Keats's representation of the name and the personality of the goddess of memory, one of the Titan goddesses, was influenced by the changes which occurred in his intuition of the "Fall of Hyperion." In his first and humanistic intuition of the subject, the intuition which he held in the first half of 1818, he followed general classical tradition, it is probable, in thinking of this goddess as Mnemosyne. Hesiod listed Mnemosyne as a daughter of Coelus and Terra and a sister of Saturn and the Titans, and he said that she was wooed by Jupiter and bore the nine Muses. Lempriere said that "the word Mnemosyne signifies memory" and that "therefore the poets have rightly called memory the mother of the muses."

When Keats swung from the humanism of Shakespeare and Milton to the humanitarianism of Wordsworth at the end of April 1818, he changed his intuition of the "Fall of Hyperion" from a humanistic and Miltonic epic into a humanitarian and Wordsworthian vision. In the introduction to the humanitarian vision, which he composed in the latter part of September 1818, he changed the name of the goddess of memory from Mnemosyne to Moneta. He believed doubtless that the simplicity of the name Moneta was more appropriate in the natural style of the vision and that its admonitory significance was more suitable to the rôle of the goddess in this poem. Moneta has a double rôle. She is not only the goddess of memory, who gives Keats a vision of the fall of the Titans, but she is also the priestess of humanitarianism, who utters a scathing denunciation of thoughtless and visionary poets and who rebukes Keats himself as an idle dreamer. Keats derived Moneta from Hyginus, who said that she was the daughter of Aether and Terra and the mother of the Muses. He learned that Moneta is the same person as Mnemosyne, the goddess of memory, from a note in the *Auctores Mythographi Latini* upon Hyginus' Moneta —

> Illa est *Mnemosyne* Hesiodo & Apollodoro. Vidit id Turnebus, cum scriberet Advers. I. xxviii. 3. *Moneta Hygino est, quae Mnemosyne a Graecis vocatur.* . . . Certe *Moneta* eadem est, quae *Mnemosyne*, nam auctor infra dicet matrem esse Musarum *Monetam*, quae a Pindaro . . . *Mnemosyne* dicitur. . . .

At the end of this long note it is stated that Hyginus' Moneta is not the same person as Juno, who was worshipped by the Romans under the name of Moneta because she warned the sleeping guards by means of the cackling of geese that the Gauls were approaching to assault the Capitol. The significance of Juno Moneta, however, may have influenced Keats's conception of Moneta (or Mnemosyne), the goddess of memory.

Keats resumed his humanistic philosophy of negative capability in the latter part of October and began, sometime thereafter, the humanistic and Miltonic *Hyperion*. In this epic version he called the goddess of memory by the more appropriate name of Mnemosyne. He listed her among the Titans in the second book, and in the third book he represented her as the foster mother of Apollo, the hero of the epic. She was the only one of the Titans whom he placed on the side of the Olympians.

In September 1819, when Keats attempted to combine the humanitarian and the humanistic versions of the poem into a third version, *The Fall of Hyperion, a Dream*, he called the goddess of memory by the name of Moneta. The name Mnemosyne was so fixed in his mind, however, that twice (in parts which he added in the reconstruction of the poem) he called the goddess Mnemosyne.

The sources of a few other Titans in *Hyperion* should be explained. In the second book (vv. 17 *et seq.*) Keats said that not all of the defeated Titans were confined in the den near the bounds of Tartarus.

> Coeus, and Gyges, and Briareüs,
> Typhon, and Dolor, and Porphyrion,
> With many more, the brawniest in assault,
> Were pent in regions of laborious breath;
> Dungeon'd in opaque element, to keep
> Their clenched teeth still clench'd, and all their limbs

Lock'd up like veins of metal, crampt and screw'd;
Without a motion, save of their big hearts
Heaving in pain, and horribly convuls'd
With sanguine feverous boiling gurge of pulse.

Keats derived the confinement of these Titans in the elements of the earth and the pain which they suffered from a passage of Hesiod's *Theogony*:

The brothers Briareus and Cottus lay,
With Gyges, bound in chains, remov'd from day,
By their hard-hearted sire, who with surprise
View'd their vast strength, their form, and monstrous size:
In the remotest parts of Earth confin'd
They sat, and silent sorrows wreck'd their mind. . . .
[Cooke's translation, vv. 916 *et seq.*]

Keats changed Hesiod's account of Cottus, Gyges, and Briareus, however. He represented them as fighting on the side of Saturn instead of on the side of Jupiter and as being confined in the earth by Jupiter instead of by their father Coelus.

Other sources of the Titans in the passage from *Hyperion* quoted above are indicated in Woodhouse's Commonplace Book and Book of Transcripts. Opposite this passage in the transcript of *Hyperion* in the Book of Transcripts, Woodhouse copied a number of verses from Ronsard's ode *A Michel de l'Hospital*. These verses, describing the battle between the Olympians and the Giants, contain the names of Cotte (Cottus), Gyge (Gyges), Briare (Briareus), Typhe (Typhoeus or Typhon), Encelade (Enceladus), and Porfyre (Porphyrion). Woodhouse had lent Keats a copy of Ronsard's works in September 1818, and he presumed that Keats had been influenced by Ronsard's list of Giants. There is no detail of these Giants (or Titans) in Ronsard's ode, however, which is not also in Keats's other sources.

Opposite this same passage in the transcript of *Hyperion* in Woodhouse's Commonplace Book, there is the following verse in Keats's handwriting: "Big-brawn'd Aegaeon mounted on a Whale." And below this verse there are the following references: "Aegaeon p. 25, S. O. Typhon or Typhoeus 90. Coeus 108." The verse "Big-brawn'd Aegaeon mounted on a Whale" occurs on page 25 of Sandys's *Ovid*, edition of 1640. A marginal gloss on "Aegaeon" says: "A Gyant drowned in the Aegaean Sea (of him so called) for assisting the Titans, and taken into the number of the Sea Gods by Tethys." Keats did not mention Aegaeon in *Hyperion* but he mentioned Briareus, whom Lempriere identifies with Aegaeon.

Keats knew Coeus in Hesiod's *Theogony*, in which he is called a Titan, as well as in Sandys's *Ovid's Metamorphosis*, in which he is called a Giant. Keats derived Dolor from Hyginus, who is the only classical mythologist who mentioned Dolor in connection with the Titans. In the passages from the *Fabulae* which I quoted above, Hyginus listed Dolor and other abstract qualities together with the Titans as sons of Aether and Terra. Keats found Porphyrion also in Hyginus' list of the sons of Aether and Terra, and he learned from Lempriere that Porphyrion was called a Titan by Horace. Keats derived Creus from Hesiod but he found Iapetus, Atlas, and Phorcus in several of his sources — Hesiod, Lempriere, and Hyginus.

The sources of Keats's Typhon and Enceladus are more complex. Hesiod said that, after Jupiter had overthrown Saturn and the Titans, Earth mated with Tartarus and bore Typhoeus, who had a hundred serpent heads, who frightened the gods with his clamor and strife, and who was overcome by a thunderbolt of Jupiter in a chasm of a mountain. And Virgil said that the body of Enceladus, half-burned by a thunderbolt, reposed underneath Mount Aetna and that, whenever he turned his weary side, the whole island of Sicily shook and the sky was veiled with smoke (*Aeneid*, III. 578 *et seq.*). Enceladus was usually but not always identified with Typhoeus or Typhon. Keats found Typhon and Enceladus represented as different persons by Hyginus and by Ronsard. He was influenced in particular, however, by a passage in Shakespeare's *Titus Andronicus* (IV. ii. 93–96) —

I tell you, younglings, not Enceladus
With all his threat'ning band of Typhon's brood,
Nor great Alcides, nor the god of war,
Shall seize this prey out of his father's hands.

His recollection of this passage is proved by the echo of "youngling" in the speech in which Enceladus exhorted the Titans to resume war against the Olympians —

Do ye forget the blows, the buffets vile?
Are ye not smitten by a youngling arm?

[II 317–18.]

Keats, taking a hint from Shakespeare, represented Enceladus as the fiercest and most warlike of the Titans:

. . . tiger-passion'd, lion-thoughted, wroth,
He meditated, plotted, and even now
Was hurling mountains in that second war,
Not long delay'd, that scar'd the younger Gods
To hide themselves in forms of beast and bird.

In this passage Keats attributed to Enceladus deeds which Ovid had assigned to Typhon. In the fifth book of the *Metamorphosis* one of the Pierides sang the wars of the Giants against the Gods —

> How *Typhon*, from earth's gloomy entrailes rais'd,
> Struck all their powr's with feare: who fled amaz'd,
> Till *Aegypts* scorched soyle the weary hides;
> And wealthy *Nile*, who in seuen channels glides.
> That thither Earth-borne *Typhon* them pursu'd:
> When as the Gods concealing shapes indu'd.
> *Ioue* turn'd himselfe, shee said, into a Ram:
> From whence the hornes of *Libyan Hammon* came.
> *Bacchus* a Goat, *Appollo* was a Crowe,
> *Phoebe* a Cat, *Ioue's* wife a Cow of snowe:
> *Venus* a Fish, a Stork did *Hermes* hide. . . .

And then one of the Muses sang the defeat and the confinement of Typhon beneath Mount Aetna in Sicily.

Keats gave Asia an unusual, perhaps an unclassical, parentage.

> Asia, born of most enormous Caf,
> Who cost her mother Tellus keener pangs,
> Though feminine, than any of her sons. . . .

Hesiod represented Asia, Clymene, and many others as daughters of Oceanus and Tethys. Hyginus represented Asia and Clymene as daughters of Nereus and Doris. And both Hesiod and Hyginus represented Clymene as the wife of Iapetus and the mother of Atlas, Prometheus, and others. Asia and Clymene were sometimes regarded as the same person, and Lempriere represented each as the wife of Iapetus. Keats distinguished clearly between the two goddesses. He represented Clymene as the daughter of Oceanus and Tethys and the wife of Iapetus, and Asia as the daughter of Caf and Tellus (or Terra). Caf is not mentioned of course by any classical mythologist. York Powell suggested to de Sélincourt that Keats derived Caf from the *Arabian Nights Entertainment* (or the *Thousand and One Nights*), in which Kaf is represented as a fabulous mountain which is "the starry girdle of the world" and which surrounds "the earth as a ring does the finger." Kaf, the mountain-god of the Arabians, is not an improper companion to Atlas, a mountain-god of the Greeks.

Keats interpreted the genesis of Greek gods by the principle of progressive evolution, according to which each generation of deities was supplanted by a generation which was more beautiful. He derived the germ of this principle from Hesiod's *Theogony*; but he explained the principle by the neo-Platonic philosophy of beauty, out of which, we remember, he had developed the theme of *Endymion*. He stated this neo-Platonic principle of evolution in the second book of the epic (vv. 173 *et seq.*). Saturn, addressing the fallen Titans, said that he had searched the universe and that he could not discover the cause of their defeat by their offspring, the Olympians. Then Oceanus, to whom Saturn turned for advice and in whose face reposed severe content, replied:

I bring proof
How ye, perforce, must be content to stoop:
And in the proof much comfort will I give,
If ye will take that comfort in its truth.
We fall by course of Nature's law, not force
Of thunder, or of Jove. Great Saturn, thou
Hast sifted well the atom-universe;
But for this reason, that thou art the King,
And only blind from sheer supremacy,
One avenue was shaded from thine eyes,
Through which I wandered to eternal truth.
And first, as thou wast not the first of powers,
So art thou not the last; it cannot be:
Thou art not the beginning nor the end.
From chaos and parental darkness came
Light, the first fruits of that intestine broil,
That sullen ferment, which for wondrous ends
Was ripening in itself. The ripe hour came,
And with it light, and light, engendering
Upon its own producer, forthwith touch'd
The whole enormous matter into life.
Upon that very hour, our parentage,
The Heavens and the Earth, were manifest:
Then thou first-born, and we the giant-race,
Found ourselves ruling new and beauteous realms.
Now comes the pain of truth, to whom 'tis pain;
O folly! *for to bear all naked truths,*
And to envisage circumstance, all calm,
That is the top of sovereignty. Mark well!
As Heaven and Earth are fairer, fairer far
Than Chaos and blank Darkness, though once chiefs;
And as we show beyond that Heaven and Earth
In form and shape compact and beautiful,
In will, in action free, companionship,
And thousand other signs of purer life;
So on our heels a fresh perfection treads,
A power more strong in beauty, born of us
And fated to excel us, as we pass
In glory that old Darkness: nor are we
Thereby more conquer'd, than by us the rule
Of shapeless Chaos. Say, doth the dull soil

Quarrel with the proud forests it hath fed,
And feedeth still, more comely than itself?
Can it deny the chiefdom of green groves?
Or shall the tree be envious of the dove
Because it cooeth, and hath snowy wings
To wander wherewithal and find its joys?
We are such forest-trees, and our fair boughs
Have bred forth, not pale solitary doves,
But eagles golden-feather'd, who do tower
Above us in their beauty, and must reign
In right thereof; for *'tis the eternal law*
That first in beauty should be first in might:
Yea, by that law, another race may drive
Our conquerors to mourn as we do now . . .
Receive the truth, and let it be your balm.

This passage, which expresses the theme of *Hyperion*, represents a significant development in Keats's philosophy of negative capability. At the end of October 1818, when he resumed this philosophy, his point of view was romantic. He began the composition of *Hyperion* under the impulse to escape, by means of his negatively capable imagination, from the world of unpleasant reality into a world of ideal beauty. He chose deliberately, I believe, to create a world of gods, which would be above natural laws, instead of to create a world of men, which would be subject to these laws. He wrote Haydon on January 23, 1818, when he was first intuiting *Hyperion*, that there would be one essential difference between *Endymion* and *Hyperion* — namely, that Endymion, the hero of the romance, being mortal, was led on by circumstance but that Apollo, the hero of the epic, being a foreseeing god, would shape his actions like one.

Keats discovered, however, that the world of the gods as represented in Hesiod's *Theogony* and other classical sources was not above natural laws — that it was in fact only the natural world in its first and elemental beginnings. He saw that the world of Saturn and Hyperion was a world of defeat and pain and grief; but he saw also, with the help of neo-Platonism, that this world was evolving toward the goal of ideal beauty through successive stages, each of which was more beautiful than that which it supplanted. And in this principle of evolution, that first in beauty should be first in might, he found comfort. The evil which the Titans suffered was a necessary step in the progress of the world toward ultimate perfection. "Receive the truth," Oceanus told his brothers, "and let it be your balm."

Keats's idealistic conception of the world was only temporary.

In April 1819, when he gave up the composition of *Hyperion* and left the epic incomplete, he rejected this idealistic humanism and developed an empirical humanism. We shall study this stage of his philosophy in the next chapter. We should observe, however, that in *Hyperion* Keats was not romantic, although he was idealistic. He was facing the unpleasant facts of life instead of fleeing from them. "To bear all naked truths," he said,

> . . . to bear all naked truths,
> And to envisage circumstance, all calm,
> That is the top of sovereignty. . . .

Hyperion represents the extreme point in Keats's reaction against the prettiness, the triviality, the colloquial idiom, and the sentimentality — in brief, the cockney qualities — of the poetry which he wrote under the influence of Leigh Hunt in 1815 and 1816. We have traced in detail the steps by which he developed an elevated style of poetry in 1817 and in 1818 by means of an intensive study of Renaissance English poets. He began his study of Shakespeare in April and his study of Milton in October and November 1817, learning intensity and negative capability (or objectivity) from the one and conciseness, intensity, and sublimity from the other.

Hyperion is a conscious and direct imitation of Milton's *Paradise Lost*, which is a classical epic in genre and which has many classical and un-English characteristics in diction, imagery, figures of speech, and sentence structure. Keats had too much creative imagination, however, to make a literal and mechanical imitation. He employed the devices of Milton's style as creatively as Virgil had employed those of Homer's style and as Milton had employed the stylistic devices of Homer and Virgil.

I shall quote and summarize Ernest de Sélincourt's[1] excellent analysis of the Miltonic qualities and devices in the style of *Hyperion*.

> One of the most characteristic and effective features of the style of *Paradise Lost* [de Selincourt pointed out] is the studied repetition of words and phrases. This is a development of the poetic device called by Dryden the "turn," by which the same word or phrase is used twice in a different relation — its repetition giving a particular significance to the part which it performs on the second occasion. The "turn" can be employed for mere emphasis, or for musical effect, or, more satisfactorily, for both combined; but its finest use is informed with a certain pathos, or subtle but telling irony, as in Vergil's lines on the fatal impatience of Orpheus to see his bride (*Georgics*, iv. 488, 489). . . . In classical literature the "turn" found most favour with Ovid, in whom it degenerated into a mere prettiness, and the early Elizabethans caught it principally from Ovid, though Spenser developed to the full its most delicate musical possibilities.

[1] Ernest de Sélincourt, pp. 489–492.

But in English poetry Milton has the most constant recourse to it; in his work it is found in all its forms, from the vulgar Ovidian pun, which fortunately Keats escaped, to its finest and highest use.

De Sélincourt gave the following examples of the repetition of words in *Paradise Lost*:

There *rest*, if any *rest* can harbour there. . . .
[I. 185.]

and feel by turns the bitter *change*
Of *fierce extreams*, *extreams* by *change* more *fierce*. . . .
[II. 598.]

faithful found
Among the *faithless*, *faithful* only hee. . . .
[V. 897.]

unchang'd
To hoarce or mute, *though fall'n on evil dayes*,
On evil dayes though fall'n, and *evil* tongues. . . . [VII. 24–26.]

This device of repetition occurs more frequently in *Hyperion* than in *Paradise Lost* itself.

How beautiful, if sorrow had not made
Sorrow more beautiful than Beauty's self. . . .
[I. 35–36.]

sometimes eagle's wings,
Unseen before by Gods or wondering men,
Darken'd the place; and neighing steeds were heard,
Not heard before by Gods or wondering men. . . .
[I. 182–185.]

Two wings this orb
Possess'd for glory, two fair argent wings. . . .
[I. 283–284.]

Unus'd to bend, by hard compulsion bent. . . .
[I. 300.]

There is a roaring in the bleak-grown pines. . . .
Such noise is like the roar of bleak-grown pines. . . .
[II. 116, 122.]

Now comes the pain of truth, to whom 'tis pain. . . .
[II. 202.]

it enforc'd me to bid sad farewell
To all my empire: farewell sad I took. . . .
[II. 238–239.]

[the brook that]
Doth fear to meet the sea: but sea it met. . . .
[II. 302.]

Perhaps the second most striking Miltonic device which Keats employed in *Hyperion* is inversion, the placing the adjective after, instead of before, the noun which it modifies. Spenser and the early Renaissance poets derived this device from classical poetry; but Milton, the last of the Renaissance poets, employed it most effectively.

> Anon out of the earth a *fabric huge*
> Rose like an exhalation, with the sound
> Of dulcet symphonies and *voices sweet* —
> [I. 710–712.]
>
> Or flocks, or herds, or *human face divine*. . . .
> [III. 44.]
>
> The *dismal situation waste and wild*. . . .
> [I. 60.]
>
> his ponderous *shield*,
> *Ethereal temper*, *massy*, *large*, *and round*. . . .
> [I. 284–285.]

Keats's inversions are peculiarly Miltonic when one adjective precedes the noun and another follows it, when there is chiasmus, and when two or more adjectives follow the noun.

> And palpitations sweet, and pleasures soft. . . .
> [I. 313.]
>
> Savour of poisonous brass and metal sick. . . .
> [I. 189.]
>
> Upon the gold clouds metropolitan. . . .
> [I. 129.]
>
> and all her forehead wan,
> Her eye-brows thin and jet, and hollow eyes. . . .
> [II. 114–115.]

Another passage, which is not an example of inversion, produces a similar effect:

> Upon the sodden ground
> His old right hand lay nerveless, listless, dead,
> Unsceptred. . . . [I. 17–19.]

Keats had employed a series of three adjectives in the fourth book of *Endymion* (verse 764 *et seq.*), which he composed in November 1817 at the beginning of his imitation of Milton's style:

> The Carian
> No word return'd: both lovelorn, silent, wan,
> Into the vallies green together went.

He used this device also in *The Eve of St. Agnes* (II. 3), which he composed in January 1819 in an interlude in the composition of *Hyperion*. The aged beadsman

> riseth from his knees,
> And back returneth, meagre, barefoot, wan.

The whole passage which I quoted from *Endymion* is Miltonic. The "vallies green" is a Miltonic inversion and it is also a reminiscence of the "silent valley" in *Paradise Lost* (II. 546–547). Keats, commenting upon Milton's use of "valley," said: "There is a cool pleasure in the very sound of vale.... Milton has put vales in heaven and hell with the very utter affection and yearning of a great Poet."

Other devices of syntax in *Hyperion* were derived from *Paradise Lost.* Keats employed elliptical constructions, such as "torrents hoarse, Pouring a constant bulk, *uncertain where*" (II. 8–9); "Who cost her mother Tellus keener pangs, *Though feminine,* than any of her sons" (II. 54–55); and "'I know the covert, for thence came I hither.' *Thus brief*; then with beseeching eyes she went With backward footing..." (I. 152–154). Keats employed also the device of redundance for the purpose of amplifying or emphasizing the melody and the imagery. De Sélincourt quoted two examples of this device — "No further than to where his feet had stray'd, And slept there since" (I. 16–17) and "I, Coelus, wonder, how they came and whence; And at the fruits thereof what shapes they be" (I. 314–15).

Keats employed the Miltonic (and classical) constructions of "save what" and "gave of" in the following passage: "his palace-door flew ope In smoothest silence, save what solemn tubes, Blown by the serious Zephyrs, gave of sweet And wandering sounds." (I. 205–208). Keats followed Milton also in the classical use of the adjective and the participle (1) as a relative clause — "the earth Knows thee not, *thus afflicted,* for a God" (I. 55–56); (2) as an adverb or an adverbial phrase — "a stream went voiceless by" (I. 11) and "let the rose glow intense" (III. 15); and (3) as an abstract noun — "barren *void*" (I. 119).

Keats, like Milton, employed the long simile of the classical epic. Suggesting the effect of Saturn's speech to Thea, he said:

As when, upon a tranced summer-night,
Those green-rob'd senators of mighty woods,
Tall oaks, branch-charmed by the earnest stars,
Dream, and so dream all night without a stir,
Save from one gradual solitary gust
Which comes upon the silence, and dies off,
As if the ebbing air had but one wave;
So came these words and went....

This intimate, vivid, magical interpretation of nature was the peculiar gift of Keats's poetic imagination. It owed much to Wordsworth's intimate, vivid, meditative naturalism and to Coleridge's romantic magic, but it was different from each of them. Many passages in Keats's poems reveal how deeply he felt the romance, the mystery, and the majesty of "the old oak forests" of England, "its tall woods with high romances blent" (*Happy is England!* and *When I have fears*).

Keats surpassed Milton in this imaginative interpretation of nature, as Sir Sidney Colvin observed; but he could not equal Milton in rich suggestive allusions to the culture of past ages — to matters of mythology, philosophy, poetry, sculpture, etc. — for he lacked Milton's erudition and maturity of mind. The following are examples of these learned allusions in *Hyperion*. Describing Thea, Keats said:

> Her face was large as that of Memphian sphinx,
> Pedestal'd haply in a palace court,
> When sages look'd to Egypt for their lore. [I. 31-33.]

And, describing the workings of the dawn when Hyperion was preparing to begin his journey across the sky, he called them

> hieroglyphics old,
> Which sages and keen-eyed astrologers
> Then living on the earth, with labouring thought
> Won from the gaze of many centuries:
> Now lost, save what we find on remnants huge
> Of stone, or marble swart; their import gone,
> Their wisdom long since fled. . . .
> [I. 277-283.]

And, in his description of Asia in the den of the defeated Titans, he said:

> More thought than woe was in her dusky face,
> For she was prophesying of her glory;
> And in her wide imagination stood
> Palm-shaded temples, and high rival fanes,
> By Oxus or in Ganges' sacred isles. [II. 56-60.]

Much of the Miltonic quality of *Hyperion* depends upon the diction. Keats adopted the diction of Renaissance poets in April 1817, we have seen, when he began the composition of *Endymion*. The influx of Miltonic words into his poetic vocabulary began in November 1817 in the fourth book of *Endymion*, increased in the poems which he composed in 1818, and came to its climax in *Hyperion*. It is difficult to distinguish the words which he derived from Milton from those which he derived from Spenser, Shakespeare, and other Renaissance poets, for the greater part of Milton's diction is the common poetic diction of his period. Some of the words which Keats employed in *Hyperion* are peculiar to Milton, however, and others are reminiscences of particular passages in *Paradise Lost.* De Sélincourt selected the following words in *Hyperion* as definitely Miltonic — argent (I. 284), colure (I. 274), essence (I. 232, II. 331, III. 104), gurge (II. 28), inlet (I. 211), lucent (I. 239), oozy (II. 170), orbed (I. 166), reluctant (I. 61), slope (I. 204), sovran (III. 115), and astonied (II. 165). "Mr. W. T. Arnold has pointed out," de Sélincourt said, "that the immense increase of adjectives in -ed, which in Keats's later work supplant the -y adjectives, is also chiefly due to the study of Milton."

Hyperion contains a great number of Miltonic reminiscences, reminiscences of words, images, allusions, ideas, incidents, and characteristics of persons from particular passages in *Paradise Lost.* It contains also an equally great number of Shakespearean reminiscences. I shall point out striking examples of these reminiscences in the following critical analysis of the epic.

Keats began his epic of the Greek gods *in medias res* in the manner of the Greek epic. All of the Titans, with the exception of Hyperion, the god of the sun, have been defeated and supplanted by their offspring, the Olympians, led by Jupiter, Neptune, and Pluto, "the rebel three." The main action of the epic, as the title indicates, is the overthrow of Hyperion by young Apollo, the son of Jupiter.

Keats expended the full force of his poetic faculties upon the beginning, for he knew that all great poems begin impressively. Commenting upon the beginning of *Paradise Lost*, he observed:

> There is always a great charm in the openings of great Poems, more particularly where the action begins — that of Dante's Hell. Of Hamlet, the first step must be heroic and full of power; and nothing can be more impressive and shaded than the commencement of the action here [in *Paradise Lost*] —
>
> "round he throws his baleful eyes."

In the first verses of *Hyperion*, Keats described the lonely vale into which the aged Saturn, king of the Titans, has retired, bewildered by his defeat and numbed by despair. He sought to create an effect of utter stillness, absolute colorlessness, and titanic despair. I quote the text of the autograph manuscript:

> Deep in the shady sadness of a Vale,
> Far sunken from the healthy breath of Morn,
> Far from the fiery noon, and ~~evening~~ Eve's one star,
> Sat grey hair'd Saturn quiet as a stone,
> Still as the silence round about his Lair.
> Forest on forest hung above his head
> ~~Like Clouds that whose bosoms thundrous bosoms~~
> Like Cloud on Cloud. No stir of air was there,

~~a young vulture's~~
~~Not so much life as what an eagle's wing~~
~~Would spread upon a field of green ear'd corn:~~
Not so much life as on a summer's day
Robs not at all the dandelion's fleece
But where the dead leaf fell, there did it rest.
A stream went voiceless by, still deadened more
By reason of his fallen divinity
~~Shading across it~~
Spreading a shade: the Naiad mid her reeds
Press'd her cold finger closer to her lips.

This autograph manuscript, which is the second draft, shows the care with which Keats revised the opening verses. He achieved at last the perfect effect which he sought in the text which he published in 1820.

Deep in the shady sadness of a vale
Far sunken from the healthy breath of morn,
Far from the fiery noon, and eve's one star,
Sat gray-hair'd Saturn, quiet as a stone,
Still as the silence round about his lair;
Forest on forest hung about his head
Like cloud on cloud. No stir of air was there,
Not so much life as on a summer's day
Robs not one light seed from the feather'd grass,
But where the dead leaf fell, there did it rest.
A stream went voiceless by, still deadened more
By reason of his fallen divinity
Spreading a shade: the Naiad 'mid her reeds
Press'd her cold finger closer to her lips.

Keats received from Milton the suggestion of the stillness and the sadness of the vale into which Saturn, overthrown by his rebel sons, retired. He marked the following passage in his copy of *Paradise Lost* (I. 318–321) —

Or have ye chosen this place
After the toil of battle to repose
Your wearied virtue, for the ease you find
To slumber here, as in the vales of Heaven?

The "vales" in this passage reminded him of another passage in which Milton described the vale in Hell into which one group of the fallen angels retreated (II. 546 *et seq.*), and he observed in an annotation:

There is a cool pleasure in the very sound of vale. The English word is of the happiest chance. Milton has put vales in heaven and hell with the very utter affection and yearning of a great Poet. It is a sort of Delphic Abstraction — a beautiful thing made more beautiful by being reflected and put in a Mist. The next mention of Vale is one of the most pathetic in the whole range of Poetry

Others, more mild,
Retreated in a silent Valley etc.

How much of the charm is in the valley! —

The innumerable compositions and decompositions by which Keats achieved the perfect effect of utter stillness and absolute colorlessness which are the setting for the titanic grief and despair which paralyze Saturn may be illustrated in the genesis of two verses. Keats composed the eighth and ninth verses originally in the following form —

Not so much life as what an eagle's wing
Would spread upon a field of green ear'd corn.

The fierce energy in the "eagle's wing" and the vivid color in "green ear'd corn" destroy the harmony of the sensuous effect which Keats was striving to produce. He altered "what an eagle's wing" into "a young vulture's wing" without, however, removing the images of energy and color. Then, being unable to improve the imagery of the verses for the moment, he left the verses in this form and continued his copying and revising of the poem. Afterwards he came back to these verses, drew a line through them, and wrote the following across the margin on the right-hand side of the page —

Not so much life as on a summer's day
Robs not at all the dandelion's fleece.

Keats did not make any further alteration of these verses in his manuscript, and Woodhouse copied them in this form in his transcript on April 20, 1819. These lines fit harmoniously into their context, for they are free from the energy and the color of the original verses. Keats was not satisfied with them, however; and in September 1819, when he attempted to combine the humanitarian vision of the "Fall of Hyperion" and the humanistic *Hyperion* into a third version, *The Fall of Hyperion, a Dream,* he altered them into the following verses —

No stir of life
Was in this shrouded vale, not so much air
As in the zoning of a Summer's day
Robs not one light seed from the feather'd Grass. . . .

Keats himself perceived that he had spoilt the verse, "Not so much life as on a summer's day," which was already perfect, by altering it into "not so much air As in the zoning of a Summer's day" but that he had improved the verse, "Robs not at all the dandelion's fleece" by altering it into "Robs not one light seed from the feath-er'd Grass." In June 1820, when he was reading the proof sheets of *Hyperion*, he combined the two perfect verses, one from each of the two last revisions, and wrote them on the proof sheet —

> Not so much life as on a summer's day
> Robs not one light seed from the feather'd grass.

We can trace the steps of the creative process in which Keats altered the verse "Robs not at all the dandelion's fleece" into "Robs not one light seed from the feather'd grass." He marked the following passage of Shakespeare's *Troilus and Cressida* (I. iii. 316 *et seq.*) in his copy of the 1808 facsimile reprint of the First Folio —

> Blunt wedges rive hard knots: the seeded Pride
> That hath to this maturity blowne up
> In ranke *Achilles*, must or now be cropt,
> Or shedding breed a Nursery of like evil
> To over-bulke us all.

The image of "the seeded Pride That hath to this maturity blowne up" stirred Keats's imagination, and he observed in an annotation:

> One's very breath while leaning over these pages is held for fear of blowing this line away — as easily as the gentlest breeze
>
> Robs dandelions of their fleecy Crowns.

The verse, "Robs dandelions of their fleecy Crowns," is obviously a variant of the rejected verse of *Hyperion*, "Robs not at all the dandelion's fleece." The image of the dandelion, through association, recalled Shakespeare's image of "the seeded Pride That hath to this maturity blowne up"; and Keats composed the verse which stands in *Hyperion*, "Robs not one light seed from the feather'd grass."

The picture of Saturn, the fallen king of the Titans, is worthy of the perfect setting which Keats created for it.

> Along the margin-sand large foot-marks went,
> No further than to where his feet had stray'd,
> And slept there since. Upon the sodden ground
> His old right hand lay nerveless, listless, dead,
> Unsceptred; and his realmless eyes were closed;
> While his bow'd head seem'd list'ning to the Earth,
> His ancient mother, for some comfort yet.

Keats drew the general appearance and the posture of Saturn from classical dictionaries. Albricus (in *Auctores Mythographi Latini*) said that Saturn is depicted as an old man with a long white beard, bent, dejected, and pallid, with veiled head and grey complexion (Saturnus . . . pingebatur, ut homo senex, canus, prolixa barba, curvus, tristis, & pallidus, tecto capite, colore glauco). And Lempriere said that "The god is generally represented as an old man bent through age and infirmity." Keats derived other characteristics, we shall see, from more inspiring sources.

The picture of Thea, the wife of Hyperion, who came to arouse Saturn from his numb despair, is as fine as that of Saturn.

> She was a Goddess of the infant world;
> By her in stature the tall Amazon
> Had stood a pigmy's height. . . .

Keats learned from Milton the art of "humanizing" his descriptions of immortal beings to mortal ears by making comparisons of earthly things. Thea placed her hand upon Saturn's bended neck and, leaning to the level of his ear, spoke "In solemn tenour and deep organ tone." O how frail, Keats said, do the the words of our feeble tongue come to the "large utterance of the early Gods."

> Saturn, look up! — though wherefore, poor old King?
> I have no comfort for thee, no not one:
> I cannot say, "O wherefore sleepest thou?"
> For heaven is parted from thee, and the earth
> Knows thee not, thus afflicted, for a God;
> And ocean too, with all its solemn noise,
> Has from thy sceptre pass'd; and all the air
> Is emptied of thine hoary majesty.

The tragic pathos of the aged Saturn, whose sons have deposed him, and his violent but impotent indignation were inspired by Shakespeare's characterization of King Lear in a similar situation. Ernest de Sélincourt, commenting upon Thea's speech, observed:

> When it is remembered that Keats's sonnet recording the profound impression made upon him by re-reading *King Lear* was written at a time when *Hyperion* was already in his mind, it is easy to believe that he was more or less consciously influenced by Shakespeare in his conception of the character of Saturn, whose kingdom, and the powers of mind necessary to rule it, have passed away from him in age. It is noticeable that the epithet *old* is applied to Lear, at least twenty times, with deeply tragic reiteration; and his weakness, whether it is viewed with contempt, or pity, or love, or referred to by Lear himself in his utter misery, is always alluded to as the weakness of age. Goneril alludes to it with a sneer (i. 3. 16–19), Regan taunts him with it (ii. 4. 148), and Gloucester twice in the same speech applies to him the epithet *poor old* (iii. 7. 57, 62), whilst Lear calls himself a *poor old* man and constantly harps upon it. (Cf. also ii. 4. 156, 194, 238; iii. 4. 20, etc.).

Saturn replied to Thea, de Sélincourt [2] pointed out, "by questions as to his own identity which recall strikingly the language and mood of Lear."

> O tender spouse of gold Hyperion,
> Thea, I feel thee ere I see thy face;
> Look up, and let me see our doom in it;
> Look up, and tell me if this feeble shape
> Is Saturn's; tell me, if thou hear'st the voice
> Of Saturn; tell me, if this wrinkling brow,
> Naked and bare of its great diadem,
> Peers like the front of Saturn. Who had power
> To make me desolate? whence came the strength?
> How was it nurtur'd to such bursting forth,
> While Fate seem'd strangled in my nervous grasp?

Saturn's speech was modelled undoubtedly upon one of King Lear's speeches (I. iv. 244–50):

> Doth any here know me? This is not Lear:
> Doth Lear walk thus? speak thus? Where are his eyes?
> Either his motion weakens, his discernings
> Are lethargied— Ha! waking? 'Tis not so.
> Who is it that can tell me who I am?

In the second part of his speech to Thea, Saturn reveals the noble and benevolent qualities of his character. He feels his loss of dominion to be a loss of power to perform acts of beneficence in the universe.

> I am smother'd up,
> And buried from all godlike exercise
> Of influence benign on planets pale,
> Of admonitions to the winds and seas,
> Of peaceful sway above man's harvesting,
> And all those acts which Deity supreme
> Doth ease its heart of love in. . . .

By recalling his benevolent rule Saturn was inspired to resolve to regain his throne. "Saturn must be King," he exclaimed to Thea.

> Yes, there must be a golden victory;
> There must be Gods thrown down, and trumpets blown
> Of triumph calm, and hymns of festival
> Upon the gold clouds metropolitan,
> Voices of soft proclaim, and silver stir
> Of strings in hollow shells; and there shall be
> Beautiful things made new, for the surprise
> Of the sky-children. . . .

[2] Ernest de Sélincourt, p. 496.

There were two traditions of Saturn which the Greek mythological poets and their commentators were never quite able to reconcile. Keats rejected the crafty and savage character which is given to Saturn in the *Theogony*, which is ascribed to Hesiod but which scholars believe was composed three quarters of a century after the time of Hesiod. He derived the evolution of the gods from the *Theogony*, but he interpreted this evolution by means of the neo-Platonic philosophy of beauty, with which craft and brutality would be inharmonious. He derived the benevolent character of Saturn from Hesiod's *Works and Days* (translations by Chapman and Cooke) and the first book of Ovid's *Metamorphosis* (Sandys's translation). He knew Lactantius Placidus' commentary upon the first book of the *Metamorphosis* as well as Sandys's commentary. He knew Diodorus Siculus' *Historical Library* (Booth's translation), in which, in a summary of the local religious traditions of the Cretans (Book V, Chapter IV), Saturn is represented as a god of culture. He knew also Lempriere's account of Saturn, in which the two conflicting traditions of the god are fused together.

Hesiod, following the tradition of Saturn as a god of fertility and culture, represented Saturn as king of gods and men in the first and golden age of the world.

When first both gods and men had one time's birth
The gods of diverse languaged men on earth
A golden world produced, that did sustain
Old Saturn's rule when he in heaven did reign:
And then lived men, like gods in pleasure here
Indued with minds secure; from toils, griefs, clear. . . .
Thus lived they long and died as seized in sleep.
All good things served them; fruits did ever keep
Their free fields crowned, that all abundance bore
All which all equal shared, and none wished more.
[Chapman's translation.]

Ovid adapted Hesiod's story of the four ages of the world; but, in his description of the golden age, as de Sélincourt pointed out, he added one detail, the beneficence of the weather, which Keats also employed.

'Twas alwaies Spring: warme *Zephyrus* sweetly blew
On smiling flowres, which without setting grew.
[Sandys's translation.]

After Jupiter overthrew Saturn, Ovid said, the silver age succeeded the golden. And

> *Joue* chang'd the Spring (which alwayes did indure)
> To Winter, Summer, Autumne hot and cold:
> The shortned Springs the year's fourth part vphold.

Diodorus Siculus quoted Hesiod's description of the golden age in his account of Saturn, and Sandys translated it in his commentary upon Ovid's adaptation of it. Keats knew, therefore, four different translations of Hesiod's description. He was more familiar with Ovid's description, however, and, it is probable, more deeply influenced by it. It seems probable also that he was influenced by Lempriere's account of Saturn as a culture-deity. Lempriere said that, when Saturn was driven from the throne of heaven by Jupiter, he fled to Italy and collaborated with Janus in ruling that country —

> . . . and the king of heaven employed himself in civilizing the barbarous manners of the people of Italy, and in teaching them agriculture and the useful and liberal arts. His reign there was so mild and popular, so beneficent and virtuous, that mankind have called it the *golden age*, to intimate the happiness and tranquillity which the earth then enjoyed.

Keats gave Saturn more benevolence of character in the Miltonic and humanistic *Hyperion* than was necessary in the development of the neo-Platonic theme of the poem. The excessive benevolence of Saturn was carried over, I believe, from the Wordsworthian and humanitarian vision of the "Fall of Hyperion" which he abandoned at the end of October 1818. The introduction to the vision indicates that Keats intended to represent the defeat of the Titans as the downfall of the humanitarian or golden age of the world and the victory of the Olympians as the triumph of social tyranny in a world degenerating through the silver, bronze, and iron ages. At the end of the vision Keats would have foreseen a restoration of the humanitarian age through education, which would expel evil out of men and injustice out of human society. And he would have represented Apollo, inspired by Moneta, goddess of memory, as the Messiah of the humanitarian millenium. This theme was a common nineteenth-century humanitarian interpretation of Greek cosmic myths. It was expressed by Shelley in *Prometheus Unbound* in 1821.

The action of *Hyperion* passes from the picture of dethroned, dejected Saturn to that of blazing Hyperion, the god of the sun, who still kept his rule and majesty but whose mind was troubled by omens of impending disaster.

> For as among us mortals omens drear
> Fright and perplex, so also shuddered he —
> Not at dog's howl, or gloom-bird's hated screech,
> Or the familiar visiting of one

Upon the first toll of his passing-bell,
Or prophesyings of the midnight lamp;
But horrors, portion'd to a giant nerve,
Oft made Hyperion ache. His palace bright
Bastion'd with pyramids of glowing gold,
And touch'd with shade of bronzed obelisks,
Glar'd a blood-red through all its thousand courts,
Arches, and domes, and fiery galleries;
And all its curtains of Aurorian clouds
Flush'd angerly: while sometimes eagle's wings,
Unseen before by Gods or wondering men,
Darken'd the place; and neighing steeds were heard,
Not heard before by Gods or wondering men.
Also, when he would taste the spicy wreaths
Of incense, breath'd aloft from sacred hills,
Instead of sweets, his ample palate took
Savour of poisonous brass and metal sick:
And so, when harbour'd in the sleepy west,
After the full completion of fair day, —
For rest divine upon exalted couch
And slumber in the arms of melody,
He pac'd away the pleasant hours of ease
With stride colossal, on from hall to hall;
While far within each aisle and deep recess,
His winged minions in close clusters stood,
Amaz'd and full of fear; like anxious men
Who on wide plains gather in panting troops,
When earthquakes jar their battlements and towers.

The description of the palace of the sun in these and other verses was inspired, H. B. Forman suggested, by the description of the palace of the sun at the beginning of the second book of Ovid's *Metamorphosis*. Keats composed in emulation instead of in imitation of Ovid, however, for the only detail of his description which can be discovered in Ovid's is the gold which adorns the palace.

Sol's loftie Palace on high Pillars rais'd,
Shone all with gold, and stones that flamelike blaz'd.
[Sandys's translation.]

An analysis of the description of the omens which perplexed and frightened Hyperion reveals the extent to which Keats was indebted to Shakespeare's plays for the matter of his poetry. The opening verses,

For as among us mortals omens drear
Fright and perplex, so also shuddered he — ,

were suggested, as Colvin pointed out, by Milton's description of the eclipse which "with fear of change Perplexes monarchs"—

> . . . as when the sun new-risen
> Looks through the horizontal misty air
> Shorn of his beams, or, from behind the moon,
> In dim eclipse, disastrous twilight sheds
> On half the nations, and with fear of change
> Perplexes monarchs. [*Paradise Lost*, I. 594 *et seq.*]

We can trace the individual omens one by one to their sources in Shakespeare's plays. The first two omens which forebode the fall of Hyperion are:

> Not at dog's howl, or gloom-bird's hated screech,

in which the "gloom-bird" is the owl. In *2 Henry VI* (I. iv. 21–22) Bolingbroke, the conjuror, speaking of unlucky signs, said:

> The time when screech-owls cry and ban-dogs howl
> And spirits walk and ghosts break up their graves;

and in *3 Henry VI* (V. vi 44 *et seq.*) King Henry said to the future Richard III:

> The owl shriek'd at thy birth, an evil sign;
> The night-crow cried, aboding luckless time;
> Dogs howl'd, and hideous tempest shook down trees.

Keats followed Shakespeare in *Henry VI* very closely in placing these two omens, dog's howl and owl's screech, in juxtaposition. It is only in *Henry VI* that Shakespeare referred to the dog's howl as a sign of evil; in his other plays he alluded to the howl of the wolf.

The obscure meaning of the third omen,

> Or the familiar visiting of one
> Upon the first toll of his passing-bell,

is made clear by its source. The "familiar visiting" was derived from a speech of Lady Macbeth, who was contemplating the murder of Duncan (I. v. 46–47):

> That no compunctuous visitings of nature
> Shake my fell purpose;

and the "passing-bell" was drawn from another passage in *Macbeth* (II. ii 3–4):

> It was the owl that shriek'd, the fatal bellman,
> Which gives the stern'st good-night.

The owl's screech, which Keats had used as his second omen, was the associative factor which recalled as his third omen the reference to the passing-bell in *Macbeth*.

The fourth omen in *Hyperion*,

> Or prophesyings of the midnight lamp,

is a fused recollection of two forebodings in different Shakespearean plays. The "prophesyings" is a reminiscence of a passage in *Macbeth* (II. iii. 62 *et seq.*) in which Lennox said that on the night of Duncan's murder he heard

> . . . prophesying with accents terrible
> Of dire combustion and confus'd events
> New hatch'd to the woeful time.

The "prophesying" in this passage was impressed in Keats's mind by its occurrence in *Antony and Cleopatra* (IV. xiv. 120–121):

> . . . She had a prophesying fear
> Of what hath come to pass. . . .

Keats's association of the midnight lamp with the prophesyings was caused doubtless by his recollection of an incident which Shakespeare derived from Plutarch. In North's translation of Plutarch's *Life of Julius Caesar*, Plutarch said that Brutus one night

> thought he heard a noise at his tent-door, and looking towards the light of the lamp that waxed dim, he saw a horrible vision of a man, of a wonderful greatness and dreadful look, which at first made him marvellously afraid.

In Shakespeare's *Julius Caesar* (IV. iii. 275 *et seq.*), in which this incident is adapted, Caesar's ghost appeared in the tent of Brutus at midnight to prophesy his death in the Battle of Philippi, and Brutus said:

> How ill this taper burns! Ha! who comes here?
> I think it is the weakness of mine eyes
> That shapes this monstrous apparition.

And in *Richard III* (V. iii. 180 *et seq.*) Shakespeare supplemented Holinshed's brief mention of Richard's dream by fusing with it the incident from Plutarch quoted above. At midnight, before the Battle of Bosworth Field, the ghosts of all the persons whom Richard had murdered appeared in his tent and cursed him. After the ghosts had vanished Richard awoke and said:

> The lights burn blue. It is now dead midnight.
> Cold fearful drops stand on my trembling flesh.
> . . . shadows to-night
> Have struck more terror to the soul of Richard
> Than can the substance of ten thousand soldiers
> Armed in proof, and led by shallow Richmond.

This passage in *Richard III* is undoubtedly the source of Keats's association of the midnight lamp with prophesyings of coming disaster.

The fifth omen in *Hyperion* is stated as follows:

> His palace bright
> Bastion'd with pyramids of glowing gold,
> And touch'd with shade of bronzed obelisks,
> Glar'd a blood-red through all its thousand courts,
> Arches, and domes, and fiery galleries;
> And all its curtains of Aurorian clouds
> Flush'd angerly. . . .

The blood-red flushing of the palace of the sun at sunrise to forebode the fall of the sun-god, Hyperion, was suggested to Keats by allusions to this unlucky portent in Shakespeare's plays. In *King John* (III. i. 326) Blanche said:

> The sun's o'ercast with blood; fair day, adieu!

and in *1 Henry IV* (V. i. 1 *et seq.*), on the morning of the Battle of Shrewsbury, King Henry said:

> How bloodily the sun begins to peer
> Above yon busky hill! The day looks pale
> At his distemperature.

Keats's association of pyramids with the palace in his statement of this omen may have been suggested by a passage in *Macbeth* (IV. i. 56 *et seq.*) in which both occur in connection with the supernatural elements from which Keats derived some of his omens. When Macbeth visited the witches to learn his fate he conjured them in part as follows:

> Though castles topple on their warders' heads;
> Though palaces and pyramids do slope
> Their heads to their foundations . . .
> Even till destruction sicken; answer me
> To what I ask you.

The "curtains of Aurorian clouds" in Keats's description of the palace of the sun is a very common poetical figure; but, since the whole passage in which it is embedded is a mass of Shakespearean reminiscences, it may have been suggested by a description of a sunrise in *Romeo and Juliet* (I. i. 140 *et seq.*):

> But all so soon as the all-cheering sun
> Should in the farthest east begin to draw
> The shady curtains from Aurora's bed.

Keats derived the word "angerly" (for "angrily"), H. B. Forman suggested, "from Shakespeare who in *King John* (Act IV, Scene I) makes Arthur promise Hubert not to 'look upon the iron angerly.'"

The sixth omen in *Hyperion*,

> . . . while sometimes eagle's wings,
> Unseen before by Gods or wondering men,
> Darken'd the place,

was derived from *Julius Caesar* (V. i. 80 *et seq.*), in which two eagles, which are birds of good omen, appear to the army of Casca. The eagles soon leave, however, and ravens, crows, and kites appear — birds of evil omen, which, Casca said,

> Fly o'er our heads and downward look on us,
> As we were sickly prey. Their shadows seem
> A canopy most fatal, under which
> Our army lies, ready to give up the ghost.

Keats may have confused the eagles with the ravens, crows, and kites because of their juxtaposition in *Julius Caesar*; or he may have consciously substituted the eagles for the ravens, crows, and kites, for the eagle, which is the bird of Jove, would be a bird of evil omen to Hyperion.

The seventh omen in *Hyperion*,

> . . . and neighing steeds were heard,
> Not heard before by Gods or wondering men,

was derived from *Julius Caesar* (II. ii. 23), in which, before the murder of Caesar,

> Horses did neigh, and dying men did groan.

The atmosphere of wonder at the actions of the steeds was suggested probably by a passage in *Macbeth* (II. iv. 14 *et seq.*) in which Ross said that on the night of Duncan's murder

> . . . Duncan's horses — a thing most strange and certain —
> Beauteous and swift, the minions of their race,
> Turn'd wild in nature, broke their stalls, flung out,
> Contending 'gainst obedience, as they would make
> War with mankind.

I have not been able to discover an undoubted source of the eighth omen in *Hyperion* —

> Also, when he would taste the spicy wreaths
> Of incense, breath'd aloft from sacred hills,
> Instead of sweets, his ample palate took
> Savour of poisonous brass and metal sick.

Hyperion's minions were amazed and affrighted by these fearful portents

. . . like anxious men
Who on wide plains gather in panting troops,
When earthquakes jar their battlements and towers.

The source of Keats's use of the earthquake as a sign of evil is found in *Macbeth* (II. iii. 65–66), in which Lennox said that on the night of Duncan's murder,

. . . some say, the earth
Was feverous and did shake,

and in *1 Henry IV* (III. i. 13 *et seq.*), in which Glendower boasted:

At my nativity
The front of heaven was full of fiery shapes,
Of burning cressets; and at my birth
The frame and huge foundation of the earth
Shak'd like a coward.

The toppling down of towers in connection with the earthquake may have been suggested to Keats by Hotspur's reply to Glendower's superstitious vaunt: oft unruly wind, imprisoned within the earth and striving for enlargement,

Shakes the old beldam earth, and topples down
Steeples and moss-grown towers.

The effect of these portents upon Hyperion is revealed by his soliloquy (I. 228 *et seq.*). His passions were agitated, his mind was bewildered, and his radiance, the symbol of his might, was diminished. He fled to the eastern gate of his palace six hours before he was due to drive the fiery orb of the sun across the sky.

And all along a dismal rack of clouds,
Upon the boundaries of day and night,
He stretch'd himself in grief and radiance faint.

Coelus and Terra had been supplanted by their offspring, the Titans, but Coelus had resigned himself to his fate. He looked down with pity upon Hyperion, who was destined to be supplanted by a more beautiful successor. His speech to Hyperion is a significant reflection of the neo-Platonic theme of the poem.

O brightest of my children dear, earth-born
And sky-engendered, Son of Mysteries
All unrevealed even to the powers
Which met at thy creating; at whose joys
And palpitations sweet, and pleasures soft,
I, Coelus, wonder, how they came and whence;

And at the fruits thereof what shapes they be,
Distinct, and visible; *symbols divine,*
Manifestations of that beauteous life
Diffus'd unseen throughout eternal space:
Of these new-form'd art thou, oh brightest child!
Of these, thy brethren and the Goddesses!

Coelus expressed pity also for Saturn, his first-born, who had already been overthrown and supplanted.

There is sad feud among ye, and rebellion
Of son against his sire. I saw him fall,
I saw my first-born tumbled from his throne!
To me his arms were spread, to me his voice
Found way from forth the thunders round his head!
Pale wox I, and in vapours hid my face.

The mortal passions which Coelus saw in the minds of his sons who had fallen and which he now saw in the mind of Hyperion were to him signs of deterioration and impending defeat.

Art thou, too, near such doom? vague fear there is:
For I have seen my sons most unlike Gods.
Divine ye were created, and divine
In sad demeanour, solemn, undisturb'd,
Unruffled, like high Gods, ye liv'd and ruled:
Now I behold in you fear, hope, and wrath;
Actions of rage and passion; even as
I see them, on the mortal world beneath,
In men who die. — This is the grief, O Son!
Sad sign of ruin, sudden dismay, and fall!

These mortal passions, signs of deterioration in gods, appeared in the mind of Saturn (in the second book) when he entered the den of the imprisoned Titans. Thea looked sidelong into Saturn's face.

There saw she direst strife; the supreme God
At war with all the frailty of grief,
Of rage, of fear, anxiety, revenge,
Remorse, spleen, hope, but most of all despair.
Against these plagues he strove in vain; for Fate
Had pour'd a mortal oil upon his head,
A disanointing poison. . . .

Plato is perhaps the ultimate source of this idea in western thought. He taught that man should keep his soul calm and unruffled by suppressing passions, which are faculties of the mortal part of his soul, and by exalting reason, which is the faculty of the immortal part of his soul. He banished poetry from his ideal commonwealth because it stirred passions and disturbed the divine calm of the soul. Keats derived the idea from Milton's *Paradise Lost* (IV. 114 *et seq.*). Satan came to the earth in the guise of an angel of God to tempt Adam and Eve to sin. In a great soliloquy he reviewed the whole course of his life and resolved to persist in his course of evil.

> Thus while he spake, each passion dimmed his face,
> Thrice changed with pale — ire, envy, and despair;
> Which marred his borrowed visage, and betrayed
> Him counterfeit, if any eye beheld:
> For Heavenly minds from such distempers foul
> Are ever clear.

Keats made this idea a fundamental principle of his humanism. In this and the following period of his poetry he strove to oppose and to solve the problems of his experience in a calm state of mind.

The action of the second book takes place in the den or covert of the defeated and imprisoned Titans. Saturn, led by Thea, came to

> that sad place
> Where Cybele and the bruised Titans mourn'd.
> It was a den where no insulting light
> Could glimmer on their tears; where their own groans
> They felt, but heard not, for the solid roar
> Of thunderous waterfalls and torrents hoarse,
> Pouring a constant bulk, uncertain where.
> Crag jutting forth to crag, and rocks that seem'd
> Ever as if just rising from a sleep,
> Forehead to forehead held their monstrous horns;
> And thus in thousand hugest phantasies
> Made a fit roofing to this nest of woe.
> Instead of thrones, hard flint they sat upon,
> Couches of rugged stone, and slaty ridge
> Stubborn'd with iron.

Some of the Titans were wandering in the world unconfined; and others, the brawniest in assault, were pent in elements of the earth.

> But for the main, here found they covert drear.
> Scarce images of life, one here, one there,
> Lay vast and edgeways; like a dismal cirque
> Of Druid stones, upon a forlorn moor,
> When the chill rain begins at shut of eve,
> In dull November, and their chancel vault,
> The Heaven itself, is blinded throughout night.
> Each one kept shroud, nor to his neighbour gave
> Or word, or look, or action of despair.

Keats described the den of the Titans according to the best Greek tradition. He received a suggestion, de Sélincourt thought, from the eighth book of Homer's *Iliad*, in which Jove, rebuking Juno, said:

> I weigh not thy displeased spleen, tho' to th' extremest bounds
> Of earth and seas it carry thee, where endless night confounds
> *Japhet*, and my dejected Sire, who sit so far beneath
> They never see the flying sun, nor hear the winds that breathe,
> Near to profoundest *Tartarus*. [Chapman's translation.]

In the fourteenth book of the *Iliad*, also, Somnus, prescribing an oath for Juno, alluded to

> . . . all the Gods of the infernal state
> Which circle Saturn. . . .

Keats drew other details — the dark gulf with jutting crags and "the solid roar of thunderous waterfalls and torrents hoarse"— from the longer description of the den of the Titans in Hesiod's *Theogony*:

> They forc'd the Titans deep beneath the ground,
> Cast from their pride, and in sad durance bound,
> Far from the surface of the Earth they lie,
> In chains, as Earth is distant from the sky. . . .
>
> . . . .
>
> A mighty chasm, horror and darkness here;
> And from the gates the journey of a year;
> Here storms in hoarse, in frightful murmurs play,
> The seat of night, where mists exclude the day.
>
> . . . .
>
> And here th' allies of Jove their captives keep,
> The Titans, who to utter darkness fell,
> And in the farthest parts of chaos dwell. [Cooke's translation.]

Keats derived other details — the name "den" and the posture of the Titans, who lie on their sides in silent dejection — from Milton's description of the fallen angels in Hell. Milton made the association for Keats by comparing the fallen angels to the Titans. Satan lifted up his head and addressed Beëlzebub, Milton said;

> his other parts besides
> Prone on the flood, extended long and large,
> Lay floating many a rood, in bulk as huge
> As whom the fables name of monstrous size,
> Titanian or Earth-born, that warred on Jove,
> Briareos or Typhon, whom the den
> By ancient Tarsus held. . . .

Keats derived still other details from Fingal's Cave on the Isle of Staffa, which he visited with Brown at the end of July 1818. The island of black basalt pillars with its huge cave hollowed out by the sea impressed him as the work of primeval giants.

I am puzzled how to give you an Idea of Staffa [he wrote his brother Tom]. . . . Suppose now the Giants who rebelled against Jove had taken a whole Mass of black Columns and bound them together like bunches of matches — and then with immense Axes had made a cavern in the body of these columns — of course the roof and floor must be composed of the broken ends of the Columns — such is fingal's Cave except that the Sea has done the work of excavations and is continually dashing there — so that we walk along the sides of the cave on the pillars which are left as if for convenient Stairs — the roof is arched somewhat gothic wise and the length of some of the entire side pillars is 50 feet. . . . The length of the Cave is 120 feet and from its extremity the view into sea through the large Arch at the entrance — the colour of the colum[n]s is a sort of black with a lurking gloom of purple therein. For solemnity and grandeur it far surpasses the finest Cathedral. At the extremity of the Cave there is a small perforation into another cave, at which the waters meeting and buffeting each other there is sometimes produced a report as of a cannon heard as far as Iona which must be 12 Miles.

His purpose in tramping through the lake country of England and the Highlands of Scotland, he wrote Bailey, was to "identify" finer scenes, to load his mind with grander mountains, and to strengthen more his reach in poetry. He was meditating upon the matter of *Hyperion* when he went on this excursion; and the grand and majestic scenes which he saw — the mountains, glens, lakes, islands, caves, and waterfalls — gave a personal identity, an individual reality, to scenes which he had read in Homer's *Iliad*, Hesiod's *Theogony*, and Milton's *Paradise Lost.* One detail in his description of the den of the Titans —"the solid roar Of thunderous waterfalls and torrents hoarse"— was a fused recollection of Hesiod's "storms in hoarse, in frightful murmurs," the dashing and roaring of the sea in Fingal's Cave, and the thunderous waterfalls near Ambleside in the lake country. He discovered the waterfalls early one morning by the "noise" which they made. They were buried in trees in the bottom of a valley.

First we stood a little below the head about half way down the first fall, buried deep in trees, and saw it streaming down two more descents to the depth of near fifty feet — then we went on a jut of rock nearly level with the tsecond [*sic*] fall-head, where the first fall was above us, and the third below our feet still — at the same time we saw that the water was divided by a sort of cataract island on whose other side burst out a glorious stream — then the thunder and the freshness.

Another detail in his description — the defeated Titans lying vast and edgeways "like a dismal cirque Of Druid stones, upon a forlorn moor When the chill rain begins at shut of eve, In dull November"— was a recollection of his impressions of the Druid stones near Keswick on June 28, 1818. He approached "those aged stones" very late in the afternoon ("at shut of eve") and saw them, he said, "on a gentle rise in the midst of the Mountains, which at that time darkened all around, except at the fresh opening of the Vale of St. John."

After describing the den of the Titans, Keats enumerated the chief Titans in imitation of Milton's list of the fallen angels in the first book of *Paradise Lost* (vv. 392 *et seq.*). He emulated Milton in rolling out melodious and resounding names, in making stimulating allusions, and in giving very brief but very vivid descriptive biographies. His Titans, unlike the Titans in the *Theogony*, are not merely primeval gods of brutal strength. They are less beautiful than their conquerors, the Olympians, but they too are symbols of that beautiful life diffused throughout eternal space. The savage passions which animated them in their den of imprisonment were caused by the rebellion by which they were overthrown. When they were the ruling gods of the universe they possessed calm and unruffled minds. Enceladus, the fiercest of the Titans, was

> once tame and mild
> As grazing ox unworried in the meads;
> Now tiger-passion'd, lion-thoughted, wroth. . . .

When Enceladus exhorted the Titans to renew the war against the Olympians, he recalled "the days of peace and slumberous calm"—

> Those days, all innocent of scathing war,
> When all the fair Existences of heaven
> Came open-eyed to guess what we would speak. . . .

The council of the Titans, in which they debated whether to accept defeat and imprisonment or to renew the war against the Olympians, was composed in emulation of the council of the fallen angels in the second book of *Paradise Lost*. Saturn began the debate by stating the question and asking for advice. Oceanus, the second speaker, explained their defeat by a neo-Platonic principle of evolution (which we have already considered) and advised them to receive the truth and let it be their balm. Clymene described, as evidence of the superior beauty of the Olympians, an enchanting melody produced by young Apollo which made her "sick Of joy and grief at once." Then the wrathful voice of huge Enceladus drowned

Clymene's timid words. He reminded the Titans of their injuries and stirred them to fierce anger. Hyperion appeared in the den of the Titans in the middle of Enceladus' speech and lighted up the vast gulf with his radiance. Despondence again seized upon the Titans, however, at sight of the dejected god of the sun. Then fierce Enceladus cast his gaze around upon his brothers and Iäpetus, Creüs, and Phorcus strode to his side and those four shouted forth the name of old Saturn.

> Thus in alternate uproar and sad peace,
> Amazed were those Titans utterly.
> O leave them, Muse! O leave them to their woes;
> For thou art weak to sing such tumults dire:
> A solitary sorrow best befits
> Thy lips, and antheming a lonely grief.

In these opening verses of the third book Keats alluded to his grief for his brother Tom's death.

J. M. Murry[3] has pointed out that the third book of *Hyperion* differs from the first two books both in thought and in style. I cannot accept his interpretation of the poem, but I do agree with him that the third book represents a new and significant development in Keats's philosophy — a development which forced him to leave the poem unfinished in the one hundred and thirty-sixth verse of the book.

The first two books, we have seen, are an idealistic interpretation of life. Keats faced the naked, unpleasant facts of life, but he found in life a principle of hope and comfort. The defeat of the Titans was grievous to them, but it was a step in the evolution of the world towards beauty and goodness and happiness. The style of the first two books, an imitation of the style of *Paradise Lost,* is concise, intense, and elevated, having something of that "naked and grecian" style which he strove to attain.

There was an interval between the composition of the first two books and that of the fragment of the third book, and there were also intervals in the composition of the third book itself. Keats completed the first two books, I believe, by the middle of January 1819. About January 18 he visited Dilke's relatives in Hampshire and composed *The Eve of St. Agnes.* In the first part of February he composed the fragment of *The Eve of St. Mark*; then, about the middle of February, he fell into a mood of doubt and despair in which he could not compose. He wrote his brother on February 14

[3] J. M. Murry, *Keats and Shakespeare*, p. 86.

that he had "not gone on with Hyperion" and that he would have to "wait for the spring to rouse [him] up a little." He completed the poem in its final form and gave the manuscript to Woodhouse by April 20, 1819.

Keats composed the fragment of the third book between February 14 and April 20, 1819. In the greater part of this period — in fact, down to the middle of April — he complained in his letters that he was unable to compose poetry. This period was, however, a period of intense intellectual activity in which he rejected the idealistic humanism of the first two books of *Hyperion*, passed through moods of doubt and despair, and developed an empirical humanism. The third book of *Hyperion* reflects this development of Keats's philosophy; and in interpreting the third book we must refer to it, but we must reserve a detailed analysis of it for the next chapter.

In the third book Keats introduced Apollo, the hero of the epic, and Mnemosyne, his foster mother. As he had suggested in the speech of Clymene in the second book, he represented Apollo as the god of poets instead of as the god of the sun. His Apollo is not a logical supplanter of his blazing Hyperion, the god of the sun, who has no connection with poetry. In representing Apollo the poet, he drew inevitably and perhaps consciously upon himself and his own experience. His Apollo expresses his own feelings and thoughts. And the style of the third book is much more subjective than that of the first two books.

> Meantime touch piously the Delphic harp,
> And not a wind of heaven but will breathe
> In aid soft warble from the Dorian flute;
> For lo! 'tis for the Father of all verse.
> Flush everything that hath a vermeil hue,
> Let the rose glow intense and warm the air,
> And let the clouds of even and of morn
> Float in voluptuous fleeces o'er the hills;
> Let the red wine within the goblet boil,
> Cold as a bubbling well; let faint-lipp'd shells,
> On sands, or in great deeps, vermilion turn
> Through all their labyrinths; and let the maid
> Blush keenly, as with some warm kiss surpris'd.
> Chief isle of the embowered Cyclades,
> Rejoice, O Delos, with thine olives green,
> And poplars, and lawn-shading palms, and beech,
> In which the Zephyr breathes the loudest song,
> And hazels thick, dark-stemm'd beneath the shade:
> Apollo is once more the golden theme!
> Where was he, when the Giant of the Sun
> Stood bright, amid the sorrow of his peers?

Together had he left his mother fair
And his twin-sister sleeping in their bower,
And in the morning twilight wandered forth
Beside the osiers of a rivulet,
Full ankle-deep in lilies of the vale.
The nightingale had ceas'd, and a few stars
Were lingering in the heavens, while the thrush
Began calm-throated. Throughout all the isle
There was no covert, no retired cave
Unhaunted by the murmurous noise of waves,
Though scarcely heard in many a green recess.

These verses are quite different from those of the first two books. They are not so concise and elevated and not so "naked and grecian." They are more sensuous, more sentimental, and more romantic. They belong, I should say, to Keats's Spenserian rather than to his Miltonic manner. They impress me as a purified, refined, and highly developed example of the style which Keats had employed in *Endymion*. Their most striking qualities, fresh natural beauty and youthful exuberant joy, were inspired doubtless by Keats's youthful, sensuous love for Fanny Brawne. They were composed, I believe, very soon after he told Miss Brawne that he loved her and just before or just after he composed *The Eve of St. Agnes*.

Woodhouse has recorded Keats's own recognition of the spontaneity of his description of Apollo in the third book. I quote from a manuscript in the Lowell Collection in the Harvard College Library.

He has said that he has often not been aware of the beauty of some thought or expres^{n}. until after he has composed & written it down — It has then struck him with astonishment — & seemed rather the prod^{n}. of another person than his own — He has wondered how he came to hit upon it. This was the case with the descr^{n}. of Apollo in the 3 b. of Hyperion. Perhaps every one in the habit of writ^{g}. verse or prose may have had a somewhat similar feeling: that of the extreme appositeness & happiness (the curiosa felicitas) of an idea, of the excellence of wh: he was unaware until he came to write it down & read it over. It seems scarcely his own; & he feels that he co^{d}. never imitate or hit upon it again: & he can not conceive how it came to him — Such was Keats's Sensation of astonishment & pleasure when he had prod^{d}. the lines "His white melod^{s}. etc." It seemed to come by chance or magic — to be as it were something given to him —

At the end of the description of the fresh, joyous beauty of the Isle of Delos, as in the description of youthful, joyous love in *The Eve of St. Agnes*, Keats struck a note of grief. Apollo listened to the song of the thrush and the murmurous noise of waves —

> He listen'd, and he wept, and his bright tears
> Went trickling down the golden bow he held.
> Thus with half-shut suffused eyes he stood,
> While from beneath some cumbrous boughs hard by
> With solemn step an awful Goddess came,
> And there was purport in her looks for him,
> Which he with eager guess began to read. . . .

This note of poignant grief in the midst of beauty appears in all of the poems which Keats composed in 1819. Melancholy, he said in the ode on that passion, "dwells with Beauty — Beauty that must die." He lost his belief that the world is progressing in beauty, as *The Eve of St. Agnes* shows, in the latter part of January 1819.

The awful goddess who came to comfort Apollo was Mnemosyne, the goddess of memory, who had forsaken old and sacred thrones for prophecies of him and who had watched over him, although he had not seen her, from his childhood to the present time. He had dreamed of her, however, and awaking he had found a golden lyre by his side. Now, meeting her in visible form, Apollo conversed with her as Keats himself had conversed with Moneta in the humanitarian version of the poem.

Mnemosyne, in whose globed brain all knowledge was enfolded, asked Apollo to tell her the cause of his grief. And Apollo, with sudden scrutiny and gloomless eyes, answered, while his white melodious throat throbbed with the syllables:

> Mnemosyne!
> Thy name is on my tongue, I know not how;
> Why should I tell thee what thou so well seest?
> Why should I strive to show what from thy lips
> Would come no mystery? For me, dark, dark,
> And painful vile oblivion seals my eyes:
> I strive to search wherefore I am so sad,
> Until a melancholy numbs my limbs;
> And then upon the grass I sit, and moan,
> Like one who once had wings. . . .

The "dark, dark, And painful vile oblivion" which sealed Apollo's eyes reflects the bitter mood of despair through which Keats passed in March 1819. Keats perceived the evil in nature, and he himself suffered pain from it, but he was unable to find a solution for it which would give him comfort or enable him to endure it in calm fortitude. The phraseology as well as the thought of Apollo's complaint is the same as that of the sonnet *Why did I laugh tonight?* which Keats composed a day or two before March 19.

> Say, wherefore did I laugh? O mortal pain!
> O Darkness! Darkness! ever must I moan
> To question Heaven and Hell and Heart in vain!

Keats composed this sonnet, he said, "with no Agony but that of ignorance" and "with no thirst of anything but Knowledge. . . ."

Apollo besought Mnemosyne to help him to escape from his environment — to point out the way to one particular beauteous star, to which he might fly with his lyre and make it pant with his melody.

> I have heard the cloudy thunder: where is power?
> Whose hand, whose essence, what divinity
> Makes this alarum in the elements,
> While I here idle listen on the shores
> In fearless yet in aching ignorance?

Mnemosyne remained silent, but in her face Apollo read the answer to the doubts and questions which inspired his grief.

> Mute thou remainest — Mute! yet I can read
> A wondrous lesson in thy silent face:
> Knowledge enormous makes a God of me.
> Names, deeds, gray legends, dire events, rebellions,
> Majesties, sovran voices, agonies,
> Creations and destroyings, all at once
> Pour into the wide hollows of my brain,
> And deify me, as if some blithe wine
> Or bright elixer peerless I had drunk,
> And so become immortal.

The knowledge which made Apollo a god represents the knowledge and wisdom which Keats acquired shortly after he had composed the sonnet *Why did I laugh tonight?* Keats expressed this new wisdom on March 19 and on April 28 in the journal letter to his brother. I shall analyze this wisdom, which I call empirical humanism, in the following chapter. In this connection, however, we should state a few of its chief principles. Keats accepted evil as an essential and necessary principle in nature; and he identified evil in animate nature — birds, animals, and men — with the instinctive and egotistic impulses. This evil or instinctive principle is necessary; for, if the hawk were a disinterested instead of an egotistic creature, he would go without his breakfast of robins. These instinctive impulses, which produce identity or personality, are beautiful; they are the very stuff of which poetry is made. Keats himself, he said, was a part of instinctive, egotistic nature; but, by virtue of his negatively capable imagination, he could also stand above and outside of nature and speculate about it. Keats considered also the evil which man suffers as well as that which he inflicts. Since man is a part of nature, he said, he cannot escape the evil which is inherent in nature. If he rises above the evil of one stage of nature, he suffers that of another stage. Therefore, since nature is as it is, man cannot attain permanent happiness. Keats acquired this new wisdom in an agony of spirit; but after he had acquired it he could bear naked truths and envisage circumstances with calm and temperate blood.

Apollo, like Keats, received this knowledge through pain and turmoil of soul; but, having received it, he was a god.

> Soon wild commotions shook him, and made flush
> All the immortal fairness of his limbs;
> Most like the struggle at the gate of death;
> Or liker still to one who should take leave
> Of pale immortal death, and with a pang
> As hot as death's is chill, with fierce convulse
> Die into life: so young Apollo anguish'd:
> His very hair, his golden tresses famed
> Kept undulation round his eager neck.

I quote the final verses from the autograph manuscript:

> During the Pain Mnemosyne upheld
> Her arms as one who prophesied. At length
> ~~Phoebus~~
> Apollo shriek d — and lo ~~he was the God!~~
> ~~And godlike~~ from all his limbs
> Celestial

The final verse was left in this incomplete form in the published version; but in Woodhouse's transcript the following words were added in pencil: "Glory dawn'd, he was a god."

The doubt which Keats felt in January, the despair through which he passed in February and March, and the new wisdom, the empirical humanism, which he acquired in the latter part of March and the first part of April forced him to abandon *Hyperion* after he had expressed this new wisdom in the opening verses of the incomplete third book. He could not proceed with the composition of the third and the remaining books because he had lost his faith in the neo-Platonic and idealistic principle in accordance with which he had intuited the poem as a whole and in accordance with which he had written the first two books. He was a remarkably sincere poet. In every poem which he composed he expressed the principles in which he believed in the period of its composition.

A dissatisfaction with Milton's style had nothing to do with his giving up the composition of *Hyperion*. He was still satisfied with Milton's style in April 1819, when he abandoned the poem. Every revision in the poem, as de Sélincourt pointed out, made the poem more Miltonic. His famous rejection of Milton's style occurred in September 1819, five months after he had given up the poem. This rejection applies, as we shall see later, to *The Fall of Hyperion, a Dream*, a third version in which he attempted to fuse the first two versions, the humanitarian and Wordsworthian vision and the humanistic and Miltonic epic. He tried without much success to remove the Miltonic qualities of style from that part of the reconstructed poem which he adapted from *Hyperion*.

In conclusion, it will satisfy our instinctive curiosity to ascertain how Keats had intended to complete *Hyperion*. He meditated upon the poem for exactly one year before he began to compose it. He changed its theme many times in this period, we have seen, and every time he changed the theme, it is probable, he changed the story. Most of his friends, perhaps all of them, were unaware of the changes which occurred in his intuition of the poem. Woodhouse's account of the scope of the poem represents doubtless the intuition of the poem which Keats formed in the first half of 1818. In his interleaved and annotated copy of *Endymion*, Woodhouse gave three extracts from *Hyperion* and observed:

> The above lines, separated from the rest, give but a faint idea of the sustained grandeur and quiet power which characterize the poem: but they are sufficient to lead us to regret that such an attempt should have been abandoned. The poem, if completed, would have treated of the dethronement of Hyperion, the former God of the Sun, by Apollo, — and incidently of those of Oceanus by Neptune, of Saturn by Jupiter etc., and of the war of the Giants for Saturn's reestablishment — with other events, of which we have but very dark hints in the mythological poets of Greece and Rome. In fact the incidents would have been pure creations of the Poet's brain.

Keats's publishers stated in the Advertisement to the 1820 volume of his poems that "the unfinished poem of Hyperion . . . was intended to have been of equal length with Endymion," which we know contains 4050 verses. This Advertisement was written probably by Woodhouse, who, since Keats was ill at that time, helped Taylor select the poems to be printed, revise them, and supervise the printing. I quote the Advertisement:

> If any apology be thought necessary for the appearance of the unfinished poem of HYPERION, the publishers beg to state that they alone are responsible, as it was printed at their particular request, and contrary to the wish

of the author. The poem was intended to have been of equal length with ENDYMION, but the reception given to that work discouraged the author from proceeding.

This Advertisement aroused Keat's indignation. In the copy of *Endymion* which he gave to B. Davenport, Esq., and which is now in the Lowell Collection in the Harvard College Library, he crossed out the Advertisement with angry strokes of his pen and wrote above it: "This is none of my doing — I was ill at the time." He bracketed the final statement of the Advertisement, "but the reception given that work discouraged the author from proceeding," and wrote below it: "This is a lie." Taylor and Woodhouse were always well disposed to Keats but they did not always understand him. The statements in their Advertisement were not only false but they also represented Keats as a weakling who was discouraged from completing *Hyperion* by hostile criticism of *Endymion*. As a matter of fact, the malignant reviews of *Endymion* appeared before Keats began *Hyperion* and they impelled him to begin the poem before he had intended.

The theory that Keats intended to make *Hyperion* as long a poem as *Endymion* falls, as de Sélincourt [4] pointed out, with Keats's repudiation of the Advertisement. It represents probably his first and discarded intuition of the poem. When he began the poem at the end of October 1818, he intuited the poem doubtless on a much smaller scale. Internal evidence in the first two books, de Sélincourt argued, shows that Keats limited the action of the poem to the defeat of Hyperion by Apollo. His allusions to the defeat of Saturn by Jupiter and that of Oceanus by Neptune indicate that he did not intend to relate these incidents in more detail in a later part of the poem. His allusion to "that second war" which Enceladus and his brother Titans waged against the Olympians suggests that this incident also was outside of the main action of the poem. De Sélincourt's conjectural summary of the unfinished part of the poem is, in my opinion, substantially right.

The view . . . which I advance tentatively . . . is that *Hyperion* would not have reached more than 1200 — 1500 lines, or four books of the length of the first and second. . . . I conceive that Apollo, now conscious of his divinity, would have gone to Olympus, heard from the lips of Jove of his newly acquired supremacy, and been called upon by the rebel three to secure the kingdom that awaited him. He would have gone forth to meet Hyperion who, struck by the power of supreme beauty, would have found resistance impossible. [There would have been no physical combat between Hyperion and Apollo, de Sélincourt

[4] Ernest de Sélincourt, pp. 487–488.

said.] A combat would have been completely alien to the whole idea of the poem as Keats conceived it, and as, in fact, it is universally interpreted from the speech of Oceanus in the second book. The resistance of Enceladus and the Giants, themselves rebels against an order already established, would have been dealt with summarily, and the poem would have closed with a description of the new age which had been inaugurated by the triumph of the Olympians, and, in particular, of Apollo the god of light and song.

4

The Eve of St. Agnes was the first poem in which Keats was inspired by his love for Fanny Brawne. In the latter half of December 1818 he was with Miss Brawne every day either in her own home or in that of the Dilkes, and his wooing progressed swiftly and prosperously. About the middle of December he and Brown accepted an invitation to pass the Christmas season with Dilke's father in Chichester and Dilke's brother-in-law, John Snook, in Bedhampton. He wrote his brother George on December 18:

> I think also of going into Hampshire this Christmas to Mr Snooks — they say I shall be very much amused. But I dont know — I think I am in too huge a Mind for study — I must do it — I must wait at home, and let those who wish come to see me. I cannot always be (how do you spell it?) trapsing.

On December 21 Keats wrote Brown, who had already gone to Chichester, that his sore throat would detain him in Hampstead. He was held in Hampstead also by his composition of *Hyperion* and by his love for Miss Brawne. A few days before Christmas he visited the Reynoldses and discovered that they expected him to pass Christmas Day with them. He wrote Mrs. Reynolds on Tuesday, December (22?):

> My dear Mrs Reynolds,
>
> When I left you yesterday, 'twas with the conviction that you thought I had received no previous invitation for Christmas day: the truth is I had, and had accepted it under the conviction that I should be in Hampshire at the time: else believe me I should not have done so, but kept in Mind my old friends. I will not speak of the proportion of pleasure I may receive at different Houses — that never enters my head — you may take for a truth that I would have given up even what I did see to be a greater pleasure, for the sake of old acquaintanceship — time is nothing — two years are as long as twenty.
>
> Yours faithfully
>
> John Keats

Keats expressed himself neither clearly nor tactfully; for he was deceiving Mrs. Reynolds and he was embarrassed. He had accepted an invitation to pass the whole Christmas season with Dilke's relatives in Hampshire, but he had already decided to postpone this visit. He was intending to pass Christmas Day either with the Brawnes or with the Dilkes in Hampstead, where he would be with Fanny Brawne. The Reynoldses suspected the truth; for Charlotte Reynolds told H. B. Forman that she believed that the other invitation to which Keats referred in his letter to Mrs. Reynolds was from Mrs. Brawne. This incident was doubtless the beginning of that jealousy which the Reynoldses cherished against Fanny Brawne.

Miss Lowell discovered the significance of Keats's visit with the Brawnes (or the Dilkes) on Christmas Day, 1818 in a letter which Fanny Brawne wrote to Fanny Keats on December 13, 1821, three years afterwards.

> I dined with Mrs. Dilke a day or two ago [Miss Brawne wrote] . . . we dine with them on Christmas day which is like most peoples Christmas days melancholy enough . . . . I cannot think it will be much worse than mine for I have to remember that three years ago was the happiest day I had ever then spent.

Christmas Day, 1818, the happiest day Miss Brawne had ever spent, was undoubtedly the day on which Keats told her he loved her.

Keats concealed his love for Miss Brawne from his brother George as well as from his friends and acquaintances; and for some time Brown, Dilke, and Mrs. Dilke were the only persons who knew that he loved her. He wrote his brother on January 2, 1819:

> Yesterday M^r^ [and] M^rs^ D and myself dined at Mrs Brawn'es — nothing particular passed.

That is, Miss Lowell observed, nothing that he cared to tell his brother. He added, however, very significantly:

> I never intend hereafter to spend any time with Ladies unless they are handsome — you lose time to no purpose. For that reason I shall beg leave to decline going again to Redall's or Butlers or any Squad where a fine feature cannot be mustered among them all.

Keats tore himself away from Miss Brawne a few days after the middle of January 1819 and joined Brown at old Mr. Dilke's in Chichester. "You will find him a very odd young man," Mrs. Dilke wrote her father-in-law, "but good-tempered, and good-hearted, and very clever indeed." On January 23 Keats and Brown walked to John Snook's in Bedhampton, where they stopped for a fortnight. Keats's visit in Hampshire was a quiet one, for he was suffering from a sore throat and his hosts were kind but staid persons. At Chichester, he said, he attended two "dowager Card parties" and at Bedhampton he drove in a chaise with Brown and John Snook junior to see the consecration of a chapel in the park of the Reverent Mr. Lewis Way, a noted converter of Jews. This quiet visit in Hampshire was one of the most productive periods of his poetic career. He wrote his brother on February 14:

> I was nearly a fortnight at M[r] John Snook's and a few days at old M[r] Dilke's. Nothing worth speaking of happened at either place. I took down some thin paper and wrote on it a little poem call'd St. Agnes' Eve, which you shall have as it is when I have finished the blank part of the rest for you.

Keats composed the first draft of *The Eve of St. Agnes*, it seems, in Bedhampton in the last week of January and the first week of February 1819. He revised the romance in Winchester in September 1819 and published it with still other revisions in his *Poems* of 1820. The autograph manuscript of the first draft is now in the Lowell Collection in the Harvard College Library. There is a transcript of this manuscript in Woodhouse's Commonplace Book and another in his Book of Transcripts. Woodhouse copied the manuscript on April 20, 1819, the day on which he copied the manuscript of *Hyperion*. On the page opposite the transcript in his Book of Transcripts, he observed:

> This copy was taken from K's original M.S. He afterwards altered it for publication, & added some stanzas & omitted others. His alterations are noticed here. The published copy differs from both in a few particulars. K. left it to his Publishers to adopt which they pleased & to revise the whole.

And at the end of the transcript he added:

> Copied from J.K.'s rough M.S. 20 Ap. 1819. Written about the latter end of 1818 & the beginning of 1819.

There is a transcript of the revised version in George Keats's Book of Autographs and Transcripts. The seven first stanzas of the romance are not in the autograph first draft but they are in the transcript which Woodhouse made on April 20, 1819, three months after the first draft was composed. H. B. Forman suggested that Severn, to whom Keats gave the first draft, clipped off these stanzas and gave them to souvenir collectors.

The Eve of St. Agnes is the only complete and perfect long poem which Keats composed in the course of his life. The two "Hyperions" and *The Eve of St. Mark* are incomplete; and *Endymion*, *The Pot of Basil*, *Lamia*, and *Otho the Great* are imperfect in some respect — in story, sentiment, imagery, or diction. *The Eve of St. Agnes* seems to us, when we first begin to consider it, to be a spontaneous expression of genius, springing like Pallas Athena full grown from the forehead of the poet. In the case of the other long poems, such as *Endymion* and *Hyperion*, we can trace the slow process of conception and growth. In the minute records of Keats's life, however, there is no mention of *The Eve of St. Agnes* before it was composed. The intuition and the composition of the romance were sudden, spontaneous, and rapid. The matter of it, however, had germinated for years in the fallow soil of the poet's mind.

H. M. MacCracken [5] suggested that Keats derived the story of *The Eve of St. Agnes* from an episode in Boccaccio's prose romance *Il Filocolo*. Boccaccio derived the story of *Il Filocolo* from the famous mediaeval romance of Floris and Blanchefleur which is preserved in mediaeval French and English versions. Boccaccio invented, however, the distinctive details which resemble those in *The Eve of St. Agnes*. I cannot accept MacCracken's argument that Keats adapted the story from Boccaccio's *Il Filocolo*; but, since his argument has been accepted by critics such as Colvin and de Sélincourt, we must consider it.

There is no external evidence that Keats had any knowledge of the story of *Il Filocolo*. There was no English translation of this long and dull romance; and in January 1819, when Keats composed *The Eve of St. Agnes*, he could not read Italian. When he adapted *The Pot of Basil* from a novel in Boccaccio's *Decameron* in the spring of 1818, he used a seventeenth-century English translation. At the end of April 1818 he expressed an ambition to learn Italian, but circumstances delayed his realization of this ambition. When he read Dante's *Divine Comedy* in the summer of 1818 he read it in Cary's English translation. It was not until September 1819 that he announced that he was studying Italian and reading Ariosto's *Orlando Furioso*, "not managing," he said, "more than six or eight stanzas at a time." It has been suggested that he might have read *Il Filocolo* in the seventeenth-century French translation; but there is no evidence that he discovered this translation. It has been suggested also that he might have learned the story of *Il Filocolo* either from Hunt, who inspired him to read Italian romance, or from Reynolds, with whom he planned in the spring of 1818 to adapt a series of metrical romances out of Boccaccio's *Decameron*. If he learned the story of *Il Filocolo* from Hunt or Reynolds, however, it is strange that they did not comment upon its influence upon *The Eve of St. Agnes*. Hunt, in his interpretation of *The Eve of St. Agnes*, suggested Brand's *Popular Antiquities* as a source but did not mention Boc-

[5] H. M. MacCracken, "The Source of Keats's *Eve of St. Agnes*," *Modern Philology*, Vol. V.

caccio. And Reynolds, in his Advertisement to *The Garden of Florence*, referred to the plan which he and Keats had made to translate a series of Boccaccio's tales into English verse and implied that *The Pot of Basil* was the only story which Keats adapted from Boccaccio.

The internal evidence that Keats derived the story of *The Eve of St. Agnes* from an episode of *Il Filocolo* is, in my judgment, inconclusive. MacCracken gave a summary of the episode as follows:

> The enamored Florio, under his new name, Filocolo, has followed Biancofiore to Alexandria. Having ingratiated himself with Sadoc, the guardian of the tower in which Biancofiore with her attendant, Glorizia, is confined, Florio arranges to be conveyed into the tower by concealing himself in a basket of flowers. On the appointed day, a gala-day, Florio gets into the tower, and when he is deposited in one of the rooms of the tower, he at once demands of Glorizia to be led to Biancofiore. Glorizia explains to him that he cannot immediately see her, on account of the dangers from scandal and too sudden joy of the lady. Therefore Glorizia arranges to conceal Florio in an adjoining chamber, from which he can observe Biancofiore and her attendants in their merry-making, and promises later to conduct him from the side-chamber and conceal him behind the curtains of Biancofiore's bed, where he must await his lady's going to sleep before revealing himself. Glorizia warns him that Biancofiore will be severely frightened when she wakes, but that her fear will soon give way to joy. Glorizia then tries to arouse the melancholy Biancofiore, sighing in the midst of the festivities, to take part in the celebration of the day, and comforts her by recounting a dream in which she saw Florio appear in Biancofiore's chamber, while Biancofiore was asleep in her bed, and that she awoke and made great joy. Thus comforted, the girl and her maids celebrate the day with flowers and music, though Biancofiore often heaves great sighs; Florio looks on through a little hole from the adjoining chamber. At night Glorizia arranges Biancofiore's bed and conceals Florio behind the curtains. While Biancofiore prepares for bed, Glorizia arouses her feelings for Florio by suggesting now the possiblity, and again the impossibility, of his coming. Glorizia goes so far as to hint that some other man might please her — a suggestion indignantly repudiated. When Glorizia leaves her, Biancofiore lies down, but only after she is exhausted by sighs for Florio does she give herself up to sleep. Florio advances and caresses her as she sleeps, and gazes with impassioned love upon her. The room is filled with magic light as bright as day, from two magic carbuncles. Florio addresses the girl in loving words, bidding her wake and enjoy her love. Biancofiore, however, does not awake until Florio clasps her in his arms. When she wakes she mistakes him at first for the Florio about whom she is that very moment dreaming, and so remains half-asleep. Growing more awake, she cries out to her dream Florio: "Who takes thee from me?" Florio at last convinces her of his identity, and, after a ring is given and vows interchanged, the lovers retire and spend the night together.

This episode from *Il Filocolo* has many details which are remarkably like those in *The Eve of St. Agnes* — the secret entrance of Florio into the castle of enemies in which his mistress Biancofiore is confined, his entrance on an occasion of festivity, the aid given him by Glorizia, Biancofiore's female attendant, his hiding in Biancofiore's bedroom, Biancofiore's sighing and longing for Florio in the midst of the festivity, her disrobing that night and her dream of him, her awakening by him, and the consummation of their love.

The episode lacks, however, the most distinctive element of *The Eve of St. Agnes* — the striking contrast between the warm, passionate love of Porphyro and Madeline and the dark, sombre setting of family feud. The conclusion of the episode, also — the lovers' passing the night together, their seizure by the sultan the next morning, and the pardon which their devoted love wins for them — is quite different from the conclusion of Keats's romance.

The genesis of *The Eve of St. Agnes* can be explained entirely, I believe, by reference to poetic materials with which we know Keats was familiar. The setting of the story, the feud between the families of Porphyro and Madeline, was suggested by the setting of Shakespeare's *Romeo and Juliet*. The persons in the story, also, correspond to those in *Romeo and Juliet*—Porphyro to Romeo, Madeline to Juliet, Angela, Madeline's nurse, to Juliet's nurse, and Madeline's relatives to Juliet's relatives, the Capulets. The character of the love of Porphyro and Madeline was influenced, as we shall see presently, by that of the love of Romeo and Juliet; and the contrast between the tone of their love and the tone of the setting was suggested likewise by that in *Romeo and Juliet*.

The incidents also were derived in part from *Romeo and Juliet*. Porphyro, like Romeo, loves a girl with whose family his own are at bitter enmity. Like Romeo, he ventures to visit her on an occasion of festivity in her father's castle, in which, if he were discovered, he would be slain by savage foes. In this visit he is helped by Angela, a faithful old servant, as Romeo is aided by Juliet's nurse. Madeline's disregard of the festivity in the castle, the ceremonies which she performs as she retires to bed, and her dream of Porphyro were suggested by the traditional rites of St. Agnes' Eve. Porphyro's hiding himself in Madeline's chamber and his gazing upon her as she slept were suggested to Keats inevitably in his development of his story on the basis of the rites of St. Agnes' Eve. This incident was influenced, however, as the details prove, by a similar incident in Shakespeare's *Cymbeline*, in which Iachimo conceals himself in Imogen's chamber and gazes upon her. And the description of Madeline's disrobing as she prepares for bed was modelled upon a similar description in Browne's *Britannia's Pastorals*. Many descriptive details with which Keats filled out his story were reminiscences of Spenser, Shakespeare, Dante, Milton, William Browne, Chatterton, Coleridge, and Mrs. Radcliffe.

The second element of the romance consists in the superstitious rites of lovers on the Eve of St. Agnes. In the following stanzas Keats related these rites, which Madeline, he said, "had heard old dames full many times declare":

They told her how, upon St. Agnes' Eve,
Young virgins might have visions of delight,
And soft adorings from their loves receive
Upon the honey'd middle of the night,
If ceremonies due they did aright;
As, supperless to bed they must retire,
And couch supine their beauties, lily white;
Nor look behind, nor sideways, but require
Of Heaven with upward eyes for all that they desire.

'Twas said her future lord would there appear
Offering as sacrifice — all in the dream —
Delicious food even to her lips brought near:
Viands and wine and fruit and sugar'd cream,
To touch her palate with the fine extreme
Of relish: then soft music heard; and then
More pleasures followed in a dizzy stream
Palpable almost: then to wake again
Warm in the virgin morn, no weeping Magdalen.

Keats added the second of these stanzas in September 1819, when he was revising the romance, to make the feast which Porphyro prepares for Madeline a necessary part of the ceremonies. He suppressed it afterwards because, we may presume, he believed that it weakened the effect of the feast by anticipating it in inferior imaginative style.

Keats learned the amorous rites of the Eve of St. Agnes from oral tradition. De Sélincourt quoted Woodhouse as saying that Keats wrote the poem "at the suggestion of Mrs. Jones"; and Colvin quoted Woodhouse as saying that "the subject was suggested by Mrs. Jones." I overlooked this note in Woodhouse's Book of Transcripts, in which I presume it occurs; and I do not now have an opportunity to ascertain the exact words of the note. Woodhouse made a second reference to Mrs. Jones in his Book of Transcripts. In a note to the song *You say you love*, he wrote in shorthand: "from Miss Reynolds and Mrs. Jones." Brown also referred to Mrs. Jones, including her in the list of persons among whom he divided Keats's books in 1821. These references show that Mrs. Jones was a friend of the Reynoldses' and that Keats knew her as early as September

1817, when he composed *You say you love.* In the first part of January 1819, I surmise, Keats encountered Mrs. Jones in the home of the Reynoldses; and, in a discussion of the Eve of St. Agnes, which would occur on January 20, she said to him, it is possible: "Why don't you write a poem upon the ceremonies of St. Agnes' Eve?" When he began to meditate upon this subject he looked it up, it is probable, in some reference book. Leigh Hunt,[6] in his commentary upon the romance, cited Brand's *Popular Antiquities* as a book in which one might find an account of the ceremonies of St. Agnes' Eve. There are also brief allusions to these ceremonies in Jonson's *Satyr*, a masque, and in Burton's *Anatomy of Melancholy* (Part 3. Sec. 2. Mem. 3. Subs. 1). Keats derived from Brand's *Popular Antiquities*, it is probable, the religious rites of St. Agnes' Day — the offering of lambs to St. Agnes, the shearing of the lambs, and the weaving of the wool by "secret sisterhood" (stanzas viii and xiii).

The third element of the romance — the creative and the controlling emotion — was Keats's love for Miss Brawne, a love which was boyish, sensuous, and passionate. With his bookish habit of associating his personal experience with analogies in the poetry which he read, his love reminded him of Romeo's. A year before he met Fanny Brawne he had regarded Juliet as the type of girl whom he desired to love. In September 1817 he engaged in a humorous argument with Jane Reynolds about the respective merits of Juliet and Imogen. He wrote her on September 14:

> Imprimis — I sincerely believe that Imogen is the finest Creature; and that I should have been disappointed at hearing you prefer Juliet. Item Yet I feel such a yearning towards Juliet and that I would rather follow her into Pandemonium than Imogen into Paradize — heartily wishing myself a Romeo to be worthy of her and to he[a]r the Devils quote the old Proverb —"Birds of a feather flock together"— Amen.

While Keats remained in Hampstead, seeing Miss Brawne every day, he was too much agitated by love to express it in poetry. When he went to Chichester about January 18, however, his imagination, freed from the overpowering emotions which she excited in him, intuited his love for her in the objective symbols of poetry, drawing these symbols from the story of Romeo and Juliet and the amorous rites of St. Agnes' Eve.

Keats's love for Miss Brawne determined the form as well as the matter of *The Eve of St. Agnes*. In December 1818 he was composing *Hyperion* in the "naked and grecian" style of Milton's *Paradise*

[6] Leigh Hunt, *The London Journal* for January 21, 1835; and *Imagination and Fancy*, London, 1844.

Lost. Love, however, lured him out of the mood of the Greek epic into the mood of the metrical romance. He composed *The Eve of St. Agnes,* accordingly, in the sensuous, romantic style of Spenser's *Faerie Queene.*

Keats's knowledge of the mediaeval metrical romance was not very extensive. His negatively capable imagination required very little knowledge, however, to reproduce the cultural atmosphere of a past age in vivid, authentic form. He had read Ellis' *Specimens of Early English Metrical Romances,* which consists of brief summaries with briefer quotations; Chaucer's *Knight's Tale*; Tasso's *Jerusalem Delivered* (in Fairfax's translation); De Moraes' *Palmerin of England* (in Munday's translation, corrected by Southey); Malory's *Morte d'Arthur,* it is probable; and Spenser's *Faerie Queene.* He had learned from Leigh Hunt something of Ariosto's *Orlando Furioso*; and in September 1819, eight months later, he studied Italian and translated a part of this romance. He had read also the Gothic romances of Mrs. Radcliffe, whom he mentioned in connection with *The Eve of St. Agnes* and *The Eve of St. Mark.* He liked Coleridge's *Christabel,* to which he was very much indebted, and he scorned Scott's metrical romances. He regarded Spenser above all as the master of the romance.

The evolution of Keats's understanding of Spenser, we have seen, was slow, proceeding through Thomson and the eighteenth-century Spenserians, Browne and the seventeenth-century Spenserians, and Hunt, the nineteenth-century Spenserian. His study of Shakespeare in 1817 and his study of Shakespeare and Milton in 1818 freed him from the sentimentality of Mary Tighe and Hunt, the colloquial diction of Hunt, and the loose versification of Hunt and Browne. In January 1819, after he had acquired a fuller and a truer understanding of Renaissance poetry, he was able to reproduce in *The Eve of St. Agnes* the quintessence of Spenser's sensuous style.

The evolution of Keats's metrical romances stands out clearly in the general evolution of his poetry. He composed his first metrical romance, the incomplete *Calidore,* in the spring of 1816 according to the formula which Hunt had developed in *The Story of Rimini* — romantic chivalry, sentimental sensuousness, colloquial diction, short narrative genre, and loose, overflowing heroic couplets. In 1817, after he had reacted against Hunt's style, he composed *Endymion,* his second metrical romance, according to a formula which he had worked out independently from Spenser, Shakespeare, Drayton, and Browne — the romance of Spenser, the sensuousness of Spenser and Shakespeare, the suggestive, erudite diction of Renaissance poets in general, the long narrative genre of Spenser and Browne, and the loose, overflowing heroic couplets of Browne. He did not free his style entirely, however, from Hunt's diction and versification. His third metrical romance, *The Pot of Basil*, which he composed in the spring of 1818, was transitional, looking backward into the past and forward into the future. It has the short narrative genre which Hunt had developed and, unfortunately, Hunt's sentimental sensuousness. The imagery in certain passages, however, is as intense as Shakespeare's and Milton's. The diction is pure and elevated, having several concise, imaginative phrases. The metre, the ottava rima of Italian metrical romances, has strength and energy as well as flexibility. *The Eve of St. Agnes*, his fourth metrical romance, has the romantic spirit, the sensuous imagery, and the subtle, intricate stanza of Spenser's *Faerie Queene*. It has the glowing, youthful love and the intensely contrasting motifs of Shakespeare's *Romeo and Juliet*. It has the pure, elevated, and erudite diction of Renaissance poetry. And it has the short narrative genre of Hunt's *Story of Rimini*.

In the first draft of *The Eve of St. Agnes* Keats set the story in Devonshire near Dartmoor. He called his hero Lionel, his heroine Madeline, and one of the baron's retainers Ferdinand. He called another retainer Francesco Mendez but, remembering that he was setting his story in England, he changed his name to Lord Maurice Lacey. In his final version, however, he changed "Dartmoor bleak" to "Southern moors," Lionel to Porphyro, Ferdinand to Hildebrand, and Lord Maurice Lacey to Lord Maurice. It has been suggested, on the basis of the names in the final version, that the story is set in Northern Italy at the end of the middle ages and that the feud between the families of Porphyro and Madeline is a part of the political struggle between the Guelphs and Ghibellines. In this interpretation Porphyro, whose name is Italian, is a Guelph and Madeline's father, whose retainers have Germanic names, is a Ghibelline. It is probable, however, that Keats intended that the setting be, as it is, the vague and universal realm of romance.

The most striking element in *The Eve of St. Agnes* is its intensely sensuous imagery. Poetry produces its effect upon men by means of sensations, images, vague moods, definite emotions, and ideas. It stimulates directly auditory sensations, and because of the association of sensations with words it stimulates images of all possible sensations. Since poets differ in the structure of their sensory systems, they differ likewise in their imagery. A difference in imagery is, therefore, one of the essential differences in poetic style. The imagery of Keats's poetry has two notable characteristics. In the first place, it is comprehensive, having images of all the sensations of the sensory system — sensations of sight, hearing, touch, temperature, pressure, taste, smell, motor sensations, and internal sensations, hunger, thirst, lust, etc. In the second place, it is sensuous, being rich in images of the intimately physical sensations of touch, temperature, pressure, taste, smell, and the internal sensations. Sensations of sight and hearing may be the most indispensable, the highest, and the noblest of sensations but they are not sensuous.

Keats's letters, as well as his poetry, abound in illustrations of the delicacy and intensity of his intimately physical sensations, especially sensations of taste. Tuberculosis, which seized upon him in the fall of 1818, intensified his inherently sensuous temperament, making the year 1819 the supremely sensuous period of his poetry. He wrote his sister on April 13, 1819:

> I hope you have good store of double violets — I think they are the Princesses of flowers and in a shower of rain, almost as fine as barley sugar drops are to a schoolboy's tongue.

He wrote her from Winchester on August 28, 1819:

> The delightful Weather we have had for two Months is the highest gratification I could receive — no chill'd red noses — no shivering — but fair atmosphere to think in. . . . I should like now to promenade round you[r] Gardens — apple tasting — pear-tasting — plum-judging — apricot nibbling — peach scrunching — nectarine-sucking and Melon carving. I have also a great feeling for antiquated cherries full of sugar cracks — and a white currant tree kept for company.

He wrote Dilke on September 22, 1819:

> Talking of Pleasure, this moment I was writing with one hand, and with the other holding to my Mouth a Nectarine — good god how fine. It went down soft[,] pulpy, slushy, oozy — all its delicious embonpoint melted down my throat like a large beatified Strawberry. I shall certainly breed.

He wrote his brother on February 19:

> I never drink now above three glasses of wine — and never any spirits and water. Though by the bye the other day — Woodhouse took me to his coffee house and ordered a Bottle of Claret — now I like Claret, whenever I can have Claret I must drink it, —'tis the only palate affair that I am at all sensual in. . . . For really 'tis so fine — it fills the mouth one's mouth [*sic*] with a gushing freshness — then goes down cool and feverless. . . .

Haydon said that Keats

> once covered his tongue and throat as far as he could reach with Cayenne pepper in order to appreciate the delicious coldness of Claret in all its glory — his own expression.

He was in his glory in the fields [Haydon said]. The humming of a bee, the sight of a flower, the glitter of the sun, seemed to make his nature tremble; then his eyes flashed, his cheek glowed, his mouth quivered.

This supremely sensuous temperament made Keats preeminently the master of sensuous poetry. In the last letter which he wrote, when he knew that he would not live to glean his teeming brain, he said that he possessed

the knowledge of contrast, feeling for light and shade, all that information (primitive sense) necessary for a poem. . . .

Keats was much more than a poet of sensuous beauty. He was a thinker, a critic, and an interpreter of life. He recognized, however, the essential value of "primitive sense" upon which poetic imagery is based. The poems which he composed in 1819, especially the great odes, are both richly sensuous and profoundly critical.

A controlling principle in Keats's composition of a metrical romance was the particular sensuous atmosphere which he desired to produce. He wrote his brother from Winchester on September 20, 1819:

The great beauty of Poetry is, that it makes every thing every place interesting — The palatine venice and the abbotine Winchester are equally interesting. Some time since I began a Poem call'd "The Eve of St Mark" quite in the spirit of Town quietude. I think it will give you the sensation of walking about an old county Town in a coolish evening.

And he wrote Taylor on November 17, 1819:

I wish to diffuse the colouring of St. Agnes Eve throughout a Poem in which Character and Sentiment would be the figures to such drapery.

The atmosphere of *The Eve of St. Agnes* combines the rich sensuousness of Spenser's Bower of Bliss and the electric passion of Shakespeare's *Romeo and Juliet.* The warm, youthful love of Porphyro and Madeline is set in a mediaeval castle of passionate hatred, ardent revelry, and drunken carousing. The castle itself is set in a world of bitter cold, raging tempest, Catholic devotion and penance, age, and death. Keats's knowledge of contrast and his feeling for light and shade were awakened and trained by his study of Shakespeare. He drew the device of setting youthful love in a background of family feud from *Romeo and Juliet*, but he invented and added from his own grim experience of life the second and enveloping background of natural decay and death. In the very midst of his prosperous love for Fanny Brawne, he expressed his abiding conviction that happiness, even happiness in love, is a transient moment in a world of unhappiness, an unhappiness which is the law of nature. *The Eve of St. Agnes* is, therefore, a stark and grim interpretation of love as well as a glowing, sensuous romance.

The impression of bitter cold with which the romance begins is expressed vividly through the owl, the hare, the flock in woolly fold, and the aged beadsman.

> St. Agnes' Eve — Ah, bitter chill it was!
> The owl, for all his feathers, was a-cold;
> The hare limp'd trembling through the frozen grass,
> And silent was the flock in woolly fold:
> Numb were the Beadsman's fingers, while he told
> His rosary, and while his frosted breath,
> Like pious incense from a censer old,
> Seem'd taking flight for heaven, without a death,
> Past the sweet Virgin's picture, while his prayer he saith.

The description of the beadsman, which continues, links the theme of coldness, age, and death with the theme of Catholic devotion and penance. As this aged, holy man walks along the chapel aisle by slow degrees,

> The sculptur'd dead, on each side, seem to freeze,
> Emprison'd in black, purgatorial rails:
> Knights, ladies, praying in dumb orat'ries,
> He passeth by; and his weak spirit fails
> To think how they may ache in icy hoods and mails.

In the meantime the silver snarling trumpets proclaim the splendid feast within the castle. And

> The carved angels, ever eager-eyed,
> Star'd, where upon their heads the cornice rests,
> With hair blown back, and wings put cross-wise on their breasts.

The pity which the beadsman feels for the "sculptur'd dead" was suggested, Hunt observed, by a passage in Dante's *Divina Commedia*, which Keats read in Cary's translation. The souls of men who expiate the sin of pride, Dante said, are bent down beneath the weight of heavy stones,

> As, to support incumbent floor or roof,
> For corbel, is a figure sometimes seen,
> That crumples up its knees unto its breast;
> With the feign'd posture, stirring ruth unfeign'd
> In the beholder's fancy. . . .

The inner setting stands out vividly in contrast to the outer setting. The friends and kinsmen of the baron assemble at a high feast in the castle.

At length burst in the argent revelry,
With plume, tiara, and all rich array,
Numerous as shadows haunting fairily
The brain, new stuff'd, in youth, with triumphs gay
Of old romance.

Madeline, the baron's daughter, attends the feast; but, thinking of the amorous rites she will try that night, she is oblivious of the feasters around her. Her lover, Porphyro, ventures into the castle at the risk of his life; for, should he be discovered, a hundred swords will storm his heart. In the composition of the inner setting, Keats drew upon *Hamlet* and *Macbeth* as well as upon *Romeo and Juliet.* When Porphyro has been hidden in Madeline's chamber by Angela, the old nurse,

The boisterous, midnight, festive clarion,
The kettle-drum, and far-heard clarionet,
Affray his ears, though but in dying tone: —
The hall door shuts again, and all the noise is gone.

The contrast between the mood of Porphyro and that of the feasters was suggested, de Sélincourt observed, by the contrast between Hamlet's refined nature and that of his uncle, King Claudius. When Horatio, hearing a flourish of trumpets, asks, "What does this mean, my lord?" Hamlet replies:

The King doth wake to-night and takes his rouse,
Keeps *wassail*, and the swaggering up-spring reels;
And, as he drains his draughts of *Rhenish* down,
The *kettle-drum* and trumpet thus bray out
The *triumph* of his pledge.

[I. iv. 8–12].

At the end of the romance, we shall see, Keats recalled again Hamlet's description of his uncle's carousing.

The amorous rites of St. Agnes' Eve, about which the action of the romance hinges, belong to the plane of the supernatural and the magical but the story is worked out in the natural and human plane. Madeline believes that by performing these rites she will see her future husband in a dream, but she is awakened from her sleep by a real lover who has been concealed in her chamber by human agency. The style of the romance, likewise, as we have seen, is vivid and sensuous instead of suggestive and magical. The verses,

Thou must hold water in a witch's sieve
And be liege-lord of all the Elves and Fays,

express beliefs in English folk-lore but they are not magical in style. In the second verse Keats alluded doubtless to Prospero, who (in

The Tempest) ruled the spirits of the enchanted isle; and in the first verse he recalled a verse in *Much Ado* (V. i. 4–5), "Which falls into mine ears as profitless As water in a sieve," or a verse in *Macbeth* (I. iii. 8), in which the First Witch said: "In a sieve I'll thither sail." As we have already observed in *Hyperion*, Keats drew much of his folk-lore from Shakespeare.

Porphyro hid himself in Madeline's chamber that he might "win that night a peerless bride,"

> While legion'd fairies pac'd the coverlet,
> And pale enchantment held her sleepy-eyed.

In *Cymbeline* (II. ii. 9–10) Imogen, retiring on the night that Iachimo concealed himself in her chamber and observed her as she slept, prayed:

> From fairies and the tempters of the night
> Guard me, beseech ye!

And in *Romeo and Juliet* (I. iv. 70–71) Mercutio, describing Mab, Queen of the fairies, said:

> she gallops night by night
> Through lovers' brains, and then they dream of love. . . .

Only two verses in *The Eve of St. Agnes* have the true quality of magic:

> Never on such a night have lovers met,
> Since Merlin paid his Demon all the monstrous debt.

These verses remind us of five verses in the Song of the Indian Maid which Keats composed in November 1817:

> Beneath my palm trees, by the river side,
> I sat a weeping: what enamour'd bride,
> Cheated by shadowy wooer from the clouds,
> But hides and shrouds
> Beneath dark palm trees by a river side?

The weird, allusive magic of these two passages was inspired partly by three verses in Coleridge's *Kubla Khan*:

> A savage place! as holy and enchanted
> As e'er beneath a waning moon was haunted
> By woman wailing for her demon-lover!

The phraseology of the first verse, "Never on such a night have lovers met," was suggested by a famous passage in *The Merchant of Venice* (V. i. 1 *et seq.*), in which Lorenzo, alluding to stories of famous lovers, began, "In such a night as this. . . ." H. B. Forman [7] ex-

[7] H. B. Forman, Variorum Edition, Vol. II, p. 74.

plained Merlin's "monstrous debt" as his monstrous existence, which he owed to the demon who begot him of a British virgin and which he repaid when he died or disappeared through the working of one of his own spells by Viviane. Forman added that the tempest which raged around the castle in which Porphyro met Madeline, like the tempest around Broceliande on the night Merlin was spell-bound, suggests the significance of the phrase, "Never on such a night, etc." The particular version of the Merlin story which Keats read has not been established definitely.

Keats expended the full force of his sensuous temperament upon the central action of the romance, which takes place in Madeline's chamber.

> A casement high and triple-arch'd there was,
> All garlanded with carven imag'ries
> Of fruits, and flowers, and bunches of knot-grass,
> And diamonded with panes of quaint device,
> Innumerable of stains and splendid dyes,
> As are the tiger-moth's deep-damask'd wings;
> And in the midst, 'mong thousand heraldries,
> And twilight saints, and dim emblazonings,
> A shielded scutcheon blush'd with blood of queens and kings.
>
> Full on this casement shone the wintry moon,
> And threw warm gules on Madeline's fair breast,
> As down she knelt for heaven's grace and boon;
> Rose-bloom fell on her hands, together prest,
> And on her silver cross soft amethyst,
> And on her hair a glory, like a saint:
> She seem'd a splendid angel, newly drest,
> Save wings, for heaven: — Porphyro grew faint:
> She knelt, so pure a thing, so free from mortal taint.

The images in these stanzas, with the exception of a few images of temperature and touch, are visual. The frame of the scene, the arch of the casement with its carven imageries of fruits and flowers and bunches of knot-grass, is sharply outlined and colorless. The "splendid dyes" and "thousand heraldries" of the stained-glass panes are suggestive but indefinite as to form and color. The picture becomes colorful gradually in the "twilight saints," the "dim emblazonings," and the "shielded scutcheon" which "blush'd with blood of queens and kings." Within this frame is the delicately and exquisitely colored picture, in which the moonlight, shining through the stained-glass panes, reflects their colors upon Madeline as she prays beside the casement. This picture may be contrary to fact, for moonlight, it is said, does not reflect distinct colors; but Keats saw this picture in his mind and he makes us see it. From truth to fact, as Aristotle observed, we can appeal to imaginative truth, which is the final criterion of art.

The verses, "She seem'd a splendid angel, newly drest, Save wings, for heaven," are a reminiscence, Mrs. Ridley [8] suggested, of some verses in *Romeo and Juliet* (II. ii. 26–28):

> O! speak again *bright angel*; for thou art
> As glorious to this night, being o'er my head,
> As is a *winged* messenger of *heaven*. . . .

In the description of Madeline's disrobing, Keats presents images of warmth, odor, touch, sight, sound, and movement.

> Anon his heart revives: her vespers done,
> Of all its wreathed pearls her hair she frees;
> Unclasps her warmed jewels one by one;
> Loosens her fragrant boddice; by degrees
> Her rich attire creeps rustling to her knees:
> Half-hidden, like a mermaid in sea-weed,
> Pensive awhile she dreams awake, and sees,
> In fancy, fair St. Agnes in her bed,
> But dares not look behind, or all the charm is fled.

We may contrast the art of this scene with that of a similar scene in *Christabel*. Keats, striving to produce a sensuous and pleasant effect, described Madeline's disrobing in full, vivid detail; and Coleridge, striving to create a magical and fearful effect, described Geraldine's disrobing in brief, suggestive detail.

> Then drawing in her breath aloud,
> Like one that shuddered, she unbound
> The cincture from beneath her breast:
> Her silken robe, and inner vest,
> Dropt to her feet, and full in view,
> Behold! her bosom and half her side —
> A sight to dream of, not to tell!

Keats drew the idea and many of the details of his description of Madeline's disrobing from a long simile in Browne's *Britannia's Pastorals* (Book I, Song 5, vv. 807 *et seq.*). Describing Riot's transformation in the House of Repentance, Browne said:

> And as a lovely maiden, pure and chaste,
> With naked iv'ry neck, and gown unlac'd,
> Within her chamber, when the day is fled,
> Makes poor her garments to enrich her bed:

[8] Ernest de Sélincourt, Fifth Edition, 1926.

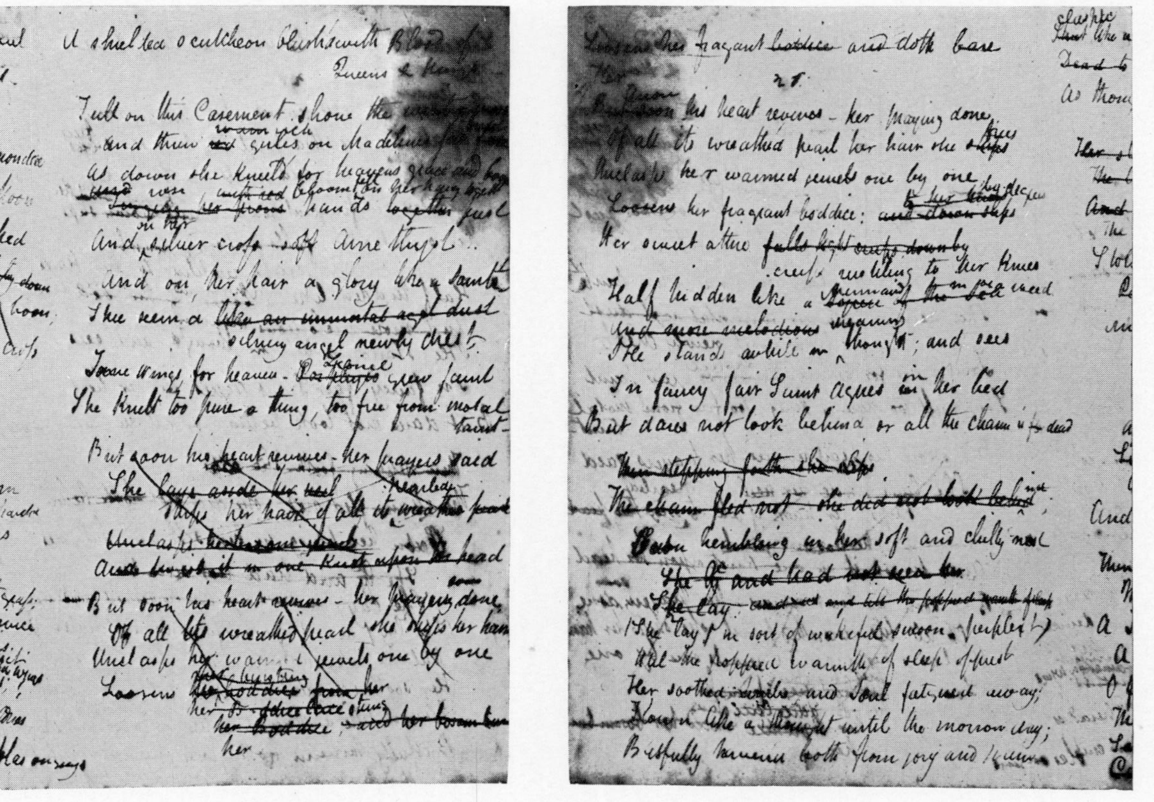

TWO PAGES OF THE FIRST DRAFT OF *THE EVE OF ST. AGNES*

Reproduced from the original autograph manuscript by permission of the Harvard College Library

First, puts she off her lily-silken gown,
That shrinks for sorrow as she lays it down;
And with her arms graceth a waistcoat fine,
Embracing her as it would ne'er untwine.
Her flaxen hair, ensnaring all beholders,
She next permits to wave about her shoulders,
And though she cast it back, the silken slips
Still forward steal and hang upon her lips:
Whereat she sweetly angry, with her laces
Binds up the wanton locks in curious traces . . .
Then on her head a dressing like a crown;
Her breasts all bare, her kirtle slipping down,
And all things off . . .
Except her last, which enviously doth seize her,
Lest any eye partake with it in pleasure,
Prepares for sweetest rest. . . .
So by degrees his shape all brutish wild,
Fell from him. . . .

Keats reduced and refined Browne's rough, diffuse ore into pure gold and stamped it with the impression of his own genius. He may have drawn one image, "Half-hidden, like a mermaid in sea-weed," from Marlowe's *Hero and Leander* (Sestyad II. v. 314 *et seq.*), in which, when Hero leaped out of the bed in which Leander lay,

He on the suddaine cling'd her so about,
That Meremaid-like vnto the floore she slid,
One half appear'd, the other halfe was hid . . .
And her all naked to his sight displayd. . . .

The description of Madeline in her bed presents images of softness, coldness, warmth, and relaxation.

Soon, trembling in her soft and chilly nest,
In sort of wakeful swoon, perplex'd she lay,
Until the poppied warmth of sleep oppress'd
Her soothed limbs, and soul fatigued away;
Flown, like a thought, until the morrow-day;
Blissfully haven'd both from joy and pain;
Clasp'd like a missal where swart Paynims pray;
Blinded alike from sunshine and from rain,
As though a rose should shut, and be a bud again.

Can the beautiful go beyond this? [Leigh Hunt[9] exclaimed]. I never saw it. And how the imagery rises! Flown like a *thought* — Blissfully *haven'd* — Clasp'd like a missal in a land of *Pagans*: that is to say, where Christian prayer books must not be seen, and are, therefore, doubly cherished for the danger. And

[9] Leigh Hunt, *The London Journal* for January 21, 1835; and *Imagination and Fancy*, London, 1844.

then, although nothing can surpass the preciousness of this idea, is the idea of the beautiful, crowning all —

> *Blinded* alike from sunshine and from rain,
> *As though a rose should shut, and be a bud again.*

Thus it is that poetry, in its intense sympathy with creation, may be said to create anew, rendering its words more impressive than the objects they speak of, and individually more lasting; the spiritual perpetuity putting them on a level (not to speak it profanely) with the fugitive compound.

The verses, "Until the poppied warmth of sleep oppress'd Her soothed limbs, and soul fatigued away," are as vividly sensuous as verses may be. Hunt preferred the suggestive figures in the second part of the stanza, however, to the sensuous images in the first part. Keats learned the art of ingenious and elaborate figures of speech from Milton's *Paradise Lost,* which he began to study intensively at the end of 1817. Milton learned the art of these figures of speech from the Greek rhetoricians, who reduced them to rule and illustrated them from Greek poetry and oratory.

Keats attained the acme of sensuousness in his description of the feast which Porphyro prepares for Madeline.

> And still she slept an azure-lidded sleep,
> In blanched linen, smooth, and lavender'd,
> While he from forth the closet brought a heap
> Of candied apple, quince, and plum, and gourd;
> With jellies soother than the creamy curd,
> And lucent syrops, tinct with cinnamon;
> Manna and dates, in argosy transferr'd
> From Fez; and spiced dainties, every one,
> From silken Samarcand to cedar'd Lebanon.

A feast was not one of the traditional rites of lovers on St. Agnes' Eve. Keats added the feast to the ceremonies to intensify the rich sensuousness of the climax of the romance. The description is rich in images of touch, taste, and hunger and in suggestive and melodious names such as "silken Samarcand" and "cedar'd Lebanon." A part of the effect depends upon the collocation of vowels and consonants by which the sound is made to echo the sense. Leigh Hunt, as well as Bailey, remembered that Keats had a definite theory of the harmony of vowels in verse. Commenting upon Keats's description of the feast, Hunt [10] said:

I remember Keats reading to me with great relish and particularity, conscious of what he had set forth, the lines describing the supper, and ending with the words,

> Lucent syrops tinct with cinnamon.

---

[10] Leigh Hunt, *Lord Byron and Some of his Contemporaries.*

Mr. Wordsworth would have said that the vowels were not varied enough; but Keats knew where his vowels were *not* to be varied. On the occasion above alluded to, Wordsworth found fault with the repetition of the concluding sound of the participles in Shakespeare's line about bees:

The *singing* masons *building* roofs of gold.

This he said, was a line which Milton would never have written. Keats thought, on the other hand, that the repetition was in harmony with the continued note of the singers, and that Shakespeare's negligence (if negligence it was) had instinctively felt the thing in the best manner. The assertion about Milton is startling, considering the tendency of that great poet to subject his nature to art; yet I have dipped, while writing this, into *Paradise Lost,* and at the second chance have lit on the following:

The gray
Dawn, and the Pleiades before him danced,
Shedding sweet influence. Less bright the moon,
But opposite, in *levelled west, was set*
His mirror, with full force borrowing her light.

The repetition of the *e* in the fourth line is an extreme case in point, being monotonous in order to express oneness and evenness. Milton would have relished the supper, which his young successor, like a page for him, has set forth. It was Keats who observed to me, that Milton, in various parts of his writings, has shown himself a bit of an epicure, and loves to talk of good eating.

In the expression of images of taste, thirst, and hunger, Keats learned more from Milton than from Spenser and Shakespeare. He was deeply impressed, we have seen, by Milton's description of the feast which Adam and Eve prepared for Raphael in the Garden of Eden. He imitated it in the introduction to *The Fall of Hyperion, a Dream*, which he composed in the latter part of September 1818, and in *The Eve of St. Agnes*, which he composed four months later. The details in his second imitation are less obviously Miltonic. They are more thoroughly transmuted and they are fused with details from other sources. He introduced, like Milton, fruits from various parts of the Orient, and he drew two of the fruits, the gourd and the creamy curd, from Milton's description. For particular images and for melodious words he was as much indebted to Shakespeare and Marlowe as to Milton.

When Keats described Porphyro gazing upon Madeline as she slept, he recalled Shakespeare's description of Iachimo gazing upon Imogen. The image,

And still she slept an azure-lidded sleep,

was a reminiscence of Shakespeare's image of Imogen's lids,

. . . white and azure, lac'd
With blue of heaven's own tinct. . . . [II. ii. 22–23.]

The phraseology of the verse,

> With jellies soother than the creamy curd,

was a reminiscence of the phraseology of a verse in *The Winter's Tale* (IV. iv. 160–161),

> Good *sooth*, she is
> The queen of *curds* and *cream* . . .

When Keats remembered Shakespeare's phraseology his imagination, working freely, converted "sooth" (truth) into "soother" (more soothing). Verbal licenses, such as the creation of new words, are among the chief defects of his poetry; but the felicitous harmony of "soother" in this case justifies its illegitimate creation. Milton's "dulcet creams," as well as Shakespeare's "curds and cream," may have entered into the phrase "creamy curd." "Dulcet" may, indeed, have had some influence upon the meaning which Keats gave to "soother." The word "tinct" in the verse, "Lucent syrops, tinct with cinnamon," was, like the phrase "azure-lidded sleep," a reminiscence of the passage from *Cymbeline* which I have already quoted.

The verses,

> Manna and dates, in argosy transferr'd
> From Fez; and spiced dainties, every one,
> From silken Samarcand to cedar'd Lebanon,

are indebted for their diction, melody, and suggestiveness to a passage in Marlowe's *Jew of Malta*:

> Mine *Argosie* from Alexandria,
> Loaden with *Spice* and *Silkes*, now vnder saile,
> Are smoothly gliding downe by Candie Shoare
> To Malta, through our Mediterranean sea.

Keats may have read and relished this fine passage with Leigh Hunt, who years afterwards quoted and analyzed it in his *Imagination and Fancy*.

The climax of the romance occurs in the stanza in which Porphyro takes the place of the lover whom Madeline expected to see in a dream.

> Beyond a mortal man impassion'd far
> At these voluptuous accents, he arose,
> Ethereal, flush'd, and like a throbbing star
> Seen mid the sapphire heaven's deep repose;
> Into her dream he melted, as the rose
> Blendeth its odour with the violet, —
> Solution sweet: meantime the frost-wind blows

> Like Love's alarum pattering the sharp sleet
> Against the window-panes; St. Agnes' moon hath set.

Woodhouse[11] wrote Taylor on September 20, 1819 that Keats had amplified this stanza into three stanzas to make it clear that Porphyro and Madeline consummated their love on St. Agnes' Eve. These three stanzas, which Keats suppressed by the advice of Woodhouse and Taylor, have not been preserved; but there are traces of them, possibly, together with other alterations to which Woodhouse objected, in the transcript in George Keats's Book of Autographs and Transcripts. These revisions were foreign to the mood in which Keats composed the romance. They were inspired, we shall see later, by the rebellious and cynical mood which was aroused in him in September 1819.

This romance of glowing, youthful love comes to an end artistically with a recurrence of the sombre notes of the two enveloping settings — the inner setting of feudal splendor, passionate hatred, and drunken carousing and the outer setting of bitter cold, raging tempest, age, and death. The lovers steal out of the castle while the iced gusts of the storm rave and beat against the window panes. They pass through the hall where the baron's retainers lie in a drunken sleep —

> The bloated wassaillers will never heed . . .
> Drown'd all in Rhenish and the sleepy mead. . . .

The description of the "bloated wassaillers," in which "drenching mead" was an earlier reading for "sleepy mead," was a reminiscence of a passage in *Macbeth* (I. vii. 63 *et seq.*), in which Macbeth, preparing for the murder of Duncan, says:

> his two chamberlains
> Will I with *wine and wassail* so convince
> That memory, the warder of the brain,
> Shall be a fume, and the receipt of reason
> A limbeck only. When in swinish *sleep*
> Their *drenched* natures lie as in a death. . . .

As the lovers leave the castle, they pass through the portal,

> Where lay the Porter, in uneasy sprawl,
> With a huge empty flaggon by his side. . . ,

a porter who is a reminiscence doubtless of the drunken porter in *Macbeth*.

[11] The manuscript of the letter is in the Pierpont Morgan Library. See below, pp. 689 *et seq.*

The atmosphere of the romance with its vividly contrasting motifs is summed up in the final stanza.

> And they are gone: ay, ages long ago
> These lovers fled away into the storm.
> That night the Baron dreamt of many a woe,
> And all his warrior-guests, with shade and form
> Of witch, and demon, and large coffin-worm,
> Were long be-nightmar'd. Angela the old
> Died palsy-twitch'd, with meagre face deform;
> The Beadsman, after thousand aves told,
> For aye unsought for slept among his ashes cold.

5

The intense happiness in love which Keats expressed in the romance of Porphyro and Madeline was, as he foreshadowed in the setting, transient and momentary. After he returned to Hampstead from Bedhampton about February 6, he was confined in Wentworth Place with a sore throat from which he had been suffering since the middle of December. He wrote his brother on February 14:

> I am still at Wentworth Place — indeed, I have kept indoors lately, resolved if possible to rid myself of my sore throat; . . . I see very little now, and very few persons, being almost tired of men and things. Brown and Dilke are very kind and considerate towards me. The Miss R's have been stopping next door lately, but are very dull. Miss Brawne and I have every now and then a chat and a tiff. . . . I am invited to Miss Millar's birthday dance on the 19th. I am nearly sure I shall not be able to go. A dance would injure my throat very much.

The situation was full of danger for Keats and Fanny Brawne. He was too ill to take part in her social amusements and she was too young to give them up for his sake. In his reference to "tiffs" with Miss Brawne, a reference which he could not suppress but which he could make casual, we have the first intimation of that jealousy which tortured him for the remainder of his life. He had these tiffs with Miss Brawne because she went to dances with other men. He had never learned to dance, although he had attended dances; and, if he had been well enough to escort her to them, he could not have danced with her. He wrote his sister on February 27:

> Keep on reading and play as much on the music and the grassplot as you can. I should like to take possession of those Gras[s]plots for a Month or so; and send Mrs A. to Town to count coffee berries instead of currant Bunches, for I want you to teach me a few common dancingsteps — and I would buy a Watch box to practise them in by myself.

His desire to learn to dance reveals the cause of his jealous tiffs with Miss Brawne.

On some night in the early part of February, when he was held at home by his sore throat while Miss Brawne was attending a dance, Keats expressed in an ode the physical jealousy which racked him.

To Fanny

1

Physician Nature! let my spirit blood!
O ease my heart of verse and let me rest;
Throw me upon thy Tripod, till the flood
Of stifling numbers ebbs from my full breast.
A theme! a theme! great nature! give a theme;
Let me begin my dream.
I come — I see thee, as thou standest there,
Beckon me not into the wintry air.

2

Ah! dearest love, sweet home of all my fears,
And hopes, and joys, and panting miseries, —
To-night, if I may guess, thy beauty wears
A smile of such delight,
As brilliant and as bright,
As when with ravish'd, aching, vassal eyes,
Lost in soft amaze,
I gaze, I gaze!

3

Who now, with greedy looks, eats up my feast?
What stare outfaces now my silver moon?
Ah! keep that hand unravish'd at the least;
Let, let, the amorous burn —
But, pr'ythee, do not turn
The current of your heart from me so soon.
O! save, in charity,
The quickest pulse for me.

4

Save it for me, sweet love! though music breathe
Voluptuous visions into the warm air,
Though swimming through the dance's dangerous wreath;
Be like an April day,
Smiling and cold and gay,
A temperate lily, temperate as fair;
Then, Heaven! there will be
A warmer June for me.

5

Why, this — you'll say, my Fanny! is not true:
Put your soft hand upon your snowy side,

Where the heart beats: confess —'tis nothing new —
Must not a woman be
A feather on the sea,
Sway'd to and fro by every wind and tide?
Of as uncertain speed
As blow-ball from the mead?

6

I know it — and to know it is despair
To one who loves you as I love, sweet Fanny!
Whose heart goes flutt'ring for you every where,
Nor, when away you roam,
Dare keep its wretched home.
Love, Love alone, has pains severe and many:
When loneliest keep me free,
From torturing jealousy.

7

Ah! if you prize my subdued soul above
The poor, the fading, brief pride of an hour;
Let none profane my Holy See of love,
Or with a rude hand break
The sacramental cake:
Let none else touch the just new-budded flower;
If not — may my eyes close,
Love! on their last repose.

Lord Houghton published this ode in 1848; and his son, the Marquess of Crewe, has a fragmentary autograph manuscript, containing stanzas 2, 3, 5, 6, and 7. The manuscript is undated; but the thought of the ode, which is very definite, establishes the approximate date. The verses, "Let none else touch the just new-budded flower" and "But, pr'ythee, do not turn The current of your heart from me so soon," indicate that Keats composed the ode very soon after he became the accepted lover of Miss Brawne. He was not jealous of Miss Brawne in January, when he composed *The Eve of St. Agnes*; but he grew jealous of her in February because she went to dances with other men. The verse, "Beckon me not into the wintry air," indicates that he composed the ode between February 6 and February 14, when he was confined in his room with a sore throat.

H. B. Forman and de Sélincourt have suggested that the substance of the ode was influenced by passages in Burton's *Anatomy of Melancholy*, which Keats was reading and, as was his habit, associating with his own experience. In the Dilke Collection there is a copy of *The Anatomy of Melancholy*, edition of 1813, which Keats marked and annotated. On the title page he wrote, "John Keats from Charles Brown 1819." He found bitter food for his jealousy in the peevish descriptions of love which Burton quoted with gusto from the physicians, philosophers, theologists, and poets of antiquity. Discussing the mental symptoms of lovers, Burton said:

> . . . though they be merry sometimes, and rapt beyond themselves for joy, yet most part, Love is a plague, a torture, an hell, a bitter sweet passion at last. . . . From it, saith *Austin*, arise *biting cares, perturbations, passions, sorrowes, feares, suspitions, discontents, contentions, discords, warres, treacheries, enmities, flattery, cosening, riot, lust, impudence, cruelty, knavery, etc.* . . . These doubts, anxieties, suspitions, are the least part of their torments, they breake many times from passions to actions, speake faire, and flatter, now most obsequious and willing, by and by they are averse, wrangle, fight, sweare, quarrell, laugh, weepe: and he that doth not so by fits, *Lucian* holds, is not throughly touched with this Loadstone of Love. . . . So that to say truth, as *Castilio* describes it, *The beginning, middle, end of Love is naught else but sorrow, vexation, torment, irksomenesse, wearisomenesse, so that to be squalid, ugly, miserable, solitary, discontent, deiected, to wish for death, to complaine, rave, and to be peevish, are the certain signes, & ordinary actions of a love-sick person.*

The verses,

> Ah! dearest love, sweet home of all my fears,
> And hopes, and joys, and panting miseries . . .
> Love, Love alone, has pains severe and many. . . ,

reflect, it seems, Burton's description of the medley passions which afflict lovers. The verses,

> Who now, with greedy looks, eats up my feast?
> What stare outfaces now my silver moon?
> Ah! keep that hand unravish'd at the least. . . ,

were inspired, as H. B. Forman suggested, by a passage in Burton's description of the physical symptoms of lovers:

> They cannot look off whom they love, they will *impregnare eam ipsis oculis*, deflowre her with their eyes, be still gazing, staring, stealing faces, smiling, glancing at her, as *Apollo* on *Leucothoe*, the *Moone* on her *Endymion*, when she stood still in *Caria*, and at *Latmos* caused her Chariot to be stayed . . . and many Lovers confesse when they came in their Mistresse presence, they could not hold off their eyes, but looked wistly and steddily on her, *inconnivo aspectu*, with much eagernes and greedinesse, as if they would looke through, or should never have enough sight of her, . . . *Fixis ardens, obtutibus haeret*; So she will doe by him, drink to him with her eyes, nay drink him up, devoure him, swallow him, as *Martials Mamurra* is remembred to have done: *Inspexit molles pueros, oculisque comedit, etc.*[12]

The painful jealousy which Keats felt because Miss Brawne went to dances was inflamed, de Sélincourt suggested, by Burton's description of dancing as an artificial allurement to the passion of burning lust.

[12] I quote from the edition printed at Oxford for Henry Cripps in 1638.

> *Incitamentum libidinis, Petrarch* calls it, the spurre of lust, *A circle of which the Divell himselfe is the Center. Many women that use it, have come dishonest home, most indifferent, none better,* Another tearmes it *the companion of all filthy delights and entisements, and 'tis not easily told what inconveniences come by it, what scurrile talke, obscene actions,* and many times such monstrous gestures, such lascivious motions, such wanton tunes, meretricious kisses, homely embracings. . . .

The phrase "ease my heart," which had already been used in *Endymion* (I. 538), was derived from *I Henry IV* (I. iii. 126). The image in the verses,

> Must not a woman be
> A feather on the sea,
> Sway'd to and fro by every wind and tide?

was composed, it is possible, from elements abstracted from three passages in Shakespeare's plays. The element of the feather blown by the wind came from *The Winter's Tale* (II. iii. 154), "I am a feather for each wind that blows"; the element of the feather moved by the tide came from *Antony and Cleopatra* (III. ii. 48), "the swan's down-feather, That stands upon the swell at full of tide"; and the element of persons, like a feather, blown to and fro came from *King Henry VI* (Part II, IV. viii. 57), "Was ever feather so lightly blown to and fro as this multitude?"

After expressing his jealousy subjectively and directly in the ode *To Fanny*, Keats attempted to express it objectively and symbolically in *The Eve of St. Mark.* He succeeded in composing, however, only the introduction to the romance. In the journal letter to his brother, in the section which he began on February 14, 1819, he said:

> We — i. e. Brown and I — sit opposite one another all day authorizing. . . . In my next packet, as this is one by the way, I shall send you my Pot of Basil, St. Agnes' Eve, and if I should have finished it, a little thing called the Eve of St. Mark. You see what fine Mother Radcliffe names I have — it is not my fault — I do not search for them. I have not gone on with Hyperion, for to tell the truth I have not been in great cue for writing lately — I must wait for the spring to rouse me up a little.

Woodhouse copied the romance into his Book of Transcripts and said in a note that it was "written 13/17 Feby 1819." Keats revised this incomplete romance in September 1819, while he was residing in Winchester, and he copied it on September 20 into the journal letter which he was writing to his brother. This autograph letter containing the romance is in the Pierpont Morgan Library. There is another autograph manuscript of it in George Keats's Book of Autographs and Transcripts, which is in the British Museum. H. B. Forman examined a fragment of a third autograph manuscript which was in the possession of Frank T. Sabin, bookseller, of 118 Shaftesbury Avenue, London. There is a transcript of the romance in Woodhouse's Book of Transcripts. Lord Houghton published the romance in 1848; and in 1906 H. B. Forman added to the published text 16 verses in Middle English. These verses are not in the first two autograph manuscripts mentioned above, but they are in the fragment of the third autograph manuscript and in Woodhouse's transcript. Woodhouse copied them at the end of his transcript as if they were new verses which Keats had not interwoven into the text. H. B. Forman suggested that Keats intended to insert them between verses 98 and 99 at the beginning of the other passage in Middle English. I believe that they were the only verses which Keats composed in September 1819.

Keats learned the rites of St. Mark's Eve, out of which he intended to build the romance, from Brand's *Popular Antiquities*, which he had consulted for the rites of St. Agnes' Eve.

> It is customary in Yorkshire [Brand said], for the common people to sit and watch in the church porch on St. Mark's Eve, April 24th, from eleven o'clock at night till one in the morning. The third year (for this must be done thrice) they are supposed to see the ghosts of all those who are to die in the next year, pass by into the church, (which they are said to do in their usual dress, and precisely in the order of time in which they are doomed to depart. Infants and young children, not yet able to walk, are said to roll in on the pavement.Those who are to die remain in the church, but those who are to recover return after a longer or shorter time, in proportion to the continuance of their future sickness.).

Keats related the rites of St. Mark's Eve in those 16 verses which he composed, I believe, in Winchester in September 1819. He simplified the legend, saying that all those whose wraiths enter the church on St. Mark's Eve will die. I quote the photograph of the autograph manuscript which was printed by H. B. Forman in *The Bookman* for October 1906.

Gif ye wol stonden hardie wight —
Amiddes of the blacke night —
Righte
~~Full~~ in the churche porch, pardie
Ye wol behold a companie
Approchen thee
Full dolourouse
For sooth to sain from everich house
Be it in City or village
wol Phantom
~~From hill~~ come the ~~feature~~ and image

Of ilka gent and ilka carle
Whom coldè Deathè hath in parle
And wol some day that very year
Touchen with ~~his~~ foulè venime spear
And sadly do them all to die —
Hem all shalt thou see verilie —
~~And they shall passen thee beside~~
~~Tho in the darke~~ pass
And everichon shall by thee ~~go~~
~~Truly mine auctour sayeth so~~
All who must die that year Alas.

Keats intended, we have seen, to add this passage in Middle English to the other passage in Middle English which he had composed in February 1819. When he copied the other passage in the letter to his brother he observed:

> What follows is an imitation of the Authors in Chaucer's time —'tis more ancient than Chaucer himself and perhaps between him and Gower.

His knowledge of the Middle English language was as uncertain and as inexact as his knowledge of the chronology of Middle English writers. He imitated Middle English very much in the manner in which Chatterton had imitated it. In September 1819, when he composed the passage quoted above, he turned to Chatterton in his search for a pure English idiom. He wrote Reynolds on September 21:

> I always somehow associate Chatterton with autumn. He is the purest writer in the English Language. He has no French idiom, or particles like Chaucer —'tis genuine English Idiom in English words.

Dante Gabriel Rossetti discovered the key to the story which Keats intended to develop out of the rites of St. Mark's Eve in a passage in a letter which Keats wrote to Fanny Brawne in August 1820:

> If my health would bear it, I could write a Poem which I have in my head, which would be a consolation for people in such a situation as mine. I would show some one in Love as I am, with a person living in such Liberty as you do.

Rossetti wrote H. B. Forman,[13] the publisher of Keats's letters to Fanny Brawne:

> I should think it very conceivable — nay, I will say, *to myself* highly probable and almost certain, — that the "Poem which I have in my head" referred to by Keats at page 106 was none other than the fragmentary *Eve of St. Mark.* By the light of the extract. . ., I judge that the heroine — remorseful after trifling

[13] H. B. Forman, Variorum Edition, Vol. III, pp. 7–8.

with a sick and now absent lover — might make her way to the minster-porch to learn his fate by the spell, and perhaps see his figure enter but not return.

Whether commenced or not with the view in question may be uncertain [Rossetti added] (though he must have *known* Miss B. when he wrote the Houghton letter); but he may (without even having at first intended it) have seen how well the scheme of the poem (which the superstition makes manifest enough) was fitted to work in with the ideas expresed in the Brawne letter.

Rossetti's conjecture has been confirmed by later discoveries of Keats's relations with Miss Brawne. When Keats composed *The Eve of St. Mark* between February 13 and 17, 1819, he was confined at home with a sore throat, suffering from jealousy because Miss Brawne was going to dances. In the same period, we have seen, he expressed his jealousy in direct and personal form in the ode *To Fanny*. His jealousy was as intense in February 1819 as in August 1820, although it was not so morbid. When he wrote Miss Brawne in August 1820, he could refer to *The Eve of St. Mark* as "a Poem which I have in my head," for he had only composed the introduction.

The substance of *The Eve of St. Mark* is "oddly muddled up," as Rossetti observed, with the substance of *The Cap and Bells; or, The Jealousies*, an incomplete satiric fairy tale which Keats composed in November and December 1819. That part of *The Cap and Bells* which Keats derived from Shakespeare's *A Midsummer Night's Dream* — the mingling of fairies and mortals; the criss-cross loves of Elfinan and Bellanaine, Hubert and Bertha Pearl; Bertha Pearl as a fairy changeling, etc. — could not have been a part of *The Eve of St. Mark*. Other elements, however — the theme of jealousy; Bertha, the name of the heroine; the figures embroidered on the sampler; the legend-leaved book; and the setting in Canterbury on St. Mark's Eve — are elements of *The Eve of St. Mark*.

The atmosphere of *The Eve of St. Mark* is as fine, although in a quite different way, as that of *The Eve of St. Agnes*. Rossetti wrote H. B. Forman that *The Eve of St. Mark* "is perhaps, with *La Belle Dame sans Merci*, the chastest and choicest example of [Keats's] maturing manner, and shows astonishingly real mediaevalism for one not bred as an artist."

Keats set the romance in an English cathedral town.

> Bertha was a Maiden fair,
> Dwelling in the old Minster square;
> From her fireside she could see
> Sidelong its rich antiquity,
> Far as the Bishop's garden wall. . . .

He drew the setting from cathedral towns which he knew. He visited Canterbury in May 1817, Chichester in January 1819, and Winchester in August, September, and October 1819. He composed the romance a month after he had left Chichester and he revised it in Winchester. He intended to set the story in Canterbury, I believe, if we may identify the setting with that of *The Cap and Bells.* He introduced vernal elements in the setting — the "wholesome drench of April rains," etc. — which he had experienced doubtless in his visit in Canterbury in May 1817. When he copied the romance for his brother on September 20, 1819, he described the atmosphere he wished to create in it.

> The great beauty of Poetry is, that it makes every thing every place interesting — The palatine venice and the abbotine Winchester are equally interesting. Some time since I began a Poem call'd "The Eve of St Mark" quite in the spirit of Town quietude. I think it will give you the sensation of walking about an old county Town in a coolish evening. I know not yet whether I shall ever finish it — I will give it far as I have gone. *Ut tibi placeat!*

I quote from the text in the letter.

> Upon a Sabbath day it fell;
> Thrice holy was the sabbath bell
> That call'd the folk to evening prayer.
> The City streets were clean and fair
> From wholesome drench of April rains,
> And on the western window pains [panes]
> The chilly sunset faintly told
> Of unmatur'd green vallies cold,
> Of the green, thorny, bloomless hedge,
> Of Rivers new with spring tide sedge,
> Of Primroses by shelter'd rills,
> And Da[i]sies on the aguish hills.
> Thrice holy was the sabbath bell:
> The silent streets were crowded well
> With staid and pious companies
> Warm from their fireside oratries,
> And moving with demurest air
> To even song and vesper prayer.
> Each arched porch and entry low
> Was fill'd with patient crowd and slow,
> With whispers hush, and shuffling feet
> While play'd the organ loud and sweet.

The atmosphere of a fresh, cool, quiet, devout English cathedral town on a Sunday evening in spring is mediaeval, modern, eternal. With a few deft touches, such as orat'ries, evensong, and vesper prayer, however, Keats converted the atmosphere of the Canterbury which he knew into the mediaeval and Catholic atmosphere of the Canterbury of the fourteenth or the fifteenth century.

Here, as in *The Eve of St. Agnes*, there is a series of enveloping settings; but here they create an effect of harmony instead of contrast. The aguish hills and green vallies cold enfold the silent streets of the cathedral town, filled with patient folk and slow, moving with whispers hush and shuffling feet to evensong and vesper prayer; and the silent streets, crowded with staid and pious companies, enfold the silent room, overlooking the minster-square, in which Bertha reads the legend of St. Mark in an illuminated manuscript.

> The Bells had ceas'd, the Prayers begun,
> And Bertha had not yet half done
> A curious volume, patch'd and torn,
> That all day long, from earliest morn,
> Had taken captive her fair eyes,
> Among its golden broideries: —
> Perplex'd her with a thousand things —
> The Stars of heaven, and Angels' wings;
> Martyrs in a fiery blaze;
> Azure Saints 'mid silver rays;
> A[a]ron's breastplate, and the seven
> Candlesticks John saw in heaven;
> The winged Lion of Saint Mark,
> And the Covenantal Arck
> With its many Misteries
> Cherubim and golden Mice.
>
> . . . .
>
> Untir'd she read the Legend page
> Of holy Mark from youth to age,
> On Land, on Sea, in pagan-chains,
> Rejoicing for his many pains.
> Sometimes the learned Eremite
> With golden star, or daggar bright,
> Refer'd to pious poesies
> Written in smallest crow quill size
> Beneath the text and thus the rhyme
> Was parcell'd out from time to time. . . .

Similar images, bright, golden, and suggestive, had appeared in three earlier passages in Keats's poetry. In the heptasyllabics on Fingal's Cave (July 26, 1818):

> Not St. John in Patmos isle
> In the passion of his toil
> When he saw the churches seven
> Golden-aisled built up in heaven
> Gazed at such a rugged wonder.

In a stanza on Skulls of Monks in Beauly Abbey (August 3/7, 1818):

Poor Skull! Thy fingers set ablaze,
With silver saint in golden rays,
The Holy Missal, thou didst craze
  'Mid bead and spangle
While others passed their idle days
  In coil and wrangle.

And in the humanitarian introduction to *The Fall of Hyperion, a Dream* (September and October 1818):

All in a mingled heap confused there lay
Robes, golden tongs, censer and chafing dish
Girdles, and chains and holy jewelries.

Keats copied the heptasyllabics on Fingal's Cave as well as *The Eve of St. Mark* into the journal letter which he wrote his brother in September 1819; and, noticing the similarity of his allusions to St. John in the two poems, he suppressed the third and fourth verses of the passage which I have quoted from Fingal's Cave. The metres of the two poems are somewhat similar, the one being heptasyllabic and the other octosyllabic with a mingling of heptasyllabic verses. *The Eve of St. Mark* represents a turning away from the regular heptasyllabics, in which under the influence of Fletcher Keats had composed many lyric poems in 1818. Robert Bridges suggested that Keats managed the four-beat metre of *The Eve of St. Mark* with that freedom which Coleridge advocated and employed in *Christabel*.

Keats represented the bright, colorful, and mystic side of mediaeval life—stained-glass windows, richly decorated vestments, holy jewelries, illuminated manuscripts, missals and legends of saints, elaborate ritual, and mystic visions — in all of the poems which he composed in this period. He was influenced undoubtedly by the cathedrals and abbeys which he visited before, during, and after his excursion into Scotland, by illuminated manuscripts and other mediaeval records which he saw in the British Museum, and by books of prints of mediaeval paintings which Haydon showed him.

The following picture in *The Eve of St. Mark* represents a distinct and original development in Keats's employment of imagery. It is perfect in its vivid, concise, sharply etched details and in its artistic contrast of light and shade.

  All was silent, all was gloom
Abroad and in the homely room; —
Down she sat, poor cheated soul,
And struck a swart Lamp from the coal,

Leaned forward with bright drooping hair
And slant book full against the glare.
Her shadow, in uneasy guise,
Hover'd about, a giant size,
On ceiling, beam, and old oak chair,
The Parrot's cage and pannel square,
And the warm-angled winter screne. . . .
   Untir'd she read — her shadow still
Glower'd about as it would fill
The room with g[h]astly forms and shades —
As though some ghostly Queen of Spades
Had come to mock behind her back,
And dance, and ruffle her garments black.

The Eve of St. Mark was one of the sources of the Pre-Raphaelite movement in English poetry, painting, and sculpture. Holman Hunt said that this movement, which was begun by John Millais, Dante Gabriel Rossetti, and himself, was inspired by engravings of the frescoes in the Campo Santo in Pisa, Ruskin's artistic principles, and Keats's poetry. The Pre-Raphaelite artists admired and imitated the simple story, the intense passion, the concise and concrete imagery, and the bright color of Keats's metrical romances.

Rossetti was delighted, when he read Keats's letters in 1848, to discover that Keats had admired early Italian painting. Keats expressed his admiration for it in the journal letter to his brother at the end of December 1818, a month and a half before he composed *The Eve of St. Mark.*

When I was last at Haydon's I look[ed] over a Book of Prints taken from the fresco of the Church at Milan the name of which I forget — in it are comprised Specimens of the first and second age of art in Italy. I do not think I ever had a greater treat out of Shakespeare. Full of Romance and the most tender feeling — magnificence of draperies beyond any I ever saw, not excepting Raphael's. But Grotesque to a curious pitch — yet still making up a fine whole — even finer to me than more accomplish'd works — as there was left so much room for Imagination.

There were no engravings of frescoes from a church in Milan, Colvin pointed out; those which Keats saw at Haydon's must have been Lasinio's engravings of frescoes of Orcagna, Benozzo Gozzoli, and the Campo Santo in Pisa — the same engravings which inspired Millais, Holman Hunt, and Rossetti thirty years later.

CHAPTER VII

THE GREAT ODES AND OTHER POEMS

I

The first great creative period of Keats's poetry, containing the two first books of *Hyperion*, *The Eve of St. Agnes*, and *The Eve of St. Mark*, extended from the latter part of October 1818 to the middle of February 1819. The second great creative period, containing the fragment of the third book of *Hyperion*, the sonnet *Bright star! would I were as stedfast as thou art!*, the ballad *La belle dame sans merci*, and the odes *To Psyche*, *To a Nightingale*, *On Melancholy*, *On a Grecian Urn*, and *On Indolence*, extended from the middle of February 1819 to the end of May.

In the first part of the second great creative period, Keats complained in his letters that he was unable to compose poetry. He wrote his brother on February (17?): "I have not gone on with Hyperion, for to tell the truth I have not been in a great cue for writing lately — I must wait for the spring to rouse me up a little." And on March 13 he wrote his brother: "I know not why Poetry and I have been so distant lately —." A day or two after March 19 he composed the sonnet *Why did I laugh tonight?* On April 13 he wrote his sister: "I have written nothing and almost read nothing — but I must turn over a new leaf." And on the same day he wrote Haydon: "I dread as much as a Plague the idle fever of two months more without any fruit." Within a few days, however, he began a great creative period, completing the fragment of the third book of *Hyperion* and composing the sonnet *Bright star!*.

The period from the middle of February to the middle of April was a period of critical activity in which Keats solved the problems of experience which had brought the preceding creative period to an end. His poetry was preeminently a criticism of life. He could not compose a particular poem until he had interpreted the fragment of experience which he expressed in that poem. The problems which obstructed his composition of poetry in February 1819 were mental rather than physical. Tuberculosis, which was attacking him in the form of a sore throat, had not yet sapped his creative vitality, although it caused him to fall at times into a state of physical and mental apathy. He had given up the composition of *Hyperion* because he had lost his belief in the theme of the poem, the idea that the world is evolving toward a goal of beauty and happiness. He had been inspired to begin *The Eve of St. Mark* by his jealousy of Fanny Brawne, but he could not complete the romance because he could not solve the problem of his jealousy.

Other problems which vexed him were the insecurity of his income and the loss of his poetic reputation. Haydon, having exhausted the patience and generosity of his patrons, begged Keats to lend him money; and, when Keats applied to Abbey for money to lend to Haydon, he discovered that the available funds from his inheritance were exhausted and that he could not obtain his share in his brother Tom's estate until his sister Fanny should come of age. Hating the routine of finance, of which he was profoundly ignorant, he was sorely tried by his efforts to satisfy Haydon's insistent demands for money. He wrote Haydon on March 8 that he had been to Abbey's and to the lawyers' about every three days — a worse ordeal to him, he said, than anything in Dante's *Inferno*.

Keats began to discover in this period that the malignant reviewers of *Endymion* had destroyed his poetic reputation and prevented the sale of copies of the poem. He wrote his brother on February 19:

> I have not said in any Letter yet a word about my affairs — in a word I am in no despair about them — my poem has not at all succeeded — in the course of a year or so I think I shall try the public again — in a selfish point of view I should suffer my pride and my contempt of public opinion to hold me silent — but for your's and fanny's sake I will pluck up a spirit and try again. I have no doubt of success in a course of years if I persevere — but it must be patience — for the Reviews have enervated and made indolent mens minds — few think for themselves. These Reviews too are getting more and more powerful, and especially the Quarterly — they are like a superstition which the more it prostrates the Crowd and the longer it continues the more powerful it becomes just in proportion to their increasing weakness. I was in hopes that when people saw, as they must do now, all the trickery and iniquity of these Plagues they would scout them, but no they are like the spectators at the Westminster cock-pit — they like the battle and do not care who wins or who loses.

Keats had endured the personal ridicule in the reviews of *Endymion* with courage and equanimity. He perceived now, however, that the reviews had made readers of poetry either hostile or indifferent to his poems, and his belief in the disinterestedness of human beings was destroyed. He felt rather bitter when he contrasted the failure of his poems with the success of Byron's.

> I was surprised [he wrote his brother] to hear from Taylor the amount of Murray the bookseller's last sale. What think you of £25,000? He sold 4000 copies of Lord Byron.

He believed that the success of Byron's poems was due to their appeal to the egotistic instincts of human beings.

Keats's loss of faith in the disinterested and benevolent qualities of human nature was caused in part by his discovery of selfish, egotistic, and animal traits in Bailey's character. He had learned Wordsworth's humanitarianism from Bailey, we remember, and he had regarded Bailey as the most disinterested of men. He wrote his brother on February 19:

> I have a long story to tell you about Bailey — I will say first the circumstances as plainly and as well as I can remember, and then I will make my comment. You know that Bailey was very much cut up about a little Jilt in the country somewhere. I thought he was in a dying state about it when at Oxford with him: little supposing as I have since heard that he was at that very time making impatient Love to Marian[ne] Reynolds — and guess my astonishment at hearing after this that he had been trying at Miss Martin. So Matters have been. So Matters stood — when he got ordained and went to a Curacy near Carlisle, where the family of the Gleigs reside. There his susceptible heart was conquered by Miss Gleig — and thereby all his connections in town have been annulled — both male and female. I do not now remember clearly the facts. These however I know — He showed his correspondence with Marian[ne] to Gleig — retur[n]ed all her Letters and asked for his own — he also wrote very abrubt [*sic*] Letters to M[rs] Reynolds. I do not know any more of the Martin affair than I have written above. No doubt his conduct has been very bad. The great thing to be considered is — whether it is want of delicacy and principle or want of knowledge and polite experience. And again Weakness — yes that is it — and the want of a Wife — yes that is it — and then Marian[ne] made great Bones of him although her Mother and sister have teased her very much about it. Her conduct has been very upright throughout the whole affair — She liked Bailey as a Brother — but not as a Husband — especially as he used to woo her with the Bible and Jeremy Taylor under his arm — they walked in no grove but Jeremy Taylors. Marian[ne']s obstinacy is some excuse — but his so quickly taking to miss Gleig can have no excuse — except that of a Ploughman who wants a wife. The thing which sways me more against him than any thing else is Rice's conduct on the occasion; Rice would not make an immature resolve: he was ardent in his friendship for Bailey, he examined the whole for and against minutely; and he has abandoned Bailey entirely. All this I am not supposed by the Reynoldses to have any hint of. It will be a good Lesson to the Mother and Daughters — nothing would serve but Bailey. If you mentioned the word Tea pot some one of them came out with an a propos about Bailey — noble fellow — fine fellow! was always in their mouths —

Mrs. Reynolds and her daughters, it is evident, had praised Bailey, the humanitarian young clergyman, much more than they had praised Keats, the sceptical young poet. Keats himself was disappointed in Bailey but he felt some satisfaction in the disappointment of the Reynoldses. He had known that Bailey was uncompromising, that Bailey could not forgive faults in other men, but he had believed that he was disinterested and benevolent. He discovered that Bailey, while professing high abstract ideals of human conduct, sought a wife in the unswerving, instinctive way in which a plowman seeks a mate. Mrs. Reynolds and her daughters, Keats said, erred in judging Bailey, an egotist, and himself, a man of negative capability, in a literal manner.

— this may teach them [he said] that the man who redicules[*sic*] romance is the most romantic of Men — that he who abuses women and slights them loves them the most — that he who talks of roasting a Man alive would not do it when it came to the push — and above all, that they are very shallow people who take every thing literally. A Man's life of any worth is a continual allegory, and very few eyes can see the Mystery of his life — a life like the scriptures, figurative — which such people can no more make out than they can the hebrew Bible. Lord Byron cuts a figure — but he is not figurative — Shakespeare led a life of Allegory: his works are the comments on it.

Keats's comments upon Bailey's conduct show the strong ethical bias of his mind. They show also the inductive, associative, and generalizing qualities of his speculation. In the final stage of his thought he chose Byron, instead of Bailey, as an illustration of the egotistic man, and Shakespeare, instead of himself, as an illustration of the negatively capable man. The egotist has a single mind which is the servant of his instinctive impulses. The negatively capable man, on the other hand, has a double mind, so to speak, one which ministers to his instinctive impulses and another which freely intuits the world. The egotistic poet expresses his own feelings and thoughts. The negatively capable poet enters into and expresses the feelings and thoughts of other men. Shakespeare, having this imaginative insight into life, lived an imaginative, figurative life, a life of allegory. Byron, being an egotist, lived a life which was striking; but, since he lacked imaginative insight, his life was without meaning and significance. He cut a figure but he was not figurative.

The vital changes which were occurring in Keats's conception of life and poetry are revealed in the letter which he wrote to Haydon on March 8. His first words reflect a passage in the letter which Milton wrote Charles Diodati on September 23, 1637. Like Milton, he was meditating instead of composing, but, unlike Milton, he was not meditating upon an immortality of fame. He could not compose poetry. He was beginning to perceive the evil in nature, the egotism in human beings, and the futility of human ambition and endeavor.

You must be wondering where I am [he said] and what I am about! I am mostly at Hampstead, and about nothing; being in a sort of qui bono temper, not exactly on the road to an epic poem.

Painful experience was making Keats very sceptical. He believed that men are governed by egotistic instead of by disinterested impulses and that they strive to exalt themselves rather than to discover truth.

> What a set of little people we live amongst! [he exclaimed]. I went the other day into an ironmonger's shop — without any change in my sensations — men and tin kettles are much the same in these days — they do not study like children at five and thirty — but they talk like men of twenty. Conversation is not a search after knowledge, but an endeavour at effect.
>
> In this respect two most opposite men, Wordsworth and Hunt, are the same. A friend of mine observed the other day that if Lord Bacon were to make any remark in a party of the present day, the conversation would stop on the sudden.

Keats had already lost his humanitarian benevolence, his love of humanity. He was now losing his humanistic magnanimity, his love of fame. He was discovering, however, the joy of self-expression. Men are not interested, he believed, in poetry which expresses truth. They are interested only in poetry which flatters their self-esteem.

> I am convinced of this [he said], and from this I have come to this resolution — never to write for the sake of writing or making a poem, but from running over with any little knowledge or experience which many years of reflection may perhaps give me; otherwise I will be dumb. What imagination I have I shall enjoy, and greatly, for I have experienced the satisfaction of having great conceptions without the trouble of sonnetteering. I will not spoil my love of gloom by writing an Ode to Darkness!

Keats was thinking of going to Edinburgh and studying medicine. He was resolved that he would not make his living by writing the kind of poetry which would please the public.

> With respect to my livelihood [he said], I will not write for it, — for I will not run with that most vulgar of all crowds, the literary. Such things I ratify by looking upon myself, and trying myself at lifting mental weights, as it were. I am three and twenty, with little knowledge and middling intellect. It is true that in the height of enthusiasm I have been cheated into some fine passages; but that is not the thing.

Keats longed to escape the fever in which he intuited truth and expressed it in his poems. He admitted that in moments of feverish inspiration he had expressed beautiful intuitions of truth; "but that," he said, "is not the thing." He longed to see life more calmly, to apprehend truth more steadily, and to express it more completely. "To bear all naked truths," he had said in *Hyperion*, "And to envisage circumstance, all calm, That is the top of sovereignty." "I see by little and little," he had written Haydon in January, "more of what is to be done, and how it is to be done, should I ever be able to do it."

In the third week of March 1819 occurred the crisis in which Keats saw the naked truths of life intensely and completely. He received this knowledge in an agony of spirit, but immediately thereafter he began to develop an empirical humanism and to attain unto a calm and temperate acceptance of these painful truths. The stages of this crisis are revealed clearly in the journal letter which he was writing to his brother.

On March 18 Keats played a game of cricket and was struck in the eye by a ball. This accident, he wrote his brother on March 19, cast him into a state of physical debility and mental apathy.

> This morning I am in a sort of temper indolent and supremely careless: I long after a stanza or two of Thompson's [*sic*] Castle of indolence. My passions are all alseep [*sic*] from my having slumbered till nearly eleven and weakened the animal fibre all over me to a delightful sensation about three degrees on this side of faintness — if I had teeth of pearl and the breath of lillies I should call it langour [*sic*] — but as I am (Especially as I have a black eye) I must call it laziness. In this state of effeminacy the fibres of the brain are relaxed in common with the rest of the body, and to such a happy degree that pleasure has no show of enticement and pain no unbearable frown. Neither Poetry, nor Ambition, nor Love have any alertness of countenance as they pass by me: they seem rather like three figures on a greek vase — a Man and two women whom no one but myself could distinguish in their disguisement. This is the only happiness, and is a rare instance of advantage in the body overpowering the Mind.

In this passage we find almost the whole substance of the *Ode on Indolence* which Keats composed in the latter part of May, two months later. Tortured by the three chief problems of his experience — love, ambition, and poetry — he welcomed that state of physical debility and mental apathy in which he was unable to feel the pain which these problems had inflicted on him.

A day or two later, after he had recovered from this apathy, Keats sank again into the depths of despair. He was in a state of "aching ignorance" in which he strove to find an answer to the problems of poetry, ambition, and love. He found the answer, and he laughed in irony, and he expressed the answer in a sonnet. The answer to his personal problems depended upon his solution of the fundamental and universal problem of evil in nature. He wrote his brother a summary of his solution of the problem of evil, and then he introduced the sonnet as follows:

> I am ever affraid [*sic*] that your anxiety for me will lead you to fear for the violence of my temperament continually smothered down: for that reason I did not intend to have sent you the following sonnet — but look over the two last pages and ask yourselves whether I have not that in me which will well

bear the buffets of the world. It will be the best comment on my sonnet; it will show you that *it was written with no Agony but that of ignorance; with no thirst of anything but Knowledge* when pushed to the point though the first steps to it were through my human passions — they went away, and I wrote with my Mind — and perhaps I must confess a little bit of my heart —

Why did I laugh tonight? No voice will tell:
  No God, no Deamon [*sic*] of severe response
Deigns to reply from heaven or from Hell. —
  Then to my human heart I turn at once —
Heart! thou and I are here sad and alone;
  Say, wherefore did I laugh? O mortal pain!
O Darkness! Darkness! ever must I moan
  To question Heaven and Hell and Heart in vain!
Why did I laugh? I know this being's lease
  My fancy to its utmost blisses spreads:
Yet could I on this very midnight cease
  And the world's gaudy ensigns see in shreds.
Verse, fame and Beauty are intense indeed
But Death intenser — Death is Life's high meed.

I went to bed, and enjoyed an uninterrupted Sleep. Sane I went to bed and sane I arose.

The sonnet, with the exception of the last four verses, is crude and amorphous. Keats composed it before his imagination had completely intuited the thought which inspired it, and he never revised it, for he expressed the thought in more perfect form in later poems. It was one of the poems to which he alluded in the sixth stanza of the *Ode to a Nightingale.* He reworked the eleventh verse of the sonnet, indeed, into the sixth verse of the stanza.

The sonnet represents the point at which Keats turned from a feverish rebellion against painful experience to a calm acceptance. The change occurrred in the middle of the poem. The octave expresses aching ignorance and the sestet a new and stoical wisdom. Death, Keats perceived, was the only solution to his problems of poetry, ambition, and love.

Let us consider now Keats's explanation of the problem of evil in nature, upon which the answer in the sonnet depended. His speculations on the problem of evil occur in the journal letter to his brother immediately after his account of the state of apathy into which he was cast by the injury to his eye from the cricket ball. The account of this state of apathy is dated March 19. There is no division in the letter between these two passages, but there was evidently an interval of time (perhaps of one or two days) between them.[1] His mind was no longer apathetic; it was active and energetic.

[1] See footnote on next page which proves there was an interval of "a few days" between the two passages.

I have this moment[2] [he said] received a note from Haslam in which he expects the death of his Father, who has been for some time in a state of insensibility — his mother bears up he says very well — I shall go to town to-morrow to see him. This is the world — thus we cannot expect to give way many hours to pleasure. Circumstances are like Clouds continually gathering and bursting. While we are laughing, the seed of some trouble is put into the wide arable land of events — while we are laughing it sprouts it grows and suddenly bears a poison fruit which we must pluck. Even so we have leisure to reason on the misfortunes of our friends; our own touch us too nearly for words.

Keats considered the problem of evil from the two opposing principles of human nature — the principle of egotism and the principle of disinterestedness. "It is an old maxim of mine," he had written Bailey in March 1818, " . . . that every point of thought is the centre of an intellectual world — the two uppermost thoughts in a Man's mind are the two poles of his World[;] he revolves on them and every thing is southward or northward to him through their means."

Very few men [he wrote his brother] have ever arrived at a complete disinterestedness of Mind: very few have been influenced by a pure desire of the benefit of others — in the greater part of the Benefactors to Humanity some meretricious motive has sullied their greatness — some melodramatic scenery has fa[s]cinated them. From the manner in which I feel Haslam's misfortune I perceive how far I am from any humble standard of disinterestedness. Yet this feeling ought to be carried to its highest pitch, as there is no fear of its ever injuring Society — which it would do I fear pushed to an extremity. For in wild nature the Hawk would loose his Breakfast of Robins and the Robin his of worms — the Lion must starve as well as the swallow.

Keats's mind had grown in knowledge and in wisdom. He had considered the problem of evil in nature in March 1818, exactly one year before; and in the *Epistle to Reynolds* he had described his imaginative intuition of the "eternal fierce destruction" which is the law of nature —

The Shark at savage prey — the hawk at pounce,
The gentle Robin, like a pard or ounce,
Ravening a worm. . . .

He had been unable to solve the problem of evil in nature and he had exclaimed in despair:

Oh never will the prize,
High reason, and the lore of good and ill
Be my award.

And in April 1818 he had distrusted his imagination, shut out his intuitions of evil, and accepted blindly Wordsworth's humanitarian optimism.

[2] On April 15 he wrote in this journal letter: "A few days after the 19th of April [for March] I received a note from Haslam containing the news of his father's death."

Now, in March 1819, he saw much farther into the problem of evil in nature. He saw that evil is not only present in nature but that, nature being as it is, evil is also inherent and necessary in it. If the hawk were a disinterested instead of an egotistic creature, he said, it would lose its breakfast of robins. Natural creatures live by destroying one another and find their good in doing evil to one another. He was learning the lore of good and ill and he was bearing naked truths with calm and stoical fortitude.

Keats perceived that the principle of egotism, the principle of evil, is as inherent in human beings as in the lower forms of nature.

> The greater part of Men [he said] make their way with the same instinctiveness, the same unwandering eye from their purposes, the same animal eagerness as the Hawk. The Hawk wants a Mate, so does the Man — look at them both [,] they set about it and procure on[e] in the same manner. They want both a nest and they both set about one in the same manner — they get their food in the same manner. The noble animal Man for his amusement smokes his pipe — the Hawk balances about the Clouds — that is the only difference of their leisures. This it is that makes the Amusement of Life — to a speculative Mind. I go among the Fields and catch a glimpse of a Stoat or a fieldmouse peeping out of the withered grass — the creature hath a purpose and its eyes are bright with it. I go amongst the buildings of a city and I see a Man hurrying along — to what? the Creature has a purpose and his eyes are bright with it.

Keats's conception of human nature, however, was not pessimistic. He believed that there is a principle of disinterestedness as well as a principle of egotism in human beings. Most men, he said, are more egotistic than disinterested but all men have impulses towards good and some few men approach the ideal of complete disinterestedness.

> But then [he continued], as Wordsworth says, "we have all one human heart"— there is an electric fire in human nature tending to purify — so that among these human creature[s] there is continually some birth of new heroism. The pity is that we must wonder at it: as we should at finding a pearl in rubbish. I have no doubt that thousands of people never heard of have had hearts completely disinterested: I can remember but two — Socrates and Jesus — their Histories evince it. What I heard a little time ago, Taylor observe with respect to Socrates, may be said of Jesus — That he was so great a man that though he transmitted no writing of his own to posterity, we have his Mind and his sayings and his greatness handed to us by others. It is to be lamented that the history of the latter was written and revised by Men interested in the pious frauds of Religion. Yet through all this I see his splendour.

Being a poet of negative capability like Shakespeare, Keats had a double mind, one part of which served the instinctive impulses of his ego, while the other part intuited the instinctive and evil nature of the world and speculated about it. "This it is," he said, "that makes the Amusement of Life — to a speculative Mind." In speculating about the principle of egotism, the principle of evil, in nature, he was, he knew, outside and above nature. At the same time, he was, he knew equally well, a part of the egotistic order of nature.

> Even here [he said] though I myself am pursuing the same instinctive course as the veriest human animal you can think of — I am however young writing at random — straining at particles of light in the midst of a great darkness — without knowing the bearing of any one assertion[,] of any one opinion. Yet may I not in this be free from sin? May there not be superior beings amused with any graceful, though instinctive attitude my mind may fall into, as I am entertained with the alertness of a Stoat or the anxiety of a Deer? Though a quarrel in the Streets is a thing to be hated, the energies displayed in it are fine; the commonest Man shows a grace in his quarrel. By a superior being our reasoning[s] may take the same tone — though erroneous they may be fine. This is the very thing in which consists poetry, and if so it is not so fine a thing as philosophy — For the same reason that an eagle is not so fine a thing as a truth.

Keats explained in this passage the new wisdom which enabled him to bear with calm stoicism the naked and painful truths which he perceived in nature. This new wisdom, which I call empirical humanism, was an empirical development of his humanistic philosophy of negative capability. In the letter which he wrote Woodhouse on October 27, 1818, we remember, he said that "The Sun, the Moon, the Sea and Men and Women who are creatures of impulse are poetical and have about them an unchangeable attribute" but that the poet (the negatively capable poet), who can escape from the control of his instinctive impulses, who has no identity, no personality, who "is continually in for and filling some other Body," is the most unpoetical of all creatures.

Now, in March 1819, Keats perceived that evil is inherent and necessary in nature and that the evil which natural creatures, including human beings, inflict upon one another is inspired by their instinctive and egotistic impulses. He perceived also, as he had perceived in October 1818, that natural phenomena and natural creatures, who are governed by instinctive impulses, are beautiful and poetical. He saw beauty in that which is instinctive; and, since the instinctive includes the egotistic and the disinterested, he saw beauty in the egotistic as well as in the disinterested. He could not only bear the naked truths of life with calm fortitude, although he was suffering from them, but he could also see beauty in them.

This general conclusion of his argument is clear. Another conclusion, however, which is based on a false assumption, obscures Keats's real meaning. He assumed, for the purpose of illustrating his general conclusion, that his own reasonings on the instinctive impulses of a stoat might seem as instinctive and therefore as beautiful to a superior being as the impulses of a stoat seemed to him. "This [the instinctive impulses of a stoat and his own reasonings] is the very thing in which consists poetry," he said, "and if so it is not so fine a thing as philosophy — For the same reason that an eagle is not so fine a thing as a truth." He knew that the impulses of a stoat are instinctive but he did not believe that his own reasonings were instinctive. He did not really mean, therefore, that poetry is not so fine a thing as philosophy.

We can approach his real meaning from another angle of his thought in this period. The contrast which he drew again and again in this period is not a contrast between instinctive poetry and pure, or abstract, philosophy but a contrast between instinctive or egotistic poetry and negatively capable poetry. The egotistic poet, such as Byron, expresses his own instinctive impulses and his own feelings and thoughts. The negatively capable poet, such as Shakespeare, enters into the instincts of birds and animals and the minds of men and expresses their instinctive impulses and their feelings and thoughts. He made this distinction, we remember, in the letter which he wrote his brother on February 19:

> A Man's life of any worth is a continual allegory, and very few eyes can see the Mystery of his life — a life like the scriptures, figurative — which such people can no more make out than they can the hebrew Bible. Lord Byron cuts a figure — but he is not figurative — Shakespeare led a life of Allegory: his works are the comments on it.

Negatively capable poetry became, in Keats's thought, negatively capable philosophy. The negatively capable poet or philosopher does exactly what Keats did in this letter which he wrote his brother in the third week of March 1819. He escapes from the instinctive plane of nature and apprehends the naked truths of nature and speculates about them in perfect freedom. This type of poetry or philosophy, Keats believed, is musical, imaginative, and figurative, or symbolic.

> Give me this credit [he wrote his brother] — Do you not think I strive — to know myself? Give me this credit, and you will not think that on my own accou[n]t I repeat Milton's lines —
>
> "How charming is divine Philosophy
> Not harsh and crabbed as dull fools suppose
> But musical as is Apollo's lute"—
>
> No — no[t] for myself — feeling grateful as I do to have got into a state of mind to relish them properly. Nothing ever becomes real till it is experienced — Even a Proverb is no proverb to you, till your Life has illustrated it.

He believed truly that he was becoming a philosophical poet. "I hope I am a little more of a Philosopher than I was," he wrote Miss Jeffrey three months later, "consequently a little less of a versifying Pet-lamb."

There is a gap of three and a half weeks, from a day or two after March 19 to April 15, in the journal letter which Keats was writing to his brother. He had thought himself out of despair into a stoical acceptance of life; but he had not begun to express his experience in poetic form. "I am still at a stand in versifying," he wrote his brother on April 15, "— I cannot do it yet with any pleasure—."

Keats's resumption of poetic composition was preceded appropriately enough by a meeting with Coleridge on Sunday, April 11. He had been influenced by Coleridge's poems in 1814, at the beginning of his poetic career. He read Coleridge's *Sibylline Leaves* in November 1817 and echoed a magical passage from *Kubla Khan* in the Song of the Indian Maid in the fourth book of *Endymion*. He was like Coleridge in sensuous and imaginative faculties: in his keen organic sensibility to natural beauty and in his imaginative intuition of the magical charm of nature. He was unlike Coleridge, however, in other mental faculties. He believed that his own mind, like Shakespeare's, was negatively capable and that Coleridge's mind was egotistic. The negatively capable mind, he said, was satisfied with the isolated particles of truth which its imagination apprehended, but the egotistic mind strove to fit imaginative intuitions of truth into a rational system. Coleridge, he said, "would let go by a fine isolated verisimilitude caught from the Penetralium of mystery, from being incapable of remaining content with half-knowledge." When he met Coleridge on Sunday, April 11, he was somewhat offended by Coleridge's interminable and, as he thought, egotistic monologue. His own ideal of conversation was an exchange of ideas between men who were striving to discover truth instead of to proclaim it *ex cathedra*. His reaction to Coleridge was influenced, also, by political prejudice; for, like Hazlitt, he believed that Coleridge, together with Wordsworth and Southey, had betrayed the liberal cause. He described his meeting with Coleridge in the section of the journal letter which he wrote to his brother on April 15.

Last Sunday I took a Walk towards highgate and in the lane that winds by the side of Lord Mansfield's park I met Mr Green our Demonstrator at Guy's in conversation with Coleridge — I joined them, after enquiring by a look whether it would be agreeable — I walked with him a[t] his alderman-after-dinner pace for near two miles I suppose. In those two Miles he broached a thousand things — let me see if I can give you a list — Nightingales, Poetry — on Poetical Sensation — Metaphysics — Different genera and species of Dreams — Nightmare — a dream accompanied by a sense of touch — single and double touch — A dream related — First and second consciousness — the difference explained between will and Volition — so m[an]y metaphysicians from a want of smoking the second consciousness — Monsters — the Kraken — Mermaids — Southey believes in them — Southey's belief too much diluted — A Ghost story — Good morning — I heard his voice as he came towards me — I heard it as he moved away — I had heard it all the interval — if it may be called so. He was civil enough to ask me to call on him at Highgate[.]

Coleridge wrote an account of his meeting with Keats in his *Table Talk* on August 14, 1832, thirteen years afterwards.

A loose, slack, not well-dressed youth met Mr. —— and myself in a lane near Highgate. —— knew him, and spoke. It was Keats. He was introduced to me, and stayed a minute or so. After he had left us a little way, he came back and said: "Let me carry away the memory, Coleridge, of having pressed your hand!" — "There is death in that hand," I said to ——, when Keats was gone; yet this was, I believe, before the consumption showed itself distinctly.

Coleridge related a somewhat more accurate account of this meeting, as Miss Lowell [3] pointed out, in a conversation with John Frere. Miss E. M. Green discovered Frere's memorandum of this conversation and published it in *The Cornhill Magazine* for April 1917. Coleridge did not retain — he probably did not receive — a vivid impression of Keats's personality; and he forgot that Keats walked two miles with him, listening to his monologue. His most vivid recollection of the meeting was his prediction of Keats's death. Like Wordsworth, he never appreciated Keats's poetry. He admitted to Frere in 1830, nine years after Keats's death, that he had read only three of Keats's poems — two sonnets and a poem with a classical name which he did not remember.

F. You have not read much of Keats, Sir, I think?

C. No, I have not. I have seen two Sonnets which I think showed marks of a great genius had he lived. I have also read a poem with a classical name — I forget what. Poor Keats, I saw him once. Mr. Green, whom you have heard me mention, and I were walking out in these parts, and we were overtaken by a young man of a very striking countenance whom Mr. Green recognised and shook hands with, mentioning my name; I wish Mr. Green had introduced me, for I did not know who it was. He passed on, but in a few moments sprung back and said, "Mr. Coleridge, allow me the honour of shaking your hand."

I was struck by the energy of his manner, and gave him my hand.

He passed on and we stood still looking after him, when Mr. Green said, "Do you know who that is? That is Keats, the poet."

---

[3] Amy Lowell, Vol. II, pp. 210–212.

"Heavens!" said I, "when I shook him by the hand there was death!" This was about two years before he died.

F. But what was it?

C. I cannot describe it. There was a heat and a dampness in the hand. To say that his death was caused by the Review is absurd, but at the same time it is impossible adequately to conceive the effect which it must have had on his mind.

It is very well for those who have a place in the world and are independent to talk of these things, they can bear such a blow, so can those who have a strong religious principle; but all men are not born Philosophers, and all men have not those advantages of birth and education.

Poor Keats had not, and it is impossible I say to conceive the effect which such a Review must have had upon him, knowing as he did that he had his way to make in the world by his own exertions, and conscious of the genius within him.

It is remarkable that Coleridge, who had reacted against the revolutionary principles of his youth, who had become a supporter of the Tory government and established religion, and who had been censured and ridiculed by liberal critics such as Hazlitt, should deplore the malignant review of Keats's *Endymion* in *The Quarterly Review*, a Tory periodical. His sympathetic toleration of the radical principles of Keats and Shelley would not have been appreciated, however, by these young rebels. He regarded their radicalism as a youthful phase through which he had passed and through which he believed he could have helped them to pass.

Poor Shelley [he told Frere], it is a pity I often think that I never met with him. I could have done him good. He went to Keswick on purpose to see me and unfortunately fell in with Southey instead. There could have been nothing so unfortunate. Southey had no understanding for a toleration of such principles as Shelley's.

I should have laughed at his Atheism. I could have sympathised with him and shown him that I did so, and he would have felt that I did so. I could have shown him that I had once been in the same state myself, and I could have guided him through it. I have often bitterly regretted in my heart of hearts that I did never meet with Shelley.

Keats was much more deeply impressed by Coleridge's conversation than he was willing to admit. The influence of Coleridge's monologue, together with the influence of his poems, is evident and significant in the poems which Keats composed in April and May 1819 — especially in the second ode *To* [*Fanny*], the ballad *La belle dame sans merci*, the *Ode to a Nightingale*, and the sonnet *The House of Mourning*.

Keats resumed poetic composition on April 15, after an interval of two months of intense and searching thought, by composing into the journal letter to his brother an incomplete set of heroic couplets of no particular importance about a princess who visited a Faery's Court with her Ape, her Dwarf, and her Fool. And on April 16 he composed a humorous character sketch of Brown in three Spenserian stanzas.

> Brown this morning [he said] is writing some spenserian stanzas against M^{rs}[,] Miss Brawne and me; so I shall amuse myself with him a little: in the manner of Spenser —

The humor of the sketch consists in the fact that each descriptive statement means the opposite of what it says. Keats was revolted by the discovery of sensual impulses in Bailey, who was a self-righteous moralist; but he regarded Brown's frankly lustful temperament with amused tolerance. Beset by men of character like Bailey, Taylor, and Woodhouse, he was strongly attracted by Brown, who was an unaffected, humorous, full-blooded fellow.

On April 17 Keats composed some doggerel verses, *Two or three Posies*, for his sister. And sometime after the middle of April he completed the fragment of the third book of *Hyperion* and gave the manuscript of the whole poem to Woodhouse, who copied it on April 20.

Love was the first problem to test Keats's stoical acceptance of life. On April 3 Dilke moved to Westminster and leased his half of Wentworth Place to Mrs. Brawne. And for nearly three months, from the early part of April to the end of June, Keats and Fanny Brawne lived in adjoining houses which were under the same roof and in the same garden. He expressed the gamut of emotions which this daily intimacy with Miss Brawne aroused in him in the poems which he composed in the latter half of April and in the letters which he wrote her in July and August, after he had left Wentworth Place. This daily intimacy stirred him above all into an ecstatic intensity of passion, giving him on the whole more pleasure than pain.

> I never knew before [he wrote Miss Brawne on July 8], what such a love as you have made me feel, was; I did not believe in it; my Fancy was afraid of it, lest it should burn me up. But if you will fully love me, though there may be some fire, 'twill not be more than we can bear when moistened and bedewed with Pleasures.

He was not in a position to marry Miss Brawne, however, and the continuous suppression of the strong physical desire which daily association with her aroused in him gave him pain. He had a feeling of relief, therefore, when he left Wentworth Place at the beginning of July. He wrote her from Shanklin on August 5:

> I shall keep it [his promise to see her in a short time] with as much sorrow as gladness: for I am not one of the Paladins of old who liv'd upon water grass and smiles for years together. What though would I not give to-night for the gratification of my eyes alone?

Sometime shortly after the middle of April 1819, Keats composed a sonnet in which he expressed a dream-consummation of his love for Miss Brawne. He composed it on a page at the end of the first volume of his copy of Cary's *Dante*, the copy which he had carried with him on his Scottish excursion; and, on April 16 or a day or two thereafter, he copied it into his journal letter to his brother. He introduced it as follows:

> The fifth canto of Dante please me more and more — it is that one in which he meets with Paulo and Franc~~h~~esca [*sic*]. I had passed many days in rather a low state of mind, and in the midst of them I dreamt of being in that region of Hell. The dream was one of the most delightful enjoyments I ever had in my life. I floated about the whirling atmosphere as it is described with a beautiful figure to whose lips mine were joined, at [as] it seemed for an age — and in the midst of all this cold and darkness I was warm — even flowery tree tops sprung up and we rested on them sometimes with the lightness of a cloud, till the wind blew us away again. I tried a Sonnet upon it — there are fourteen lines but nothing of what I felt in it — O that I could dream it every night —
>
> As Hermes once took to his feathers light
> When lulled Argus, baffled, swoon'd and slept
> So on a delphic reed my idle spright
> So play'd, so charm'd[,] so conquer'd, so bereft
> The dragon world of all its hundred eyes
> And seeing it asleep so fled away: —
> Not to pure Ida with its snow ~~clad~~ cold skies,
> Nor unto Tempe where Jove grieved that day,
> But to that second circle of sad hell,
> Where in the gust, the whirlwind and the flaw
> Of Rain and hailstones lovers need not tell
> Their sorrows. Pale were the sweet lips I saw
> Pale were the lips I kiss'd and fair the form
> I floated with about that melancholy storm.

The copy of Cary's *Dante*, containing the original autograph of the sonnet, was possessed by the late H. B. Forman but I do not know who owns it now. Forman[4] described the original draft, however, which is almost identical with that which Keats copied into the journal letter to his brother. The journal letter is in the Marquess of Crewe's Collection. There are transcripts with slight variations in Dilke's copy of *Endymion* and in Woodhouse's Commonplace Book, Scrap-book, and Book of Transcripts. Woodhouse dated the sonnet

[4] H. B. Forman, Variorum Edition, Vol. III, p. 17.

"April 1819." It was published by Hunt in *The Indicator* for June 28, 1820.

Keats had some difficulty in composing the sonnet, for in the original draft there are three rejected beginnings. And he did not succeed, as he admitted, in expressing the sensuous beauty of his nympholeptic dream. The classical comparisons of the octave, which have no vital relation to the dream, produce an effect of cold intellectual ingenuity. The images of the sestet, however, give a vivid impression of warm, imaginative passion in a cold, windy, murky setting, reminding us of similarly contrasting effects in *The Eve of St. Agnes*.

In this period Keats felt himself to be an unstable atom in a world of instability. He was intensely conscious of the inseparable relationship of beauty and decay, joy and sorrow, life and death. Considering happiness to be mutable and transient, he longed to enjoy love in its richest bloom and to die.

> For myself [he wrote Miss Brawne on July 1, 1819] I know not how to express my devotion to so fair a form: I want a brighter word than bright, a fairer word than fair. I almost wish we were butterflies and liv'd but three summer days — three such days with you I could fill with more delight than fifty common years could ever contain.

And again on July 25 he wrote her:

> I have two luxuries to brood over in my walks, your Loveliness and the hour of my death. O that I could have possession of them both in the same minute. I hate the world: it batters too much the wings of my self-will, and would I could take a sweet poison from your lips to send me out of it. . . . I am distracted with a thousand thoughts. I will imagine you Venus to-night and pray, pray, pray to your star like a He[a]then.
>
> Your's ever, fair Star,
>
> John Keats

In these letters Keats repeated the sentiment and to some extent the phraseology of the sonnet *Bright Star!* the first great poem which he composed in April 1819. I quote the original version,[5] which is preserved in Brown's transcript in the Marquess of Crewe's Collection.

> Bright star! would I were stedfast as thou art!
> Not in lone splendour hung amid the night;
> Not watching, with eternal lids apart,
> Like Nature's devout sleepless Eremite,
> The morning waters at their priestlike task
> Of pure ablution round earth's human shores;
> Or, gazing on the new soft fallen mask
> Of snow upon the mountains and the moors: —

[5] This version is quoted by Sir Sidney Colvin, p. 493.

No; — yet still steadfast, still unchangeable,
  Cheek-pillow'd on my Love's white ripening breast,
To touch, for ever, its warm sink and swell,
  Awake, for ever, in a sweet unrest;
To hear, to feel her tender-taken breath,
  Half passionless, and so swoon on to death.

The position of this beautiful sonnet in the evolution of Keats's poetry has been established gradually by scholars. Colvin discovered and printed Brown's transcript of the original version, which is dated "1819." R. L. Rusk [6] discovered that Keats had used the image of the North Star as a symbol of steadfastness in the journal letter which he wrote his brother Tom on June 25, 26, and 27, 1818, the first three days of his excursion into Wordsworth's lake country.

The two views we have had of it [Windermere] are of the most noble tenderness — they can never fade away — they make one forget the divisions of life; age, youth, poverty and riches; and refine one's sensual vision into a sort of north star which can never cease to be open lidded and stedfast over the wonders of the great Power.

Miss Lowell [7] discovered that in the middle of April 1819 Keats went to his former lodgings in Well Walk and looked over the letters which he had left there.

I have been to Mrs Bentley's this morning [he wrote his brother on April 15] and put all the Letters two [*sic*] and from you and poor Tom and me [in order]. I found some of the correspondence between him and that degraded Wells and Amena. . . . I found also this morning in a note from George to you my dear sister a lock of your hair which I shall this moment put in the miniature case. . . .

When Keats looked over these letters, Miss Lowell suggested, he read the journal letter which he had written his brother Tom from Windermere. His imagination, excited by the image of the North Star as a symbol of steadfastness, crystallized those sentiments which were floating in solution in his mind — in particular, that longing for steadfastness as well as intensity in love. He composed the sonnet, we may conjecture, within a few days after the middle of April.

This sonnet is an interesting example of the processes of poetic composition. Keats expressed the emotions of his present experience by means of images of his past experience. He recalled his past experience by reading a letter which he had written instead of by unconscious association. He enlarged and enriched the experience of gazing at the waters of Windermere with a vision as open lidded and

[6] R. L. Rusk, *North American Review* for March 1924.

[7] Amy Lowell, Vol. II, pp. 202–203.

as steadfast as that of the North Star by metamorphosing the North Star into nature's devout sleepless eremite watching with eternal lids apart and by metamorphosing the waters of Windermere into the universal waters of the ocean performing their priestlike task of pure ablution around earth's human shores. He drew the image of the mountains and the moors from his experience in Scotland, to which he went from the lake country; and he added the image of the *mask* of snow to have a word to rhyme with *task*.

Keats copied the final version of the sonnet about the end of September 1820, while he was on his voyage to Italy. The ship was becalmed off the Dorset coast and Keats and Severn went ashore. When they returned to the ship Keats transcribed the sonnet in a copy of Shakespeare's *Poems* which Reynolds had given him, on a blank page opposite the *Lover's Complaint*. He gave this volume, which is now in the Dilke Collection, to Severn in memory of the voyage. Some of the changes which he made in the sonnet, such as "morning waters" into "moving waters" and "devout sleepless eremite" into "patient sleepless eremite," improve the imagery and the rhythm. The change of "cheek-pillow'd" into "pillow'd," however, removes a striking compound; and the revision of the final couplet into

> Still, still to hear her tender-taken breath,
> And so live ever — or else swoon to death

alters the meaning of the sonnet, making death an alternative instead of a fulfillment.

Keats and Miss Brawne, as Miss Lowell pointed out, had a particular and a secret sentiment for the sonnets on the dream and on the bright star. He gave her the copy of Cary's *Dante*, into the first volume of which he had composed the sonnet on the dream; and she copied the sonnet on the bright star into the same volume.

Keats expressed another emotional phase of his love for Fanny Brawne in the second ode *To* [*Fanny*] and in the ballad *La belle dame sans merci*, which he composed into the journal letter to his brother on Wednesday evening, April 28, 1819. He was intensely amorous; he was, at the same time, intensely distrustful and jealous. There was a continuous struggle in his mind between sex-passion and sex-antagonism. In his rebellious moments he regarded love as a possessive, enslaving, destructive passion. It restrained his personal liberty, he felt, it separated him from his friends, it distracted him from his poetry. We must observe, however, that love spurred him as well as checked him in the composition of poetry. It inspired him (in some cases pleasantly, in other cases painfully) in the composition of some of his greatest poems — *The Eve of St. Agnes, The Eve of St. Mark, Bright star!* and *La belle dame sans merci.* He composed his great odes also in the period of his daily association with Miss Brawne.

Keats felt this rebellion against love most strongly in the spring and summer of 1819. On July 1, a few days after he had left Hampstead, he wrote Miss Brawne:

> I have never known any unalloy'd Happiness for many days together: the death or sickness of some one has always spoilt my hours — and now when none such troubles oppress me, it is you must confess very hard that another sort of pain should haunt me. Ask yourself my love whether you are not very cruel to have so entrammelled me, so destroyed my freedom.

And he wrote her again on July 25:

> You absorb me in spite of myself — you alone: for I look not forward with any pleasure to what is call'd being settled in the world; I tremble at domestic cares — yet for you I would meet them, though if it would leave you the happier I would rather die than do so. . . . I am indeed astonish'd to find myself so careless of all cha[r]ms but yours — rememb[e]ring as I do the time when even a bit of ribband was a matter of interest with me.

The second ode *To [Fanny]* is the first poem in which Keats expressed his rebellion against the trammels of love.

To — — — —

What can I do to drive away
Remembrance from my eyes? for they have seen,
Aye, an hour ago, my brilliant Queen!
Touch has a memory. O say, love, say,
What can I do to kill it and be free
In my old liberty?
When every fair one that I saw was fair
Enough to catch me in but half a snare,
Not keep me there:
When, howe'er poor or particolour'd things,
My muse had wings,
And ever ready was to take her course
Whither I bent her force,
Unintellectual, yet divine to me; —
Divine, I say! — What sea-bird o'er the sea
Is a philosopher the while he goes
Winging along where the great water throes?
How shall I do
To get anew
Those moulted feathers, and so mount once more
Above, above
The reach of fluttering Love,
And make him cower lowly while I soar?

Shall I gulp wine? No, that is vulgarism,
A heresy and schism,
Foisted into the canon-law of love; —
No, — wine is only sweet to happy men;
More dismal cares
Seize on me unawares, —
Where shall I learn to get my peace again?
To banish thoughts of that most hateful land,
Dungeoner of my friends, that wicked strand
Where they were wreck'd and live a wrecked life;
That monstrous region, whose dull rivers pour,
Ever from their sordid urns unto the shore,
Unown'd of any weedy-haired gods;
Whose winds, all zephyrless, hold scourging rods,
Iced in the great lakes, to afflict mankind;
Whose rank-grown forests, frosted, black, and blind,
Would fright a Dryad; whose harsh herbaged meads
Make lean and lank the starv'd ox while he feeds;
There bad flowers have no scent, birds no sweet song,
And great unerring Nature once seems wrong.

O, for some sunny spell
To dissipate the shadows of this hell!
Say they are gone, — with the new dawning light
Steps forth my lady bright!
O, let me once more rest
My soul upon that dazzling breast!
Let once again these aching arms be placed,
The tender gaolers of thy waist!
And let me feel that warm breath here and there
To spread a rapture in my very hair, —
O, the sweetness of the pain!
Give me those lips again!
Enough! Enough! it is enough for me
To dream of thee!

Keats's description of that "hateful land" of love, that "wicked strand," upon which his friends were "wreck'd and live a wrecked life" and on which "birds [have] no sweet song," was suggested, I believe, by Spenser's description of the Rock of Vile Reproach, the rock of sensual pleasures (*Faerie Queene*, II. xii. 7 and 8):

On whose sharp cliftes the ribs of vessels broke,
And shivered ships, which had beene wrecked late,
Yet stuck, with carcases exanimate
Of such, as having all their substance spent
In wanton joyes and lustes intemperate,
Did afterwardes make shipwrack violent,
Both of their life, and fame for ever fowly blent.

. . . .

A daungerous and detestable place,
To which nor fish nor fowle did once approch,
But yelling meawes, with seagulles hoars and bace,
And cormoyraunts, with birds of ravenous race. . . .

Lord Houghton published the only known version of the ode and dated it "October, 1819" without citing his authority. As far as I can ascertain, there is no extant manuscript.

Keats composed the ode one evening in April 1819, it is evident, while he was living in one half of Wentworth Place and Miss Brawne was living in the other half; for at the beginning of the ode he said that he had seen Miss Brawne an hour ago and at the end he imagined that he saw her step forth into the garden the next morning. The last two verses — "Enough! Enough! it is enough for me To dream of thee!" — refer to the nympholeptic dream of Miss Brawne which he expressed on April 16 in the sonnet *As Hermes once took to his feathers light.* And the phrase in the third verse — "Touch has a memory" — is a reminiscence of his conversation with Coleridge on April 11. Among the subjects which Coleridge discussed were

Different genera and species of Dreams — Nightmare — *a dream accompanied by a sense of touch* — single and double touch — A dream related —

The sentiment of the ode proves that Keats composed it in the spring of 1819 instead of in the fall. In the spring he felt rebellious against love; but in the fall he surrendered unconditionally to it. He wrote Miss Brawne on October 13, 1819 that he could no longer reason against the reasons of his love because it gave him too much pain. Instead of being tortured by the fear that love would enslave him, he was tortured by the fears that Miss Brawne did not love him as much as he loved her and that he would die before he could marry her.

The second ode *To* [*Fanny*] is an exact and complete interpretation of *La belle dame sans merci.* The one expresses a rebellion against the trammels of love in direct, personal style; the other expresses the same sentiment in objective symbols. Since, in the very nature of things, direct expression of experience precedes symbolic, the ode, I believe, precedes the ballad.

Keats copied (possibly composed) *La belle dame sans merci* into the journal letter to his brother on Wednesday evening, April 28, 1819.

La belle dame sans merci —

O what can ail thee Knight at arms
Alone and palely loitering?

The sedge has withered from the Lake
And no birds sing!

O what can ail thee Knight at arms
So haggard, and so woe begone?
The Squirrel's granary is full
And the harvest's done.

I see ~~death's~~ a lilly on thy brow
With anguish moist and fever dew,
And on thy cheeks ~~death's~~ a fading rose
Fast Withereth too —

I met a Lady in the ~~Wilds~~ Meads
Full beautiful, a faery's child
Her hair was long, her foot was light
And her eyes were wild —

I made a Garland for her head,
And bracelets too, and fragrant Zone
She look'd at me as she did love
And made sweet moan —

I set her on my pacing steed
And nothing else saw all day long
For sidelong would she bend and sing
A faery's song —

She found me roots of relish sweet
And honey wild and ~~honey~~ manna dew
And sure in language strange she said
I love thee true —

She took me to her elfin grot
and sigh'd full sore,
And there she wept ~~and there she sighed~~
And there I shut her wild wild eyes
With Kisses four —

And there she lulled me asleep
And there I dream'd Ah Woe betide!
The latest dream I ever dreamt
On the cold hill side.

I saw pale Kings and Princes too
Pale warriors death pale were they all
Who cried La belle dame sans merci
Thee hath in thrall.

I saw their starv'd lips in the gloam
~~All tremble~~ gaped wide
With horrid warning ~~wide agape~~,
And I awoke, and found me here
On the cold hill's side

And this is why I ~~wither~~ sojourn here
Alone and palely loitering;
Though the sedge is withered from the Lake
And no birds sing —

Keats drew the details of this ballad from various sources, adding to them, subtracting from them, and altering them freely. He took the title, Leigh Hunt said, from *La Belle Dame Sans Mercie,* a poem composed by Alain Chartier, court poet of Charles II of France. He read the poem in an English translation into rhyme royal which, it was believed, was made by Chaucer. Chartier feigned that he rode into the country at an easy pace to muse over the death of his mistress, that he met a group of friends who tried to divert him from his grief, and that he overheard a dialogue between an amorous gentleman and a gentlewoman without mercy. Keats took nothing from this conventional mediaeval erotic dialogue except possibly the "pacing steed." He was fascinated by the title, however, making it, we remember, the title of the Provençal ditty with which Porphyro awoke Madeline on St. Agnes' Eve. In the ballad, we may imagine, he restored this ditty which was long since mute.

Keats derived the setting and the persons of the ballad from Spenser's story of Cymochles, a knight of fierce and fickle passion, and Phaedra, a wicked faery who enchanted him with sensual pleasures (*Faerie Queene*, II. vi. 2 *et seq.*). When Cymochles met Phaedra she was sitting in a little gondelay by the shore of the Idle Lake,

Making sweete solace to herselfe alone.

As she transported the knight to her island she entertained him with light behavior and loose dalliance.

Sometime her head she fondly would aguize
With gaudy girlonds, or fresh flowrets dight
About her necke, or rings of rushes plight. . . .

When they came to the island,

Into a shady dale she soft him led,
And laid him downe upon a grassy playn;
And her sweete selfe without dread or disdayn
She sett beside, laying his head disarmd
In her loose lap, it softly to sustayn,
Where soone he slumbred, fearing not be harmd,
The whiles with a love lay she thus him sweetly charm'd:

. . . .

By this she had him lulled fast a sleepe,
That of no worldly thing he care did take. . . .

Keats retained the lake in the setting of the story, but he converted the gondelay into a pacing steed. He knew many episodes in *The Faerie Queene* and in other chivalric romances, such as *Palmerin of England*, in which knights convey ladies on steeds. He made the lady of the ballad a faery of romance, like Phaedra, a lady of mortal stature, exceeding beauty, and supernatural powers. He had the knight, instead of the lady, weave a garland for her head; and he had the lady look at the knight as though she loved him, sing him a song, lead him to her elfin grot, and lull him asleep.

Keats suffused his ballad in an atmosphere which is far more weird and sinister than that of Spenser's episode of Cymochles and Phaedra. He presented the destructive effects of love by means of the knight's dream.

> I saw pale Kings and Princes too
> Pale warriors death pale were they all
> Who cried La belle dame sans merci
> Thee hath in thrall.
>
> I saw their starv'd lips in the gloam
> With horrid warning gaped wide,
> And I awoke, and found me here
> On the cold hill's side.

Keats derived the thought and the details of these stanzas from three sources. The first is Spenser's description of the Rock of Vile Reproach, which, as we have seen, is the source of a part of the second ode *To* [*Fanny*]. The second is Spenser's story of the adventure of Britomartis, the maiden knight of chastity, in the Castle of Busirane, the castle of lust (III. xi. xxviii *et seq.*). When Britomartis entered the castle, she saw arras depicting the conquests which Cupid had won against the gods —

> On mighty *kings* and kesars, into *thraldome* brought.
>
> . . . .
>
> Kings, queenes, lords, ladies, knights, and damsels gent
> Were heap'd together with the vulgar sort,
>
> . . . .
>
> To shew Dan Cupids powre and great effort. . . .

The third source, as de Sélincourt pointed out, is a passage in Shakespeare's *Pericles, Prince of Tyre* (I. i. 34 *et seq.*). When Pericles ventured to stake his life to win the princess, her father Antiochus warned him:

Yon sometimes famous *princes*, like thyself,
Drawn by report, adventurous by desire,
Tell thee, with speechless tongues and *semblance pale*,
That without covering, save yon field of stars,
Here they stand martyrs, slain in Cupid's wars;
And with *dead cheeks* advise thee to desist
For going on death's net, whom none resist.

Keats composed *La belle dame sans merci* in the magical style which is the peculiar achievement of romantic genius. The magical style, Matthew Arnold said, was the contribution of the Celts to English poetry. It was introduced into mediaeval English poetry, it is probable, from Breton lays through the medium of Norman-French lays and romances. It is found in a few mediaeval English romances, such as *Sir Gawain and the Green Knight*, which were ultimately of Celtic derivation. It is found in short passages in the poetry of the Renaissance poets, Spenser, Shakespeare, and Milton. It attained its greatest effects finally in the first quarter of the nineteenth century in Coleridge's *Christabel* and *Kubla Khan* and Keats's *La belle dame sans merci.*

The magical style, as Matthew Arnold perceived, is the gift of a poet who has keen sensibility and nervous exaltation; it consists in a representation of "the intimate life of Nature, her weird power and her fairy charm." Milton defined and at the same time illustrated the magical style in two verses in *L'Allegro* —

Such sights as youthful Poets dream
On summer eves by haunted stream.

The weird but pleasing atmosphere of the magical style may be created either by suggestive general words or by vivid concrete images. Those verses in the *Ode to a Nightingale* which are the finest examples of the magical style have vague and indefinite images —

The same that oft-times hath
Charm'd magic casements, opening on the foam
Of perilous seas, in faery lands forlorn.

Whenever the magical style has concrete images, it has them for what they suggest rather than for what they are. The concrete images in *La belle dame sans merci* suggest an atmosphere that is sad, sombre, chivalric, and weird.

It is unnecessary to explain the way in which each word in the ballad, harmonizing with every other word, does its part in suggesting the atmosphere. We should observe, however, the symbolic harmony between the knight-at-arms and his autumnal setting. His way of life, like that of the sedge, has fallen into the sere, the yellow leaf. The red fades from his cheeks as the rose withers on its stem. We should observe, also, that Keats so arranged and infused the phrases which he remembered from various sources that they suggest the peculiar atmosphere which he desired. He constructed the felicitous and unique phrase "knight-at-arms" from Milton's "knight in arms" (sonnet *When the Assault Was Intended to the City*) on analogy with the common "man-at-arms." He drew the conception of "faery's child" from Spenser's faeries of romance. He built the verse "And honey wild and ~~honey~~ manna dew" from Spenser's "hony dew" (episode of Britomartis in Castle of Busirane, *Faerie Queene*, III. xi. xxx. 4) reinforced by Coleridge's "honey dew" (*Kubla Khan*, v. 53). His "And there she lulled me asleep" was a reminiscence of Spenser's "By this she had him lulled fast a sleepe" (episode of Cymochles and Phaedra, *Faerie Queene*, II. vi. xviii. 1). He recalled "woe begone" and "sigh'd full sore" from Spenser's *Faerie Queene* (*passim*); "pacing steed" possibly from Alain Chartier's *La Belle Dame Sans Mercie*; "her hair was long" from "her hair grew lang" in the folk ballad *Kemp Owyne*; "her eyes were wild" from Wordsworth's "Her eyes are wild, her head is bare"; and "anguish moist" from Leigh Hunt's "moist anguish" (*Story of Rimini*, IV. 65). It has been suggested that the verse "And no birds sing" was a reminiscence of William Browne's "Let no bird sing" (*Britannia's Pastorals*, I. 2. 894). Keats had employed an earlier variant of this verse, however, in the second ode *To* [*Fanny*], "There bad flowers have no scent, birds no sweet song," in which he recalled Spenser's description of the Rock of Vile Reproach, a detestable place which was approached only by hoarse and ravenous birds such as cormorants, mews, and sea gulls.

The form of the folk ballad, in which Keats composed *La belle dame sans merci*, helps to produce the peculiar effect of the poem. He presented the bare dramatic outlines of the story, giving each detail a weird significance. He told the story as a dialogue, representing the knight as the poet saw him and as he saw himself. He used the device of repetition, making the last stanza repeat and enforce the tone of weird tragedy which the first stanza had sounded. He shortened the fourth verse of the ballad stanza, producing a rhythm of haunting and ominous slowness. He gave some of his images the vivid simplicity of ballad imagery:

Her hair was long, her foot was light
And her eyes were wild —

and the magical numerical definiteness of ballad imagery:

> And there I shut her wild wild eyes
> With Kisses four —

He feared that his readers would misunderstand the imaginative connotations of this last image and ridicule it as they had ridiculed similar images in Wordsworth's *Lyrical Ballads*. In the letter to his brother in which he copied the ballad, he anticipated objections to the image and answered them jestingly.

> Why four kisses — you will say — why four[?] because I wish to restrain the headlong impetuosity of my Muse — she would have fain said "score" without hurting the rhyme — but we must temper the Imagination as the Critics say with Judgment. I was obliged to choose an even number that both eyes might have fair play: and to speak truly I think two a piece quite sufficient. Suppose I had said seven; there would have been three and a half a piece — a very awkward affair and well got out of on my side.

Woodhouse copied the original version of *La belle dame sans merci* into his Commonplace Book and into his Book of Transcripts. Leigh Hunt printed a revised version in his *Indicator* for May 10, 1820. The revisions destroy much of the magical charm of the ballad. Keats made the revisions at the beginning of May 1820, it is probable, while he was lodging in Kentish Town to be near Leigh Hunt. He was warned by Hunt doubtless that the unique and striking phrases of the original version might be ridiculed, and he was too ill at the time to trust his own judgment.

On April 28, 1819 Keats composed an *ex tempore Chorus of Four Fairies* into his journal letter to his brother immediately after he had composed and commented on *La belle dame sans merci*. This *Chorus* is a dialogue, in heptasyllabic verse, between fairies of the four elements — Salamander, spright of fire, Zephyr, spright of air, Dusketha, spright of earth, and Breama, spright of water. Keats was almost equally intrigued by Spenser's faeries of romance and Shakespeare's fairies, who were a composite of faeries of romance, elves of popular tradition, and spirits of the elements. He drew, on the same day, *La belle dame* from the one and the *Chorus* from the other.

On April 28, after he had composed these two poems, he completed his explanation of that empirical and stoical humanism which he had begun a day or two after March 19. He had accepted with calm stoicism, we remember, the fact that man is a part of the instinctive and egotistic nature of the world. A few days after

March 19 he had considered the evil which natural creatures, including human beings, inflict. Now, on April 28, he considered the evil which they suffer. Since man is a part of nature, he said, he cannot escape the evil which is inherent and necessary in nature. In every stage of nature there is an evil which is peculiar to that stage. If man rises above the evil of one stage of nature, he suffers the evil of another stage. Keats denied specifically the Rousseauistic theory of the goodness and the happiness of natural man and the Godwinian theory of the perfectibility of human nature and the progress of society to a state of happiness. He was at the farthest point in his reaction against those principles which he had expressed in the introduction to a humanitarian version of the "Fall of Hyperion."

> I have been reading lately [he wrote his brother] two very different books, Robertson's America and Voltaire's Siecle De Louis XIV. It is like walking arm and arm between Pizarro and the great-little Monarch. In How lementable [*sic*] a case do we see the great body of the people in both instances: in the first where Men might seem to inherit quiet of Mind from unsophisticated senses; from uncontamination of civilisation; and especially from their being as it were estranged from the mutual helps of Society and its mutual injuries — and thereby more immediately under the Protection of Providence — even there they had mortal pains to bear as bad, or even worse than Ba[i]liffs, Debts and Poverties of civilised Life.
>
> The whole appears to resolve into this — that Man is originally "a poor forked creature" subject to the same mischances as the beasts of the forest, destined to hardships and disquietude of some kind or other. If he improves by degrees his bodily accom[m]odations and comforts — at each stage, at each accent [ascent] there are waiting for him a fresh set of annoyances — he is mortal and there is still a heaven with its Stars above his head.
>
> The most interesting question that can come before us is, How far by the persevering endeavours of a seldom appearing Socrates Mankind may be made happy — I can imagine such happiness carried to an extreme — but what must it end in? — Death — and who could in such a case bear with death — the whole troubles of life which are now frittered away in a series of years, would the[n] be accumulated for the last days of a being who instead of hailing its approach would leave this world as Eve left Paradise.
>
> But in truth I do not at all believe in this sort of perfectibility — the nature of the world will not admit of it — the inhabitants of the world will correspond to itself. Let the fish Philosophise the ice away from the Rivers in winter time and they shall be at continual play in the tepid delight of Summer. Look at the Poles and at the Sands of Africa, Whirlpools and volcanoes. Let men exterminate them and I will say that they may arrive at earthly Happiness. The point at which Man may arrive is as far as the paralel[*sic*] state in inanimate nature and no further. For instance suppose a rose to have sensation, it blooms on a beautiful morning, it enjoys itself — but there comes a cold wind, a hot sun — it cannot escape it, it cannot destroy its annoyances — they are as native to the world as itself — no more can man be happy in spite, the worldly elements will prey upon his nature.

Keats was neither pessimistic nor cynical but empirical and realistic. He perceived that there are forces for good as well as forces for evil in nature. He believed that the world with its inherent evil is necessary for the creation of human identities, individualities, or souls. The soul of a man is formed, he said, by the reaction of his faculties to the world in which he lives. In this process of soul-making, three elements are involved — the intelligence, the heart, and the world. The intelligence, which comes from God or Original Essence, has no individuality or soul. The heart is the seat of sensuous experience and of the passions which are stimulated by sensuous experience. The intelligence acquires its ideas of the world through the heart, it is shaped and colored by the passions of the heart, and it develops into a soul. "Do you not see," Keats asked his brother, "how necessary a World of Pains and troubles is to school an Intelligence and make it a Soul?" He entangled this empirical principle of the creation of mortal souls, in which he believed, with the theological principle of the creation of immortal souls, which he assumed for the purpose of attacking the Christian doctrine of the immortality of the human soul.

The common cognomen of this world among the misguided and superstitious is "a vale of tears" from which we are to be redeemed by a certain arbit[r]ary interposition of God and taken to Heaven. What a little circumscribed straightened [*sic*] notion! Call the world if you Please "The vale of Soul-making." Then you will find out the use of the world (I am speaking now in the highest terms for human nature admitting it to be immortal which I will here take for granted for the purpose of showing a thought which has struck me concerning it) I say "*Soul-making*" [—] Soul as distinguished from an Intelligence. There may be intelligences or sparks of the divinity in millions — but they are not Souls till they acquire identities, till each one is personally itself. I[n]telligences are atoms of perception — they know and they see and they are pure, in short they are God. —

How then are Souls to be made? How then are these sparks which are God to have identity given them — so as ever to possess a bliss peculiar to each one's individual existence? How, but by the medium of a world like this? This point I sincerely wish to consider because I think it a grander system of salvation than the chrystiain [*sic*] religion — or rather it is a system of Spirit-creation. This is effected by three grand materials acting the one upon the other for a series of years. These three Materials are the *Intelligence* — the *human heart* (as distinguished from intelligence or Mind) and the *World* or *Elemental space* suited for the proper action of *Mind and Heart* on each other for the purpose of forming the *Soul* or *Intelligence destined to possess the sense of Identity*.

I can scarcely express what I but dimly perceive — and yet I think I perceive it — that you may judge the more clearly I will put it in the most homely form possible. I will call the *world* a School instituted for the purpose of teaching little children to read — I will call the *human heart* the *horn Book* read in that

School — and I will call the *Child able to read, the Soul* made from that *School* and its *hornbook*.

Do you not see how necessary a World of Pains and troubles is to school an Intelligence and make it a Soul? A Place where the heart must feel and suffer in a thousand diverse ways. Not merely is the Heart a Hornbook, It is the Minds Bible, it is the Minds experience, it is the text from which the Mind or intelligence sucks its identity. As various as the Lives of Men are — so various become their Souls, and thus does God make individual beings, Souls, Identical Souls of the Sparks of its own essence.

This appears to me a faint sketch of a system of Salvation which does not affront our reason and humanity — I am convinced that many difficulties which christians labour under would vanish before it — there is one which even now Strikes me — the Salvation of Children. In them the Spark or intelligence returns to God without any identity — it having had no time to learn of and be altered by the heart — or seat of the human Passions. It is pretty generally suspected that the chr[i]stian scheme has been coppied [*sic*] from the ancient persian and greek Philosophers. Why may they not have made this simple thing even more simple for common apprehension by introducing Mediators and Personages in the same manner as in the heathen mythology abstractions are personified[?] Seriously I think it probable that this System of Soul-making — may have been the Parent of all the more palpable and personal Schemes of Redemption among the Zoroastrians[,] the Christians and the Hindoos. For as one part of the human species must have their carved Jupiter; so another part must have the palpable and named Mediatior [*sic*] and Saviour, their Christ[,] their Oromanes and their Vishnu.

If what I have said should not be plain enough, as I fear it may not be, I will but [put] you in the place where I began in this series of thoughts — I mean, I began by seeing how man was formed by circumstances — and what are circumstances? — but touchstones of his heart? and what are touchstones? but proovings [*sic*] of his heart? and what are proovings [*sic*] of his heart but fortifiers or alterers of his nature? and what is his altered nature but his Soul? — and what was his Soul before it came into the world and had these provings and alterations and perfectionings? — An intelligence — without Identity — and how is this Identity to be made? Through the medium of the Heart? And how is the heart to become this Medium but in a world of Circumstances? There now I think what with Poetry and Theology you may thank your Stars that my pen is not very long winded.

Keats derived this principle of soul-making, it is probable, from Leigh Hunt's sentimental deism, but he developed it on the basis of empirical psychology. Hunt was constantly attacking the superstition and the injustice of Christian theology and evolving new systems of theology to supplant the Christian. He believed that there is a God, that evil is transient, that good is eternal, and that the human soul is immortal. Hunt and Shelley agreed in a hatred of Christian theology, but they differed in their own theological principles. Shelley, who was a Platonic panpsychist, believed that the soul, when the body died, returned to the world-soul, or soul of the universe, from which it had come, and reunited with the world-soul, losing its personal identity. In July 1819, two months after Keats had explained the principle of soul-making in the letter to his brother, Hunt [8] expressed the same principle in a letter of condolence to Shelley, whose little son William had died.

> I had received the news of your misfortune [Hunt wrote Shelley], and thought of all which you and Mary must suffer. Marianne, I assure you, wept hearty tears of sympathy. He was a fine little fellow, was William; and for my part I cannot conceive that the young intellectual spirit which sat thinking out of his eye, and seemed to comprehend so much in his smile, can perish like the house it inhabited. *I do not know that a soul is born with us; but we seem, to me, to attain to a soul, some later, some earlier;* and when we have got that, there is a look in our eye, a sympathy in our cheerfulness, and a yearning and grave beauty in our thoughtfulness that seems to say, "Our mortal dress may fall off when it will; our trunk and our leaves may go; we have shot up our blossom into an immortal air." This is poetry, you will say, and not argument: but then there comes upon me another fancy, which would fain persuade me that poetry is the argument of a higher sphere.

Keats received this principle of soul-making from Hunt, it would seem, in a theological form. We must distinguish carefully between that part of the theory which Keats assumed for the purpose of argument and that part in which he believed. The principle that the souls or personal identities of men are created by the reaction of their mental faculties to their sensuous and emotional experience in the world became the most consoling principle in his empirical humanism. It soothed his feverish rebellion against the painful facts of life into a calm, deliberate acceptance. The principle that the souls so created were immortal — that they possessed personal identity after the death of their bodies — had no part in his philosophy. It was an assumption instead of a conviction. "I am speaking now," he told his brother, "in the highest terms for human nature admitting it to be immortal which I will here take for granted for the purpose of showing a thought which has struck me concerning it." After this period as well as before it he expressed poignant regret that he could not believe in the conscious immortality of the human soul.

Keats's empirical and humanistic philosophy of life and poetry manifests itself in the four sonnets which he composed at the end of April 1819 and in the five odes which he composed in May. He copied the sonnets into his journal letter to his brother.

> Friday — April 30 — Brown has been here rummaging up some of my old sins — that is to say sonnets. I do not think you remember them so I will copy

[8] Thornton Hunt, *The Correspondence of Leigh Hunt*, Vol. I, pp. 130–131.

them out as well as two or three lately written. I have just written one on Fame — which Brown is transcribing and he has his book and mine. I must employ myself perhaps in a sonnet on the same subject —

Keats composed the second sonnet *On Fame* into the journal letter to his brother; and, after Brown had transcribed the first sonnet *On Fame*, he copied it also into the journal letter. There are transcripts of both sonnets in Keats's copy of *Endymion* and in Woodhouse's Book of Transcripts, and there is a transcript of the first sonnet in Woodhouse's Commonplace Book.

Fame, we remember, was one of the three problems — love, fame, and poetry — which had afflicted him in March 1819. The ridicule of *Endymion* by the reviewers and the indifference of the public to the poem had cast him into a state of morbid despair, polluting his love of fame, that humanistic magnanimity which had inspired him in 1817 and the first part of 1818. Now on April 30, 1819, after he had mastered the disagreeable facts of experience, he dismissed fame, paying her scorn for scorn.

On Fame

Fame like a wayward girl will still be coy
  To those who woo her with too slavish knees
  But makes surrender to some thoughtless boy
And dotes the more upon a heart at ease —
She is a Gipsey will not speak to those
  Who have not learnt to be content without her
A Jilt whose ear was never whisper'd close
  Who think they scandal her who talk about her —
A very Gipsey is she Nilus born,
Sister in law to jealous Potiphar:
Ye lovesick Bards, repay her scorn for scorn.
Ye lovelorn Artists madmen that ye are,
Make your best bow to her and bid adieu
Then if she likes it she will follow you.

Keats may have derived the comparison of fame to a wayward jilt, as E. H. Meyerstein [9] suggested, from Dryden's description of fame in the epilogue to the first part of *The Conquest of Granada* —

Fame, like a little mistress of the town,
Is gain'd with *ease*, but then she's lost as soon:
For as those tawdry misses, soon or late,
Jilt such as keep 'em at the highest rate . . .
So, Fame is false to all that keep her long;
And turns up to the fop that's brisk and *young*.

---

[9] Ernest de Sélincourt, Fifth Edition, 1926.

His study of Dryden in 1818 and in 1819 not only strengthened the fibre of his verse but gave him also poetic ideas and images. He derived the metaphor of fame as a gipsy, it is probable, from Shakespeare's *Antony and Cleopatra* (IV. xii. 28–29), in which Antony said that Cleopatra

> Like a right gipsy, hath, at fast and loose,
> Beguil'd me to the very heart of loss.

And just as coy jilt reminded him of Cleopatra, so Cleopatra, by a similar process of association, reminded him of jealous Potiphar.

The second sonnet *On Fame*, which is more imaginative and passionate than the first, is a poetic version of those intense philosophic reflections which Keats wrote in the journal letter to his brother on March 19 and April 28. He looked back upon that morbid despair which he had suffered in March and anathematized that love of fame, that fierce miscreed, which had caused it.

On Fame

You cannot eat your cake and have it too. — Proverb.

~~How is that Man misled~~ }
How fever'd is that Man } who cannot look
  Upon his mortal days with temperate blood
Who vexes all the leaves of his Life's book
  And robs his fair name of its maidenhood[:]
It is as if the rose should pluck herself
  Or the ripe plum~~b~~ finger its misty bloom
As if a clear Lake meddling with itself
  Should ~~fill~~ cloud its pureness with a muddy gloom.
But the rose leaves herself upon the Briar
For winds to kiss and grateful Bees to ~~taste~~ feed
And the ripe plumb ~~will wear~~ still wears its dim attire[,]
The undisturbed Lake has crystal space —
{ teasing the world for grace
Why then should man { ~~his own bright name deface~~
{ ~~spoil~~ }
~~And~~ { ~~burn~~ } ~~our pleasures in his selfish fire~~
Spoil his salvation by a fierce miscreed[?]

Keats copied the sonnet *To Sleep* in the journal letter to his brother immediately after the two sonnets *On Fame*. He composed the incomplete first draft, which ends with the twelfth verse, on the flyleaf of the second volume of the annotated copy of *Paradise Lost* which he gave afterwards to Mrs. Dilke and which is now in the Dilke Collection. The transcripts of the sonnet in Keats's copy of *Endymion* and in Woodhouse's Commonplace Book and Book of Transcripts are dated merely "1819." *To Sleep* is not one of the "old sins" which Brown was rummaging up; it is one of the new "sins" which Keats had composed lately — perhaps a day or two before he composed the sonnets *On Fame.* After copying the new sonnets Keats closed his letter without fulfilling his promise to copy the old ones.

The autographs and transcripts of the sonnet reveal Keats's imagination at work in the different stages of composition. The first draft represents the first effort of the imagination.

To Sleep

O soft embalmer of the still Midnight
Shutting with careful fingers and benign
Our gloom-pleas'd eyes embowered from the light
~~Of sun or teasing candles~~
As wearisome as darkness is divine
O soothest sleep, if so it please thee close
Mine willing eyes in midst of this thine hymn
Or wait the amen, ere thy poppy throws
Its sweet-death dews o'er every pulse and limb —
Then shut the hushed Casket of my soul
And turn the Key round in the oiled wards
And let it rest until the morn ~~has stole~~
grey east's
Bright tressed From the ~~west's~~ shuddering bourn

Keats longed for sleep, as he had longed for mental apathy (or indolence) and death, to give him a respite from the painful experience through which he was passing. He began to write down the sonnet before his imagination had finished selecting and shaping its materials and he was forced to stop with the twelfth verse. The fourth verse of the first quatrain, the fourth verse of the second quatrain, and the last six verses were in an amorphous state. The autograph of the sonnet in the journal letter represents the finished work of the imagination.

To Sleep

O soft embalmer of the still midnight
Shutting with careful fingers and benign
Our gloom-pleas'd eyes embowered from the light,
Enshaded in forgetfulness divine —
O soothest sleep, if so it please the[e] close
In midst of this thine hymn my willing eyes,
Or wait the amen, ere thy poppy throws
Around my bed its dewy Charities —
Then save me or the passed day will shine
Upon my pillow breeding many woes:
Save me from curious conscience that still lords

Its strength for darkness, borrowing [burrowing] like ~~the~~ a Mole —
 Turn the key deftly in the oiled wards
And seal the hushed Casket of my soul.

Keats perfected the fourth verses of the first and second quatrains by changing "As wearisome as darkness is divine" into "Enshaded in forgetfulness divine" and "Its sweet-death dews o'er every pulse and limb" into "Around my bed its dewy Charities." The difficulty of rhyming caused him to reconstruct the last six verses. He changed the imagery of the eleventh and twelfth verses because it was too bright in color and moved these verses up into the position of the ninth and tenth verses. He inserted a new thought with striking imagery in the eleventh and twelfth verses. He perfected the ninth and tenth verses and moved them down into the position of the thirteenth and fourteenth verses.

In the various transcripts, "the" (v. 5) and "borrowing" (v. 12), which were misspelled in the autograph in the journal letter, are corrected into "thee" and "burrowing." In the transcript in Woodhouse's Book of Transcripts, "dewy" (v. 8) is crossed out and "lulling" is written above it.

The word "lulling" [Woodhouse said in a note] is in K.'s handwriting. The correction was made when he borrowed this book to select a small poem to write in an album, intended to consist of original poetry, for a lady.

In this transcript, also, "hoards" is written in the place of "lords" (v. 11). Woodhouse may have misread "hoards" for "lords" or he may have derived it from an autograph which has not survived. It is significant, however, that, when Keats read Woodhouse's transcript, he left "hoards" untouched although he revised "dewy" into "lulling." The substitution of "hoards" for "lords," as H. B. Forman observed, makes the image more felicitous and harmonious:

Save me from curious conscience that still hoards
Its strength for darkness, burrowing like a mole —

Keats composed the sonnet in the style and in the thought of Renaissance poetry on Sleep. It is a worthy companion to Sidney's sonnet *Come Sleepe, O Sleepe, the certaine knot of peace* and Daniel's sonnet *Care-charmer Sleep, son of the sable night.* The imagery and the phraseology of the first quatrain were a reminiscence of the famous invocation of sleep in Shakespeare's *Henry IV, Part II* (III. i. 5. *et seq.*) —

O *Sleep*, O gentle Sleep,
Nature's *soft* nurse, how have I frighted thee,
That thou no more wilt *weigh my eyelids down*
And steep my senses *in forgetfulness*?

And later in this passage occur the words "lull'd" and "seal." Keats may have remembered also Mary Tighe's adaptation of Shakespeare's invocation of sleep —

> Oh! thou best comforter of that sad heart
> Whom fortune's spite assails; come, gentle *Sleep,*
> The weary mourner *sooth*! for well the art
> Thou knowest in *soft forgetfulness* to steep
> The *eyes* which sorrow taught to watch and weep. . . .

Keats's phrase "soothest sleep" (most soothing sleep) was not suggested by Mrs. Tighe's "sooth" (true). He had already used the comparative form of "soothest" in *The Eve of St. Agnes* ("With jellies soother than the creamy curd"), in which we saw he derived the word from a passage in Shakespeare's *Winter's Tale* (IV. iv. 160–161).

The fourth sonnet which Keats composed at the end of April 1819 expresses his rebellion against the restrictive form of the sonnet. For more than a year he had been seeking to discover or to invent a poetic genre which would be a perfect medium for the expression of small units of his personal experience. In January 1818, we remember, he had turned from the Petrarcan to the Shakespearean form of the sonnet. In January, also, he experimented with heptasyllabics and on February 3 he invented a rondeau in heptasyllabics. On January 2, 1819 he said that he preferred the rondeau to the sonnet because he could "amplify" in it a single idea "with greater ease and more delight and freedom than in the sonnet." He returned to the sonnet on March 19, 1819, and composed *Why did I laugh to-night?* in the Shakespearean form. In the latter half of April he composed three Shakespearean sonnets — *As Hermes once, Bright star!* and the first *On Fame*; two irregular Shakespearean sonnets — *To Sleep* (ababcdcdbcefef) and the second *On Fame* (ababcdcdefeggf); and one completely irregular sonnet — *If by dull rhymes* (abcabdcabcdede).

Keats introduced this irregular sonnet as follows:

> I have been endeavouring to discover a better Sonnet Stanza than we have. The legitimate does not suit the language over-well from the pouncing rhymes — the other kind [the Shakespearean] appears too elegiac — and the couplet at the end of it has seldom a pleasing effect — I do not pretend to have succeeded—it will explain itself.

> If by dull rhymes our English must be chaind
> And, like Andromeda, the Sonnet sweet,
> Fetterd, in spite of pained Loveliness;
> Let us find out, if we must be constrain'd,

Sandals more interwoven and complete
To fit the naked foot of poesy;
Let us inspect the Lyre, and weigh the stress
Of every chord, and see what may be gain'd
By ear industrious, and attention meet;
Misers of sound and syllable, no less
Than Midas of his coinage, let us be
Jealous of dead leaves in the bay wreath crown,
So, if we may not let the muse be free,
She will be bound with Garlands of her own.

The autograph fragment of the journal letter ends with the fourth verse of the sonnet and the rest of the letter, including the last ten verses of the sonnet, is preserved in the transcript which was made by John Jeffrey for Lord Houghton. There are transcripts of the sonnet, all dated merely "1819," in Keats's copy of *Endymion* and in Woodhouse's Commonplace Book and Book of Transcripts.

Keats's censure of the Shakespearean sonnet as too elegiac is illuminating. Very few of the English or Shakespearean sonnets of the Renaissance, from those of Surrey to those of Drummond, are notably elegiac. Most of the elegiac sonnets of the eighteenth century, however — the sweet, sad, pensive sonnets of Charlotte Smith, William Hayley, the Della Cruscans, Coleridge, and Hunt (of the *Juvenilia*) — are Shakespearean in form. Keats imitated Shakespeare's sonnets directly, but he was influenced also by the sentimental tone of the Shakespearean sonnets of the eighteenth century. He elevated and ennobled the Shakespearean form of the sonnet — he stands next to Shakespeare in this type of poetry — but all of his sonnets, those which are Petrarcan as well as those which are Shakespearean, are more or less elegiac.

Keats was not successful in his experiments with the form of the sonnet. He gained freedom by violating form, but he lost the subtle correspondence between thought and form which is the peculiar virtue of Petrarcan and Shakespearean sonnets. He composed only three sonnets after April 1819; for he had developed the ode, the perfect genre which he had been seeking.

2

The five great odes which Keats composed at the end of April and in May represent the summit of his lyric poetry and perhaps the summit of all his poetry. All recent study of the odes has hinged about the question whether they are realistic or romantic. They express indeed the inadequacy and the futility of all romantic and idealistic attempts to escape from the disagreeable facts of real life. They are realistic interpretations of Keats's personal experience in accordance with that empirical humanism which he thought out in March and April 1819. He had perceived, we remember, a harmony between good and evil in that unity of nature of which he was a part. A world of pains and troubles, a place where the heart must feel and suffer in a thousand diverse ways, is necessary, he wrote his brother on April 28, to school an intelligence and make it a soul. He had attained that "top of sovereignty" for which he had striven: he could apprehend the "naked truths" of life with calm and temperate blood. He saw life steadily and he saw it whole. "In the height of enthusiasm," he had said on March 8, "I have been cheated into some fine passages; but that is not the thing." Now he had achieved that clear, steady vision of life in which he could compose poems which would be the thing.

There has been a great deal of discussion among critics about the order in which Keats composed the five odes. External evidence, the only absolutely sure evidence, establishes the order of only two of them. Keats brought the journal letter to his brother to an end on May 3, and between May 3 and May 31 he wrote only three brief notes, one to Haslam and two to Fanny Keats. If he had continued the journal letter through May, we could fix the dates of the odes more exactly and interpret the ebb and flow of the thought of the odes more subtly. The letters which he wrote to Miss Jeffrey of Teignmouth on May 31 and June 9 show, however, that there was no essential change in his philosophy in May.

The *Ode to Psyche* is undoubtedly the first of these odes and the *Ode on Indolence* the last. Keats composed the *Ode to Psyche* at the end of April 1819; for he copied it into the journal letter to his brother near the end of the section which he dated Friday, April 30. And Woodhouse said, in his Book of Transcripts, that the *Ode to Psyche* was "Given by J. K. to J. H. R. 4 May 1819." Keats composed the *Ode on Indolence*, it is probable, at the end of May; for he referred to it in the letter which he wrote to Miss Jeffrey on June 9 and repeated sentiments which he had expressed in it. Transcripts of the *Ode to a Nightingale* are dated "May 1819" in Keats's copy of *Endymion* and in Woodhouse's Commonplace Book and Book of Transcripts. The various transcripts of the odes *On Melancholy* and *On a Grecian Urn* are dated merely "1819."

We can establish the relative order of the odes, however, by means of evidence of Keats's progressive development of the metrical form of the odes. He developed the form of his odes out of the form of

Spenser's nuptial ode *Epithalamion*, which he admired and quoted from the beginning of his poetic career. The *Epithalamion* belongs in the tradition of the Greek choral ode, although it is not so elaborate and not so regular as the choral ode with its triple movement of strophe, antistrophe, and epode. The *Epithalamion* is divided into stanzas of 17, 18, and 19 verses. A normal stanza of 19 verses has the following rhyme scheme — ababccdcdeefggfhhii. The sixth, eleventh, and seventeenth verses have three stresses and the other verses have five.

Keats began the development of the form of his great odes in the Hymn to Pan which he composed for the first book of *Endymion* in April 1817. This hymn, or ode, is divided into stanzas of 14, 15, and 16 verses. The last verse and sometimes the third to the last verse of each stanza have three stresses and the other verses have five. The verses are rhymed in couplets, for the hymn was composed to be inserted into *Endymion*, a poem in heroic couplets. The prothalamion in the fourth book of *Endymion*, which was composed in November 1817, has a similar metrical form.

The *Ode to Maia*, which Keats composed on May 1, 1818, represents the second stage in his development of the form of his great odes. When he composed it he called it a fragment; but he never continued it, for he saw that it was complete in thought and form. It consists of a single stanza of 14 verses; the second, fourth, eleventh, and thirteenth verses have three stresses and the other verses have five; and the rhyme scheme is ababccdedefgfg. Keats composed this ode in 14 verses, I believe, because he was accustomed to express brief intuitions of personal experience in the 14 verses of the sonnet. He adapted the rhyme scheme of Spenser's *Epithalamion* and the device of inserting verses of three stresses in a pattern of verses of five stresses. He gave an appearance of completeness to the form of the ode by repeating the metrical pattern of the first quatrain in the last quatrain.

Keats began a rapid development of the ode in April 1819, after he had become dissatisfied with the restrictive form of the sonnet. In his desire for freedom of form, he composed the most irregular of his odes, the second ode *To* [*Fanny*], which consists in two stanzas of 43 and 14 verses, with a most irregular mingling of verses of two and three stresses in the pattern of pentameters. The rhyme scheme of the first stanza is abbaccdddeeffccgg, etc.

The *Ode to Psyche*, the first of the five great odes, represents the next stage in Keats's development of the ode. In the journal letter to his brother he divided the ode by means of spacing into three stanzas of 23, 12, and 32 verses. The last stanza, however, consists in form in two stanzas of 14 and 18 verses. Throughout the ode there is a mingling of verses of two and three stresses in the pattern of pentameters. The twelfth and twenty-first verses of the first stanza have three stresses and the twenty-third verse has two stresses; the sixth, eighth, tenth, and twelfth verses of the second stanza have three stresses; the tenth, twelfth, and fourteenth verses of the third stanza have three stresses; and the sixteenth and eighteenth verses of the last stanza have three stresses. The rhyme scheme of the first stanza is ababcdcdeffeefghhiijhjh; of the second stanza, ababcdcdefef; of the third stanza, ababcdcdefghgh; and of the last stanza, ababcdcdeeafafghgh. In the revised form of the ode Keats removed the rhyme of the tenth and fourteenth verses by changing "fan" into "roof." This ode is more elaborate than the second ode *To* [*Fanny*] but is also more regular.

Keats perceived that the irregular and elaborate form of the *Ode to Psyche* was not effective. In his next ode, the *Ode to a Nightingale,* he developed the same basic ode form in the direction of simplicity and regularity. He reduced the number of verses in each stanza to ten and inserted one verse of three stresses, the eighth, in the pattern of his pentameters. The rhyme scheme of every stanza except the second is ababcdecde; the rhyme scheme of the second stanza has one less rhyme — ababcadcad.

Keats employed this essential form in the three other odes, but he made one progressive alteration: he rejected the device of inserting verses of three stresses in the pattern of his pentameters and made all of the verses pentameters. The *Ode to a Nightingale* stands, therefore, between the *Ode to Psyche* and the three other odes. These later odes, the *Ode on Melancholy*, the *Ode on a Grecian Urn*, and the *Ode on Indolence*, have the same metrical form. Each stanza has 10 iambic pentameter verses and is divided into a quatrain of two invariable and alternating rhymes (abab) and a sestet of three rhymes, the first tercet of which has an invariable rhyme scheme (cde) and the second tercet a variable rhyme scheme (cde, or dce, or ced). Metrical form does not reveal, therefore, the relative order of these three odes; but external evidence, as we have seen, shows that the *Ode on Indolence* is the last of these odes, and the theme of the *Ode on Melancholy* indicates, we shall see, that this ode follows the *Ode to a Nightingale* and precedes the *Ode on a Grecian Urn.*

Keats was a better artist in this period as well as a better philosopher. He began to compose with judgment, we remember, in November 1818, after *Endymion* had been censured by the reviewers.

We have observed in *Hyperion* and *The Eve of St. Agnes* those "innumerable compositions and decompositions" by which he achieved that snailhorn beauty of perfect art. He had conquered the fitful, feverish moods in which he had composed his earlier poems. Intuiting his experience with a clear and controlled vision, he made each of his odes beautiful as a whole as well as in parts. Introducing the *Ode to Psyche* to his brother, he said:

> The following Poem — the last I have written[—] is the first and the only one with which I have taken even moderate pains. I have for the most part dash'd of[f] my lines in a hurry. This I have done leisurely — I think it reads the more richly for it and will I hope encourage me to write other thing[s] in even a more peac[e]able and healthy spirit.

We cannot study the pains with which Keats composed the *Ode to Psyche*, for the first draft has not survived. The earliest version is that which he copied into the journal letter to his brother on May 31, 1819. The second version is that which he gave to Reynolds on May 4 and which Woodhouse copied into his Book of Transcripts. And the third version is that which he published in his *Poems* of 1820. While he was copying the ode for his brother, he changed "to" into "into" (v. 4), "charm'd" into "lull'd" (v. 57), and "frame" into "feign" (v. 62); and he transposed the "n" and "m" in "name" (v. 61). Comparing this version with that which he published, we find that he changed "awaked" into "awaken'd" (v. 6), "fan" into "roof" (v. 10), "freckle-pink" into "silver-white" (v. 14), "syrian" into "Tyrian" (v. 10), "bloomiest" into "brightest" (v. 36), and "O" into "So" (v. 44). By changing "bloomiest" into "brightest" he removed the only improperly formed and objectionable word in the ode. He improved the color harmony of the picture by changing "freckle-pink" into "silver-white," but he removed an unusual compound which is beautiful in itself. This ode is not so fine either in form or in content as the three odes which follow it. The form of the ode is too irregular to make a single metrical effect and the tone is slightly sentimental.

Keats expressed in the *Ode to Psyche*, as in the earlier odes, the Hymn to Pan and the *Ode to Maia*, his yearning love for the serene beauty of Greek deities. Following Wordsworth, we remember, he believed that Greek gods had been created by Greek poets who were inspired by sensations of natural beauty. In *Endymion* and in *Hyperion* he had emulated the myth-making poets of ancient Greece. He was attracted by Psyche because, since she was the latest deity in the Greek pantheon, he could create as well as revive her.

> You must recollect [he wrote his brother] that Psyche was not embodied as a goddess before the time of Apulieus [*sic*] the Platonist who lived after the A[u]gustan age, and consequently the Goddess was never worshipped or sacrificed to with any of the ancient fervour — and perhaps never thought of in the old religion — I am more orthodox that [than] to let a heathen Goddess be so neglected —

Keats's statement was based, as the phraseology indicates, upon the definition of "Psyche" in Lempriere's *Classical Dictionary* —

> The word [Psyche] signifies *the soul*, and this personification of Psyche first mentioned by Apuleius, is posterior to the Augustan age, though still it is connected with ancient mythology.

Keats first read the myth of Cupid and Psyche in Mary Tighe's *Psyche*, the sentimental allegory which had fascinated him in 1815 and 1816. He had read recently, however, William Adlington's translation of Apuleius' *Golden Ass*, the ancient source of the myth. He was chiefly indebted to Apuleius, but he recalled some of Mrs. Tighe's sentimental phrases.

Keats saw a vision of Psyche, he said, and sang to her by his own eyes inspired. His imagination intuited this vision by fusing descriptive details which he had read with his own impressions of natural beauty. He described this vision of Psyche in the first stanza of the ode.

> O Goddess! hear these tuneless numbers, wrung
> By sweet enforcement and remembrance dear,
> And pardon that thy secrets should be sung
> Even into thine own soft-chonched ear:
> Surely I dreamt to-day, or did I see
> The winged Psyche with awaken'd eyes?
> I wander'd in a forest thoughtlessly,
> And, on the sudden, fainting with surprise,
> Saw two fair creatures, couched side by side
> In deepest grass, beneath the whisp'ring roof
> Of leaves and trembled blossoms, where there ran
> A brooklet, scarce espied:
> 'Mid hush'd, cool-rooted flowers, fragrant-eyed,
> Blue, silver-white, and budded Tyrian,
> They lay calm-breathing on the bedded grass;
> Their arms embraced, and their pinions too;
> Their lips touch'd not, but had not bade adieu,
> As if disjoined by soft-handed slumber,
> And ready still past kisses to outnumber
> At tender eye-dawn of aurorean love:
> The winged boy I knew;
> But who wast thou, O happy, happy dove?
> His Psyche true!

We can follow Keats's imagination in its process of intuiting this vision. He recalled a phrase in the sentimental verse, "By sweet enforcement and remembrance dear," from a verse in the first stanza of Mary Tighe's *Psyche* —

> While *dear remembrance* bade her ever weep. . . .

He drew the picture of Cupid and Psyche with their arms embraced and their pinions too and their lips not touching but yet not bidding adieu from prints of the sculptured group which he saw probably in Spence's *Polymetis* and in the *Musée Napoléon*. He may have recalled the phrases "arms embraced," "fainting with surprise," and "on the sudden" from Mary Tighe's *Psyche* (VI. 53. 6–7) —

> Thus, in her lover's circling *arms embraced*,
> The *fainting* Psyche's soul, by *sudden* flight. . . .

Keats set Cupid and Psyche, then, in a scene the details of which he derived from Apuleius' description of the transportation of Psyche to the palace of Cupid in a secluded valley —

> Thus poore Psyches being left alone weeping and trembling on the top of the rocke, was blowne by the gentle aire and of shrilling Zephyrus, and carride from the hill with a meeke wind, which retained her garments vp, and by little and little brought her downe into a deepe valie, where she was laid in a *bed of most sweet and fragrant floures. Thus faire Psyches being sweetly couched among the soft and tender hearbes, as in a bed of sweete and fragrant flowres*, and hauing qualified the troubles and thoughts of her restlesse mind, was now wel reposed: And when she had refreshed her selfe sufficiently with sleepe, she rose with a more quiet and pacified minde, and fortuned to *espie a pleasant wood inuironed with great and mighty trees*: she *espied likewise a running riuer* as cleere as christal: In the middest of the wood, welnigh at the fal of the riuer was a Princelie edifice. . . .

In this description we find the details which Keats employed in his picture of Cupid and Psyche,

> couched side by side
> In deepest grass, beneath the whisp'ring roof
> Of leaves and trembled blossoms, where there ran
> A brooklet, scarce espied:
> 'Mid hush'd, cool-rooted flowers, fragrant-eyed,
> Blue, silver-white, and budded Tyrian,
> They lay calm-breathing on the bedded grass. . . .

This whole passage (especially the verses "'Mid hush'd, cool-rooted flowers, fragrant-eyed, Blue, silver-white, and budded Tyrian)" is richly sensuous, presenting images of temperature, touch, pressure, strain, odor, color, and outline. It is a fine example of the way in which Keats enriched images of other writers with his own sensuous experience.

Keats constructed the final verses of the stanza,

> But who wast thou, O happy, happy dove?
> His Psyche true!

from a reminiscence of Mary Tighe's *Psyche*:

> *Oh happy* you! who blest with present bliss. . . .
> [II. 1. 1.]
> *Oh, Psyche, happy* in thine ignorance! . . .
> Pure spotless *dove*! . . .
> [II. 3. 1, 5.]

He repeated this play upon "happy" most effectively in the *Ode to a Nightingale* and the *Ode on a Grecian Urn.*

In the second and third stanzas of the ode Keats praised Psyche's loveliness and expressed regret that she was created too late to have been worshipped with "antique vows" and the "believing lyre." In the six verses which he employed at the end of both stanzas, he revelled in the Renaissance device of creating imaginative compounds and phrases.

> O latest born and loveliest vision far
> Of all Olympus' faded hierarchy!
> Fairer than Phoebe's sapphire-region'd star,
> Or Vesper, amorous glow-worm of the sky;
> Fairer than these, though temple thou hast none,
> Nor altar heap'd with flowers;
> Nor virgin-choir to make delicious moan
> Upon the midnight hours;
> No voice, no lute, no pipe, no incense sweet
> From chain-swung censer teeming;
> No shrine, no grove, no oracle, no heat
> Of pale-mouth'd prophet dreaming.

Keats constructed many of these fine phrases out of his reminiscenses of the nineteenth stanza of Milton's ode *On the Morning of Christ's Nativity* —

> The *Oracles* are dumb;
> *No voice* or hideous hum
> Runs through the archèd roof in words deceiving.
> Apollo from his *shrine*
> Can no more divine,
> With hollow shriek the steep of Delphos leaving.
> No nightly trance, or breathèd spell,
> Inspires the *pale-eyed* Priest from the *prophetic* cell.

Keats dissolved Milton's stanza into its primal elements and shaped these elements into a new and original whole.

In the final stanza Keats promised Psyche:

> Yes, I will be thy priest, and build a fane
>   In some untrodden region of my mind,
> Where branched thoughts, new grown with pleasant pain,
>   Instead of pines shall murmur in the wind:
> Far, far around shall those dark-cluster'd trees
>   Fledge the wild-ridged mountains steep by steep;
> And there by zephyrs, streams, and birds, and bees,
>   The moss-lain Dryads shall be lull'd to sleep;
> And in the midst of this wide quietness
> A rosy sanctuary will I dress
> With the wreath'd trellis of a working brain,
>   With buds, and bells, and stars without a name,
> With all the gardener Fancy e'er could feign,
>   Who breeding flowers, will never breed the same:
> And there shall be for thee all soft delight
>   That shadowy thought can win,
> A bright torch, and a casement ope at night,
>   To let the warm Love in!

The central idea of the stanza, the idea of building a fane for Psyche in some untrodden region of his mind, was original as well as felicitous. The adjective "untrodden" may have been a reminiscence of a verse in the first stanza of Mary Tighe's *Psyche* —

> Fair Psyche through *untrodden* forests went. . . .

The finest image in the stanza is that of the pines, "those dark-cluster'd trees" which "Fledge the wild-ridged mountains steep by steep." The genesis of this image reveals the way in which Keats "identified" or gave individual character to the images which he read. In his earlier years, before he had seen mountains, he was intrigued by images of mountain pines which he read in the poetry of his Renaissance masters. Shakespeare's *Cymbeline* (IV. ii. 174–175) —

> as the rud'st wind,
> That by the top doth take the mountain pine.

Shakespeare's *Merchant of Venice* (IV. i. 75 *et seq.*) —

> You may as well forbid the mountain pines
> To wag their high tops and to make no noise,
> When they are fretten with the gusts of heaven. . . .

Fletcher's *Faithful Shepherdess* —

> Straighter than the straightest pine upon the steep
> Head of an aged mountain. . . . [I. ii. 65–66.]
> . . . a brim
> Of sailing pines, that edge yon mountain in.
> [IV. iii. 57.]

Milton's *Paradise Lost* (I. 292–293) —

> . . . the tallest pine
> Hewn on Norwegian hills. . . .

Keats imitated these images in December 1816 in *I stood tip-toe* (v. 128) —

> In the calm grandeur of a sober line,
> We see the waving of the mountain pine.

He imitated them also in April 1817 in a description of Mount Latmos in *Endymion* (I. 85–86) —

> The freshness of the space of heaven above,
> Edg'd round with dark tree tops? . . .

and in the Hymn to Pan in *Endymion* (I. 261–262) —

> By every wind that nods the mountain pine,
> O forester divine!

In the summer of 1818 Keats made an excursion to the lakes and mountains of Cumberland and Westmorland and the mountains of Scotland to "identify finer scenes" in his mind. When he saw Windermere, in the lake country, he was astonished at the slate, the moss, the rock-weed, the coloring, or, as he called it, the countenance or intellectual tone of the scene. "The space, the magnitude of mountains and waterfalls are well imagined before one sees them," he wrote his brother Tom; "but this countenance or intellectual tone must surpass every imagination and defy any remembrance." When he climbed the "rich-toned Mountains" to see the Falls of Lodore, he identified the image of trees on a mountain peak — that is, he experienced with his own senses a scene which he had imagined from descriptions in poetry.

> I had an easy climb [he wrote his brother Tom on June 29, 1818] among the streams, about the fragments of Rocks, and should have got I think to the summit, but unfortunately I was damped by slipping one leg into a squashy hole. There is no great body of water, but the accompaniment is delightful; for it oozes out from a cleft in *perpendicular Rocks, all fledged with ash and other beautiful trees*. It is a strange thing how they got there.

Having identified this image in his own sensuous experience, he could express its countenance, its intellectual tone, in the *Ode to Psyche*:

> Far, far around shall those dark-cluster'd trees
> Fledge the wild-ridged mountains steep by steep.

He may have recalled this scene, as he recalled another scene in the sonnet *Bright star!*, by rereading the letters which he had written his brother Tom.

The symbolism of the final verses of the ode —

> And there shall be for thee all soft delight
> That shadowy thought can win,
> A bright torch, and a casement ope at night,
> To let the warm Love in!

has been interpreted by H. W. Garrod.[10] In the shrine which he built for Psyche in some untrodden region of his mind, Keats set an open casement and a bright torch to admit and to attract Psyche, the timorous moth-goddess, who symbolizes melancholic love. He identified Psyche the soul with Psyche the moth. In the *Ode on Melancholy* he said:

> Nor let the beetle, nor the death-moth be
> Your mournful Psyche. . . .

He learned this symbolism from Lempriere's *Classical Dictionary*.

> Psyche is generally represented [Lempriere said] with the wings of a butterfly to intimate the lightness of the soul, of which the butterfly is a symbol, and on that account, among the ancients, when a man had just expired, a butterfly appeared fluttering above, as if rising from the mouth of the deceased.

The butterfly which arises from the mouth of the deceased explains Keats's "death-moth" in the *Ode on Melancholy*.

Keats composed the five odes in a homogeneous state of mind. As we read the odes in succession, we meet images, emotions, and ideas which occur and recur in subtly varied phrases and which, echoing and enforcing one another, build a background of infinite imaginative suggestiveness. Keats did not express the principles of his empirical humanism in the *Ode to Psyche*, but he composed the ode, as he said, in the healthy state of mind which this philosophy had engendered in him. In the other four odes, however, he expressed different phases of his empirical humanism.

[10] H. W. Garrod, *Keats*, p. 99.

Brown, with whom Keats was living in Wentworth Place, related the circumstances of the composition of the *Ode to a Nightingale* as follows:

> In the spring of 1819 a nightingale had built her nest near my house. Keats felt a tranquil and continual joy in her song; and one morning he took his chair from the breakfast table to the grass-plot under a plum-tree, where he sat for two or three hours. When he came into the house, I perceived he had some scraps of paper in his hand, and these he was quietly thrusting behind the books. On inquiry, I found those scraps, four or five in number, contained his poetic feeling on the song of our nightingale. The writing was not well legible; and it was difficult to arrange the stanzas on so many scraps. With his assistance I succeeded, and this was his *Ode to a Nightingale*, a poem which has been the delight of every one. [Manuscript, Houghton-Crewe Collection; quoted by Colvin.]

Keats gave these scraps of paper, it seems, to Reynolds. They were possessed in turn by Marianne Reynolds and her son Townley Green; and when Townley Green died they were bought by the Marquess of Crewe, who now owns them. They were published in photographic facsimile by Sir Sidney Colvin in the *Monthly Review* for March 1903. The ode exists in every stage of composition and revision. There are transcripts in Keats's copy of *Endymion*, Woodhouse's Commonplace Book and Book of Transcripts, and George Keats's Book of Autographs and Transcripts. Keats was induced by Haydon to publish the ode in July 1819 in the *Annals of the Fine Arts*, a quarterly magazine edited by James Elmes; he published it also in his *Poems* of 1820.

Brown's story of the composition of the ode is right in the main, Sir Sidney Colvin pointed out, although, since he wrote it twenty years afterwards, it is inaccurate in details. The manuscript consists of two half sheets of note-paper, inscribed on both sides, instead of the four or five scraps which Brown remembered. On the recto of leaf 2 Keats began the ode as follows: "Small winged Dryad"; but, rejecting this beginning after he had written the three words, he made a second beginning on the recto of leaf 1, on which he composed the first and second stanzas and 6 verses of the third stanza. On the recto of leaf 2, which he turned upside down to avoid the first false beginning, he completed the third stanza and composed the fourth and fifth stanzas. On the verso of leaf 1 he composed the sixth and seventh stanzas; and on the verso of leaf 2, the eighth stanza. Brown remembered his difficulty in reading this first draft, Sir Sidney Colvin pointed out, but he forgot the cause of the difficulty. The writing is not illegible but the order of the stanzas is confusing at first. Evidences of composition and "decomposition," which the first stanza will illustrate, prove that these two half sheets of note-paper contain the first draft of the ode.

Ode to the Nightingale

drowsy
~~My~~ Heart aches and a ~~painful~~ numbness ~~falls~~
pains
My sense as though of hemlock I had dunk
Or empted some dull opiate to the drains
past
One minute ~~hence~~ and Lethe-wards had sunk:
'Tis not through envy of thy happy lot,
But being too happy in thine happiness
That thou light-winged dryad of the trees
In some melodious plot
Of beechen green and shadows numberss
Singest of summer in full-throated ease.

Keats began the first stanza as follows: "My Heart aches and a painful numbness falls." He crossed out "My," intending for a moment, it seems, to make "Heart aches" a noun but he rejected this alteration. He changed "falls" into "pains" and, to avoid repetition in sound, changed "painful" into "drowsy." To have a rhyme for "pains," he chose "drains," which he used inexactly for "dregs." In this stanza, therefore, we see him in the process of selecting basic rhyme words. We see evidence of composition, also, in the omission of letters in words, as "dunk" for "drunk" and "numberss" for "numberless."

The *Ode to a Nightingale* has, as H. W. Garrod pointed out, an interesting position in the tradition of the nightingale in English poetry. In mediaeval English poetry the nightingale is represented as the bird of love; and in debates, such as *The Owl and the Nightingale* and *The Cuckoo and the Nightingale*, the nightingale defends the pleasures of the senses. In the Renaissance, when classical culture was revived and assimilated, English poets adopted the Greek legend of Tereus, Procne, and Philomela, according to which Philomela, having been violated and mutilated by her brother-in-law Tereus, was transformed into a nightingale. In English poetry of the sixteenth, seventeenth, and eighteenth centuries, the nightingale, or Philomela, is represented as a melancholy bird eternally lamenting her woes in sad but sweet melody. These two traditions of the nightingale converged in Milton's poetry. In his *Sonnet to the Nightingale*, he followed the mediaeval tradition, representing the nightingale as the bird of love and the cuckoo as the bird of hate. The nightingale, he said, fills the lover's heart with fresh hopes. In *Il Penseroso*, however, he followed the classical tradition, calling the nightingale —

> Sweet bird, that shunn'st the noise of folly,
> Most musical, most melancholy!

At the end of the eighteenth century Coleridge and Wordsworth revolted against the classical tradition of the nightingale and revived the mediaeval tradition in a more natural form. In April 1798 Coleridge composed a poem on the nightingales which he heard singing on the estate of Alfoxden, which Wordsworth had leased from the noble family of St. Albyn. Alluding to Milton's description of the nightingale as "Most musical, most melancholy," he said:

> A melancholy Bird? O idle thought!
> In nature there is nothing melancholy.

After rebuking those poets who followed servilely the false convention of "Philomela's pity-pleading strains," he addressed William and Dorothy Wordsworth as follows:

> My Friend, and my Friend's Sister! we have learnt
> A different lore: we may not thus profane
> Nature's sweet voices always full of love
> And joyance! 'Tis the merry Nightingale
> That crowds, and hurries, and precipitates
> With fast thick warble his delicious notes,
> As he were fearful, that an April night
> Would be too short for him to utter forth
> His love chant, and disburthen his full soul
> Of all its music!

Wordsworth expressed a similar conception of the nightingale as a bird of joy in the poem beginning —

> O nightingale! thou surely art
> A creature of a "fiery heart" . . .

which he composed in 1807. Coleridge and Wordsworth were influenced in their conception of the nightingale by the mediaeval debate *The Cuckoo and the Nightingale*, which Wordsworth translated in 1801 and published in 1842.

Keats, like Coleridge and Wordsworth, represented the nightingale as a happy bird singing of summer in full-throated ease. His description of the world of natural beauty and mystery in which he imagined the nightingale lived and sang was influenced slightly, we shall see, by Coleridge's description of the grove in Alfoxden in which he heard the nightingales sing. Both poets expressed also their perception of the fading anthem of the nightingale. Keats had known Coleridge's poem for three years at the least. He had already echoed it twice before — in *Endymion* (III. 142 *et seq.*) and in *The Pot of Basil* (liv. 8). And on Sunday, April 11, three or four weeks before he composed the *Ode to a Nightingale*, he met Coleridge in Millfield Lane and walked two miles with him at a slow pace. Among the subjects which Coleridge discussed were "Nightingales, Poetry — on Poetical Sensation —." Professor Garrod suggested that there was a subtle connection between Coleridge's conversation on nightingales and Keats's *Ode to a Nightingale.* Coleridge doubtless discussed the history of the nightingale in poetry and explained, as he had explained in his poem *The Nightingale*, that it is a happy instead of a melancholy bird. Coleridge's discussion of the nightingale in poetry reminded Keats probably of the nightingale which was singing in his garden and started a process of creation in the subconscious depths of his mind.

Keats expressed in his *Ode to a Nightingale* the inadequacy of a romantic escape from painful reality into an ideal world of natural beauty. He considered this problem in the light of the empirical humanism, the new wisdom which he had acquired in the latter half of March 1819.

The consoling power of natural beauty was an essential principle of that philosophy of nature which he had learned from Wordsworth in the fall of 1815. He said in the opening verses of *Endymion* that "A thing of beauty is a joy for ever" and that, in spite of despondence, "Some shape of beauty moves away the pall From our dark spirits." "The setting Sun will always set me to rights," he wrote Bailey in November 1817, "— or if a Sparrow come before my Window I take part in its existence and pick about the Gravel." Like Wordsworth, he explained this principle of consolation by means of the empirical principle of sensation; and, like Wordsworth also, he fused or confused it with the neo-Platonic ecstasy. In *Endymion* he described ecstasies in which his soul, stimulated by sensations of natural beauty, escaped from his body with its mortal cares and entered into communion with Original Essence. As he grew older he substituted a principle of objective imagination, which he deduced from Shakespeare's plays with Hazlitt's assistance, for the principle of neo-Platonic mysticism, which he had learned from Spenser. He wrote his brother George in October 1818 that, as his imagination strengthened, he lived not in this world alone but in a thousand worlds. He was impelled to begin *Hyperion*, we remember, to escape from the painful consciousness of his dying brother into the ideal world of Greek beauty. Imaginative intuitions of beauty had enabled him to escape momentarily from petty cares but they could not enable him to escape, he discovered, from the serious ills "that flesh is heir to." He fell into despair in February 1819; but in March, we remember, he developed an empirical and stoical humanism which enabled him to endure the painful ills of life with calm fortitude.

As Keats sat under the plum tree in the garden of Wentworth Place one morning in May and listened to the song of the nightingale, he was stoically, almost apathetically, despondent. His heart ached and a drowsy numbness pained his sense as though of hemlock he had drunk. He did not envy the happy lot of the nightingale who sang of summer in full-throated ease, but her happiness made him intensely conscious of his own sorrows. The effective play on the word "happy," repeated and developed from the *Ode to Psyche*, was suggested, we have seen, by a verse in Mary Tighe's *Psyche* (II. 3. 1). Another phrase, "a drowsy numbness pains My sense," may be also a reminiscence of Mrs. Tighe's *Psyche* (VI. 16) —

> A *drowsy* dullness seems o'er all to creep . . .
> while deep repose
> *Benumbs* each torpid *sense* and bids her eyelids close.

And the phrase "as though of hemlock I had drunk" is almost identical to a verse in Marlowe's translation of Ovid's *Love Elegies* (Bk. III. El. 6):

> Yet like as if cold Hemlock I had drunke. . . .

In the second stanza of the ode Keats longed for a draught of wine that on the wings of intoxication he might escape from his sorrows into the happy world of the nightingale.

> O, for a draught of vintage! that hath been
> Cool'd a long age in the deep-delved earth,
> Tasting of Flora and the country green,
> Dance, and Provencal song, and sunburnt mirth!
> O for a beaker full of the warm South,
> Full of the true, the blushful Hippocrene,
> With beaded bubbles winking at the brim,
> And purple-stained mouth;
> That I might drink, and leave the world unseen,
> And with thee fade away into the forest dim:

In the fourth stanza, however, he exclaimed:

> Away! away! for I will fly to thee,
> Not charioted by Bacchus and his pards,
> But on the viewless wings of Poesy,
> Though the dull brain perplexes and retards: . . .

A contrast between the intoxication produced by wine and the ecstasy engendered by sensations of beauty runs through the poems which Keats composed in 1818 and 1819. The passage in the *Ode to a Nightingale* is the quintessence of two earlier passages which he had composed in a lower degree of imagination. In some heptasyllabics which he composed *ex tempore* on January 31, 1818, he said:

Hence Burgundy, Claret and Port,
 Away with old Hock and Madeira,
Two earthly ye are for my sport;
 There's a beverage brighter and clearer.
Instead of a pitiful rummer,
My wine overbrims a whole summer;
 My bowl is the sky,
 And I drink at my eye,
 Till I feel in the brain
 A Delphian pain —

He drank sensations of natural beauty, he said, until he fell into an ecstasy in which his soul flew to Apollo and his body pressed to the earth. The second passage occurs in the second ode *To* [*Fanny*], which he composed in April 1819, three or four weeks before he composed the *Ode to a Nightingale*. Longing to escape from the painful fetters of love, he said:

Shall I gulp wine? No, that is vulgarism,
A heresy and schism,
Foisted into the canon-law of love. . . .

In the second stanza of the *Ode to a Nightingale*, Keats expressed this idea in images and rhythms of imperishable beauty. He sublimated that love of wine for which he has been censured, transforming it into sensuous images of a pure and exalted kind. He infused the love of wine, also, with poetic associations, making it as suggestive as it is sensuous. The wine which he invoked tastes of Flora and the country green, dance, and Provençal song, and sunburnt mirth. With three or four suggestive details he re-created the gay, warm, glamorous atmosphere of mediaeval Provence. In the verses —

O for a beaker full of the warm South,
 Full of the true, the blushful Hippocrene,
  With beaded bubbles winking at the brim,
   And purple-stained mouth. . .

he employed a style which the Greek rhetoricians, who were Milton's masters, called the elegant, a style which is replete with figures of speech, which stirs the reader's imagination with its sheer, concentrated artistry. Few readers would call this style obscure; but Leigh Hunt,[11] being malicious, said that Byron, living in Italy, drinking its wine, and basking in its sunshine, asked him what was the meaning of a beaker "full of the warm South."

Keats drew a part of his phraseology from the poetry which he was reading, but he "identified" these phrases in his own sensuous experience. The verse "Cool'd a long age in the deep-delved earth" is a fine example of this process. He created the compound "deep-delved" on analogy with Milton's "low-delved" — "Hid from the world in a low-delved tomb" (*On the Death of a Fair Infant*, v. 32). And two or three weeks before he composed the ode he associated wine "Cool'd a long age" with "Flora and the country green." He wrote his sister on April 17:

> O there is nothing like fine weather, and health, and Books, and a fine country, and a contented Mind, and Diligent habit of reading and thinking . . . and, please heaven, *a little claret-wine cool out of a cellar a mile deep* — with a few or a good many ratafia cakes — a rocky basin to bathe in, a strawberry bed to say your prayers to *Flora* in. . . .

The phrases "the true, the blushful Hippocrene" and the "dull brain" may have been suggested to Keats by two verses in Drayton's *Ode 9* — "Which to the colder brayne Is the true Hypocrene." And the verse "With beaded bubbles winking at the brim" may have been a reminiscence of a verse in Dryden's *Oedipus* (IV. i) — "Seething like rising bubbles on the brim." The phrase "charioted by Bacchus and his pards" was a reminiscence of Rabelais' description of Bacchus' conquest of India — "*Bacchus* marchoit en bataille, & estoit sur *un char* magnifique, tiré par trois couples de jeune *pards*, joints ensemble."

In the third stanza of the ode Keats described the painful facts of life from which he longed to escape.

> Fade far away, dissolve, and quite forget
> What thou among the leaves hast never known,
> The weariness, the fever, and the fret
> Here, where men sit and hear each other groan;
> Where palsy shakes a few, sad, last gray hairs,
> Where youth grows pale, and spectre-thin, and dies;
> Where but to think is to be full of sorrow
> And leaden-eyed despairs,
> Where Beauty cannot keep her lustrous eyes,
> Or new Love pine at them beyond to-morrow.

After Keats had mastered the "naked truths" of life in the latter part of March 1819, he could contemplate them with temperate

[11] Leigh Hunt, *Lord Byron and Some of his Contemporaries.*

blood, intuit them, and express them in the objective form of poetry. He alluded to "The weariness, the fever, and the fret" which he had experienced in February and March before he had mastered the painful problems of his experience. The phraseology of this verse may have been suggested by a passage in *Tintern Abbey* (vv. 52–53), in which Wordsworth said that, "When the fretful stir Unprofitable, and the fever of the world" hung upon the beatings of his heart, his spirit turned to the natural beauty of sylvan Wye for consolation. In the verse "Where youth grows pale, and spectre-thin and dies," Keats referred to his brother Tom, who died a slow and lingering death, wasting away under the ravages of consumption. And in the verses "Where Beauty cannot keep her lustrous eyes, Or new Love pine at them beyond to-morrow," he alluded, more truly than he thought, to his love for Fanny Brawne.

Keats's imagination bore him into the world of beauty in which he imagined the nightingale lived and sang; but his painful consciousness of real life accompanied him. His description of the world of the nightingale is richly sensuous but it is also sombre and sad. The mood of sorrow through which he views the scene makes the beauty of the scene more intense and poignant.

Already with thee! tender is the night,
  And haply the Queen-Moon is on her throne,
    Cluster'd around by all her starry Fays;
      But here there is no light,
  Save what from heaven is with the breezes blown
    Through verdurous glooms and winding mossy ways.

5

I cannot see what flowers are at my feet,
  Nor what soft incense hangs upon the boughs,
But, in embalmed darkness, guess each sweet
  Wherewith the seasonable month endows
The grass, the thicket, and the fruit-tree wild;
  White hawthorn, and the pastoral eglantine;
    Fast fading violets cover'd up in leaves;
      And mid-May's eldest child,
  The coming musk-rose, full of dewy wine,
    The murmurous haunt of flies on summer eves.

There are two settings in the ode, as A. W. Crawford[12] has pointed out, and the change from the one setting to the other occurs at the beginning of the sestet of the fourth stanza. In the first part of the ode Keats is sitting one morning in May under the plum tree in the garden of Wentworth Place. In the second part of the ode he flies on

[12] A. W. Crawford, *The Genius of Keats*, pp. 103 *et seq.*

the wings of the imagination to the ideal world of the nightingale, a forest in May in the early hours of the night. "Haply the Queen-Moon is on her throne. . . But here there is no light, Save what from heaven is with the breezes blown Through verdurous glooms and winding mossy ways."

This description is perhaps the richest expression of natural beauty in Keats's poetry. He recalled many details from Coleridge's *Nightingale* but he enriched and heightened every detail which he remembered. The imaginative effects of the two poems are therefore entirely different. The sources of the phrases, the "forest dim," the "verdurous glooms," the "mossy ways," the "grass," the "thicket," the "fruit-tree wild," etc., may be found in the following passages in Coleridge's poem. Near the beginning of the poem Coleridge said:

Come, we will rest on this old *mossy* Bridge!
You see the glimmer of the stream beneath,
But hear no *murmuring*: it flows silently
O'er its soft bed of *verdure*. All is still,
A balmy night! and tho' the stars be *dim*,
Yet let us think upon the vernal showers
That gladden the green earth, and we shall find
A pleasure in the *dimness* of the stars.
And hark! the Nightingale begins its song. . . .

In the middle of the poem Coleridge described the grove in which he heard the nightingales sing.

This *grove* is *wild* with tangling underwood,
And the trim *walks are broken up*, and *grass*,
Thin *grass* and king-cups grow within the *paths*.
But never elsewhere in one place I knew
So many Nightingales: and far and near
In *wood* and *thicket* over the wide *grove*
They answer and provoke each other's songs —
. . . .
Beside a brook in *mossy forest-dell*. . . .

In the sixth stanza Keats described the effect of the nightingale's song upon him.

Darkling I listen; and, for many a time
  I have been half in love with easeful Death,
Call'd him soft names in many a mused rhyme,
  To take into the air my quiet breath;
    Now more than ever seems it rich to die,
  To cease upon the midnight with no pain,
    While thou art pouring forth thy soul abroad
        In such an ecstasy!
  Still wouldst thou sing, and I have ears in vain —
    To thy high requiem become a sod.

This stanza relates the ode definitely to that empirical humanism by means of which he overcame his despair in the latter part of March 1819. It seemed to him "rich to die, To cease upon the midnight with no pain," while the nightingale was "pouring forth" her "soul abroad In such an ecstasy." He recalled that "many a time" he had "been half in love with easeful Death" and had "Call'd him soft names in many a mused rhyme." One of the mused rhymes in which he had invoked death is the sonnet *Why did I laugh tonight?* which he composed on March 19 or a day or two thereafter. In this sonnet he considered the painful problems of his experience — the problems of poetry, ambition, and love — and he decided, after an empirical analysis of the problem of evil in nature, that death was the only solution to these problems.

> Verse, fame and Beauty are intense indeed
> But Death intenser — Death is Life's high meed.

Keats adapted the eleventh verse of the sonnet,

> Yet could I on this very midnight cease,

into the sixth verse of the sixth stanza of the ode,

> To cease upon the midnight with no pain. . . .

Another mused rhyme in which he had invoked death is the sonnet *Bright star!* which he composed a day or two after the middle of April 1819. Considering the problem of his love for Fanny Brawne, he longed to possess Miss Brawne steadfastly and completely and to die in the same instant.

> To hear, to feel her tender-taken breath,
> Half passionless, and so swoon on to death.

In the seventh stanza of the ode Keats expressed his impression of the immortality of the nightingale's song.

> Thou wast not born for death, immortal Bird!
> No hungry generations tread thee down;
> The voice I hear this passing night was heard
> In ancient days by emperor and clown:
> Perhaps the self-same song that found a path
> Through the sad heart of Ruth, when, sick for home,
> She stood in tears amid the alien corn;
> The same that oft-times hath
> Charm'd magic casements, opening on the foam
> Of perilous seas, in faery lands forlorn.

The idea of this stanza, the contrast between the mortality of man and the immortality of the nightingale, has provoked a great deal of discussion. Robert Bridges [13] said that "the thought is fanciful or superficial — man being as immortal as the bird in every sense but sameness, which is assumed and does not satisfy." This sameness does satisfy us, however, for, although it may not be a truth of fact, it is a truth of impression. In *The Round Table* and in *The Lectures on the English Poets* Hazlitt said, de Sélincourt [13] pointed out, that we connect the idea of the individual with human beings and the idea of the class with natural objects and creatures of the lower orders. We think of human beings as individuals, differing from one another in personality, each having within himself impulses and ideas of which we know nothing. We think of birds, however, as members of classes, each bird being identical with all other birds of the same class. And we think of the voice of the bird, even more than of the bird itself, as always and eternally the same. Wordsworth was also impressed, as de Sélincourt pointed out, by the eternal sameness of the voice of birds; and he said in his poem *To the Cuckoo*:

> O Cuckoo! shall I call thee Bird,
> Or but a wandering Voice? . . .
> Even yet thou art to me
> No bird, but an invisible thing,
> A voice, a mystery;
> *The same whom in my school-boy days*
> *I listened to*. . . .

The sestet of the seventh stanza has stirred the imaginations of readers to a greater degree perhaps than any other passage in Keats's poetry. It consists in two tercets which are equally vivid but entirely different types of poetry. The first tercet, which distills the essence of the story of Ruth from the Hebrew Bible, is poetry of human emotions. It is as intense and as poignant as the allusion to Ceres and Proserpine in *Paradise Lost* (IV. 268–272), an allusion which Keats quoted and praised as uniquely Miltonic.

The second tercet suggests the magical atmosphere of romance. In the first draft of the ode we see Keats in the process of selecting the magically suggestive words of the tercet —

> The same that oftimes hath
> magic
> Charm'd ~~the wide~~ casements opening on the foam
> Of ~~keelless~~ perilous seas in fairy lands folorn [*sic*].

Keats substituted "magic" for the unimaginative "the wide" and "perilous" for the inharmonious "keelless." He did not intro-

[13] Ernest de Sélincourt, p. 475.

duce the third most suggestive word, "faery," which calls up the world of mediaeval romance, until he published the ode in his *Poems* of 1820. In his intermediate versions, as in the first draft, he retained "fairy," which suggests the very different world of Shakespeare's fairies, the fairies of *A Midsummer Night's Dream.*

Keats composed the picture of the "magic casements" out of many diverse elements, fusing them together so thoroughly that it is difficult to discover the sources from which he drew them. Sir Sidney Colvin [14] suggested that Keats recalled Claude's *Enchanted Castle*, which he had described in his *Epistle to Reynolds* —

> You know the Enchanted Castle[, —] it doth stand
> Upon a Rock on the Border of a Lake,
> Nested in Trees, which all do seem to shake
> From some old Magic like Urganda's Sword . . .
> A mossy place, a Merlin's Hall, a dream . . .
> The doors all look as if they oped themselves,
> The windows as if latch'd by fays & elves. . . .

The lake or sea in this painting, however, is clear and calm and peaceful; it does not foam and it is neither "keelless" nor "perilous."

Mrs. Katherine Ridley [15] suggested that Keats remembered casements opening upon foaming seas from Mrs. Radcliffe's Gothic romances.

> From her *casement* she look'd out from . . . Alpine steeps . . . into the valley, along which *foamed* a broad and rapid stream . . . in one broad sheet of *foam*. . . . [*Mysteries of Udolpho*, Ch. XX.]
> . . . *casements* thrown *open* . . . . Beyond appeared the *waters of the Mediterranean*, stretching far to the south and to the east, where they were lost in the horizon. [*Mysteries of Udolpho*, Ch. XXXVIII.]
>
> The countess was sitting . . . in a room the *windows* of which looked upon the *sea*. . . . The moon shone faintly by intervals through broken clouds upon the waters, illuming the white *foam* which burst around. [*Castles of Athlin and Dunbayne.*]

Miss Lowell,[16] following Professor John Livingston Lowes, suggested that Keats derived certain details, especially the "perilous seas," from a description of the Arabian Gulf in Diodorus Siculus' *Historical Library* (in Booth's translation).

> . . . by the continual dashing of the floods . . . it *foams* terribly. . . . The waves dashing against these huge rocks, mount up in a curl, and *foam* to admiration. . . . Next adjoining to this *perilous sea*. . . . [Book III, Ch. III.]

---

[14] Sir Sidney Colvin, pp. 264–265, 291.
[15] Ernest de Sélincourt, Fifth Edition, 1926.
[16] Amy Lowell, Vol. II, p. 253.

I do not believe, however, that Keats derived any of these details either from Mrs. Radcliffe or from Diodorus Siculus. I believe that the whole magic picture was formed in his mind by a fusion of his remembrance of Claude's *Enchanted Castle* and his recollection of Spenser's story of Marinel in *The Faerie Queene* (Book III, Canto IV). He drew the image of magic casements opening on a sea from Claude's *Enchanted Castle* and "the foam Of perilous seas, in faery lands forlorn" from Spenser's story of Marinel. Marinel, the son of the knight Dumarin and the sea-nymph Cymoent, was the guardian of the Rich Strand, defending it against all who attempted to pass over it.

An hundred knights of honorable name
He had subdew'd, and them his vassals made,
That through all *Farie Lond* his noble fame
Now blazed was, and feare did all invade,
That none durst passen through that *perilous* glade.

When Marinel was overthrown and wounded by Britomart, the maiden knight, his mother, accompanied by sea-nymphs, came to his assistance.

Soone as they bene arriv'd upon the brim
Of the Rich Strond, their charets they *forlore*,
And let their temed fishes softly swim
Along the margent of the *fomy shore*. . . .

Cymoent found her son lying in a deadly swoon,

. . . a lumpe of earth *forlorne*. . . .

In the final stanza of the ode Keats described his return to the world of reality.

Forlorn! the very word is like a bell
To toll me back from thee to my sole self!
Adieu! the fancy cannot cheat so well
As she is fam'd to do, deceiving elf.
Adieu! adieu! thy plaintive anthem fades
Past the near meadows, over the still stream,
Up the hill-side; and now 'tis buried deep
In the next valley-glades:
Was it a vision, or a waking dream?
Fled is that music: — Do I wake or sleep?

Keats admitted the inadequacy of the romantic escape from the world of reality to the world of ideal beauty. "Adieu!" he said to the nightingale, "the fancy cannot cheat so well As she is fam'd to do, deceiving elf." A return to consciousness of reality was the necessary end of each romantic escape into an imaginary world. In his earlier poems this escape had given him a momentary forgetfulness of reality and a momentary happiness. In the *Ode to a Nightingale,* however, the consciousness of painful reality had accompanied him into the ideal world of the nightingale. The final stanza is perfect except for a single inconsistency in the representation of feeling. Up to this point in the ode, Professor Garrod [17] pointed out, Keats made a clear contrast between his own sadness and the happiness of the nightingale; but in the final stanza he called the nightingale's song a "plaintive anthem," reading his own sadness into the song of the nightingale.

The *Ode on Melancholy* is very closely connected with the *Ode to a Nightingale.* It explains the cause of the sadness which Keats felt in the beautiful world of the nightingale. He was becoming intensely conscious of the close interrelation of beauty and decay, joy and sorrow, and life and death. Beauty made him sad, for he perceived that beauty is evanescent. Like Shakespeare, he wept to have that which he feared to lose.

There is no autograph manuscript of the *Ode on Melancholy.* There is a transcript in George Keats's Book of Autographs and Transcripts and another in Woodhouse's Book of Transcripts. The ode was published by Keats in his *Poems* of 1820 and by Lord Houghton in 1848.

Two traditions of melancholy, the one poetic and the other philosophic and medical, converged in the *Ode on Melancholy.* Keats derived the theme of the ode, that melancholy arises from a consciousness of the decay of beauty, from sensuous poets of the Renaissance, Spenser, Shakespeare, and others. This theme had descended from the poets of Greece and Rome, Anacreon, Catullus, Ausonius, etc. Keats had expressed a consciousness of the flux of life and the mutability of beauty in *Sleep and Poetry,* which he had composed in November and December 1816. At that time, being young, full of hope, and looking upon life as a delightful adventure, he questioned that sadness which the flux of life inspired in Spenser and Shakespeare.

Stop and consider! life is but a day;
A fragile dew-drop on its perilous way
From a tree's summit; a poor Indian's sleep
While his boat hastens to the monstrous steep
Of Montmorency. Why so sad a moan?
Life is the rose's hope while yet unblown;
The reading of an ever-changing tale;

[17] H. W. Garrod, *Keats,* p. 116.

The light uplifting of a maiden's veil;
A pigeon tumbling in clear summer air;
A laughing school-boy, without grief or care,
Riding the springy branches of an elm.

Keats suffered from the flux of life in the latter half of 1818 and in the first half of 1819. He saw his brother Tom, who had an exquisite love of life, grow pale and spectre-thin, and die. His painful experience sharpened his imagination, deepened his emotions, and matured his intellect. He became empirical and realistic in his interpretation of the nature of the world. Life, he believed, is a strenuous discipline which must be endured with stoical fortitude. It may school an intelligence and make it a soul but it does not give permanent happiness. In the *Ode on Melancholy*, therefore, he expressed a more poignant sadness than that which he found in *The Faerie Queene.* We read fine things, he said, but we do not feel them until we have gone the same steps as the writers.

Keats derived details of the ode from Burton's *Anatomy of Melancholy*, a compendium of the philosophic tradition of melancholy. He steeped his mind in this period, we have seen, in Burton's summary of the theories of ancient, mediaeval, and Renaissance physicians, philosophers, and poets upon the subject of the causes, symptoms, and cures of melancholia. He had read also Fletcher's song on melancholy and Milton's *Il Penseroso*, which represent the mood of a man who has the melancholic temperament.

Keats began the ode, Lord Houghton said, as follows:

Though you should build a bark of dead men's bones,
  And rear a phantom gibbet for a mast,
Stitch shrouds together for a sail, with groans
  To fill it out, blood-stained and aghast;
Although your rudder be a dragon's tail
  Long sever'd, yet still hard with agony,
    Your cordage large uprootings from the skull
Of bald Medusa, certes you would fail
  To find the Melancholy — whether she
    Dreameth in any isle of Lethe dull. . . .

Woodhouse, who preserved this rejected stanza, copied "creeds" for "shrouds" in verse 3. Keats derived the character and, to some extent, the details of this grisly imagery from *The Anatomy of Melancholy.* Those terrors which arise from the apprehension of horrible objects, Burton said, produce a fierce and grievous melancholy. Among the examples which Burton cited the following is pertinent:

Hercules de Saxonia, calls this kinde of Melancholy (*ab agitatione spirituum*) by a peculiar name, it comes from the agitation, motion, contraction, dilation of spirits, not from any distemperature of humors, and produceth strong effects. This terrour is most usually caused, as *Plutarch* will have, *from some imminent danger, when a terrible object is at hand*, heard, seen, or conceived, *truly appearing, or in a dream*. . . . Many lose their wits *by the sudden sight of some spectrum or devill, a thing very common in all ages* . . . as *Orestes* did at the sight of the *Furies*. . . . Some by sudden fires, earthquakes, inundations, or any such dismall objects. . . or by the sight of a monster, a *carcase*, they are disquieted many months following, and cannot endure the roome where a *coarse* hath been, for a world would not be alone with a *dead man*. . . . At *Basil* a many little children in the spring time, went to gather flowers in a meddow at the townes end, where a malefactor hung in *gibbets*; all gazing at it, one by chance flung a stone, and made it stir, by which accident, the children affrighted ran away; one slower than the rest, looking back, and seeing the stirred *carcase* wag towards her, cryed out it came after, and was so terribly affrighted, that for many dayes she could not rest, eat or sleepe, she could not be pacified, but melancholy, died.

[Part I. Sec. 2. Mem. 4. Subs. 3.]

By the time that Keats had come to the end of the stanza he perceived that his imagination had conjured up images which were too grisly for the mood which he intended to express — a mood which was similar to that which he had expressed in the first stanza of the *Ode to a Nightingale*, a drowsy numbness which pained his sense as though he had emptied some dull opiate to the dregs and Lethewards had sunk. In the last verse of the stanza, "Dreameth in any isle of Lethe dull," he struck the tone of the mood which he felt by recalling a phrase from the *Ode to a Nightingale*. With this image as a beginning, he composed the first stanza:

No, no, go not to Lethe, neither twist
Wolf's-bane, tight-rooted, for its poisonous wine;
Nor suffer thy pale forehead to be kiss'd
By nightshade, ruby grape of Proserpine;
Make not your rosary of yew-berries,
Nor let the beetle, nor the death-moth be
Your mournful Psyche, nor the downy owl
A partner in your sorrow's mysteries;
For shade to shade will come too drowsily,
And drown the wakeful anguish of the soul.

Keats disagreed with Burton. You cannot nourish your melancholy, he said, on melancholy and horrible things, such as wolf's-bane, nightshade, death-moth, and downy owl. On the contrary, you must gorge your melancholy on things of beauty —

But when the melancholy fit shall fall
Sudden from heaven like a weeping cloud,

That fosters the droop-headed flowers all,
And hides the green hill in an April shroud;
Then glut thy sorrow on a morning rose,
Or on the rainbow of the salt sand-wave,
Or on the wealth of globed peonies;
Or if thy mistress some rich anger shows,
Emprison her soft hand, and let her rave,
And feed deep, deep upon her peerless eyes.

To the man who has the sensuous temperament, Keats said, to the man "whose strenuous tongue Can burst Joy's grape against his palate fine," melancholy arises from a perception of the decay of beauty:

She dwells with Beauty — Beauty that must die;
And Joy, whose hand is ever at his lips
Bidding adieu; and aching Pleasure nigh,
Turning to poison while the bee-mouth sips:
Ay, in the very temple of Delight
Veil'd Melancholy has her sovran shrine,
Though seen of none save him whose strenuous tongue
Can burst Joy's grape against his palate fine;
His soul shall taste the sadness of her might,
And be among her cloudy trophies hung.

Keats represented Melancholy as a goddess who has her sovran shrine in the very temple of Delight. Floyd Dell [18] suggested that Keats found this symbolism recorded as a literal fact in *The Anatomy of Melancholy*. "Sorrow" was worshiped by the Romans, Burton said, "under the name of Angerona Dea."

As *Macrobius* records 1. 10. *Saturnalium*; *In the Calends of January, Angerona had her holy day, to whom in the Temple of Volupia, or Goddesse of pleasure, their Augures and Bishops did yearely sacrifice; that being propitious to them, she might expell all cares, anguish, and vexation of the minde for that yeare following.* [Part I. Sec. 2. Mem. 3. Subs. 5.]

And, in the third partition of *The Anatomy* (Sec. 4. Mem. 1. Subs. 3), Burton called Angerona Dea "our goddess of Melancholy." Burton's literal statement that Angerona Dea, the goddess of melancholy, had her shrine in the temple of Volupia, the goddess of delight, inspired Keats to compose the ode by giving him a symbol through which he could express the emotion which had been engendered in him by painful experience.

The *Ode on a Grecian Urn* follows closely and logically in thought after the *Ode on Melancholy*. Keats attempted to solve the problem

[18] Floyd Dell, "Keats's Debt to Robert Burton," *The Bookman* (New York), for March 1928.

of beauty and decay which caused his melancholy. Saddened by the mutability of natural beauty, he sought consolation in the more permanent beauty of art. The artist is a part of flowing nature, he knew, but the artist can arrest the fleeting beauty of nature and express it in the relatively eternal form of art. He became aware of this idea in 1817, when he was steeping himself in English poetry of the Renaissance. He read the boasts of sonneteers, such as Shakespeare, that the beauty of their mistresses would live forever in their powerful rhymes. He drew a clear distinction in *Endymion*, we have seen, between the beauty of nature and the beauty of art. And on June 26, 1818, while he was visiting the lakes and mountains of Westmorland, he wrote his brother Tom:

> I shall learn poetry here and shall henceforth write more than ever, for the abstract endeavor of being able to add a mite to that mass of beauty which is harvested from these grand materials, by the finest spirits, and put into etherial existence for the relish of one's fellows.

Keats discussed poetry, painting, and sculpture with his friends, Haydon, Hazlitt, and Severn, and he learned to distinguish between the functions of these three arts. He may have been influenced, de Sélincourt [19] suggested, by the sonnet which Wordsworth composed in 1811 upon sight of a picture which Sir George Beaumont had painted. Wordsworth said that painting has the peculiar faculty of arresting and fixing a moment of fleeting time and of giving it the calm serenity of eternity.

> Praised be the Art whose subtle power could stay
> Yon cloud, and fix it in that glorious shape;
> Nor would permit the thin smoke to escape,
> Nor those bright sunbeams to forsake the day;
> Which stopped that band of travellers on their way,
> Ere they were lost within the shady wood;
> And showed the Bark upon the glassy flood
> For ever anchored in her sheltering bay.
> Soul-soothing Art! whom Morning, Noontide, Even,
> Do serve with all their changeful pageantry;
> Thou, with ambition modest yet sublime,
> Here, for the sight of mortal man, hast given
> To one brief moment caught from fleeting time
> The appropriate calm of blest eternity.

Keats expressed in the first stanza of the ode the peculiar impression which sculpture makes upon us. Addressing the Grecian urn, he said:

[19] Ernest de Sélincourt, p. 476.

Thou still unravish'd bride of quietness,
Thou foster-child of silence and slow time,
Sylvan historian, who canst thus express
A flowery tale more sweetly than our rhyme: . . .

The first moment which the sculptor had fixed upon the urn was a moment of Bacchic energy and ecstatic joy.

What leaf-fring'd legend haunts about thy shape
Of deities or mortals, or of both,
In Tempe or the dales of Arcady?
What men or gods are these? What maidens loth?
What mad pursuit? What struggle to escape?
What pipes and timbrels? What wild ecstasy?

These men and maidens live, however, in the ethereal world of art. Their ecstasy is an ethereal ecstasy. The melody of their pipes and timbrels touches our imagination but not our ears.

Heard melodies are sweet, but those unheard
Are sweeter; therefore, ye soft pipes, play on;
Not to the sensual ear, but, more endear'd,
Pipe to the spirit ditties of no tone: . . .

As in the *Ode to a Nightingale* Keats contrasted the mortal world of pain, decay, and death with the immortal world of beauty and joy in which the nightingale sang, so in the *Ode on a Grecian Urn* he contrasted mortal life with the immortal life of art. The persons carved on the urn have advantages as well as limitations. They are held immovable and immortal in a moment of ecstatic endeavor. They cannot achieve the objects for which they strive, but they will not suffer the decay and death of mortal life. They feel passion more than human, but they will not have, like mortal men, the aftermath of passion—"a heart high-sorrowful and cloy'd, A burning forehead, and a parching tongue."

Fair youth, beneath the trees, thou canst not leave
Thy song, nor ever can those trees be bare;
Bold Lover, never, never canst thou kiss,
Though winning near the goal — yet, do not grieve;
She cannot fade, though thou hast not thy bliss,
For ever wilt thou love, and she be fair!

Ah, happy, happy boughs! that cannot shed
Your leaves, nor ever bid the Spring adieu;
And, happy melodist, unwearied,
For ever piping songs for ever new;
More happy love! more happy, happy love!
For ever warm and still to be enjoy'd,
For ever panting, and for ever young;

All breathing human passion far above,
That leaves a heart high-sorrowful and cloy'd,
A burning forehead, and a parching tongue.

The *Ode on a Grecian Urn* is a rich mosaic of Keats's experience in life and in art. The urn [20] which he described is an imaginary urn which he intuited out of his recollections of various vases, friezes, paintings, and poems. He saw some vases, including the Townley Vase, in original form in the British Museum. He saw other vases in books of engravings—the Sosibios Vase in the *Musée Napoléon*, a four-volume collection of engravings of the works of art which Napoleon pillaged from Italy, and the Holland House Vase and the Borghese Vase in Piranesi's *Vasi e Candalabri*. Dilke possessed a tracing which Keats made of the engraving of the Sosibios Vase. Keats saw these books of engravings of vases, it is probable, in Haydon's studio, in which he had seen the book of engravings of the frescoes of the Campo Santo.

The "leaf-fringed legend" in the first stanza refers to the fringe of leaves which is carved around the neck of many vases, the Sosibios Vase and the Borghese Vase, for example. The Bacchic throng with its "wild ecstasy" was suggested by the Townley Vase and the Borghese Vase. The "maiden loth," the "mad pursuit," and the "struggle to escape" were suggested by details in the Townley Vase. In one group in this vase a maenad is fleeing from a man who is pursuing. The "pipes and timbrels" were suggested by the Borghese Vase, on which a youth plays on pipes and a maiden shakes a timbrel over her head and left shoulder. "Tempe" was derived, as de Selincourt pointed out, from Collins' ode *The Passions*. The Bacchic scenes on these vases reminded Keats of a similar scene in Collins' ode, in which Joy, playing on the pipe, inspired such ecstasy that they who heard the strain thought that they saw the maids of Tempe's vale dancing to some unwearied minstrel.

The description of the fair youth in the second stanza who is singing a song which he cannot leave beneath trees which will never be bare is a fusion of details which Keats remembered from vases and poetry. In the Borghese Vase there is a youth who is dancing and apparently singing; there are no trees but there is a fringe of leaves above his head. The trees which will never be bare were a reminiscence, however, of some verses in Shakespeare's sonnet 12. Keats

[20] I am indebted to two excellent studies of the influence of Greek vases upon Keats's ode: Sir Sidney Colvin, pp. 416 *et seq.*; and Paul Wolters, an article in *Archiv für des Studien der neueren Sprachen*, CXX. Band, der neuen Serie XX. Band. 1908. pp. 53-61.

quoted these verses in a letter which he wrote to Reynolds on November 22, 1817:

> When lofty trees I see barren of leaves
>   Which erst from heat did canopy the herd,
> And Summer's green all girded up in sheaves,
>   Borne on the bier with white and bristly beard. . . .

Keats recalled these verses because he too was thinking about the mutability of life. The bold lover who cannot kiss his mistress, though winning near the goal, was suggested by a group in the Townley Vase in which a youth and a maiden in a half-embrace are on the point of kissing.

In the third stanza Keats expressed the happiness of the world of art most effectively by a word-play — "Ah, happy, happy boughs!" "happy melodist," and "more happy love! more happy, happy love!" He had already employed this device, we remember, in the *Ode to Psyche* and the *Ode to a Nightingale*.

The second moment of life which the sculptor had fixed upon the Grecian urn was a moment of pastoral peace and serene piety.

> Who are these coming to the sacrifice?
>   To what green altar, O mysterious priest,
> Lead'st thou that heifer lowing at the skies,
>   And all her silken flanks with garlands drest?
> What little town by river or sea shore,
>   Or mountain-built with peaceful citadel,
>   Is emptied of this folk, this pious morn?
> And, little town, thy streets for evermore
>   Will silent be; and not a soul to tell
>   Why thou art desolate, can e'er return.

In the final tercet, Colvin observed, Keats's imagination suddenly and lightly shifted its ground, viewing the artistic arrest of life as though it were an infliction in the sphere of reality.

The style of this stanza, as Matthew Arnold perceived, has the clear radiance of Greek style. The first tercet, he said, "is Greek, as Greek as a thing from Homer or Theocritus; it is composed with the eye on the object, a radiancy and light clearness being added."

The chief source of the quiet pastoral sacrifice which Keats described in the fourth stanza is Claude's painting, the *Sacrifice to Apollo*, which Sir Sidney Colvin described as follows:

> It shows to the right an altar in front of a temple of Apollo, and about the altar a group including king and priest and a young man holding down a victim ox by the horns; people with baskets and offerings coming up from behind the temple; and to the left tall trees with a priest leading in another victim by the

horns, and a woman with a jar bringing in libation; a little back, two herdsmen with their goats; a river spanned by a bridge and winding towards a sea-bay partly encircled by mountains which close the view, and on the edge of the bay the tower and roofs of a little town indistinctly seen.

Keats had described this painting briefly in the epistle which he wrote to Reynolds on March 25, 1818:

The sacrifice goes on; the pontif knife
Gleams in the sun, the milk-white heifer lows,
The pipes go shrilly, the libation flows:
A white sail shews above the green-head cliff
Moves round the point, and throws her anchor stiff.
The Mariners join hymn with those on land.

There is neither a "white sail" nor a group of "mariners" in the *Sacrifice to Apollo*. Keats always mingled details from various sources with the details of the particular scene which he was describing.

From this painting were derived the chief details of the sacrifice in the *Ode on a Grecian Urn* — the crowd of people coming to the sacrifice, the mysterious priest leading a lowing heifer to the altar, and the "little town by . . . sea shore, Or mountain-built with peaceful citadel." These details may have been influenced and enforced by the Roman *suovetaurilia* (the sacrifice of a hog, a sheep, and a bull) which is depicted on the Holland House Vase. The side of the vase which Piranesi engraved shows a veiled priest (the "mysterious priest") standing at the left of a metal tripod and making a preliminary sacrifice of wine and incense; two youths behind the tripod, one of them holding pipes before his breast; at the left, behind the priest, a small group of people approaching the tripod; and at the right a group of youths leading the sacrificial victims, which are apparently a sow and a heifer. The details in Keats's description, especially the heifer lowing at the skies, may have been influenced also by the sacrificial procession in the south frieze of the Parthenon. Fragments of this frieze are among the Elgin Marbles, which he studied with Haydon. He had a more discriminating knowledge of the friezes of the Parthenon than of Greek vases. In the *Ode on Indolence* he admitted that the figures on a Greek vase were "strange" to him, "as may betide," he said, "to one deep in Phidian lore."

In the *Ode on a Grecian Urn* Keats represented, as we have seen, two kinds of beauty in Greek life: the beauty of the Bacchic throng, a beauty of youth and energy and joy; and the beauty of the pastoral sacrifice, a beauty of clear serenity and quiet piety. He learned the beauty which he associated with Greek life from Greek sculpture, which he saw in fragmentary but original form, rather than from Greek poetry, which he read in warped and colored translations. He studied the Elgin Marbles with Haydon, who knew more about them than any other man in that age. He went to see these fragments again and again, gazing at them in a state of ecstasy. On one occasion Severn discovered him before the marbles, his "eyes shining so brightly" and his "face so lit up by some visionary rapture" that the painter stole quietly away without intruding.

> Keats made me in love with the real living Spirit of the past [Severn said]. He was the first to point out to me how essentially modern that Spirit is: "It's an immortal youth," he would say, "just as there is no *Now* or *Then* for the Holy Ghost." [21]
>
> Rome, the *real* Rome [Severn said again] would never have become a joy to me — not, at any rate, for a very long time, and even then with difficulty and at best obscurely — had it not been for Keats's talks with me about the Greek spirit, — the Religion of the Beautiful, the Religion of Joy, as he used to call it. All that was finest in sculpture — and, as I came to see directly or indirectly, all that was finest too in painting, in *everything* — was due to that supreme influence. "I never cease to wonder at all that incarnate Delight," Keats remarked to me once: nor do I either, now that in inferior measure I too see something of what he saw.[21]

Keats began to appreciate the youth and the energy and the joy of Greek life in 1817 when he was viewing the Elgin Marbles with Haydon, studying Renaissance poetry, and composing *Endymion*. His appreciation of the quiet, radiant serenity of Greek life began at the end of 1818, when, oppressed by painful experience and stirred into a restless fever, he longed for serenity. The top of sovereignty, he said again and again in the letters and poems which he wrote in the first half of 1819, is to view circumstances in a calm state of mind, to behold the naked truths of life with temperate blood. The calm, stoical fortitude which he attained in April and May of 1819 is the truest phase of humanism in his whole poetic career.

The imaginary Grecian urn which Keats described is untrue, as Paul Wolters pointed out, to the pure conventions of Greek art. A Greek sculptor would no more think of mingling a Bacchic throng with a pious sacrifice than a Greek dramatist would think of mingling tragedy and comedy in a play. The vase which Keats described belongs in the tradition of the new-Attic or Roman type of vase instead of in the tradition of the pure Attic type. He had a precedent for the incongruous scenes on his vase, however, in the scene which Sosibios, a sculptor of the late Greek or Roman period, carved on a

[21] William Sharp, *Life and Letters of Joseph Severn*, p. 29.

vase. He was sufficiently impressed by the Sosibios Vase, we have seen, to make a tracing of the engraving of the vase in the *Musée Napoléon*. On this vase is depicted a blazing altar with four figures on each side of it, three facing it and one turned away. At the right of the altar are Artemis holding a bow in her left hand and leading a fawn with her right, a maenad with a harp, a satyr playing on pipes, and a maenad turning away from the altar and leaning on a staff. At the left of the altar are Hermes holding his caduceus aloft, a maenad with a pitcher, a Pyrrhic dancer, and a maenad with a large tambourine.

In the final stanza of the *Ode on a Grecian Urn* Keats's imagination shifted its ground again and considered the empirical message which the figures carved on the urn will give to one generation of men after another.

O Attic shape! Fair attitude! with brede
  Of marble men and maidens overwrought,
With forest branches and the trodden weed;
  Thou, silent form, dost tease us out of thought
As doth eternity: Cold Pastoral!
  When old age shall this generation waste,
    Thou shalt remain, in midst of other woe
Than ours, a friend to man, to whom thou say'st,
  "Beauty is truth, truth beauty,"— that is all
    Ye know on earth, and all ye need to know.

This final stanza is not so perfect as the other stanzas of the ode. The transitions in thought are not sufficiently clear and there is no strict correspondence between the units of thought and the metrical units of quatrain and two tercets. "Attic shape" and "Fair attitude" remind us of the artificial epithets of eighteenth-century poetry. "Brede," used in the sense of "embroidery," is too unusual to be a typical eighteenth-century word but it is a reminiscence of Collins' *Ode to Evening*.

The thought of the stanza is intelligible although it is not very clearly expressed. We can understand it best by considering it as the final stage, or the conclusion, of the thought of the preceding stanzas. The development of thought in the *Ode on a Grecian Urn* is very similar to that in the *Ode to a Nightingale*. At the beginning of the ode he escaped by means of his imagination from the world of reality into the world of art. He entered imaginatively into the two pictures of Greek life which the sculptor had carved upon the urn, experiencing that artistic illusion, "that willing suspension of disbelief," as Coleridge called it, "which constitutes poetic faith." As in the *Ode to a Nightingale*, however, a consciousness of painful reality accompanied him into the world of art and he contrasted the happiness of the figures on the urn with the unhappiness of mortal men. The carved figures in the Bacchic throng are immovable and immortal in a moment of ecstatic endeavor. They are warm and intense with the spirit of life. The bold lover will never kiss the maiden whom he is pursuing but, unlike mortal lovers, he will ever love and she be fair. Happy lovers! Keats exclaimed,

All breathing human passion far above,
That leaves a heart high-sorrowful and cloy'd,
A burning forehead, and a parching tongue.

A consciousness of reality intruded also into Keats's contemplation of the pastoral sacrifice, the second picture on the urn. The little town, whose inhabitants were attending the sacrifice, seemed silent and desolate. The artistic arrest of life seemed an infliction in the sphere of reality.

And, little town, thy streets for evermore
Will silent be; and not a soul to tell
Why thou art desolate, can e'er return.

At this point in the ode, as at the corresponding point in the *Ode to a Nightingale*, thoughts of reality came doubly strong and dissolved the artistic illusion which the carved figures on the urn had inspired in him. The word "desolate," like the word "forlorn," may have been the element which recalled him to reality. The final stanza represents his thoughts and feelings on his return to reality. When the artistic illusion was dissolved, the urn with its carved figures seemed cold, silent, and inanimate.

Thou, silent form, dost tease us out of thought
As doth eternity: Cold Pastoral!

The Grecian urn, which symbolizes artistic beauty, like the song of the nightingale, which symbolizes natural beauty, failed to give him surcease from the pain of reality. In the epistle which he wrote to Reynolds more than a year before he expressed the same thought in the same words. At that time his imagination was beginning to reveal to him the evil in nature. It revealed, in the first place, the flux of all natural things and, above all, the mutability of beauty, spoiling the singing of the nightingale and forcing him in summer skies to mourn. And it revealed, in the second place, "an eternal fierce destruction" among natural creatures — "The Shark at savage prey — the hawk at pounce, The gentle Robin, like a pard or ounce, Ravening a worm." At that time, however, he could not find a satisfactory solution for the intuitions of evil which his imagination formed.

> — but my flag is not unfurl'd
> On the Admiral staff, — and to philosophize
> I dare not yet! — Oh never will the prize,
> High reason, and the lore of good and ill
> Be my award. *Things cannot to the will*
> *Be settled, but they tease us out of thought.*

Now, in May 1819, when he composed the *Ode on a Grecian Urn*, he had philosophized and he had learned the "lore of good and ill." He had perceived that evil, which is connected in natural creatures with egotistic instincts, is inherent and necessary in nature. He had discovered that he could not escape this evil by fleeing either into the world of natural beauty (the *Ode to a Nightingale*) or into the world of artistic beauty (the *Ode on a Grecian Urn*). He had learned, however, to endure evil with stoical fortitude and to look upon the naked truths of life with temperate blood. He had learned also that the egotistic instincts of natural creatures, which produce much of the evil in nature, are beautiful, that they are the very thing in which poetry consists. The figures in the Bacchic throng on the Grecian urn are animated by natural instincts. The bold lover pursues the fleeing maiden with the same instinctive eagerness with which a hawk or a stoat pursues its mate. These instinctive actions, Keats perceived, are true and they are beautiful. And so, contemplating the Grecian urn with its true and beautiful representations of life, he said:

> When old age shall this generation waste,
> Thou shalt remain, in midst of other woe
> Than ours, a friend to man, to whom thou say'st,
> "Beauty is truth, truth beauty,"— that is all
> Ye know on earth, and all ye need to know.

The *Ode on Indolence* has not survived in Keats's autograph. It was preserved by Woodhouse, who obtained it "from C. B" (Charles Brown), transcribed it into his Book of Transcripts, and dated it "1819." It was published by Lord Houghton in 1848 from a transcript which was made, it is probable, either by Brown or by Woodhouse.

Keats described the pleasures of indolence in two earlier passages in his poetry, the Cave of Quietude in the fourth book of *Endymion* (November 1817) and the sonnet *What the thrush said* (February 19, 1818). Consumption, which had seized upon him in the autumn of

1817, was slowly sapping his vitality; and any physical or mental strain cast him into a state of physical debility and mental apathy. He was struck in the eye by a cricket ball on March 18, 1819, and the next morning he experienced a fit of apathy or, as he called it, indolence.

> This morning [he wrote his brother on March 19] I am in a sort of temper indolent and supremely careless: I long after a stanza or two of Thompson's [*sic*] Castle of indolence. My passions are all alseep[*sic*] from my having slumbered till nearly eleven and weakened the animal fibre all over me to a delightful sensation about three degrees on this side of faintness — if I had teeth of pearl and the breath of lillies I should call it langour[*sic*] — but as I am (Especially as I have a black eye) I must call it laziness. In this state of effeminacy the fibres of the brain are relaxed in common with the rest of the body, and to such a happy degree that pleasure has no show of enticement and pain no unbearable frown. Neither Poetry, nor Ambition, nor Love have any alertness of countenance as they pass by me: they seem rather like three figures on a greek vase — a Man and two women whom no one but myself could distinguish in their disguisement. This is the only happiness, and is a rare instance of advantage in the body overpowering the Mind.

Keats composed the *Ode on Indolence* at the end of May, it is probable, in a fit of indolence which was caused, I presume, by the strain of six weeks of intense composition. He recalled naturally the ideas, emotions, and images which he had experienced in that earlier fit of indolence on March 19. The Greek vase to which he alluded in the letter on March 19 and which he described in more detail in the ode was engraved in Piranesi's *Vasi e Candalabri*. The engraving shows three figures, a man and two women, in single file, hands joined together, and heads slightly bowed. In this same book of engravings Keats saw the Borghese Vase and the Holland House Vase, two of the vases which he had in his mind in the composition of his *Ode on a Grecian Urn*.

1

One morn before me were three figures seen,
  With bowed necks, and joined hands, side-faced;
And one behind the other stepp'd serene,
  In placid sandals, and in white robes graced;
    They pass'd, like figures on a marble urn,
  When shifted round to see the other side;
They came again; as when the urn once more
    Is shifted round, the first seen shades return;
  And they were strange to me, as may betide
With vases, to one deep in Phidian lore.

2

How is it, Shadows! that I knew ye not?
  How came ye muffled in so hush a mask?

Was it a silent deep-disguised plot
To steal away, and leave without a task
My idle days? Ripe was the drowsy hour;
The blissful cloud of summer-indolence
Benumb'd my eyes; my pulse grew less and less;
Pain had no sting, and pleasure's wreath no flower:
O, why did ye not melt, and leave my sense
Unhaunted quite of all but — nothingness?

3

A third time pass'd they by, and, passing, turn'd
Each one the face a moment whiles to me;
Then faded, and to follow them I burn'd
And ached for wings, because I knew the three;
The first was a fair Maid, and Love her name;
The second was Ambition, pale of cheek,
And ever watchful with fatigued eye;
The last, whom I love more, the more of blame
Is heap'd upon her, maiden most unmeek, —
I knew to be my demon Poesy.

4

They faded, and, forsooth! I wanted wings:
O folly! What is Love? and where is it?
And for that poor Ambition! it springs
From a man's little heart's short fever-fit;
For Poesy! — no, — she has not a joy, —
At least for me, — so sweet as drowsy noons,
And evenings steep'd in honied indolence;
O, for an age so shelter'd from annoy,
That I may never know how change the moons,
Or hear the voice of busy common sense!

The *Ode on Indolence* does not present a new phase of Keats's criticism of life. It is little more than a metrical paraphrase of that fit of apathy which he described in the journal letter to his brother on March 19, 1819. He considered the three chief problems of his experience — poetry, ambition, and love — in the sonnet *Why did I laugh tonight?* which he composed on March 19 or a day or two thereafter. He considered the problem of ambition in the two sonnets *On Fame,* which he composed on April 30; and he considered the problem of love in a series of poems which he composed in the latter half of April — the sonnets *As Hermes once,* and *Bright star!*, the second ode *To* [*Fanny*], and the ballad *La belle dame.* And he considered the problem of poetry both philosophically and technically in his letters and in his poems. Although he mastered the painful truths of life and accepted them with stoical fortitude, he welcomed sleep and mental apathy, which gave him a momentary relief from pain, and death, which would give him complete and final relief.

In the final stanza of the ode Keats bade farewell to love, ambition, and poetry:

> So, ye three Ghosts, adieu! Ye cannot raise
> My head cool-bedded in the flowery grass;
> For I would not be dieted with praise,
> A pet-lamb in a sentimental farce!
> Fade softly from my eyes, and be once more
> In masque-like figures on the dreamy urn. . . .

Keats repeated phrases from these verses in the letter which he wrote Miss Jeffrey of Teignmouth on June 9. He was still suffering from the apathetic mood in which he had composed the *Ode on Indolence* at the end of May, for he complained that he was idle and averse to writing.

> I have been very idle lately, very averse to writing; both from the overpowering idea of our dead poets and from abatement of my love of fame. I hope I am a little more of a Philosopher than I was, consequently a little less of a versifying Pet-lamb. . . . You will judge of my 1819 temper when I tell you that the thing I have most enjoyed this year has been writing an ode to Indolence.

Keats enjoyed the *Ode on Indolence* while he was in the apathetic mood in which he composed it; but he realized afterwards that it is inferior to the other odes which he composed in this period, for he did not publish it in his *Poems* of 1820. The ode is a mosaic of imaginative phrases from the preceding odes, but the intense feeling which had animated them is dissipated.

Keats ended the *Ode on Indolence* and this period of his poetry on a faint note of hope. "Farewell!" he told the phantoms of love, ambition, and poetry,

> Farewell! I yet have visions for the night,
> And for the day faint visions there is store. . . .

He still had hope of attaining some measure of fame in poetry and some measure of happiness in love. He was resolving at this time, we shall see, to compose poems, such as *Lamia*, which the public would like and buy and plays, such as *Otho the Great*, which the public would pay to see.

CHAPTER VIII

OTHO THE GREAT AND *LAMIA*

I

Otho the Great and *Lamia* were the first poems which Keats composed under the necessity of earning his living by means of his poetry. Up to the summer of 1819 he had never tried to compose poems which the public would like. He not only scorned writing for money but he also scorned financial matters in general. As long as Richard Abbey, the trustee of his estate, supplied him with the money which he needed, he did not investigate the state of his finances. He was compelled to consider it, at length, by a series of circumstances. In December 1818 he wrote Haydon, who had asked him for a loan, that he had barely enough money to support himself for three or four years. He was resolved, he said, to study, to travel, and to refrain from publication. When he applied to Abbey for money to lend to Haydon he discovered that the residue of his estate was much less than he had supposed and that he could not secure his share of his brother Tom's estate until his sister, the youngest of the heirs, came of age. During the past three years he had spent not only the income but a part of the principal of his estate. With reckless generosity he had lent £200 to his friends. It was a vice, Woodhouse [1] complained, for a man in Keats's circumstances to lend money.

At the end of May 1819, when his funds were exhausted, Keats was forced to consider means by which he could earn his living. On May 31 he wrote Miss Jeffrey of Teignmouth:

> I have been always till now almost as careless of the world as a fly — my troubles were all of the Imagination — My Brother George always stood between me and any dealings with the world. Now I find I must buffet it —I must take my stand upon some vantage ground and begin to fight — I must choose between despair & Energy — I choose the latter — though the world has taken on a quakerish look with me, which I once thought was impossible —
>
> "Nothing can bring back the hour
> Of splendour in the grass and glory in the flower."
>
> I once thought this a Melancholist's dream —

Keats considered two alternatives in this crisis — taking a position as a surgeon on an Indiaman and earning his living with his poetry.

[1] Woodhouse's letter to Taylor, August 31, 1819, Woodhouse's Scrap-book.

I have the choice as it were of two Poisons [he wrote Miss Jeffrey] (yet I ought not to call this a Poison) the one is voyaging to and from India for a few years; the other is leading a fevrous life alone with Poetry — This latter will suit me best; for I cannot resolve to give up my Studies. . . I would rather conquer my indolence and strain my nerves at some grand Poem — than be in a dunderheaded indiaman.

Keats was compelled also to seek a lodging for the summer; for Brown, with whom he had been living, had leased his house, as was his custom, for the months of July, August, and September. Keats could not bear to return to his former lodging in Well Walk, he wrote Miss Jeffrey, because it would remind him constantly of his brother who had died in it. He resolved to leave Hampstead and to retire into the country to study and to compose. He asked Miss Jeffrey to inquire about a cheap lodging in the villages around Teignmouth, and she replied promptly that she had found one for him in the beautiful village of Bradley. On June 8, however, Rice called on him and proposed that they take a lodging together for a month in Shanklin in the Isle of Wight, and he accepted Rice's proposal at once.

Keats's plan to retire to Shanklin to compose poetry was very nearly wrecked on June 15. When he called on Abbey to ask for money he was told that his aunt, Mrs. Midgley John Jennings, had threatened to file a suit in Chancery against Abbey as trustee of the Jennings estate.

I was the day before yesterday much in want of Money [he wrote Haydon on June 17]: but some news I had yesterday has driven me into necessity. I went to Abbey's for some Cash, and he put into my hand a letter from my Aunt's Solicitor containing the pleasant information that she was about to file a Bill in Chancery against us. Now in case of a defeat Abbey will be very undeservedly in the wrong box; so I could not ask him for any more money, nor can I till the affair is decided; and if it goes against him I must in conscience make over to him what little he may have remaining.

Keats was in a desperate situation. He had no money at all and, if his aunt filed the suit in Chancery, he would not receive any money from his estate for a very long while. He decided at once to inquire for a position with an apothecary. He had the courage, in spite of his false pride, to resolve to do that which he despised — to sell pills over a counter.

Brown persuaded Keats, however, to try the press again. He proposed that they collaborate in the composition of a tragedy, sharing equally whatever profits they might gain, and he lent Keats money for his maintenance in the meantime. Brown's motives were mixed:

they were partly altruistic, for he liked Keats; and they were partly selfish, for, believing in Keats's genius, he desired to share in the fame and money which he expected the tragedy would earn.

Keats wrote his sister on June 16:

I have not run quite aground yet I hope, having written this morning to several people to whom I have lent money, requesting repayment. I shall hencefore [*sic*] shake off my indolent fits, and among other reformation be more diligent in writing to you. . . .

In the letter which he wrote to Haydon on June 17 he explained the circumstances which caused him to need money and said:

My purpose is now to make one more attempt in the Press — if that fail, "ye hear no more of me" as Chaucer says. Brown has lent me some money for the present. Do borrow or beg some how what you can for me.

None of the persons to whom Keats had lent money repaid any part of his indebtedness. Haydon, in particular, was selfishly insensible to Keats's need. He believed that he was a great painter, and that, being such, he had the right to levy upon other men for his support. To art, with which he identified himself, he sacrificed ruthlessly everyone and everything. He borrowed money from all sorts of men — wealthy patrons of art, fellow artists, friends, his landlord, and his servant — without any intention of repayment. Keats was bitterly disappointed by Haydon's selfish insensibility.

I have a few words to say about Haydon [he wrote his brother in September 1819, three months later]. Before this Chancery threat had cut of[f] every legitimate supp[l]y of Cash from me I had a little at my disposal: Haydon being very much in want I lent him 30£ of it. Now in this se[e]-saw game of Life I got nearest to the ground and this chancery business rivetted me there so that I was sitting in that uneasy position where the seat slants so abominably. I applied to him for payment — he could not — that was no wonder; but goodman Delver, where was the wonder then, why marry, in this, he did not seem to care much about it — and let me go without my money with almost non-chalance when he ought to have sold his drawings to supply me. I shall perhaps still be acquainted with him, but for friendship that is at an end. Brown has been my friend in this — he got him to sign a Bond payable at three Months.

Keats associated with Haydon after this, but he was never intimate with him again. Haydon never repaid the loan, although he knew that Keats remained in dire need of money. In after years he disparaged Keats in his letters and in his journals, striving, we may presume, to justify to his own conscience the injury which he had done to Keats.

I am placing tentatively in this period an unpublished sonnet which is preserved in the Pierpont Morgan Library in a small volume of autographs and transcripts of a few of Keats's poems. The transcript of this sonnet was made, as far as I can judge, by Woodhouse.

> The House of Mourning written by Mr Scott, —
> A sermon at the Magdalen, — A tear
> Dropt on a greasy novel, — Want of cheer
> After a walk up hill to a friend's cot, —
> Tea with a maiden Lady — A curs'd lot
> Of worthy poems with the Author near, —
> A patron lord — A drunkenness from beer, —
> Haydon's great picture, — A cold coffee pot
> At midnight, when the Muse is ripe for labour, —
> The voice of Mr Coleridge, — A french Bonnet, —
> Before you in the pit, — A pipe & tabour, —
> A damn'd inseparable flute and neighbour, —
> All these are vile, — But viler Wordsworth's sonnet
> On Dover: — Dover! — Who *could* write upon it?

The sonnet is evidently an *ex tempore* jest which Keats had no intention of preserving. He was in the habit, in his letters, of making lists of things which he disliked. In the journal letter which he wrote his brother in March 1819, he drew up a mock petition in which he said:

> . . . forasmuch as he . . . doth not admire Shiel's play, Leigh Hunt, Tom Moore, Bob Southey and Mr Rogers; and does admire Wm. Hazlitt; more overer for as more as he liketh half of Wordsworth, and none of Crabbe . . .
> . . . (signed) Count de Cockaigne.

This sonnet is the first Petrarcan sonnet which Keats had composed since July 10, 1818, almost a year before. The natural, conversational phraseology is closer to that of his letters than to that of his poems. The "voice of Mr Coleridge," which he listed among the things which are vile, proves that he composed the sonnet after he met Coleridge in Millfield Lane on Sunday, April 11, 1819. He was impressed, we remember, by the interminable flow of Coleridge's voice.

> I heard his voice as he came towards me — I heard it as he moved away — I had heard it all the interval — if it may be called so. . . .

The inclusion of "Haydon's great picture" among the things which are vile indicates, if it does not prove, that Keats composed the sonnet after Haydon had refused to repay the loan at the middle of June 1819 and had been insensible to his desperate need of money. It is possible that Keats composed the sonnet in Shanklin in July and August or in Winchester in August and September. I am inclined,

80'

The House of Mourning written by Mr Scott, —
A sermon at the Magdalen, — a tear
Dropt on a greasy novel, — want of cheer
After a walk up hill to a friend's cot, —
Tea with a Maiden Lady — a curs'd lot
Of worthy poems with the Author near, —
A patron lord — a drunkenness from beer, —
Haydon's great picture, — a cold coffee pot
At midnight when the Muse is ripe for labour, —
The voice of Mr Coleridge, — a french Bonnet, —
Before you in the pit, — a pipe & tabour, —
A damn'd inseparable flute and neighbour, —
All these are vile, — But viler Wordsworth's Sonnet
On Dover: — Dover! — who *could* write upon it?

Sonnets to Liberty Pt 1 Son X. Vol 2 p 200.

A TRANSCRIPT OF A HITHERTO UNPUBLISHED SONNET BY KEATS

Reproduced from the manuscript by permission of the Pierpont Morgan Library

however, to think that he composed it at the end of June before he left Hampstead.

The sonnet was inspired by Keats's dislike of the praise of Dover in one of the sonnets which Wordsworth composed near Dover in 1802 and published in 1807. Keats did not visit Dover in 1819, as far as I know, but he probably passed through it in 1817 on his way from the Isle of Wight to Margate. He was probably reading Wordsworth's poems in June 1819, for he quoted a passage from the *Ode on the Intimations of Immortality* in the letter which he wrote Miss Jeffrey on May 31.

Keats and Rice departed for the Isle of Wight on the Portsmouth coach, it is probable, on Sunday, June 27. Both were unwell. Keats was suffering another attack of laryngeal tuberculosis. For a month he had complained of a fit of indolence. On June 14 he wrote his sister that he had a sore throat; and on Tuesday, July 6, nine days after he had arrived in Shanklin, Isle of Wight, he wrote her:

> I was on the Portsmouth Coach the Sunday before last in that heavy shower — and I may say I went to Portsmouth by water — I got a little cold and as it always flies to my throat I am a little out of sorts that way.

Keats and Rice were witty, unselfish, and congenial friends; but, being ill and alone, they had a depressing effect upon each other. After Rice left and Brown arrived, Keats became more cheerful and optimistic.

> Rice and I passed rather a dull time of it [Keats wrote Dilke on July 31]. I hope he will not repent coming with me. He was unwell and I was not in very good health: and I am affraid we made each other worse by acting upon each others spirits. We would grow as melancholy as need be. I confess I cannot bear a sick person in a House especially alone — it weighs upon me day and night. . . .

Rice tried to conquer his melancholy, Keats wrote Dilke, and to conceal it with a pun. "I know him better since we have liv'd a month together in the isle of Wight," Keats wrote his brother afterwards. "He is the most sensible, and even wise Man I know — he has a few John Bull prejudices; but they improve him."

Keats was too ill to explore the Isle of Wight and he was not in the mood to appreciate its picturesque beauty. He needed, as he realized later, the quiet, restful atmosphere of an old cathedral town. He regarded with amusement and superiority the tourists who came "hunting after the picturesque like beagles." "It is astonishing," he said, "how they raven down scenery like children do sweetmeats." He perceived the picturesque beauty of the island but he did not feel it. He believed that his excursion into the Highlands of Scotland had sated his responsiveness to picturesque scenes.

I have been no further than Steephill [he wrote Dilke on July 31]. If I may guess I should [say] that there is no finer part in the Island than from this Place to Steephill — I do not hesitate to say it is fine. Bonchurch is the best. But I have been so many finer walks, with a back ground of lake and mountain instead of the sea, that I am not much touch'd with it, though I credit it for all the Surprise I should have felt if it had taken my cockney maidenhead. But I may call myself an old Stager in the picturesque, and unless it be something very large and overpowering I cannot receive any extraordinary relish.

Keats tried to drown his morbid thoughts of Miss Brawne in the composition of *Otho* and *Lamia.* He left Hampstead and retired to the Isle of Wight because he knew that, being ill and without money, he would not be able to marry Miss Brawne in the immediate future. He believed that, since he could not marry her, it would not be honorable to remain near her; and he felt that it would be a nervous and emotional strain to be with her without marrying her. He took leave of her in a desperate state of mind. He told her a day or two before he left Hampstead that he would never return to London if his fate did not "turn up Pam or at least a Court-card." In the sequel, separation from her, in which his imagination had full sway over his feelings, tortured him more than his intimate association with her in the last three months had done. On Thursday, July 1, four days after he had arrived in Shanklin, he wrote her in a lonely and miserable mood.

My dearest Lady,

I am glad I had not an opportunity of sending off a Letter which I wrote for you on Tuesday night — 'twas too much like one out of Ro[u]sseau's Heloise. I am more reasonable this morning. The morning is the only proper time for me to write to a beautiful Girl whom I love so much: for at night, when the lonely day has closed, and the lonely, silent, unmusical Chamber is waiting to receive me as into a Sepulchre, then believe me my passion gets entirely the sway, then I would not have you see those R[h]apsodies which I once thought it impossible I should ever give way to, and which I have often laughed at in another, for fear you should [think me] either too unhappy or perhaps a little mad.

Keats complained that he had never known "unalloy'd Happiness for many days together" and accused Miss Brawne of cruelty in destroying his freedom and inflicting new pain upon him. He was still feeling that rebellion against the trammels of love which he had expressed in the second ode *To* [*Fanny*] and the ballad *La belle dame sans merci.* He believed that Miss Brawne did not love him so much as he loved her, and he was tortured by the fear that she might love another.

Though I could centre my Happiness in you [he told her], I cannot expect to engross your heart so entirely — indeed if I thought you felt as much for me as I do for you at this moment I do not think I could restrain myself from seeing you again tomorrow for the delight of one embrace. But no — I must live upon hope and Chance. In case of the worst that can happen, I shall still love you — but what hatred shall I have for another! Some lines I read the other day are continually ringing a peal in my ears:

To see those eyes I prize above mine own
Dart favors on another —
And those sweet lips (yielding immortal nectar)
Be gently press'd by any but myself —
Think, think Francesca, what a cursed thing
It were beyond expression!

[Massinger's *Duke of Milan*, I. iii. 200–207.]

It is clear from the letters which Keats wrote to Miss Brawne in this period that she was either too superficial or too immature to give him that sympathetic understanding which he needed; for she met his morbid complaints with affected reproaches and arch coquetry.

Keats composed an amazing amount of poetry during his residence in the Isle of Wight. He and Brown worked out the outline of the first act of *Otho the Great* before he left Hampstead, it is probable; and he composed the first act before Brown joined him in Shanklin. "I am so hard at work," Keats wrote his sister on July 6, "that perhaps I should not have written to you for a day or two if Georges Letter had not diverted my attention to the interests and pleasure of those I love." "I am at the diligent use of my faculties here," he wrote Miss Brawne on July 8, "I do not pass a day without sprawling some blank verse or tagging some rhymes." And on July 11 he wrote Reynolds:

You will be glad to hear, under my own hand (tho' Rice says we are like Sauntering Jack and Idle Joe) how diligent I have been, and am being. I have finish'd the Act, and in the interval of beginning the 2d have proceeded pretty well with Lamia, finishing the 1st part which consists of about 400 lines.

Brown and Martin arrived in Shanklin in the latter part of July, and Rice and Martin returned to London on Sunday, July 25. As soon as they were alone Keats and Brown began work on the second act of their tragedy. Keats wrote Dilke on July 31: "Brown and I are pretty well harnessed again to our dog-cart. I mean the Tragedy which goes on sinkingly." They composed the fourth act before they left Shanklin on August 12; and Keats composed the fifth act independently in Winchester before August 23.

Some twenty years afterwards Brown described their method of collaboration as follows:

At Shanklin he undertook a difficult task; I engaged to furnish him with the title, characters, and dramatic conduct of a tragedy, and he was to enwrap it in poetry. The progress of this work was curious, for while I sat opposite to him, he caught my description of each scene entire, with the characters to be brought forward, the events, and everything connected with it. Thus he went on, scene after scene, never knowing nor inquiring into the scene which was to follow, until four acts were completed. It was then he required to know at once all the events that were to occupy the fifth act; I explained them to him, but, after patient hearing and some thought, he insisted that many incidents in it were too humorous, or, as he termed them, too melodramatic. He wrote the fifth act in accordance with his own views, and so contented was I with his poetry that at the time, and for a long time after, I thought he was in the right. [Brown's Memoir of Keats, Houghton-Crewe Collection.] [2]

Keats's brief references rather support Brown's story of the collaboration.

Brown likes the Tragedy very much [he wrote Taylor humorously on September 5]: but he is not a fit judge, as I have only acted as Midwife to his plot, and of course he will be fond of his child.

Keats himself thought that the tragedy would be successful on the stage and that it would enhance his poetic reputation.

Mine I am sure is a tolerable tragedy [he wrote his brother on September 17] — it would have been a bank to me, if just as I had finish'd it I had not heard of Kean's resolution to go to America.

Brown's story of the collaboration has caused critics to dismiss the tragedy as mere hack-work. "When all this is taken into consideration," Ernest de Sélincourt observed, "it will be seen that it is futile to look for anything like dramatic unity or close relation between language and characterisation." It is uncritical, however, to dismiss the tragedy without studying it. The analysis which I shall make presently shows a close correspondence between plot, characterization, and language and proves that Keats's creative faculties were more vitally engaged in the composition than Brown in his vanity was willing to admit.

Before analyzing *Otho*, however, we must understand Keats's attitude towards dramatic composition in general and the composition of *Otho* in particular. His immediate purpose in composing *Otho*, as we have seen, was financial. He believed that he could earn money more quickly by composing a tragedy than by composing any other kind of poetry. He believed also that a successful tragedy would lift his poetic reputation out of the mire into which it had been trampled by the reviewers of *Endymion* and enable him to sell to advantage

[2] Quoted by Ernest de Sélincourt, p. 552.

the poems which he had in manuscript. He found that writing for money was not so disagreeable as he had supposed it would be.

The first time I sat down to write, I co^{d} scarcely believe in the necessity for so doing [he wrote Reynolds on July 11]. It struck me as a great oddity. Yet the very corn which is now so beautiful, as if it had only took to ripening yesterday, is for the market; so, why sho^{d} I be delicate[?] —

Keats and Brown jested with their friends over incidents which they pretended they were thinking of introducing into the tragedy.

We are thinking of introducing an Elephant [Keats wrote Dilke on July 31] but have not historical referance [*sic*] within reach to determine us as to Otho's Menagerie. When Brown first mention'd this I took it for a joke; however he brings such plausible reasons, and discourses so eloquently on the dramatic effect that I am giving it a serious consideration.

Keats is very industrious [Brown wrote Dilke on August 12], but I swear by the prompter's whistle, and by the bangs of stage-doors, he is obstinately monstrous. What think you of Otho's threatening cold pig to the newly-married couple? He says the Emperor must have a spice of drollery. His introduction of Grimm's adventure, lying three days on his back for love, though it spoils the unity of time, is not out of the way for the character of Ludolf, so I have consented to it; but I cannot endure his fancy of making the princess blow up her hairdresser, for smearing her cheek with pomatum and spoiling her rouge. It may be natural, as he observes, but so might many things. However, such as it is, it has advanced to nearly the end of the fourth act.[3]

Keats's fundamental purpose in composing *Otho* was artistic. The composition of dramatic poetry, we have seen, was the goal toward which he had been evolving consciously since the spring of 1817, when he began to study Shakespeare's plays. In the autumn of 1817, when he was completing *Endymion*, he thought out the first principles of his philosophy of negatively capable or dramatic poetry. On January 30, 1818 he wrote Taylor that the passage in *Endymion* (I. 777 *et seq.*) in which he explained the allegory of the poem was "a regular stepping of the Imagination towards a Truth."

My having written that Argument [he said] will perhaps be of the greatest Service to me of any thing I ever did. It set before me at once the gradations of Happiness even like a kind of Pleasure Thermometer — and is *my first step towards the chief attempt in the Drama* — the playing of different Natures with Joy and Sorrow.

Keats resolved to postpone dramatic composition until he had more experience in life and more knowledge of human nature. In the course of 1818 he was diverted intermittently by romance and humanitarianism from the development of his philosophy of negative capability, the goal of which was dramatic composition. He

[3] H. B. Forman, Variorum Edition, Vol. III, p. 35.

studied himself and experimented with egotistic genres, the lyric, the romance, and the humanitarian vision. His interest in human beings increased during his excursion into Scotland in the summer of 1818. In December 1818, after he had rejected humanitarianism and resumed his philosophy of negative capability, he began an epic, *Hyperion*, in objective or dramatic style. As his imagination strengthened, he said, he lived not in this world alone but in a thousand worlds. In the spring of 1819 he established his philosophy of negative capability upon a sound empirical basis.

The empirical humanism which Keats had thought out in March and April 1819 was tested and strengthened by the adversity which he suffered in June. In April, we remember, he had denounced the humanitarian principles of the natural goodness of men, the perfectibility of human nature, and the progress of the world through education to a state of happiness. Evil, he had concluded, is inherent in the nature of the world and in man, who is a part of nature. Evil also is necessary in the world for the maintenance of existence and for the development of the souls or personalities of men. A world of pains and troubles, a world in which the heart must feel and suffer in a thousand ways, is necessary, he said, to school an intelligence and make it a soul. There is beauty, he perceived, in the world with its conflicting principles of egotism and disinterestedness. To the negatively capable poet, such as Shakespeare, who has imaginative insight, the instinctive impulses of men are the very thing in which poetry consists.

Keats reiterated these principles in June 1819, when new troubles were coming upon him, and in July, after they were besetting him in full force. On June 9, when he was considering taking a position as surgeon on an Indiaman, he wrote Miss Jeffrey:

> Your advice about the Indiaman is a very wise advice, because it just suits me, though you are a little in the wrong concerning its destroying the energies of Mind: on the contrary it would be the finest thing in the world to strengthen them — To be thrown among people who care not for you, with whom you have no sympathies forces the Mind upon its own resources, and leaves it free to make its speculations of the differences of human character and to class them with the calmness of a Botanist. An Indiaman is a little world. One of the great reasons that the English have produced the finest writers in the world is, that the English world has ill-treated them during their lives and foster'd them after their deaths. They have in general been trampled aside into the bye paths of life and seen the festerings of Society. They have not been treated like the Raphaels of Italy. And where is the Englishman and Poet who has given a magnificent Entertainment at the christening of one of his Hero's Horses as Boyardo did? He had a Castle in the Appenine. He was a noble Poet of Romance; not a miserable and mighty Poet of the human Heart. The middle age of

Shakespeare was all c[l]ouded over; his days were not more happy than Hamlet's who is perhaps more like Shakespeare himself in his common every day Life than any other of his Characters — Ben Johnson was a common Soldier and in the Low countries, in the face of two armies, fought a single combat with a french Trooper and slew him — For all this I will not go on board an Indiaman, nor for example's sake run my head into dark alleys: I dare say my discipline is to come, and plenty of it too.

Keats was turning again from the poetry of romance to the poetry of human character, despite *The Eve of St. Agnes* and *The Eve of St. Mark*, which he had composed six months before, and *Lamia*, which he was intending to compose in July.

In the passage which I have quoted from his letter to Miss Jeffrey, Keats applied to poetry the principles of that empirical humanism which he had developed in March and April 1819. He perceived that a world of pains and troubles is necessary for the schooling of a negatively capable poet, such as Shakespeare, who, entering sympathetically into the minds of other men, expresses their emotions, ideas, and actions in objective form.

Keats's empirical humanism enabled him to endure the buffets of adversity with that healthy calmness which he called the top of sovereignty and to compose his poetry with that deliberate judgment which he had desired. On July 11, after he had composed the first act of his tragedy, he wrote Reynolds:

I have great hopes of success, because I make use of my Judgment more deliberately than I yet have done; but in case of failure with the world, I shall find my content. And here (as I know you have my good at heart as much as a Brother), I can only repeat to you what I have said to George — that however I sho[d] like to enjoy what the competences of life procure, I am in no wise dashed at a different prospect. I have spent too many thoughtful days and moralized thro' too many nights for that, and fruitless wo[d] they be indeed, if they did not by degrees make me look upon the affairs of the world with a healthy deliberation. I have of late been moulting: not for fresh feathers and wings: they are gone, and in their stead I hope to have a pair of patient sublunary legs. I have altered, not from a Chrysalis into a butterfly, but the contrary; having two little loopholes, whence I may look out into the stage of the world: and that world on our coming here [Shanklin] I almost forgot.

In composing *Otho the Great*, Keats believed that he was approaching the goal of his poetic evolution, that he was putting into practice those principles of negative capability, those principles of dramatic composition, which he had developed out of his long and intensive study of Shakespeare's plays. On August 14, after he had composed four acts of his tragedy, he wrote Bailey:

It was the opinion of most of my friends that I should never be able to write a scene. I will endeavour to wipe away the prejudice. . . . One of my Ambitions is to make as great a revolution in modern dramatic writing as Kean has done in acting.

It was Keats's ambition to establish a school of Shakespearean playwriting as Kean had established a school of Shakespearean acting. The first quarter of the nineteenth century was the culmination of the great revival of Shakespeare's plays upon the English stage. It was an era of great Shakespearean actors, such as Sarah Siddons, John Kemble, Charles Kemble, Edmund Kean, Edwin Booth, Eliza O'Neil, and William Charles Macready. Keats never mentioned Mrs. Siddons in his letters, although he may have seen her in one of her farewell performances. When he came to London in the fall of 1815, Kean was enthralling playgoers with his fiery passion and eclipsing the frigid stateliness of John Kemble. He expressed his admiration for Kean's acting, we remember, in the reviews which he wrote for *The Champion* in December 1817. "The acting of Kean is Shakespearian," he said, "— he will fully understand what we mean."

The age in which Keats lived was also a great period of dramatic criticism, the period in which Coleridge, Lamb, and Hazlitt established a new school of Shakespearean criticism. It was, however, the poorest period of playwriting in the whole course of English drama. There was, as Keats perceived, a great need and a great opportunity for a revolution in dramatic composition. The men of greatest literary genius — Wordsworth, Coleridge, Southey, Scott, Byron, Shelley, and Keats — were drawn either by nature or by circumstances into other fields of literature. They despised contemporary plays and they composed closet plays — such as Wordsworth's *Borderers* and Coleridge's *Zapolya* — in Shakespearean style; but, being separated from the stage and having little knowledge of theatric technique, they had no influence upon contemporary playwriting.

The contemporary plays which were produced upon the stage were, for the most part, translations, adaptations, and imitations of sentimental and melodramatic German plays, especially those of Kotzebue. Wordsworth protested in 1800:

> The invaluable works of our elder writers, I had almost said the works of Shakespear and Milton, are driven into neglect by frantic novels, *sickly and stupid German Tragedies*, and deluges of idle and extravagant stories in verse.

Keats and his friends censured these sentimental plays savagely. In *The Champion* for March 2, 1817 Reynolds published a review of a production of Kotzebue's *Stranger*. He defined this type of play as follows:

As to the play itself, it is in truth one of the worst of a species of drama, the best of which is far from excellent. It is *essentially* German — that is, not merely German in its original language, but of a certain style, which, whether exported from abroad, or imitated at home, is directly in opposition to truth and nature. Our own country can furnish several specimens of German artists. Our Lewises, Dimonds, and Skeffingtons, what are they but so many Spitalfields playwrights, who, think it the perfection of their art to imitate the clumsy, grotesque, and unnatural figures of foreign manufactures? — Bertram, and the Robbers are among the better specimens of German plays — The Stranger, Lovers Vows, and the late production of Adelaide among the worst.

These German plays, Reynolds said, are written according to the following formula:

Let there be some heart-breaking scene of domestic misery presented to our view — be it a fond husband deserted by a faithless wife, a generous son disinherited by his father, or a sick mother turned out of doors to perish by hunger, and thus discovered by her own son. What can be more interesting? — Then let the hero as the *natural* consequence of such a situation be driven to some act of desperation, for which the laws of his country would award him a halter — but let him "so offend to make offence a skill," that is, let his crime be varnished over with so much pretty morality, and appear to be so naturally resulting from the circumstances in which he is placed, that the audience, dear souls! are won over to sympathy, and "quite forget his vices in his woe;" — instead of the merited rope, he comes off with their applause, leaving them with a pitying tear for his misfortunes, and an approving smile for the spirit which makes him break through the petty prejudices of society.

When Keats was walking through Scotland in the summer of 1818 he witnessed a production of *The Stranger* in a barn in Inverary on the evening of July 17.

There they went on [he said] about "interesting creaters" and "human nater" till the Curtain fell and then Came the Bag pipe . . . at the heartrending, shoemending reconciliation the Piper blew amain. I never read or saw this play before; not the Bag pipe, nor the wretched players themselves were little in comparison with it — thank heaven it has been scoffed at lately almost to a fashion.

On Monday, March 15, 1819, Keats, Brown, and Cawthorn went to see Sheil's *Evadne*, a tragedy of this sentimental and melodramatic type.

The play was bad [Keats said] even in comparison with 1818, the Augustan age of the Drama, "comme on sait," as Voltaire says, the whole was made up of a virtuous young woman, an indignant brother, a suspecting lover, a libertine prince, a gratuitous villain, a street in Naples, a Cypress grove, lilies and roses, virtue and vice, a bloody sword, a spangled jacket. . . .

It was Keats's ambition to establish a Shakespearean school of playwriting which would supplant the German school. He was willing to collaborate with Brown, because he believed that Brown, who had written a successful serio-comic opera, had some knowledge of theatric technique. An analysis of *Otho* shows that he not only wrote the speeches but that he also intuited the characters and that he had some part in selecting the incidents.

Keats and Brown built the plot of *Otho* around the tragic marriage of Ludolph, son of Otho, Emperor of Germany, to Auranthe, sister of Conrad, Duke of Franconia. The antecedent circumstances out of which the plot evolved are as follows: the abortive rebellion of Ludolph, which had been caused by Otho's refusal to permit him to wed Auranthe; the immoral intrigue of Auranthe with Albert, a knight in Otho's service; the disgrace of Erminia, whom Otho had chosen to be Ludolph's bride; the defeat of an invading army of Hungarians; the pardon of Conrad, who had supported the rebellion of Ludolph, as a reward for his assistance in repulsing the Hungarians; and the courageous exploits of Ludolph, who in the guise of an Arab was the individual hero of the victory. These antecedent circumstances are revealed skilfully as the plot develops.

The plot of *Otho*, like the plots of Shakespeare's tragedies, is divided into five acts, the climax comes at the middle of the third act, and the action is continuous from scene to scene. Like Shakespeare's plots, also, it has a sub-plot, the love of Gersa and Erminia, which is in vivid contrast to the main plot, the love of Ludolph and Auranthe.

Several episodes of the plot are strikingly similar to episodes in Shakespeare's plays. In *Otho*, as in *Much Ado About Nothing*, the dramatic action begins immediately after the successful conclusion of a war with a foreign foe; and Ludolph, the hero of *Otho*, like Claudio, the hero of *Much Ado*, has distinguished himself in battle. But Ludolph, who had rebelled against his father the emperor, fights against the invaders in the guise of an Arab. This episode was suggested probably by an episode in *Cymbeline*, in which Posthumus, who has been banished, fights against the Roman invaders in the guise of a common soldier. In both plays the disguise is discovered and the hero is rewarded. Keats's indebtedness to Shakespeare is proved by similarities in phraseology and idea. (Compare *Cymbeline*, V. v. 405 *et seq.* with *Otho*, I. ii. 51 *et seq.*)

In the central episode of *Otho*, Abbot Ethelbert defends Erminia from a false charge of immorality, from a

whisper'd tale
About a midnight gallant, seen to climb
A window to her chamber neighbour'd near. . . .
[III. ii. 140–142.]

This episode was suggested probably by the central episode in *Much Ado*, in which Friar Francis defends Hero from a similar charge of immorality. Don Pedro, who had been deceived by a stratagem of the villain, Don John, testifies:

Myself, my brother, and this grieved count
Did see her, hear her, at that hour last night
Talk with a ruffian at her chamber-window.
[IV. i. 90–92.]

There is a striking resemblance also in the speeches of Ludolph, the husband of Auranthe, and Claudio, the betrothed of Hero. When Ludolph discovers that it is Auranthe instead of Erminia who is guilty of immorality, he exclaims ironically:

Am I not married to a paragon
" Of personal beauty and untainted soul? "
A blushing fair-eyed Purity! A Sylph,
Whose snowy timid hand has never sinn'd
Beyond a flower pluck'd, white as itself?
[V. ii. 21 *et seq.*]

And Claudio says:

Behold how like a maid she blushes here!
O, what authority and show of truth
Can cunning sin cover itself withal! . . .
But fare thee well, most foul, most fair! Farewell,
Thou pure impiety and impious purity!
[IV. i. 35 *et seq.*]

In the scene after the death of Conrad and Albert and the disclosure of the immorality of Auranthe, the courtiers discuss the dire events of the past night:

THEODORE. Was ever such a night?
SIGIFRED. What horrors more?
Things unbelieved one hour, so strange they are,
The next hour stamps with credit.

This scene is a reminiscence of a vivid scene in *Macbeth* (II. iv. 1 *et seq.*) in which, on the morning after the murder of Duncan, an old man and Ross discuss the dreadful incidents of the past night:

OLD MAN. Three score and ten I can remember well;
Within the volume of which time I have seen
Hours dreadful and things strange; but this sore night
Hath trifled former knowings.

In the final scene of *Otho* Ludolph broods over his wrongs until in a state of mad fury he sees a dagger in the air which leads him to the door of the chamber of his faithless wife. The obvious source of the incident in *Macbeth* is revealed in a letter which Keats wrote John Taylor, September 5, a few days after he had composed the fifth act.

> If you were to walk leisurely through an unwholesome path in the fens, with a little horror of them you would be sure to have your ague. But let macbeth cross the same path, with the dagger in the air leading him on, and he would never have an ague or any thing like it.

Since Keats enwrapped these episodes which are borrowed from Shakespeare's plays with reminiscences of Shakespeare's phraseology, it is evident either that he supplied the episodes himself or that, if Brown suggested them, he recognized their sources in Shakespeare's plays and recalled Shakespeare's phraseology. In either case, there is a close connection between the episodes and the phraseology in which they are expressed. Keats did not compose the tragedy, it is clear, in the mechanical manner which Brown described.

The plot of *Otho* is melodramatic after the fashion of the plots of Shakespeare's plays; but, like Shakespeare's plays, *Otho* is redeemed from melodrama by convincing characterization. The character of Ludolph, the protagonist, is individual in the highest degree. He is a hot, proud, obstinate boy who has been spoiled by an indulgent but autocratic father. His tragic trait is an excessive emotional instability which makes him oscillate between the extremes of feeling. He lacks that balance of character, that harmony between emotion and reason, that even commingling of blood and judgment, which Hamlet admired in his friend Horatio. He betrays his fatal emotional instability in every scene of the play in which he appears. In the scene after his marriage he indulges in such an excess of joy that his father, his wife, and his friends find it a little painful. When Abbot Ethelbert accuses Auranthe of having foisted her guilt of immorality upon Erminia, he swings through a gamut of emotions from murderous rage to scornful indifference; and, when Auranthe shows her guilt by flight, he gives away to an excess of jealous fury. In the final scene his emotions are stimulated until his reason topples. With the super-heated imagination of a madman, he sees a dagger in the air leading him on to revenge; and, when he discovers that his wife has committed suicide, his emotions subside and he dies, the victim of over-stimulated feelings.

Keats drew the character of Ludolph in accordance with his interpretation of the characters of Shakespeare's tragic heroes. In the first place, Ludolph is of royal rank and his tragic death spreads ruin far and wide in the empire. In the second place, his tragedy is clearly the result of the reaction of his tragic trait, his emotional instability, to the circumstances in which he is involved.

The character of Ludolph is objective, although on the surface it may seem subjective. Keats had a tendency to swing from one extreme of feeling to the other; but he had the power to control his temperamental impulses and emotions. He recognized the similarity of Ludolph's character to his own. "The Lover is madder than I am," he wrote Miss Brawne on August 5, 1819, "— I am nothing to him — he has a figure like the Statue of Maleager [*sic*] and double distilled fire in his heart."

Keats's intuition of Ludolph's character was inspired by Kean's interpretation of the characters of Shakespeare's tragic heroes. In his essay *On Edmund Kean as a Shakespearian Actor* he made a vivid analysis of the emotional force of Kean's acting.

> The sensual life of verse springs warm from the lips of Kean, and to one learned in Shakespearian hieroglyphics — learned in the spiritual portion of those lines to which Kean adds a sensual grandeur; his tongue must seem to have robbed the Hybla bees and left them honeyless! There is an indescribable *gusto* in his voice. . . . When he says in Othello "Put up your bright swords, for the dew will rust them," we feel that his throat had commanded where swords were as thick as reeds. From eternal risk, he speaks as though his body were unassailable. Again, his exclamation of "blood, blood, blood!" is direful and slaughterous to the deepest degree; the very words appear stained and gory. His nature hangs over them, making a prophetic repast. The voice is loosed on them, like the wild dog on the savage relics of an eastern conflict; and we can distinctly hear it "gorging and growling o'er carcase and limb." In Richard, "Be stirring with the lark to-morrow, gentle Norfolk!" comes from him, as through the morning atmosphere, towards which he yearns. . . . Surely this intense power of anatomizing the passions of every syllable, of taking to himself the wings of verse, is the means by which he becomes a storm with such fiery decision. . . . Other actors are continually thinking of their sum-total effect throughout a play. Kean delivers himself up to the instant feeling, without a shadow of a thought about anything else.

Ludolph's abnormal emotional instability was suggested to Keats, I have no doubt, by Kean's emotional interpretation of Shakespeare's tragic heroes. Ludolph's death from an excess of emotion was inspired, in particular, by Kean's representation of dying heroes. In his essay *On Kean in "Richard Duke of York"* Keats said:

> Kean always "dies as erring men do die." The bodily functions wither up, and the mental faculties hold out till they crack. It is an extinguishment, not a decay. The hand is agonized with death; the lip trembles with a last breath, as we see the autumn leaf thrill in the cold wind of evening. The very eye-lid dies. The acting of Kean is Shakespearian — he will fully understand what we mean.

We might almost say that Keats composed the rôle of Ludolph for Kean. He believed at least that Kean was the only actor who could enact the rôle successfully. In the latter part of August, a few days after he had completed the tragedy, he heard that Kean was planning to make an American tour and he was very much disappointed. "I fear all my labour will be thrown away for the present . . .," he wrote Dilke on August 28. "I had hoped," he added, "to give Kean another opportunity to shine." On September 27 he wrote his brother:

> The report runs now more in favor of Kean stopping in England. If he should I have confident hopes of our Tragedy — If he smokes the hotblooded character of Ludolph — and he is the only actor that can do it — He will add to his own fame, and improve my fortune.

Keats wrote his sister on December 20, 1819 that *Otho* had been "accepted at Drury Lane with a promise of coming out next season" and that he believed that "Kean has perceived how suitable the principal Character will be for him." Keats and Brown were unwilling to wait until the next season for their play to be produced, however, and they withdrew it from Drury Lane with the intention of submitting it to Covent Garden. In the end, it was never produced.

Since *Otho* is a tragedy of character rather than of incident, the interest of the reader is attracted by the struggles in the minds of the *dramatis personae.* These mental conflicts, as in Shakespeare's tragedies, are represented chiefly by means of soliloquies. The most effective of these soliloquies expresses the struggle in the mind of Albert between loyalty to his guilty mistress and loyalty to his emperor (III. i. 1 *et seq.*). This soliloquy is modelled closely upon the famous soliloquies of *Hamlet.* There is the same formal address, the same rhetorical questions, the same desire of death, and the same fatal indecision.

The blank verse of *Otho* is an imitation of the blank verse of Shakespeare's plays. It has verses of great imaginative effect, but passages of great length are usually marred by verses which are either weak in intuition or imperfect in expression. *Otho* contains many reminiscences of the phraseology, imagery, and ideas of the poetry of Shakespeare's plays. I have collected forty passages from *Otho* that are closely parallel either in phraseology and imagery or in phraseology and idea to passages in seventeen of Shakespeare's plays. *Otho* does not contain a much greater proportion of Shakespearean reminiscenses, however, than *Endymion* and *Hyperion.* All of the poetry which Keats composed after March 1817 is more indebted to Shakespeare than to any other one of his poetic masters.

Otho the Great is not a good play but it shows a closer correspondence between plot and characterization and speech than critics have perceived. Dramatic composition, we have seen, was the goal of the evolution of Keats's poetic art and his greatest ambition was to revive the Shakespearean type of playwriting. A desperate need of money compelled him, however, to begin dramatic composition before he was prepared for it. He composed *Otho* also in too great haste to make it as good a tragedy as he could have made it.

2

Keats chose the subject of *Lamia*, intuited it, and began to compose it, it is probable, before he left Hampstead on June 27. He completed the first part of the romance in Shanklin in July, after he had composed the first act of *Otho* and while he was waiting for Brown to arrive before beginning the second act. He wrote Reynolds from Shanklin, we have seen, on July 11:

> I have finish'd the Act, and in the interval of beginning the 2d have proceeded pretty well with Lamia, finishing the 1st part which consists of about 400 lines.

He composed the second part of the romance between August 23, when he wrote Taylor that he had just completed his tragedy, and September 5, when he wrote Taylor:

> Since I finish'd it [the tragedy] I have finish'd Lamia: and am now occupied in revising St. Agnes' Eve and studying Italian.

There were nearly six weeks of time and four acts of *Otho* between the first and second parts of *Lamia*. In this interval there occurred a change in Keats's attitude to life and poetry; and, as a consequence, the two parts of *Lamia* are different in theme and in sentiment and, to some extent, in style. We can understand the romance better, I believe, by interpreting each part separately and in its own setting in Keats's life.

Keats composed *Lamia*, as well as *Otho*, with the purpose of winning the patronage of the public. The first part of the romance, like *Otho*, reflects the healthy, resolute mood in which he went to Shanklin to compose poetry which would please the public. He had hopes of success, he wrote Reynolds on July 11, because he made use of his judgment more deliberately than he had done before. He was ardent in his love for Miss Brawne, although somewhat rebellious and morbid, and he was tolerant of the public for whom he was composing. There is a vague symbolism in the first part of the romance but there is no satire.

The first draft of the first part of the romance has not survived; but there are two incomplete fragments of the first draft of the second part. The one, which consists of two leaves, is in the Marquess of Crewe's Collection; and the other, which consists of 59 verses, is quoted in the letter which Keats wrote Taylor on September 5, 1819 and which is in the Lowell Collection in the Harvard College Library. There is finally the complete autograph manuscript which Keats revised for the press. It was preserved in Taylor's family until it was sold by public auction in 1897, and it is now in the Bemis Collection. Before it was sold H. B. Forman collated it with the printed text and published its variant readings in his editions.

The source of the story of *Lamia* is stated in a footnote on page 1 of the complete autograph manuscript:

> The ground work of this story will be found in Burton's "Anatomy of Melancholy" Part 3. Sect. 3. Memb. 1st Subs. 1st.

This source was quoted at the end of the romance in the volume of 1820.

> Philostratus, in his fourth book *de Vita Apollonii*, hath a memorable instance in this kind, which I may not omit, of one Menippus Lycius, a young man twenty-five years of age, that going betwixt Cenchreas and Corinth, met such a phantasm in the habit of a fair gentlewoman, which taking him by the hand, carried him home to her house, in the suburbs of Corinth, and told him she was a Phoenician by birth, and if he would tarry with her, he should hear her sing and play, and drink such wine as never any drank, and no man should molest him; but she, being fair and lovely, would live and die with him, that was fair and lovely to behold. The young man, a philosopher, otherwise staid and discreet, able to moderate his passions, though not this of love, tarried with her a while to his great content, and at last married her, to whose wedding, amongst other guests, came Apollonius; who, by some probable conjectures, found her out to be a serpent, a lamia; and that all her furniture was, like Tantalus' gold, described by Homer, no substance but mere illusions. When she saw herself descried, she wept, and desired Apollonius to be silent, but he would not be moved, and thereupon she, plate, house, and all that was in it, vanished in an instant: many thousands took notice of this fact, for it was done in the midst of Greece.
>
> Burton's 'Anatomy of Melancholy.' *Part* 3. *Sect.* 2. *Memb.* 1. *Subs.* 1.

Keats composed a swift, flashing, multi-colored romance upon the bare framework of Burton's brief summary of this incident of Greek folk-lore. He shortened the hero's name from Menippus Lycius to Lycius and he had Lamia tell Lycius that she was a Corinthian instead of a Phoenician. He amplified and enriched the romance with words, images, and incidents which he recalled from his reading of English poetry of the Renaissance.

Keats composed *Lamia* under the combined influences of Shakespeare and Milton. On August 14, after he had composed the first part of the romance and before he had begun the second part, he wrote Bailey:

> I am convinced more and more every day that (excepting the human friend Philosopher) a fine writer is the most genuine Being in the World. Shakspeare and the paradise Lost every day become greater wonders to me. I look upon fine Phrases like a Lover.

And, on August 25, when he was beginning the second part of *Lamia*, he wrote Reynolds:

> I am convinced more and more day by day that fine writing is, next to fine doing the top thing in the world; the Paradise Lost becomes a greater wonder.

Keats loved the sensuous and melodious words, compounds, and phrases which abound in the poetry of Shakespeare and Milton. Many of these melodious words he knew were of Greek and Roman derivation. He described the "fluent Greek" in which the guests at the nuptial feast of Lycius and Lamia conversed as "a vowel'd undersong." He employed melodious Greek names such as Hermes, Lycius, Apollonius, Lamia, Ariadne, Lethe, and Cleone and melodious adjectives of Greek and Roman derivation such as Elysian, Aeolian, Adonian, Vulcanian, Phoebean, Circean, Peraean, Cretan, Sicilian, and gordian. He employed a very large number of imaginative compounds which he formed on analogy with Shakespeare's. Some of the more striking of these compounds are soft-brushing, cirque-couchant, vermilion-spotted, rainbow-sided, lute-finger'd, green-recessed, milder-mooned, rubious-argent, tress-lifting, moth-time, flitter-winged, purple-lined, silent-blessing, wide-swerv'd, and branch-rent. He constructed also imaginative metaphors such as "the star of Lethe" for Hermes. Charles Lamb, commenting on this metaphor, said that it is

> one of these prodigal phrases which Mr Keats abounds in, which are each a poem in a word, and which in this instance lays open to us at once, like a picture, all the dim regions and their inhabitants, and the sudden coming of a celestial among them. . . .[4]

Lamia, which comes at the end of the Miltonic period of Keats's poetry, is almost as Miltonic in style as *Hyperion*. There are nearly

[4] Charles Lamb's review of the *Poems* of 1820, *The New Times* for July 19, 1820.

thirty examples of Miltonic inversion such as "blossoms blown," "brilliance feminine," "gardens palatine," "indifference drear," "palaces imperial," "temples lewd," "pavement white," "revels rude," "twin-clouds odorous," "eye severe," "vales deflower'd," and "forest trees branch-rent." There are examples in which two or more adjectives follow the nouns or pronouns which they modify — "Summer heaven, blue and clear," "shut the chamber up, close, hush'd and still," and "So they hurried all, maz'd, curious and keen." There are also several examples of Miltonic repetition — "Soft went the music the soft air along," "bright eyes double bright," and "pale contented sort of discontent."

Keats drew the beautiful and appropriate introduction of *Lamia* from Renaissance poetry.

> Upon a time, before the faery broods
> Drove Nymph and Satyr from the prosperous woods,
> Before King Oberon's bright diadem,
> Sceptre, and mantle, clasp'd with dewy gem,
> Frighted away the Dryads and the Fauns
> From rushes green, and brakes, and cowslip'd lawns. . . .

The poets of the Renaissance, inspired by the assimilative principle of neo-Platonism, explained and reconciled Egyptian, Indian, Greek, Hebrew, Teutonic, Celtic, and Christian deities as successive symbols by which men have intuited and worshiped that divine spirit which pervades the universe. Chaucer began *The Tale of the Wife of Bath* by saying that in the days of King Arthur the land was full of fairies but that now they have been driven away by the incantations of the friars. And, in the ode *On the Morning of Christ's Nativity*, Milton represented heathen deities as fading away at the birth of Christ.

Keats introduced the episode of Hermes and the nymph to account for the transformation of Lamia from a serpent into a woman and to amplify the romance with vivid descriptive and narrative details. He had a precedent in Marlowe's *Hero and Leander* for introducing an amorous episode of Hermes; and, as Douglas Bush[5] has pointed out, he very probably found a suggestion for this episode in Ovid's story of Mercury and Herse and Aglauros at the end of the second book of the *Metamorphosis*. He made considerable changes in Ovid's story of Mercury and Herse in adapting it into the plot of his romance of Lycius and Lamia; but his description of Hermes' love for the nymph echoes very definitely Ovid's description of

[5] See footnote on p. 674.

Mercury's love for Herse. (Cp. *Lamia*, I. 22–26 and Sandys's *Ovid*, ed. 1640, p. 31.)

The description of Lamia as a serpent is a fine example of the style of the romance. Hermes heard a mournful voice and, gliding softly among the bushes and trees, he discovered

a palpitating snake,
Bright, and cirque-couchant in a dusky brake.
She was a gordian shape of dazzling hue,
Vermilion-spotted, golden, green, and blue;
Striped like a zebra, freckled like a pard,
Eyed like a peacock, and all crimson barr'd;
And full of silver moons, that, as she breathed,
Dissolv'd, or brighter shone, or interwreathed
Their lustres with the gloomier tapestries —
So rainbow-sided, touch'd with miseries,
She seem'd, at once, some penanced lady elf,
Some demon's mistress, or the demon's self.
Upon her crest she wore a wannish fire
Sprinkled with stars, like Ariadne's tiar:
Her head was serpent, but ah, bitter-sweet!
She had a woman's mouth with all its pearls complete:
And for her eyes: what could such eyes do there
But weep, and weep, that they were born so fair?
As Proserpine still weeps for her Sicilian air.
Her throat was serpent, but the words she spake
Came, as through bubbling honey, for Love's sake. . . .

Leigh Hunt expressed exactly the impression which this description makes upon us:

The admiration, pity, and horror, to be excited by humanity in a brute shape, were never perhaps called upon by a greater mixture of beauty and deformity than in the picture of this creature. Our pity and suspicions are begged by the first word: the profuse and vital beauties with which she is covered seem proportioned to her misery and natural rights; and lest we should lose sight of them in this gorgeousness, the "woman's mouth" fills us at once with shuddering and compassion.[6]

The picture of Lamia as a serpent is the most gorgeous mass of colors in Keats's poetry. It is as scintillating and flashing as the picture of the water snakes in Coleridge's *Rime of the Ancient Mariner*. Keats drew his picture of Lamia in emulation both of Coleridge's picture of the water snakes and of Milton's picture of the serpent which Satan entered to tempt Eve. He may have derived the colors of Lamia, especially the blue and the green, from Coleridge and her crest from Milton. The waning and brightening and inter-

[6] Leigh Hunt's review of the *Poems* of 1820, *The Indicator* for August 2 and 9, 1820.

wreathing of the colors as Lamia breathed is a device which he had employed in his description of the mantle of Glaucus in *Endymion* and which he had derived from Drayton's description of the robe of Phoebe in *The Man in the Moone.* He followed his source in Burton's *Anatomy of Melancholy* in representing Lamia as a female demon in serpent form. In comparing Lamia to "some penanced lady elf, Some demon's mistress, or the demon's self," however, he was indebted doubtless to a passage in Coleridge's *Kubla Khan* (v. 16) — "woman wailing for her demon-lover." He had already drawn upon this passage, we remember, in *Endymion* (IV. 188 *et seq.*) and in *The Eve of St. Agnes* (xix. 9). He produced a shuddering compassion for Lamia by giving her "a woman's mouth" and eyes which weep —

> what could such eyes do there
> But weep, and weep, that they were born so fair?
> As Proserpine still weeps for her Sicilian air.

He was indebted doubtless to a passage in *Paradise Lost* (IV. 268-272) for this poignant allusion to Proserpine —

> that faire field
> Of *Enna*, where *Proserpin* gathring flours
> Her self a fairer Floure by gloomie *Dis*
> Was gatherd, which cost *Ceres* all that pain
> To seek her through the world. . . .

He was deeply impressed by the pathos of this passage. He wrote Bailey from Scotland on July 18, 1818 that the first thing he would do when he saw him would be "to read that about Milton and Ceres and Proserpine." And, in his notes on *Paradise Lost*, he said:

> There are two specimens of a very extraordinary beauty in the Paradise Lost; they are of a nature as far as I have read, unexampled elsewhere — they are entirely distinct from the brief pathos of Dante — and they are not to be found even in Shakespeare — these are according to the great prerogative of poetry better described in themselves than by a volume. The one is in the fol[lowing] — "which cost Ceres all that pain" — the other is that ending "Nor could the Muse defend her son" — they appear exclusively Miltonic without the shadow of another mind ancient or Modern.

We find other qualities of style in Keats's description of Corinth in early evening.

> As men talk in a dream, so Corinth all,
> Throughout her palaces imperial,
> And all her populous streets and temples lewd,
> Mutter'd, like tempest in the distance brew'd,

To the wide-spreaded night above her towers.
Men, women, rich and poor, in the cool hours,
Shuffled their sandals o'er the pavement white,
Companion'd or alone; while many a light
Flared, here and there, from wealthy festivals,
And threw their moving shadows on the walls,
Or found them cluster'd in the corniced shade
Of some arch'd temple door, or dusky colonnade.

This picture of Corinth in early evening reminds us of the picture of Canterbury in early evening in *The Eve of St. Mark.*

The silent streets were crowded well
With staid and pious companies,
Warm from their fire-side orat'ries,
And moving, with demurest air,
To even-song and vesper prayer.
Each arched porch, and entry low,
Was fill'd with patient folk and slow,
With whispers hush, and shuffling feet,
While play'd the organ loud and sweet.

The two pictures have the same imaginative atmosphere — cool, dark, quiet streets, filled with people, the mutter of voices, and the shuffle of feet. The two scenes are distinguished only by religious details which place the one in ancient Greece and the other in mediaeval England. Even the moving shadows in the picture of Corinth had appeared in slightly different form in *The Eve of St. Mark,* in which Bertha, striking a lamp from the dismal coal,

Lean'd forward, with bright drooping hair
And slant book, full against the glare.
Her shadow, in uneasy guise,
Hover'd about, a giant size,
On ceiling-beam and old oak chair. . . .

The architectural details of Lamia's palace — the "pillar'd porch," the "lofty portal door," and the "silver lamp" with the "phosphor glow" — were suggested to Keats by Milton's description of Pandemonium in *Paradise Lost* (I. 710 *et seq.*). Milton said that Pandemonium was designed by a fallen angel who was worshiped afterwards in Ausonian land (Italy) under the name of Mulciber. And Keats, in an earlier part of *Lamia* (I. 211–212), alluded to Mulciber and Pandemonium:

Or where in Pluto's gardens palatine
Mulciber's columns gleam in far piazzian line.

Milton represented Pandemonium as built by the magical power of music —

> Anon out of the earth a fabric huge
> Rose like an exhalation, with the sound
> Of dulcet symphonies and voices sweet —
> Built like a temple, where pilasters round
> Were set, and Doric pillars overlaid
> With golden architrave. . . .

And Keats represented Lamia's palace as built and supported in the same way —

> Sounds Aeolian
> Breath'd from the hinges, as the ample span
> Of the wide doors disclos'd a place unknown
> Some time to any . . .
> [I. 386–389].
>
> A haunting music, sole perhaps and lone
> Supportress of the faery-roof, made moan
> Throughout, as fearful the whole charm might fade.
> [II. 122–124].

Douglas Bush [7] has discovered that Greek manners and customs in *Lamia*, especially Greek manners in feasts, were derived by Keats from John Potter's *Archaeologia Graeca, or The Antiquities of Greece*, a very learned treatise, which Charles Brown listed among the books which Keats owned at the time of his death. Keats delineated Greek manners accurately according to his source and transmuted bare details into sensuous vivid images, making ancient Corinth come alive before the eyes of his readers. "Now to me," he wrote his brother in December 1818, "manners and customs long since passed whether among the Babylonians or the Bactrians are as real, or eveven [*sic*] more real than those among which I now live."

Keats was especially indebted to Potter for details of the nuptial feast of Lycius and Lamia in the second part of the romance. I quote several parallels from Mr. Bush's excellent analysis.[7]

> It was the custom then to bring away
> The bride from home at blushing shut of day,
> Veil'd, in a chariot, heralded along
> By strewn flowers, torches, and a marriage song,
> With other pageants. . . .
> [Part II, vv. 106–110.]

Potter said that, after the marriage was celebrated with appropriate sacrifices to the nuptial deities, the bride was conveyed in a

[7] Douglas Bush, "Notes on Keats's Reading," *PMLA*, Vol. L (Sept. 1935), pp. 785–806.

chariot to the home of the bridegroom in the evening and a banquet was given for relatives and friends.

The bridegroom's garments were all dyed . . . both the married persons and their attendants were richly adorned, according to their quality. . . . They were likewise decked with garlands of various herbs and flowers . . . [Potter, ed. of 1818, Vol. II, p. 280].

The house where the nuptials were celebrated was likewise decked with garlands . . . [p. 281].

The bride was usually conducted in a chariot from her father's house to her husband's in the evening, that time being chosen to conceal her blushes. [p. 281].

One thing farther may be observed in the bride's passage to her husband's house, viz. that torches were carried before her. . . . They were sometimes attended with singers and dancers . . . [p. 282].

Since Lamia was a demon, however, she had no human kinsmen in Corinth to perform their part in the ceremonies and her nuptial rites were limited to the banquet which was held in the palace which she had built with her magic arts.

> Of wealthy lustre was the banquet-room,
> Fill'd with pervading brilliance and perfume:
> Before each lucid pannel fuming stood
> A censer fed with myrrh and spiced wood . . .
>
> [Part II, vv. 173–176].

And the room wherein the entertainment was made [Potter said] was sometimes perfumed by burning myrrh or frankincense, or with other odours. [p. 383].

> Twelve sphered tables, by silk seats insphered,
> High as the level of a man's breast rear'd
> On libbard's paws, upheld the heavy gold
> Of cups and goblets, and the store thrice told
> Of Ceres' horn, and, in huge vessels, wine
> Come from the gloomy tun with merry shine.
> Thus loaded with a feast the tables stood,
> Each shrining in the midst the image of a God.
>
> [Part II, vv. 183–190].

The form [of tables] was round [Potter said] if we may believe Myrleanus in Athenaeus, who reports that the ancient Greeks made their tables, and several other things, spherical, in imitation of the world, which they believed to be of that figure. [p. 376].

They [the tables] were also adorned with plates of silver or other metals, and supported by one or more feet, curiously wrought. . . . The most common support of these tables was an ivory foot, cast in the form of a lion, a leopard, or some other animal. [p. 377].

When they began to imitate the pride and vanity of the Asiatics, their cups were made of silver, gold, and other costly materials, curiously wrought, inlaid with precious stones, and otherwise adorned . . . [p. 390].

It was customary to place the statues of the gods upon the table . . . [p. 376].

When in an antichamber every guest
Had felt the cold full sponge to pleasure press'd,
By minist'ring slaves, upon his hands and feet,
And fragrant oils with ceremony meet
Pour'd on his hair, they all mov'd to the feast
In white robes, and themselves in order placed
Around the silken couches . . . [Part II, vv. 191–197].

The tables in those days [Potter said] were not covered with linen, but only carefully cleansed with wet sponges. [p. 377].

Before they went to an entertainment, they washed and anointed themselves . . . [p. 364].

They who came off a journey were washed and clothed with apparel suitable to the occasion, in the house of the entertainer, before they were admitted to the feast . . . [p. 365].

Lastly, it must not be omitted, that the feet being most exposed to dust and filth, were oftener washed and anointed than other parts of the body . . . [p. 370].

Lastly, after washing, the hands were perfumed with odours . . . [p. 366].

The chief part to which ointments were applied was the head . . . [p. 383].

During the entertainment, all the guests were apparelled in white, or some other cheerful colour . . . [p. 380].

The manner of lying at meat was thus: the table was placed in the middle, round which stood the beds covered with cloth or tapestry, according to the quality of the master of the house: upon these they lay, inclining the superior part of their bodies upon their left arms, the lower part being stretched out at length, or a little bent . . . [p. 373].

It was customary, from the heroical ages downwards, for the guests to be ranked according to their quality. [p. 374].

Soft went the music the soft air along,
While fluent Greek a vowel'd undersong
Kept up among the guests, discoursing low
At first, for scarcely was the wine at flow . . .
[Part II, vv. 199–202].

From the most ancient times [Potter said], music and dancing were the diversions at entertainments . . . [p. 400].

But when the happy vintage touch'd their brains,
Louder they talk, and louder come the strains
Of powerful instruments: — the gorgeous dyes,
The space, the splendour of the draperies,
The roof of awful richness, nectarous cheer,
Beautiful slaves, and Lamia's self, appear . . .
[Part II, vv. 203–208].

Potter gave an elaborate discussion of Greek manners of drinking, singing, and conversing at entertainments and banquets [pp. 389 *et seq.*]. Keats's reference to beautiful slaves was derived from the following passage:

Philo the Jew . . . tells us, that it was usual to procure most beautiful slaves to attend at entertainments, not so much for any service they were to do, as to gratify the eyes of the beholders . . . [p. 389].

> Garlands of every green, and every scent
> From vales deflower'd, or forest-trees branch-rent,
> In baskets of bright osier'd gold were brought
> High as the handles heap'd, to suit the thought
> Of every guest; that each, as he did please,
> Might fancy-fit his brows, silk-pillow'd at his ease.
> [Part II, vv. 215–220].

It was also customary [Potter said] to deck themselves with flowers, or garlands composed of flowers, which were provided by the master of the feast, and brought in before the second course, or, as some are of opinion, at the beginning of the entertainment. [p. 380].

The flowers and greens whereof garlands were composed were various. [p. 382].

. . . their heads were raised up, and their backs sometimes supported with pillows. [p. 373].

The metres of Keats's romances offer an interesting study in progressive experimentation. He composed *Calidore*, his first romance, in the loose heroic couplets which Leigh Hunt had developed by combining the alexandrines and triplets of Dryden's heroic couplets with the variable caesura, run-on verses, and feminine rhymes of the heroic couplets of the seventeenth-century Spenserians. After he had reacted against Hunt's poetic principles he composed *Endymion* in the loose heroic couplets of William Browne and other seventeenth-century Spenserians. He did not, however, either change or improve his couplets very much, and for a time he stopped experimenting with them. He composed *The Pot of Basil* in the ottava rima of Fairfax's translation of Tasso's *Jerusalem Delivered*, and he strengthened the structure of his verse by studying Dryden's heroic couplets and heroic stanzas. He composed *The Eve of St. Agnes* in Spenserian stanzas and *The Eve of St. Mark* in the short, or octosyllabic, couplet. Finally he composed *Lamia* in heroic couplets, correcting the loose structure of his earlier couplets by adapting elements of the firm, vigorous, epigrammatic couplets of Dryden.

Keats adapted several structural devices from Dryden's heroic couplets. He employed twelve triplets, one quadruplet, and thirty-four alexandrines. In the following verses the third verse of the triplet and the second verse of the couplet are alexandrines —

> And as he from one trance was wakening
> Into another, she began to sing,

Happy in beauty, life, and love, and every thing,
A song of love, too sweet for earthly lyres,
While, like held breath, the stars drew in their panting fires.

In this and in other passages in the romance Keats made the metrical rhythm, as he explained to Woodhouse, harmonize with and reinforce the emotions and thoughts which he was expressing. In one passage, as de Sélincourt pointed out, he reproduced Dryden's epigrammatic and antithetical style of couplets —

So threw the goddess off, and won his heart
More pleasantly by playing woman's part,
With no more awe than what her beauty gave,
That, while it smote, still guaranteed to save.
[I. 336–339].

He maintained in his couplets as a whole a balance between looseness and rigidity. The worst defect in his metre is the large number of imperfect rhymes such as broods / woods, wont / haunt, muse / house, and voice / destroys. The proportion of imperfect rhymes, which is greater in *Lamia* than in his earlier poems, was due, I believe, to Dryden's influence.

3

The second part of *Lamia* reflects the mood of defiant egotism which was engendered in Keats in the second half of August and the first half of September 1819. An analysis of the causes and the character of this egotistic and defiant mood will explain the symbolic satire of the romance.

Keats and Brown moved from Shanklin, Isle of Wight, to Winchester on August 12; for Keats felt the need of a library and he was irritated, in his present mood, by the picturesque scenery of the Isle of Wight. On August 5, a week before he left Shanklin, he wrote Miss Brawne:

This day week we shall move to Winchester; for I feel the want of a Library. Brown will leave me there to pay a visit to Mr Snook at Bedhampton: in his absence I will flit to you and back. I will stay very little while, for as I am in a train of writing now I fear to disturb it — let it have its course bad or good — in it I shall try my own strength and the public pulse.

In the letter which he wrote Miss Brawne on August 16, four days after he had arrived in Winchester, he compared Shanklin with Winchester:

This Winchester is a fine place: a beautiful Cathedral and many other ancient building[s] in the Environs. The little coffin of a room at Shanklin is changed for a large room, where I can promenade at my pleasure — looks out onto a beautiful — blank side of a house. It is strange I should like it better than the view of the sea from our window at Shanklin. I began to hate the very posts there — the voice of the old Lady over the way was getting a great Plague. The Fisherman's face never altered any more than our black teapot — the [k]nob however was knock'd off to my little relief. I am getting a great dislike of the picturesque; and can only relish it over again by seeing you enjoy it.

When he arrived in Winchester, Keats was still maintaining courageously his struggle against adverse circumstances. He was confident of earning an income from the poems which he was composing, he was friendly towards the public whose favor he was striving to win, and he was ardent and tender in his love for Miss Brawne. In the letter which he wrote Bailey on August 14 he mentioned the poems which he had composed since he had written to Bailey and intimated that he would publish them by the following winter.

Within these two Months I have written 1500 Lines, most of which besides many more of prior composition you will probably see by next Winter. I have written two Tales, one from Boccac[c]io call'd the Pot of Basil; and another call'd S^{t}. Agnes' Eve on a popular superstition; and a third call'd Lamia — half finished. I have also been writing parts of my Hyperion and completed 4 Acts of a Tragedy.

He was ambitious, he said, to make a revolution in modern playwriting and to upset the drawling of the bluestocking literary world.

If in the course of a few years I do these two things [he added] I ought to die content — and my friends should drink a dozen of Claret on my Tomb.

Keats had written more than 1500 lines within the last two months. The first part of *Lamia* and four acts of *Otho* together comprise 1860 verses. His statement is ambiguous, also, because he lumped together the poems which he had composed within the last two months and those which he had composed since he had last written Bailey on July 18, 1818, nearly thirteen months before. He did not mean, therefore, that he had composed *The Pot of Basil*, *Hyperion*, and *The Eve of St. Agnes* within the last two months. It is necessary to explain his statement; for certain critics have believed on the basis of his statement that he was working on some version of "Hyperion" in July and August 1819.

Although Keats wrote Bailey in a confident and resolute spirit, he had reached the limit of his endurance. For two months and a half he had been in a desperate need of money. For two months he had been suffering from another attack of laryngeal tuberculosis. And for a month and a half he had been separated from Miss Brawne, tortured by thwarted desire, frustrated hopes, and corroding jealousy. These physical and mental troubles, which he had been resisting with fortitude, were sapping his vitality. He was undergoing also the exhausting labor of steady composition. Within the last two months, we have seen, he had composed 1860 verses.

On August 16, two days after he had written Bailey, Keats succumbed to a mood of irritable defiance. Every change in his attitude to life, we have observed, came with the startling suddenness of a flash of lightning. He reacted first of all against love, and he wrote a "flint-worded" letter to Miss Brawne. He told her harshly that he was forgetting her and that he must forget her for the sake of his poetry. He was not resolving at this time, however, as he resolved a month later, to wean himself away from her. He was resolving merely to forget her for the present so that he could concentrate more effectively upon the composition of poems, by means of which he hoped to retrieve his fortunes and put himself in a position to marry her.

> My dear Girl — what shall I say for myself? I have been here four days and not yet written you —'tis true I have had many teasing letters of business to dismiss — and I have been in the Claws, like a Serpent in an Eagle's, of the last act of our Tragedy. This is no excuse; I know it; I do not presume to offer it. I have no right either to ask a speedy answer to let me know how lenient you are — I must remain some days in a Mist — I see you through a Mist: as I dare say you do me by this time. Believe in the first Letters I wrote you: I assure you I felt as I wrote — I could not write so now. The thousand images I have had pass through my brain — my uneasy spirits — my unguess'd fate — all spread as a veil between me and you — Remember I have had no idle leisure to brood over you — 'tis well perhaps I have not. I could not have endured the throng of Jealousies that used to haunt me before I had plunged so deeply into imaginary interests. I would feign, as my sails are set, sail on without an interruption for a Brace of Months longer — I am in complete cue — in the fever; and shall in these four Months do an immense deal — This Page as my eye skims over it I see is excessively unloverlike and ungallant — I cannot help it — I am no officer in yawning quarters; no Parson-romeo. My Mind is heap'd to the full; stuff'd like a cricket ball — if I strive to fill it more it would burst. I know the generallity of women would hate me for this; that I should have so unsoften'd so hard a Mind as to forget them; forget the brightest realities for the dull imaginations of my own Brain. But I conjure you to give it a fair thinking; and ask yourself whether 'tis not better to explain my feelings to you, than write artificial Passion — Besides you would see through it. It would be vain to strive to deceive you. 'Tis harsh, harsh, I know it — My heart seems now made of iron — I could not write a proper answer to an invitation to Idalia. You are my Judge: my forehead is on the ground.

Keats was egotistic as well as harsh and defiant. He was thinking of his own feelings instead of Miss Brawne's. She was too immature to understand him and to comfort him in his struggle against adverse circumstances; but he responded to her petty coquetry with greater harshness than it deserved.

> You seem offended [he said] at a little simple innocent childish playfulness in my last [letter]. I did not seriously mean to say that you were endeavouring to make me keep my promise [that is, his promise to see her in a short time]. I beg your pardon for it. 'Tis but *just* you[r] Pride should take the alarm — *seriously*. You say I may do as I please — I do not think with any conscience I can; my cash resourses [*sic*] are for the present stopp'd; I fear for some time. I spend no money but it increases my debts. I have all my life thought very little of these matters — they seem not to belong to me. It may be a proud sentence; but, by heaven, I am as entirely above all matters of interest as the Sun is above the Earth — and though of my own money I should be careless; of my Friends I must be spare.

Keats derived a morbid satisfaction, it seems, from expressing his painful reaction against love.

> You see how I go on — like so many strokes of a Hammer. I cannot help it — I am impell'd, driven to it. I am not happy enough for silken Phrases, and silver sentences. I can no more use soothing words to you than if I were at this moment engaged in a charge of Cavalry — Then you will say I should not write at all — Should I not?

At the end of the letter, after he had relieved somewhat his painful feelings, he revealed a glimpse of that ardent love for Miss Brawne which he could not quench. He must forget her for the present, he told her, and compose poems which would earn him an income and enable him to marry her.

> Forgive me for this flint-worded Letter, and believe and see that I cannot think of you without some sort of energy — though mal à propos — Even as I leave off, it seems to me that a few more moments thought of you would uncrystallize and dissolve me. I must not give way to it — but turn to my writing again — if I fail I shall die hard. O my love, your lips are growing sweet again to my fancy — I must forget them. Ever your affectionate
>
> Keats —

By this time Keats and Brown had spent almost all of their money. Keats wrote to the friends to whom he had lent money and asked them to repay him; and Brown sought to borrow money from his friends. They received no reply, however, to their letters; and, as a last resort, Keats wrote a letter to Taylor, his publisher, and asked for a loan and Brown wrote a note on the doublings of the letter and offered to stand surety for the loan.

He still had hopes of gaining moderate profits from the tragedy which he had just completed, he told Taylor; and he still believed that he could become a popular poet. The tolerance of the public which he had expressed in Shanklin was converted, however, into irritable and defiant hatred.

I feel every confidence [he said] that if I choose I may be a popular writer; that I will never be; but for all that I will get a livelihood — I equally dislike the favour of the public with the love of a woman — they are both a cloying treacle to the wings of independence. I shall ever consider them (People) as debtors to me for verses, not myself to them for admiration — which I can do without. I have of late been indulging my spleen by composing a preface *at* them: after all resolving never to write a preface at all. "There are so many verses," would I have said to them, "give me so much means to buy pleasure with as a relief to my hours of labour" —

Perceiving that he was writing in a proud spirit, Keats exaggerated and defended his pride.

You will observe at the end of this if you put down the Letter "How a solitary life engenders pride and egotism!" True: I know it does — but this Pride and egotism will enable me to write finer things than any thing else could — so I will indulge it. Just so much as I am hu[m]bled by the genius above my grasp, am I exalted and look with hate and contempt upon the literary world — A Drummer boy who holds out his hand familiarly to a field marshall [*sic*] — that Drummer boy with me is the good word and favour of the public. Who would wish to be among the commonplace crowd of the little-famous — who are each individually lost in a throng made up of themselves? is this worth louting or playing the hypocrite for? To beg suffrages for a seat on the benches of a myriad-aristocracy in Letters? This is not wise — I am not a wise man — 'Tis Pride. I will give you a definition of a proud Man. He is a Man who has neither vanity nor wisdom — one fill'd with hatreds cannot be vain — neither can he be wise. Pardon me for hammering instead of writing. Remember me to Woodhouse Hessey and all in Percy street.

Keats explained his defiant egotism more clearly in the letter which he wrote Reynolds on August 25.

The more I know what my diligence may in time probably effect; the more does my heart distend with Pride and Obstinacy — I feel it in my strength to become a popular writer — I feel it in my power to refuse the poisonous suffrage of a public. My own being which I know to be becomes of more consequence to me than the crowds of Shadows in the shape of Man and Woman that inhabit a Kingdom. The soul is a world of itself, and has enough to do in its own home. Those whom I know already, and who have grown as it were a part of myself, I could not do without: but for the rest of mankind, they are as much a dream to me as Milton's Hierarchies. I think if I had a free and healthy and lasting organization of heart, and lungs as strong as an ox's so as to be able to bear unhurt the shock of extreme thought and sensation without weariness, I could pass my life very nearly alone though it should last eighty years. But I feel my body too weak to support me to the height, I am obliged continually to check myself and strive to be nothing. It would be vain for me to endeavour after a more reasonable manner of writing to you. I have nothing to speak of but myself, and what can I say but what I feel? If you should have any reason to regret this state of excitement in me, I will turn the tide of your feelings in the right Channel, by mentioning that it is the only state for the best sort of Poetry — that is all I care for, all I live for.

Keats waited anxiously for Taylor's answer to his request for a loan. He had addressed his letter to Taylor to the shop in Fleet Street, London, from which it had been forwarded to Retford, Nottingham, where Taylor was passing his vacation. Taylor delayed his answer for almost two weeks. He was perturbed by the irritable and defiant pride which Keats evinced and was inclined to refuse to lend him any money. He was a moderate and just man, however; he was not sure that he understood Keats; and, before coming to a decision, he sent Keats's letter to Woodhouse, who was in London, and asked his advice.

Woodhouse wrote Taylor a long letter on August 31. He did not understand the real causes of Keats's defiant pride; but he was sympathetic and loyal to Keats in all circumstances; and he interpreted Keats's pride as magnanimity. He offered generously to lend Taylor money to lend to Keats. His letter is a model of tactful and persuasive eloquence.

My dear John,

Though I have let a post elapse, I apprehend this letter, which will go in a parcel to you, will reach you as soon as Keats's answer. I have read his letter; and I did it before I had read yours, and with my usual disposition to understand his terms in that sense in which he uses them. Now I apprehend his word Pride to mean nothing more than literary Pride, — that disposition which arises out of a consciousness of superior and improving poetical Powers, & which would keep him, even in his present state of comparative imperfectness, from writing so as to minister to the depraved taste of the Age. — It is not in my opinion personal pride, but literary pride which his letter shows; — That he has some of the former also, I believe; But his letter does not evince it, further than it displays a solitary spirit. The Pride contained in his letter, as I understand it, is a noble pride, akin to that Indication which Milton pours forth in language of such "solemn tenour & deep organ tone" at the beginning of his 2[d] book on "the reason of Ch. Government," and for which I honor him. And I am not quite certain whether your Post Script was not added in consequence of a new ray of light breaking in upon you on this subject. Is he wrong to be dissatisfied with the Prospect of a mere "Seat on the Bench of a myriad-aristocracy in Letters?" or to keep aloof from them and their works, — or to dislike the favour of such a "public," as bepraises the Crabbes, & the Barretts, & the Codruses of the day. — I wonder how he came to stumble upon that deep truth that "people are debtors to him for verses & not he to them for admiration." Methinks such a conviction on any one's mind is enough to make half a Milton of him.

I agree with you in every syllable you say about Pride. But I do not think it applies to Keats, as he shows himself in his letter. And if you were to cull out a person upon whom to fit your summary of the whole (neither self praise nor man's praise can turn the scale either way, — nor can unmerited neglect or censure weight a feather) I think, as far as Poetry is concerned, that very man would be Keats as evidenced in his letter.

Having complied with your wish of telling you what I thought of his letter, I come now to his request. I doubt whether he will want as much as you mention. I apprehend 50[l] or 60 would suffice him, but this his next letter will shew. I think I mentioned to you how I was situated as to Cash, that I had scraped all I could together, to pay my Father, whose two calls lately had run him close. That I expected nothing till winter, and had made my calculation upon wanting little till that time. Under these circumstances I could not command £100. But I can spare £50, which shall be at your disposal, at what time & place you think proper. You are well acquainted with my good wishes towards Keats as well as with their complete disinterestedness — Whatever People regret that they could not do for Shakespeare or Chatterton, because he did not live in their time, that I would embody into a Rational principle, and (with due regard to certain expediences) do for Keats. But one's means are not unlimited, and one would not wish to give rise to expectations, which should end in disappointment, nor would one like to have the oats eaten by other cattle. I wish he could be cured of the vice of lending — for the poor man, it is a vice.

I think with you about the offer of Brown's name, and about the nonsense of the note. But would it be or not beneficial to K. that it should be taken? And is any part of the money to go to Brown? The sum will perhaps enable you to judge.

Hessey spoke about Keats's letter, & wants, & quoted your intimation to him, so that I could not do less than say he should see the letter. He will not "peach" about the Tragedy, and there is no other secret in it. I think to shew him your letter too. Perhaps he may think with me, and contrary to you, that the obligation to K. may prove beneficial to the business.

I can say nothing about what is best to be done, for K. — I am tempest tost on the subject, and even with the light of his next letter I may be as much in the dark. I think (and you need not make a bow for the compliment) that you are the prudenter man of the two, to judge in this case. But take this with you. 1st I really can't spare more "as in presenti," than the sum I have named. And 2[d] my friendship for the poor fellow wo[d] willingly go, if need is, greater lengths than merely lending you money to lend him.

I shall be out of town in about 10 Days, but I can send you (or Hessey) a draft from any place. . . .

I like Brown's few lines much . . . .

Reynolds is off, but before he went he called and left me the Sonnet — and a letter he had received from Keats. I send it to you: It will be a comment on parts of his to you. *Please return it me through the first parcel you send*. . . .

Yours affectionately
Richd. Woodhouse
Temple Tuesday Evg.
31, Augt 1819
[Woodhouse's Scrap-book.]

Woodhouse's loyalty, generosity, and disinterestedness have endeared him to Keats's biographers and critics. His disinterestedness is summed up in one sentence in his letter to Taylor. "Whatever People regret that they could not do for Shakespeare or Chatterton, because he did not live in their time," he said, "that I would embody into a Rational principle, and (with due regard to certain expediences) do for Keats."

In the meantime, Keats and Brown were becoming desperate. They owed for a month's expenses and they had not received a single answer from the friends to whom they had written for assistance. On August 31 Keats wrote another letter to Taylor. "Do answer me soon," he urged, "for I really must know something."

Taylor was persuaded by Woodhouse's letter, I presume, that Keats's pride was literary instead of personal and that, therefore, he deserved assistance. He wrote Woodhouse that £50 might be lent to Keats, that £30 might be sent him at once, and that the remainder should be held for his future needs. Woodhouse immediately turned over £50 to Hessey, who sent £30 to Keats. The receipt of this money dissipated some of the gloom in Keats's spirit. He wrote Hessey on September 5:

Winchester, Sunday Sep[tr] 5th

My dear Hessey,

I received this morning yours of yesterday enclosing a 30£ bank post bill. I have been in fear of the Winchester Jail for some time: neither Brown nor myself could get an answer from any one. This morning I hear that some unknown part of a Sum due to me and for which I had been waiting three weeks has been sent to Chichester by mistake. Brown has borrow'd money of a friend of his in Hampshire. A few days ago we had but a few shillings left — and now between us we have 60£ besides what is waiting in the Chichester post office. To be a complete Midas I suppose some one will send me a pair of asses ears by the waggon. There has been such an embargo laid on our correspondence that I can scarrcely [*sic*] believe your Letter was only dated yesterday. It seems miraculous.

Ever yours sincerely
John Keats.

I am sorry to hear such a bad account of himself from Taylor.

Keats wrote Taylor also on September 5, acknowledging the receipt of the loan and quoting 59 verses of the second part of *Lamia* which he had just completed. He was made to believe, it seems, that Taylor's delay in sending the money to him was due to Taylor's illness; and he never knew that he was really indebted to Woodhouse for the money. Woodhouse, who was content that his generosity should be unknown, was delighted with Keats's letter to Hessey. He wrote Taylor on September 7:

My dear John,

I was favored with your last on Saturday, & saw off a Bk. p. Bill for 30£ to Keats. Hessey holds the rest at his disposal. The fund of this Beaumont & Fletcher pair,

"Who with combined powers, their wit employ'd
To raise a trophy to the Drama's muses" (Poems p. 53)

were at a low, — verily at a silver, ebb. But, with your supply, there came an announcement that some Cash was gone to *Chichester*, by mistake, in payment of one of the Debts due to K. so that he was quite flush; and he supposes some one, to make a complete Midas of him, will send him down a pair of Ass's ears by the waggon. If Hessey sends you Keats's letter, you will have this joke twice over: but it is too good to be lost. I roared aloud over it, to the astonishment of some male & female "natives," who were book buying in the back shop.

[Woodhouse's Scrap-book.]

These letters which I have quoted give us the background of the second part of *Lamia*, which Keats composed between August 23 and September 5, 1819. In the first place, the stream of creative composition was flowing deeply and strongly within him. "I am in complete cue — in the fever," he wrote Miss Brawne; "and shall in these four Months do an immense deal . . . . My Mind is heap'd to the full; stuff'd like a cricket ball — if I strive to fill it more it would burst." But he did not have, he wrote Reynolds, a sufficiently "healthy and lasting organization of heart, and lungs . . . to be able to bear unhurt the shock of extreme thought and sensation without weariness." This, the last great period of his poetry, was brought to an end in the latter part of September, we shall see, by the debilitating ravages of tuberculosis.

In the second place, lack of money, thwarted love, frustrated ambition, and steady composition stirred him into an intensity of feeling and thought, exhausted his diseased and weakened vitality, and cast him into a mood of defiant egotism. He became irritable, defiant, almost cynical, in his reaction against his fiancée, Fanny Brawne, and against the public for whom he was writing poems in this period. In his defiant mood he became indifferent, almost hostile, to human beings in general and he took refuge in the world of his own ego. "The soul is a world of itself," he wrote Reynolds, "and has enough to do in its own home. Those whom I know already, and who have grown as it were a part of myself, I could not do without: but for the rest of mankind, they are as much a dream to me as Milton's Hierarchies." He was at the extreme point of his progressive reaction against those humanitarian principles — that love for humanity, that pity for the giant agony of the world, and that Messianic passion to labor, like a slave to poor humanity, for mortal good — which he had expressed in the introduction to the humanitarian version of the "Fall of Hyperion." In this period, therefore, he could not have composed this humanitarian introduction.

His empirical humanism, his philosophy of negative capability, was submerged for the moment in this rising tide of egotism. In June, two months before, he had thought that adversity would increase his negative capability, his sympathetic insight into the feelings and thoughts of other men. If he had had a "healthy and lasting organization of heart, and lungs," adversity would have had this effect upon him; but, in his diseased and debilitated condition, adversity destroyed his calm self-control and released his egotistic impulses. He succumbed to egotism for only a month, however; on September 18, we shall see, he subdued his egotistic impulses and resumed his empirical humanism.

This egotism to which Keats surrendered on August 16 changed his philosophy of poetry. He had believed, we remember, that natural instincts, which are either disinterested or egotistic, are "the very thing in which consists poetry" — that is, that natural instincts are the subject matter of poetry. He had distinguished between egotistic poets, such as Byron, who express their own instinctive impulses, feelings, and thoughts, and negatively capable poets, such as Shakespeare, who escape from the dominance of their own instincts, and who express the feelings and thoughts of other men in perfect freedom. He had regarded the negatively capable poet as the higher type of poet and he had believed that his own genius was negatively capable. Now, however, since adversity had released his egotistic impulses, he turned from negatively capable poetry to egotistic poetry. "This Pride and egotism," he wrote Taylor, "will enable me to write finer things than any thing else could — so I will indulge it." "It is the only state for the best sort of Poetry," he wrote Reynolds, "— that is all I care for, all I live for."

Before we interpret the second part of *Lamia*, however, let us consider Woodhouse's memorandum of a conversation with Keats which occurred on September 12, one week after Keats had completed *Lamia*.

Keats was relieved of his immediate need of money by the loan which he received from Taylor on September 5. He remained in Winchester to revise his poems and Brown departed ostensibly to visit Dilke's father in Chichester and Dilke's brother-in-law, Mr. Snook, in Bedhampton. On September 10 Keats was disturbed by a letter of bad news from his brother George. After George Keats had settled in Henderson, Kentucky, he had invested his capital in a boat which carried merchandise on the Mississippi River. At the time of the investment, he discovered afterwards, the boat was lying on the bottom of the river; but Audubon, the naturalist, from whom he had bought shares in the boat, was unable or unwilling to return the money. He believed that Audubon had swindled him. A friend, a Mr. Bakewell, lent him some money to support his family until he could receive funds from England.

This bad news dispelled Keats's morbid broodings and aroused him into action. That evening, after he received the letter from his brother, he took the coach to London to urge Abbey to confer with Mrs. Jennings' solicitors and to try to settle the suit which she had filed in Chancery. If this suit could be settled, he believed, Abbey would send George the remaining part of his share in the estate.

Keats arrived in London on Saturday morning, September 11, and visited 93 Fleet Street, where he saw Hessey and Woodhouse. He passed the greater part of Sunday with Woodhouse, having breakfast with him in the morning and seeing him off on the coach to Weymouth at 3 o'clock in the afternoon. He dined with Mrs. Wylie on Sunday evening and visited his sister in Walthamstow on Monday morning. On Monday evening at 7 o'clock he had an interview with Abbey, who promised to try to settle Mrs. Jennings' claim and to send money to George. He passed some time with Rice and Haslam and returned to Winchester on Wednesday, September 15.

Keats did not go to Hampstead to see Fanny Brawne while he was in London, because he was endeavoring to wean himself away from her. He wrote her a letter from Fleet Street on Monday morning, September 13.

My dear Girl,

I have been hurried to town by a Letter from my brother George; it is not of the brightest intelligence. Am I mad or not? I came by the Friday night coach and have not yet been to Ham[p]stead. Upon my soul it is not my fault. I cannot resolve to mix any pleasure with my days: they go one like another, undistinguishable. If I were to see you to-day it would destroy the half comfortable sullenness I enjoy at present into dow[n]right perplexities. I love you too much to venture to Hampstead, I feel it is not paying a visit, but venturing into a fire. *Que feraije?* as the french novel writers say in fun, and I in earnest: really what can I do? Knowing well that my life must be passed in fatigue and trouble, I have been endeavouring to wean myself from you: for to myself alone what can be much of a misery? As far as they regard myself I can despise all events: but I cannot cease to love you. This morning I scarcely know what I am doing. I am going to Walthamstow. I shall return to Winchester to-morrow; whence you shall hear from me in a few days. I am a Coward, I cannot bear the pain of being happy: 'tis out of the question: I must admit no thought of it.

Yours ever affectionately

John Keats

Keats had recovered somewhat from the irritable mood in which he had written Miss Brawne on August 16. He was thinking a little more of her and a little less of himself. The news of his brother's predicament made him keenly conscious of the desperate state of his own affairs. It would not be honorable, he decided, to hold Miss Brawne to her promise to marry him. He was resolved to give her up — at least for the present — for her own sake. "Knowing well that my life must be passed in fatigue and trouble," he told her, "I have been endeavouring to wean myself from you."

> I have forgot how to lay plans for enjoyment of any Pleasure [he wrote his brother on September 17]. I feel I can bear any thing, — any misery, even imprisonment — so long as I have neither wife nor child. Perhaps you will say yours are your only comfort — they must be.

There was a queer quirk in Keats's reasoning. It would be more unselfish, he believed, to use whatever money he might earn from his poems for the relief of his brother George than to use it for his own marriage to Miss Brawne.

> Your wants will be a fresh spur to me [he wrote his brother]. I assure you you shall more than share what I can get, whilst I am still young — the time may come when age will make me more selfish.

The effect of Keats's defiant egotism on the second part of *Lamia* comes out in Woodhouse's report of Keats's comments on his romances, *The Pot of Basil*, *The Eve of St. Agnes*, and *Lamia*, which he read and revised between September 5 and September 10, just before he left Winchester. From Weymouth on Monday, September 20, Woodhouse wrote Taylor a summary of his conversation with Keats in London on Saturday, September 11, and Sunday, September 12.

> Keats was in Town the day before I left. He came into 93 unexpectedly, while I was in the midst of a recapitulation to Hessey of the strong points of the matter between yourselves & the Captn. . . . K. came about his Chancery Suit that is to be: or rather that is not to be, if he succeeds in the object of his Journey to London; which is to dissuade some old aunt from going into that Court. — He took his breakfast with me on the Sunday, and remained with me till I stept into the Coach for this place at 3 oClock. I was much gratified with his Company. He wanted I believe to publish the Eve of S^{t}. Agnes & Lamia *immediately*: but Hessey told him it could not answer to do so now. I wondered why he said nothing of Isabella: & assured him it would please more than the Eve of S^{t}. Agnes—He said he could not bear the former now. It appeared to him mawkish. This certainly cannot be so. the feeling is very likely to come across an author on review of a former work of his own, particularly where the object of his present meditations are of a more sobered & unpassionate Character. The feeling of mawkishness seems to me to be that which comes upon us where any thing of great tenderness & excessive simplicity is met with when we are not in a

sufficiently tender & simple frame of mind to bear it: when we experience a sort of revulsion, or resiliency (if there be such a word) from the sentiment or expression. Now I believe there is nothing in any of the most passionate parts of Isabella to excite this feeling. It may, as may Lear, leave the reader far behind: but there is none of that sugar & butter sentiment, that cloys & disgusts. —

[Manuscript, Pierpont Morgan Library.]

We have also Keats's judgment of *The Pot of Basil* in his own words. On September 21, six days after he had returned to Winchester, he wrote Woodhouse:

I will give you a few reasons why I shall persist in not publishing The Pot of Basil. It is too smokeable. I can get it smoak'd at the Carpenters shaving chimney much more cheaply. There is too much inexperience of live [life], and simplicity of knowledge in it — which might do very well after one's death — but not while one is alive. There are very few would look to the reality. I intend to use more finesse with the Public. It is possible to write fine things which cannot be laugh'd at in any way. Isabella is what I should call were I a reviewer "A weak-sided Poem" with an amusing sober-sadness about it. Not that I do not think Reynolds and you are quite right about it — it is enough for me. But this will not do to be public. If I may so say, in my dramatic capacity I enter fully into the feeling: but in Propria Persona I should be apt to quiz it myself. There is no objection of this kind to Lamia — A good deal to St. Agnes Eve — only not so glaring.

The more sentimental of Keats's friends, Taylor, Woodhouse, Reynolds, and Charles Lamb, regarded *The Pot of Basil* as the best of his poems. Modern critics of his poetry are inclined, however, to accept his judgment of the romance. His reaction against its sentimentality was inspired partly by the development of his poetic taste, partly by his fear of the censure of the reviewers, and partly by the mood of defiant egotism through which he was passing. He did not attempt to remove the sentimentality from *The Pot of Basil*, for he perceived doubtless that it was diffused inextricably throughout the romance.

Keats's defiant, almost cynical, egotism stands out in his revision of *The Eve of St. Agnes*.

He had the Eve of St. A. copied fair [Woodhouse said]: He has made trifling alterations, inserted an additional stanza early in the poem to make the legend more intelligible, and correspondent with what afterwards takes place, particularly with respect to the supper & the playing on the Lute. — he retains the name of Porphyro — has altered the last 3 lines to leave on the reader a sense of pettish disgust, by bringing old Angela in (only) dead stiff & ugly. — He says he likes that the poem should leave off with this Change of sentiment — it was what he aimed at, & was glad to find from my objections to it that he had succeeded. — I apprehend he had a fancy for trying his hand at an attempt to play with his reader, & fling him off at last — I sho.d have thought he affected the "Don Juan" style of mingling up sentiment & sneering: but that he had before asked Hessey if he co.d procure him a sight of that work, as he had not met with it, and if the E. of St. A. had not in all probability been altered before his Lordship had thus flown in the face of the public. There was another alteration, which I abused for "a full hour by the *Temple* clock." You know if a thing has a decent side, I generally look no further — As the Poem was origy. written, *we* innocent ones (ladies & myself) might very well have supposed that Porphyro, when acquainted with Madeline's love for him, & when "he arose, Etherial flushd. etc. etc. (turn to it) set himself at once to persuade her to go off with him, & succeeded & went over the "Dartmoor black" (now changed for some other place) to be married, in right honest chaste & sober wise. But, as it is now altered, as soon as M. has confessed her love, P. winds by degrees his arm round her, proper breast to breast, and acts all the acts of a bonâ fide husband, while she fancies she is only playing the part of a Wife in a dream. This alteration is of about 3 stanzas; and tho' there are no improper expressions, but all is left to inference, and tho' profanely speaking, the Interest on the reader's imagination is greatly heightened, yet I do apprehend it will render the poem unfit for ladies, & indeed scarcely to be mentioned to them among the "things that are." — He says he does not want ladies to read his poetry: that he writes for men, & that if in the former poem there was an opening for a doubt what took place, it was his fault for not writing clearly & comprehensibly — that he shd. despise a man who would be such an eunuch in sentiment as to leave a maid, with that Character about her, in such a situation: & shod. despise himself to write about it etc etc etc — and all this sort of Keats-like rhodomontade. — But you will see the work I dare say. —

The sweet sentimentality and the maidenly morality which Woodhouse manifested in this letter explain doubtless why Keats did not admit him into the inner circle of his friendship. He was flattered by Woodhouse's admiration for his poetry but he was not aware of Woodhouse's disinterested loyalty and generosity. In a letter to Dilke on September 22, 1819 he said:

Do you know him [Woodhouse]? He is a Friend of Taylors at whom Brown has taken one of his funny odd dislikes. I'm sure he's wrong, because Woodhouse likes my Poetry — conclusive.

Keats revised *The Eve of St. Agnes* in a spirit of cynical defiance of the public. "I shod. have thought," Woodhouse said, "he affected the 'Don Juan' style of mingling up sentiment & sneering: but that he had before asked Hessey if he cod. procure him a sight of that work, as he had not met with it. . . ." Woodhouse was mistaken in believing that Keats said that he had not "met with" a copy of Byron's *Don Juan*. Keats was influenced by *Don Juan*, we shall see, in *Lamia*, which he completed before he revised *The Eve of St. Agnes*.

Keats was persuaded by Taylor and Woodhouse to suppress these cynical and Byronic alterations in the version which was printed in the *Poems* of 1820. But most of these alterations — probably all of them — survive in the version which George Keats copied into his

Book of Autographs and Transcripts during his visit in England in January 1820. The stanza which Woodhouse said that Keats inserted in the first part of the romance to make the legend more intelligible is the seventh stanza of this version. I believe that Woodhouse, who did not read the revised manuscript but who only heard Keats read it, was mistaken in thinking that Keats added three stanzas in the climax of the romance. A comparison of the original autograph manuscript with George Keats's transcript of the revised manuscript shows that Keats merely made a few alterations in the phraseology of the original stanzas to make clear, as Woodhouse said, that Porphyro acted the acts of a *bona fide* husband. Woodhouse's statement that Porphyro "winds by degrees his arm round her, proper breast to breast" was a remembrance of the eighth and ninth verses of the thirty-sixth stanza of the revised version. These verses are written in George Keats's transcript as follows:

> See while she speaks his arms encroaching slow
> Have zon'd her, heart to heart — loud, loud the dark winds blow.

The alteration of the last three verses "to leave on the reader a sense of pettish disgust, by bringing old Angela in (only) dead stiff & ugly" appears in George Keats's transcript as follows:

> Angela went off
> Twitch'd with the Palsy; and with face deform
> The beadsman stiffen'd, twixt a sigh and laugh
> Ta'en sudden from his beads by one weak little cough.

It is indeed fortunate that Keats was persuaded to abandon these trivial and ludicrous alterations and to restore the imaginative and serious phraseology of the original version.

Woodhouse's report of Keats's reading of *Lamia* helps us to understand the romance. Keats composed the second part of *Lamia* in the Byronic style in which he revised *The Eve of St. Agnes.*

> He then read to me Lamia, which he has half fair copied: the rest is rough. I was much pleased with it. I can use no other terms for you know how badly he reads his own poetry: & you know how slow I am in Catching even the sense of poetry read by the best reader for the 1st. time. And his poetry really must be studied to be properly appretiated [*sic*]. The story is to this effect. Hermes is hunting for a Nymph, when from a wood he hears his name & a song relating to his loss — Mercury finds out that it comes from a serpent, who promises to shew him his Nymph if he will turn the serpent into a woman; this he agrees to: upon which the serpent breathes on his eyes when he sees his Nymph who had been beside them listening invisibly — The serpent had seen a young Man of Corinth with whom she had fallen desperately in Love — She is metamorphosed into a beautiful woman, the change is quite Ovidian, but better, — She then finds the youth, & they live together in a palace in the middle of Corinth (de-

scribed, or rather pictured out in very good costume) the entrance of which no one can see (like the Cavern Prince Ahmed found in the Arabian Nights, when searching for his lost arrow) — Here they live & love, "the world forgetting; of the world forgot"— He wishes to marry her & introduce her to his friends as his wife, But this would be a forfeiture of her immortality & she refuses; at length (for says K—"women love to be forced to do a thing, by a fine fellow — *such as this* — I forget his name — *was*") she consents. The Palace door becomes visible — to the "astonishment of the Natives"— the friends are invited to the wedding feast — & K. wipes the cits & the low lived ones: of some of whom he says "who make their mouth a napkin to their thumb" in the midst of this Imperial splendour. — The lover had seen his tutor Appollonius [*sic*] that morning, while in a car with his Lamia; he had a scowl on his brow, which makes the hearts of the lovers sink: & she asks him, who that frowning old fellow was, as soon as A. passsed.—He appears at the feast: damps the joy of the two by his presence — sits over against the woman: He is a Magician. He looks earnestly at the woman: so intently & to such effect, that she reads in his eyes that she is discovered: & vanishes away, shrieking.—The lover is told she was a "Lamia" & goes mad for the loss of her, & dies — You may suppose all these Events have given K. scope for some beautiful poetry: which even in this cursory hearing of it, came every now & then upon me, & made me "start, as tho' a sea Nymph quired." The metre is Drydenian heroic — with many triplets, & many alexandrines. But this K. observed, & I agreed, was required, or rather quite in Character with the language & sentiment in those particular parts. — K. has a fine feeling when & where he may use poetical licences with effect —

Woodhouse caught, despite his modest denial, a very accurate outline of *Lamia*; and he retained a vivid impression of the descriptions, especially the realistic description of the Glutton making "his shiny mouth a napkin for his thumb." Woodhouse's disinterested affection for Keats permeated and softened his disapprobation of Keats's defiant and cynical egotism. His puritanic moral sense was pleasurably shocked indeed by the realistic and cynical passages which Keats had introduced into his romances.

He very kindly reproach'd me with never writing to him [Woodhouse concluded]: You may suppose I promised amendment, & stipulated (as Paddy says) "that all the reciprocity should not be on one side"— The last thing, as he shook me by the hand, he promised to drop me a line to Bath: "and if (said he) it *should be in verse*, I dare say you will forgive me."—He parted with me at the coach door — I had the inside all to myself: and I amused myself with diving into a deep reverie, & recalling all that had passed during the 6 hours we were tête à tête.—I make no apology for stuffing my letter with these Keatsiana. I am sure nothing else I could say wo[d]. have half the Interest. — And I deem myself in luck to have such a subject to write about. . . . This letter tho' dated on Monday was written thus far on Sunday night to the Music of some one snoring. . . .

Taylor was unpleasantly perturbed by Woodhouse's account of Keats's defiant cynicism. He wrote Woodhouse on September 25:

Bakewell Sat 25th Sep 1819.

My dear Dick,

Your welcome Letter has just reached me, having been forwarded in a parcel from Retford, which place I left last Tuesday. — I sit down to reply to it, more perhaps to express my regret at what you tell me of the Changes in the Eve of St. Agnes, than for any deliberate purpose of saying my say on things in general. — This Folly of Keats is the most Stupid piece of Folly I can conceive. — He does not bear the ill opinion of the world calmly, & yet he will not allow it to form a good opinion of Him & his writings. He repented of this Conduct when Endymion was published as much as a Man can repent, who shows by the accidental Expression of Disappointment, Mortification & Disgust that he has met with a Result different from that which he had anticipated — Yet he will again challenge the same Neglect or Censure, & again (I pledge my Discernment on it) be vexed at the Reception he has prepared for himself. — This Vaporing is as far from sound Fortitude, as the Conduct itself in the Instances before us, is devoid of good Feeling and good Sense. — I don't know how the Meaning of the new Stanzas is wrapped up, but I will not be accessory (I can answer also for H. I think) towards publishing anything which can only be read by Men, since even on their Minds a bad Effect must follow the Encouragement of those thoughts which cannot be raised without Impropriety. —

If it was so natural a process in Keats's Mind to carry on the Train of his Story in the way he has done, that he could not write decently, if he had that Disease of the Mind which renders the Perception too dull to discover Right from Wrong in Matters of moral Taste, I should object equally then as now to the Sanctioning of the Infirmity by an act of cool Encouragement on my part, but then he would be personally perhaps excusable — As it is, the flying in the Face of all Decency & Discretion is doubly offensive from its being accompanied with so preposterous a Conceit on his part of being able to overcome the best found Habits of our Nature. — Had he known truly what the Society and what the Suffrages of Women are worth, he would never have thought of depriving himself of them. — So far as he is unconsciously silly in this Proceeding I am sorry for him, but for the rest I cannot but confess to you that it excites in me the Strongest Sentiments of Disapprobation — Therefore my dear Dick if he will not so far concede to my wishes as to leave the passage as it originally stood, I must be content to admire his Poems with some other Imprint, & in so doing I can reap as much Delight from the Perusal of them as if they were our own property, without having the disquieting Consideration attached to them of our approving, by the "Imprimateur," those Parts which are unfit for publication.—

You will think me too severe again. Well then; I will suspend my Judgment till I see or hear more, but if these my present Views are shown to be no Illusion I must act as I have described — How strange too that he should have taken such a Dislike to Isabella — I still think of it exactly as you do, & from what he copied out of Lamia in a late Letter I fancy I shall prefer it to that poem also. — The Extract he gave me was from the Feast: I did not enter so well into it as to be qualified to criticise, but whether it be a want of Taste for such Subjects as Fairy Tales, or that I do not perceive true Poetry except it is in Conjunction with good Sentiment I cannot tell but it did not promise to please me. —

[Manuscript, Harvard College Library. Quoted by Miss Lowell. Vol. II, pp. 321–322.]

Taylor was such a bigoted moralist that he resolved self-righteously to refuse to publish Keats's poems unless they conformed to the rigid standards of middle-class English morality. Despite his bigotry, however, he was just. He knew that he did not have Woodhouse's sympathetic understanding of Keats and he was willing to suspend his judgment. We know the outcome of this matter but we do not know the means by which it was brought about. Keats suppressed the passages to which Taylor and Woodhouse objected and Taylor published the poems in 1820. Woodhouse allayed Taylor's suspicions of Keats's moral character, I presume, in the same tactful way in which he had appeased Taylor's disapprobation of Keats's pride a month before. And, with equal tact, he induced Keats to suppress the realistic and cynical passages in his romances. Keats never knew that Taylor had threatened to refuse to publish his poems.

This analysis of the period of defiant and cynical egotism in which Keats composed the second part of *Lamia* enables us to interpret the symbolic satire in the romance. Keats disliked the public but he tried consciously to compose a romance which the public would buy. "The more I know what my diligence may in time probably effect," he wrote Reynolds on August 25; "the more does my heart distend with Pride and Obstinacy — I feel it in my strength to become a popular writer — I feel it in my power to refuse the poisonous suffrage of a public." "I equally dislike the favour of the public with the love of a woman," he wrote Taylor on August 23, "— they are both a cloying treacle to the wings of independence. I shall ever consider them (People) as debtors to me for verses, not myself to them for admiration — which I can do without. I have of late been indulging my spleen by composing a preface *at* them. . . . 'There are so many verses,' would I have said to them, 'give me so much means to buy pleasure with as a relief to my hours of labour.'"

Keats regarded Byron as the chief contemporary example of the popular poet. He wrote his brother on February 14, 1819 that four thousand copies of Byron's poems were sold in Murray's last sale. He described Byron as an egotistic poet with a striking personality, who expressed his own instinctive impulses, feelings, and thoughts and who "cut a figure," therefore, but who was not "figurative" because, living and expressing himself instinctively, he did not interpret the significance of life. He believed that Byron won the favor of the public by stimulating their instinctive passions and by shocking their moral sensibilities — in a word, by giving them violent sensations both pleasant and unpleasant. When he composed the second part of *Lamia* he resolved to give the public the violent sensations which they seemed to like in Byron's romances. He wrote his brother on September 18:

> I have been reading over a part of a short poem I have composed lately call'd "Lamia"— and I am certain there is that sort of fire in it which must take hold of people in some way — give them either pleasant or unpleasant sensation. What they want is a sensation of some sort.

Keats composed the first part of *Lamia,* as we have seen, in a healthy and deliberate spirit. He made the style striking and flashing but he did not make it realistic and cynical. There is one passage, however, which is mildly sportive and Byronic.

> Let the mad poets say whate'er they please
> Of the sweets of Fairies, Peris, Goddesses,
> There is not such a treat among them all,
> Haunters of cavern, lake, and waterfall,
> As a real woman, lineal indeed
> From Pyrrha's pebbles or old Adam's seed.

Many critics have remarked that this passage breaks the imaginative tone of the romance. I believe that it was not in the first draft, which has not survived, and that it was added to the fair copy which Keats made in Winchester in the first part of September. The passage may have been suggested to Keats by a similar passage in Byron's description of Haidee in *Don Juan* (Canto II, stanza cxviii) —

> she was one
> Fit for the model of a statuary
> (A race of mere impostors, when all's done —
> I've seen much finer women, ripe and real,
> Than all the nonsense of their stone ideal).

Keats began the second part of *Lamia* with a cynical and Byronic comment on love —

> Love in a hut, with water and a crust,
> Is — Love, forgive us! — cinders, ashes, dust;
> Love in a palace is perhaps at last
> More grievous torment than a hermit's fast: —
> That is a doubtful tale from faery land,
> Hard for the non-elect to understand.
> Had Lycius liv'd to hand his story down,
> He might have given the moral a fresh frown,
> Or clench'd it quite: but too short was their bliss
> To breed distrust and hate, that make the soft voice hiss.

This cynicism strikes a discordant note in the harmony of the romance. It is also inartistic in and for itself, for it is insincere. Keats's reaction against his love for Fanny Brawne was harsh and defiant but it was not cynical. The phrases "Love, forgive us!" and "make the soft voice hiss" reveal an undercurrent of sentimentality and indicate the insincerity of the cynicism. The metaphor of giving "the moral a fresh frown" and the rhyme of bliss and hiss are reversions to the cockney style of his early poems. He did not have the temperament, the character, and the social experience to emulate Byron's cynical sentiments. He did not indeed like Byron's proud cynicism. Writing his brother on September 18, two weeks after he had completed the second part of *Lamia*, he referred to *Don Juan* as Byron's "last flash poem."

Keats suppressed most of the realistic and cynical passages in the version which he published in 1820. There exists, however, a passage from the first draft which he quoted in his letter to Taylor on September 5, 1819. In this passage he gave the public the unpleasant sensations which he thought they liked. Lamia prepared the nuptial feast, to which Lycius had invited the citizens of Corinth, and she

> . . . shut the chamber up close hush'd and still,
> Complete, and ready for the revels rude,
> When dreadful guests would come to spoil her solitude
> The day came soon and all the gossip rout.
> O senseless Lycius! Dolt! Fool! Madman! Lout!
> Why would you murder happiness like yours,
> And show to common eyes these secret bowers?
> The Herd came, and each guest, with buzzy brain,
> Arriving at the Portal, gaz'd amain,
> And enter'd wondring; for they knew the Street,
> Remember'd it from childhood all complete,
> Without a gap, but ne'er before had seen
> That royal Porch, that high-built fair demesne;
> So in went one and all maz'd, curious and keen.
> Save one; who look'd thereon with eye severe,
> And, with calm-planted steps, walk'd in austere;
> 'Twas Appolonius: — something to[o] he laught;
> As though some knotty problem, that had daft
> His patient thought, had now begun to thaw,
> And solve, and melt; —'twas just as he foresaw!
> Soft went the music, and the tables all
> Sparkled beneath the viewless banneral
> Of Magic; and dispos'd in double row
> Seem'd edged Parterres of white bedded snow,
> Adorn'd along the sides with living flowers
> Conversing, laughing after sunny showers:
> And, as the pleasant appetite entic'd,
> Gush came the wine, and sheer the meats were slic'd.
> Soft went the Music; the flat salver sang
> Kiss'd by the emptied goblet, — and again it rang:

Swift bustled by the servants: — here's a health
Cries one — another — then, as if by stealth,
A Glutton drains a cup of Helicon,
Too fast down, down his throat the brief delight is gone.
"Where is that Music?" cries a Lady fair.
"Aye, where is it my dear? Up in the air?"
Another whispers. "Poo!" saith Glutton "Mum!"
Then makes his shiny mouth a napkin for his thumb. etc. etc. etc.

"This," Keats remarked to Taylor, "is a good sample of the Story." It is the passage which impressed Woodhouse when Keats read the romance to him on September 12 and it is doubtless the climax of the unpleasant sensations in the first draft. The Glutton, who made "his shiny mouth a napkin for his thumb," might have lived in ancient Corinth. He appears at least in Aristophanes' comedies of Athenian life. The ladies who made simpering remarks about the music would be more at home, however, in middle-class society in England. Keats not only gave the public the unpleasant sensations which he thought they liked but he also satirized them for their indifference to the poems which he had published. The "herd" of "dreadful guests" who attended the nuptial feast of Lycius and Lamia represent the coarse and superficial public who could not appreciate his poems and who accepted the verdict of the reviewers.

This passage introduces us into the very heart of the symbolic satire of *Lamia*. In the first part of the romance there is symbolism but there is no satire; in the second part the satire breaks through the symbolism. Lycius represents a poet such as Keats, and Lamia represents the poetic imagination —

she could muse
And dream, when in the serpent prison-house,
Of all she list, strange or magnificent:
How, ever, where she will'd, her spirit went;
Whether to faint Elysium, or where
Down through tress-lifting waves the Nereids fair
Wind into Thetis' bower by many a pearly stair;
Or where God Bacchus drains his cups divine,
Stretch'd out, at ease, beneath a glutinous pine;
Or where in Pluto's gardens palatine
Mulciber's columns gleam in far piazzian line.
And sometimes into cities she would send
Her dream, with feast and rioting to blend;
And once, while among mortals dreaming thus,
She saw the young Corinthian Lycius

Charioting foremost in the envious race,
Like a young Jove with calm uneager face,
And fell into a swooning love of him.

[Part I, vv. 202–219.]

Keats had formulated this theory of imagination, we remember, in October 1818.

I feel more and more every day, as my imagination strengthens, that I do not live in this world alone but in a thousand worlds. No sooner am I alone than shapes of epic greatness are stationed around me, and serve my Spirit the office which is equivalent to a King's body guard — then "Tragedy with scepter'd pall, comes sweeping by." According to my state of mind I am with Achilles shouting in the Trenches, or with Theocritus in the Vales of Sicily. . . .

Keats believed that the chief function of the imagination is to understand and to represent the instincts, the passions, and the thoughts of human beings. Lamia has this imaginative insight into human nature and she has in particular an intuitive knowledge of love.

A virgin purest lipp'd, yet in the lore
Of love deep learned to the red heart's core:
Not one hour old, yet of sciential brain
To unperplex bliss from its neighbour pain;
Define their pettish limits, and estrange
Their points of contact, and swift counterchange;
Intrigue with the specious chaos, and dispart
Its most ambiguous atoms with sure art. . . .

[Part I, vv. 189–196.]

When Lamia revealed herself to Lycius on the road to Corinth, he adored her as a goddess and besought her to remain with him always; but she reminded him that, being of heavenly essence, she could not live in the mortal world.

Thou art a scholar, Lycius, and must know
That finer spirits cannot breathe below
In human climes, and live: Alas! poor youth,
What taste of purer air hast thou to soothe
My essence? What serener palaces,
Where I may all my many senses please,
And by mysterious sleights a hundred thirsts appease?

[Part I, vv. 279–285.]

Lamia consented, however, to remain with Lycius. She told him that she loved him, and she assured him that she was a woman and that she lived in Corinth. She "threw the goddess off, and won his heart More pleasantly by playing woman's part." The imagination,

Keats meant perhaps, strives to become real and to live in the real world.

The palace which Lamia built and supported in Corinth by means of the magical power of music represents the poems which Keats had created by means of his imagination. For a time Lycius lived happily with Lamia in the palace which she had built, but at length a sound of trumpets recalled him to a consciousness of reality. So in *Endymion*, the *Ode to a Nightingale*, and other poems, Keats was recalled from the world of beauty created by his imagination to the world of reality. When Lycius returned to a consciousness of reality, egotistic passions possessed his mind and he desired to invite his kinsmen and friends to a nuptial feast and show them his beautiful bride and her magnificent palace. "What mortal hath a prize," Lycius explained to Lamia,

> What mortal hath a prize, that other men
> May be confounded and abash'd withal,
> But lets it sometimes pace abroad majestical,
> And triumph, as in thee I should rejoice
> Amid the hoarse alarm of Corinth's voice.
> Let my foes choke, and my friends shout afar,
> While through the thronged streets your bridal car
> Wheels round its dazzling spokes.
>
> [Part II, vv. 57–64.]

Lamia foresaw the consequences of entertaining the citizens of Corinth in her magic palace. Pale, trembling, and meek, she knelt before Lycius, wept tears of anguish, and besought him to change his purpose. He became fierce and sanguineous in his insistence; and she, loving him and his tyranny, submitted to his will and made preparations for the nuptial feast. She begged him, however, not to invite old Apollonius, his instructor in philosophy, to the feast.

Lycius' desire to show his bride to the citizens of Corinth represents that love of fame which impelled Keats to publish his poems; and the nuptial feast of Lycius and Lamia represents the publication of Keats's poems. The dreadful guests, whom Keats described contemptuously, represent the public who did not appreciate Keats's poems; and old Apollonius, the bald-head philosopher who forced his way into the feast without an invitation and who made Lamia and her palace fade and vanish, represents the reviewers who judged Keats's poems by the standard of common sense and reason and who destroyed the imaginative illusion which the public might have found in them.

At the end of the romance, after Lamia is dissolved by the piercing glance of Apollonius, Lycius dies.

And Lycius' arms were empty of delight,
As were his limbs of life, from that same night.
On the high couch he lay! — his friends came round —
Supported him — no pulse, or breath they found,
And, in its marriage robe, the heavy body wound.
[Part II, vv. 307–311.]

The character which Lycius manifests in his death is quite different from Keats's character. Keats's reaction to the ridicule and censure of his poems by the Tory reviewers was virile and courageous. It was only in the last days of his life, when he was dying of consumption, that his reaction to the reviewers became morbid and hysterical. Lycius, like Ludolph in *Otho the Great*, is a perfect illustration, however, of the traditional Keats whom Shelley described in *Adonais*.

Many critics who have not studied the mental crisis through which Keats was passing when he composed *Lamia* have misinterpreted the symbolism of the romance. They have been bewildered by his daring inversion of the traditional significance of the myth of the serpent-woman. In religious and poetic tradition, from the Hebrew myth of Adam and Eve to Coleridge's *Christabel*, the serpent has been represented as a form of natural life in which evil demons, especially female demons, are condemned to pass a part of their existence. And in Burton's *Anatomy of Melancholy*, from which Keats derived the story of his romance, Lamia is an evil demon whose essential form is that of a serpent. Keats's sympathy throughout the romance is with Lamia. When she yielded to Lycius' fierce demand that the citizens of Corinth be invited to their nuptial feast, Keats exclaimed:

The serpent — Ha, the serpent! certes, she
Was none. She burnt, she lov'd the tyranny,
And, all subdued, consented to the hour
When to the bridal he should lead his paramour.
[Part II, vv. 80–83.]

Critics have been misled also by the passage in which Keats expressed his antipathy to Apollonius and the philosophy which Apollonius professed.

Do not all charms fly
At the mere touch of cold philosophy?
There was an awful rainbow once in heaven:
We know her woof, her texture; she is given
In the dull catalogue of common things.
Philosophy will clip an Angel's wings,

Conquer all mysteries by rule and line,
Empty the haunted air, and gnomed mine —
Unweave a rainbow, as it erewhile made
The tender-person'd Lamia melt into a shade.
[Part II, vv. 229–238.]

Leigh Hunt, who was not closely associated with Keats in the period in which *Lamia* was composed, misinterpreted this passage.

Mr. Keats has departed as much from common-place in the character and moral of this story, as he has in the poetry of it. He would see fair play to the serpent, and makes the power of the philosopher an ill-natured and disturbing thing. Lamia though liable to be turned into painful shapes had a soul of humanity; and the poet does not see why she should not have her pleasures accordingly, merely because a philosopher saw that she was not a mathematical truth. This is fine and good. It is vindicating the greater philosophy of poetry. At the same time, we wish that for the purpose of his story he had not appeared to give into the common-place of supposing that Apollonius's sophistry must always prevail, and that modern experiment has done a deadly thing to poetry by discovering the nature of the rainbow, the air, etc.: that is to say, that the knowledge of natural history and physics, by shewing us the nature of things, does away the imaginations that once adorned them. This is a condescension to a learned vulgarism, which so excellent a poet as Mr. Keats ought not to have made. The world will always have fine poetry, so long as it has events, passions, affections, and a philosophy that sees deeper than this philosophy. There will be a poetry of the heart, as long as there are tears and smiles: there will be a poetry of the imagination as long as the first causes of things remain a mystery.[8]

Hunt understood the meaning of Lamia but he misunderstood the meaning of Apollonius. He thought that Keats was making a sweeping censure of natural philosophy or experimental science. Later critics likewise have objected to Keats's apparent censure of natural philosophy. Robert Bridges said:

I consider it a blot that Lycius should die at the end; because he is killed by Apollonius, who, if he could not rescue him, should have let him alone. Philosophy or Reason is made unamiable: but I am afraid that Keats may have intended this; and he makes Apollonius laugh, which is almost diabolic. The general meaning is, no doubt, the antagonism of reason and pleasure, or of science and imagination, or both; and that reason should take delight in destroying pleasure is only one of the ugly doctrines that lurk beneath the text if it be read as a parable. But it is very uncertain how much Keats intended.[9]

On December 28, 1817 at the dinner party which Haydon gave for Wordsworth, Keats and Lamb agreed, Haydon said, that Newton "had destroyed all the poetry of the rainbow by reducing it to the

[8] Leigh Hunt's review of the *Poems* of 1820, *The Indicator* for August 2 and 9, 1820.
[9] Robert Bridges, *Keats, A Critical Essay.*

prismatic colours." But Keats had no quarrel with natural philosophy or science in the period in which he composed *Lamia.* He had outgrown his earlier conception of the antagonism of imagination and reason and of poetry and philosophy. In May 1818, when he professed humanitarianism, he said: "Every department of Knowledge we see excellent and calculated towards a great whole. I am so convinced of this, that I am glad at not having given away my medical Books, which I shall again look over to keep alive the little I know thitherwards." In the autumn of 1818, when he resumed his philosophy of negative capability, he retained his belief that an extensive knowledge is necessary to thinking people. And in the spring of 1819 he made use of the facts of natural philosophy — especially the facts of biology and psychology — to develop his philosophy of negative capability into what I have called empirical humanism. He wrote his brother in the latter part of March 1819 that he was grateful that he had got into a state of mind in which he could relish Milton's lines — "How charming is divine Philosophy," etc.

Keats did not mean to condemn natural philosophy in the passage which I have quoted from *Lamia.* He condemned the misapplication of the principles of natural philosophy. As I have showed in my analysis of the romance, Apollonius, the bald-head philosopher, represents the reviewer or critic who judges poetry by philosophical standards — that is, by the standards of fact and reason. If Lamia and her palace represent the imagination and its creations and if the coarse and rude citizens of Corinth who attended the nuptial feast represent the public who did not appreciate Keats's poems, then Apollonius must represent the reviewers who judged Keats's poems by the standard of fact and reason.

In working out the symbolism of *Lamia*, Keats may have been influenced by Hazlitt, from whom he derived many of his poetic principles. There is a perfect explanation of the symbolism of *Lamia* in a passage in the introductory lecture of the *Lectures on the English Poets*, which Keats heard Hazlitt deliver in the Surrey Institution in February 1818. Hazlitt said:

> Poetry is in all its shapes the language of the imagination and the passions, of fancy and will. *Nothing, therefore, can be more absurd than the outcry which has been sometimes raised by frigid and pedantic critics, for reducing the language of poetry to the standard of common sense and reason;* for the end and use of poetry, "both at the first and now, was and is to hold the mirror up to nature," seen through the medium of passion and imagination, not divested of that medium by means of literal truth or abstract reason. . . .

CHAPTER IX

ODE TO AUTUMN, *FALL OF HYPERION*, ETC.

I

THE last poems which Keats composed fall into two groups: those which he composed in Winchester in the latter part of September 1819 and those which he composed in Hampstead in October and November. These poems represent a recovery from the defiant egotism in which he had composed the second part of *Lamia* and a resumption of his calm and deliberate empirical humanism. This change in his philosophy of poetry, like the preceding changes, was startlingly sudden.

Keats began a long journal letter to his brother on Friday, September 17, two days after he had returned to Winchester from London. He related the incidents of his journey to London and discussed their tangled financial affairs in a depressed and dispirited mood. He said that Haslam was in love and observed:

> Nothing strikes me so forcibly with a sense of the ridiculous as love. A Man in love I do think cuts the sorryest figure in the world. Even when I know a poor fool to be really in pain about it, I could burst out laughing in his face. His pathetic visage becomes irrisistable [*sic*].

With this as an introduction, he composed *ex tempore* a set of satiric verses on a party of modern lovers: "Pensive they sit, and roll their languid eyes," etc.

The sudden change in Keats's state of mind manifested itself on Saturday, September 18.

> With my inconstant disposition [he wrote his brother on September 18] it is no wonder that this morning, amid all our bad times and misfortunes, I should feel so alert and well spirited. At this moment you are perhaps in a very different state of Mind. It is because my hopes are very [ever] paramount to my despair.

From this point to the end of the letter, Keats was gay, gossipy, imaginative, witty, and speculative by turns. He described Winchester vividly, quoted a humorous passage on lovers from the *Anatomy of Melancholy*, discussed political progress, copied a part of a letter which he had written on his excursion into Scotland, transcribed several of his poems, told jokes on himself and his friends, related a great deal of gossip, and speculated about life and poetry. The jests in this letter should be read by those persons who believe that he did not have a sense of humor.

The change in Keats's mood was caused in part by his active efforts to raise money for his brother (action always aroused him out of moods of brooding melancholy) and in part by a temporary improvement in his health. He wrote his brother on September 18 that he had got rid of his "haunting sore throat" and that he would conduct himself in a manner not to catch another. As soon as his health improved he began to take an intense delight in the fine autumn weather, the quiet old cathedral town, and the gardens, meadows, and stubble-fields around the town.

This Winchester is a place tolerably well suited to me [he wrote his brother on September 18]: there is a fine Cathedral, a College, a Roman-Catholic Chapel, a Methodist d°, an independent d°, — and there is not one loom or anything like manufacturing beyond bread & butter in the whole City. There are a number of rich Catholic[s] in the place. It is a respectable, ancient, aristocratical place — and moreover it contains a nunnery.

The side streets here are excessively maiden-lady like [he wrote Reynolds on September 21]: the door steps always fresh from the flannel. The knockers have a staid serious, nay almost awful quietness about them. — I never saw so quiet a collection of Lions' and Rams' heads. The doors most part black, with a little brass handle just above the keyhole, so that in Winchester a man may very quietly shut himself out of his own house.

I take a walk every day for an hour before dinner [he wrote his brother on September 21] and this is generally my walk. I go out at the back gate across one street, into the Cathedral yard, which is always interesting; then I pass under the trees along a paved path, pass the beautiful front of the Cathedral, turn to the left under a stone door way, — then I am on the other side of the building — which leaving behind me I pass on through two college-like squares seemingly built for the dwelling place of Deans and Prebendaries — garnished with grass and shaded with trees. Then I pass through one of the old city gates and then you are in one College Street through which I pass and at the end thereof crossing some meadows and at last a country alley of gardens I arrive, that is, my worship arrives at the foundation of Saint Cross, which is a very interesting old place, both for its gothic tower and alms-square, and for the appropriation of its rich rents to a relation of the Bishop of Winchester. Then I pass across St. Cross meadows till you come to the most beautifully clear river — now this is only one mile of my walk I will spare you the other two till after supper when they would do you more good.

While Keats was taking this walk on Sunday, September 19, he experienced the sensation which he expressed in the *Ode to Autumn*. In each one of his odes and romances, we remember, he developed a particular sensuous atmosphere or sensation.

How beautiful the season is now [he wrote Reynolds on Tuesday, September 21] — How fine the air. A temperate sharpness about it. Really, without joking, chaste weather — Dian skies — I never lik'd stubble-fields so much as now — Aye better than the chilly green of the Spring. Somehow a stubble-plain looks warm — in the same way that some pictures look warm. This struck me so much in my Sunday's walk that I composed upon it.

Woodhouse said in a note in his copy of the *Poems* of 1817 that Keats composed the *Ode to Autumn* on Sunday, September 19; and Keats implied that he composed the ode immediately after he had returned from his walk on this Sunday.

Keats copied the ode into the letter which he wrote to Woodhouse on September 21; and at some later time he gave the original manuscript to his brother George. These two autograph manuscripts are now in the Lowell Collection in the Harvard College Library. There is a transcript in George Keats's Book of Autographs and Transcripts and another in Woodhouse's Book of Transcripts. Comparing these manuscripts, we find some revision of phraseology but no essential change in imagery, emotion, and thought. I quote therefore the version which Keats published in his *Poems* of 1820.

TO AUTUMN

1.

Season of mists and mellow fruitfulness,
Close bosom-friend of the maturing sun;
Conspiring with him how to load and bless
With fruit the vines that round the thatch-eves run;
To bend with apples the moss'd cottage-trees,
And fill all fruit with ripeness to the core;
To swell the gourd, and plump the hazel shells
With a sweet kernel; to set budding more,
And still more, later flowers for the bees,
Until they think warm days will never cease,
For Summer has o'er-brimm'd their clammy cells.

2.

Who hath not seen thee oft amid thy store?
Sometimes whoever seeks abroad may find
Thee sitting careless on a granary floor,
Thy hair soft-lifted by the winnowing wind;
Or on a half-reap'd furrow sound asleep,
Drows'd with the fume of poppies, while thy hook
Spares the next swath and all its twined flowers:
And sometimes like a gleaner thou dost keep
Steady thy laden head across a brook;
Or by a cyder-press, with patient look,
Thou watchest the last oozings hours by hours.

FIRST DRAFT OF THE *ODE TO AUTUMN*

Reproduced from the original autograph manuscript by permission of the Harvard College Library

Where are the songs of Spring? Aye, where are they?
Think not of them thou hast thy music too—
While ~~a gold~~ [barred] clouds ~~gild~~ [bloom] the soft dying day
~~And~~ [and] Touch~~ing~~ ~~the~~ the stubble plains [with] rosy hue—
Then in a wailful quire the small gnats mourn
Among the river sallows, ~~on the~~ borne aloft
Or sinking as the light wind lives and dies;
~~Then~~ full grown Lambs loud bleat from hilly bourn,
Hedge crickets sing, and now again full soft
The Redbreast whistles from a garden croft:
~~And now flock still~~
And Gathering Swallows twitter in the Skies—

Original manuscript of John Keats
Poem to Autumn— Presented to
Miss A Barker by the author's Brother.
[illegible] Nov 15 1839

Given to my Granddaughter
Elizabeth Ward May 14th 96
from H. B. Ward

FIRST DRAFT OF THE *ODE TO AUTUMN*

Reproduced from the original autograph manuscript by permission of the Harvard College Library

3.

Where are the songs of Spring? Ay, where are they?
  Think not of them, thou hast thy music too, —
While barred clouds bloom the soft-dying day,
  And touch the stubble-plains with rosy hue;
Then in a wailful choir the small gnats mourn
  Among the river sallows, borne aloft
    Or sinking as the light wind lives or dies;
And full-grown lambs loud bleat from hilly bourn;
  Hedge-crickets sing; and now with treble soft
  The red-breast whistles from a garden-croft;
    And gathering swallows twitter in the skies.

The *Ode to Autumn* represents the final stage in Keats's development of the form of the ode. Comparing it with the *Ode on Indolence*, the last of the five odes which he composed in May 1819, we find that each stanza has eleven iambic pentameter verses instead of ten and that as a consequence each stanza is divided into a quatrain, a tercet, and a quatrain instead of a quatrain and two tercets. The rhyme scheme of the first quatrain and the tercet (abab cde) is invariable and that of the second quatrain (cdde and dcce) is variable.

The *Ode to Autumn* is the most purely sensuous and imaginative of Keats's odes. Unlike his earlier odes, such as the *Ode to a Nightingale*, it is not an interpretation of a problem of his experience. It is, as he wrote Reynolds, an expression of the sensation, or sensuous impression, which he received from the warm, golden stubble fields during his walk into the country around Winchester on Sunday, September 19.

The images and ideas by which Keats developed and expressed this sensation were suggested to him by an interesting process of association. The ode was very closely connected with other poems which he was copying and revising. On September 18, after he had looked over letters which he had written during his excursion into Scotland, he copied into his journal letter to his brother George an acrostic which he had addressed to Georgiana Augusta Keats on June 27, 1818 and a description of the Isle of Staffa and Fingal's Cave which he had written to his brother Tom on July 26, 1818. He copied also the heptasyllabics which he had composed on Fingal's Cave, omitting two verses which he had adapted afterwards into *The Eve of St. Mark*. Being reminded of this romance, which he had never completed, he worked on it on Sunday, September 19; and on Monday, September 20 he copied it into the journal letter to his brother. The setting of *The Eve of St. Mark*, the cathedral town of Canterbury in spring, which was like and yet unlike his present environment, the cathedral town of Winchester in autumn, suggested the theme of the third stanza of the *Ode to Autumn*, the contrast between the warm, golden tints of autumn and the chilly, green tints of spring.

There were 16 verses in spurious Middle English at the end of the incomplete first draft of *The Eve of St. Mark*, which Keats composed between February 13 and February 17, 1819. In September 1819 — on Sunday, September 19, it is probable — he composed another passage of 16 verses in Middle English, but he did not perfect these verses and fit them into the romance; he did not copy them, therefore, into the version in the journal letter. They exist in an autograph fragment, which H. B. Forman examined, and in a transcript in Woodhouse's Book of Transcripts. Woodhouse did not insert them into their proper place in the romance. He copied them at the end of his transcript, leaving a blank space between them and the body of the romance.

These verses in Middle English in *The Eve of St. Mark* reminded Keats, it is probable, of Chatterton. Later in the day, when he was taking a walk before dinner, he associated his impression of autumn with the description of autumn in the Third Minstrel's Song in Chatterton's *Aella, a Tragical Interlude.*

THYRDE MYNSTRELLE.

Whanne Autumpne blake and sonne-brente doe appere,
With hys goulde honde guylteynge the falleynge lefe,
Bryngeynge oppe Wynterr to folfylle the yere,
Beerynge uponne hys backe the riped shefe;
Whan al the hyls wythe woddie sede ys whyte;
Whanne levynne-fyres and lemes do mete from far the syghte;

Whann the fayre apple, rudde as even skie,
Do bende the tree unto the fructyle grounde;
When joicie peres, and berries of blacke die,
Do daunce yn ayre, and call the eyne arounde;
Thann, bee the even foule, or even fayre,
Meethynckes mie hartys joie ys steynced wyth somme care.

The personification of autumn as a reaper, the most essential element in Keats's ode, was derived from Chatterton's song. The image of the apples bending down the trees,

To bend with apples the moss'd cottage-trees,

was suggested by Chatterton's image,

Whann the fayre apple, rudde as even skie,
Do bende the tree unto the fructyle grounde. . . .

The first draft of the ode reproduces some of Chatterton's words, especially words depicting the colors of autumn. The verses,

> While a *gold* cloud *gilds* the soft dying day
> Touching the stubble plains with rosy hue —,

are reminiscent of Chatterton's verse,

> With hys *goulde* honde *guylteynge* the falleynge lefe. . . .

The phraseology of the beautiful image of Autumn "sitting careless on a granary floor," his "hair soft lifted by the winnowing wind," was derived from a passage in Shakespeare's *Henry IV, Part I* (IV. i. 194–195) —

> We shall be *winnow'd* with so rough a *wind*
> That even our *corn* shall seem as light as chaff . . . .

The *Ode to Autumn* represents a sudden and significant change in Keats's style. About September 5, we remember, he completed *Lamia* in a style which was strongly influenced by Milton's artificial style. On August 25 he wrote Reynolds:

> I am convinced more and more day by day that fine writing is, next to fine doing the top thing in the world; the Paradise Lost becomes a greater wonder.

The sensations of autumnal beauty, which inspired him to compose the *Ode to Autumn* on Sunday, September 19, caused him to react suddenly from the artificial style of Milton to the natural style of Chatterton. On September 21 he wrote Reynolds:

> I always somehow associate Chatterton with autumn. He is the purest writer in the English Language. He has no French idiom, or particles like Chaucer —'tis genuine English Idiom in English words. I have given up Hyperion — there were too many Miltonic inversions in it — Miltonic verse cannot be written but in an artful or rather artist's humour. I wish to give myself up to other sensations. English ought to be kept up. It may be interesting to you to pick out some lines from Hyperion and put a mark X to the false beauty proceeding from art, and one | | to the true voice of feeling. Upon my soul 'twas imagination [—] I cannot make the distinction — Every now and then there is a Miltonic intonation — But I cannot make the division properly.

And he wrote his brother on the same day:

> I shall never become attach'd to a foreign idiom so as to put it into my writings. The Paradise lost though so fine in itself is a currruption [*sic*] of our Language — it should be kept as it is unique — a curiosity —a beautiful and grand Curiosity. The most remarkable Production of the world. A northern dialect accommodating itself to greek and latin inversions and intonations. The

purest english I think — or what ought to be the purest — is Chatterton's. The Language had existed long enough to be entirely uncorrupted of Chaucer's gallicisms, and still the old words are used. Chatterton's language is entirely northern. I prefer the native music of it to Milton's cut by feet. I have but lately stood on my guard against Milton. Life to him would be death to me. Miltonic verse cannot be written but is the verse of art. I wish to devote myself to another sensation.

The *Ode to Autumn*, which Keats had composed on Sunday, September 19 in Chatterton's natural style, inspired and encouraged him to remove the artificial Miltonic qualities from the style of the humanistic *Hyperion*, which he had begun in December 1818 and left incomplete in April 1819. The natural style which he intended to employ reminded him of the humanitarian "Hyperion," which he had begun in September 1818 in Wordsworth's natural style. On Sunday, September 19, after he had composed the *Ode to Autumn*, he got out these two incomplete versions of "Hyperion"— the natural and humanitarian vision and the artificial and humanistic epic — and began to combine them into a third version, *The Fall of Hyperion, a Dream*. On Tuesday, September 21, when he wrote letters to Reynolds, Woodhouse, and his brother, Keats had proceeded with this reconstruction to the fifth verse of Canto II. After he had copied the *Ode to Autumn* in his letter to Woodhouse, he continued:

I will give you a few lines from Hyperion on account of a word in the last line of a fine sound —

Mortal! that thou may'st understand aright
I humanize my sayings to thine ear,
Making comparisons of earthly things;
Or thou might'st better listen to the wind
Though it blows *legend-laden* th [r]ough the trees.

I think you will like the following description of the Temple of Saturn —

I look'd around upon the carved sides
Of an old Sanctuary, with roof august
Builded so high, it seem'd that filmed clouds
Might sail beneath, as o'er the stars of heaven.
So old the place was I remember none
The like upon the earth; what I had seen
Of grey Cathedrals, buttress'd walls, rent towers,
The superan[n]uations of sunk realms,
Or nature's rocks hard toil'd in winds and waves,
Seem'd but the failing of decrepit things
To that eternal-domed monument.
Upon the marble, at my feet, there lay
Store of strange vessels and large draperies
Which needs had been of dyed asbestus wove,

Or in that place the moth could not corrupt,
So white the linen, so, in some, distinct
Ran imageries from a sombre loom.
All in a mingled heap confused there lay
Robes, golden tongs, censer and chafing dish
Girdles, and chains and holy jewelries.
Turning from these, with awe once more I rais'd
My eyes to fathom the space every way;
The embossed roof, the silent massive range
Of Columns north and south, ending in Mist
Of nothing; then to the eastward where black gates
Were shut against the Sunrise evermore.

I see I have completely lost my direction. So I e'n make you pay double postage. I had begun a Sonnet in french of Ronsard — on my word 'tis very capable of poetry — I was stop'd by a circumstance not worth mentioning — I intended to call it La Platonique Chevalresque — I like the second line —

Non ne suis si audace a languire
  De m'empresser au coeur vos tendres mains. etc.

Here is what I had written for a sort of induction —

Fanatics have their dreams wherewith they weave
A Paradise for a Sect; the savage too
From forth the loftiest fashion of his sleep
Guesses at Heaven: pity these have not
Trac'd upon vellum or wild indian leaf
The shadows of melodious utterance:
But bare of laurel they live, dream, and die,
For Poesy alone can tell her dreams,
With the fine spell of words alone can save
Imagination from the sable charm
And dumb enchantment.

My Poetry will never be fit for any thing it does n't cover its ground well. You see he she is off her guard and does n't move a peg though Prose is coming up in an awkward style enough. Now a blow in the spondee will finish her — But let it get over this line of circumvallation if it can. These are unpleasant Phrase[s].

The first passage which Keats copied from *The Fall of Hyperion, a Dream* contains verses 1–6 of Canto II (with the fifth verse omitted); the second, verses 61–86 of Canto I; and the third, verses 1–11 of Canto I. On September 21, when he wrote to Woodhouse, Reynolds, and his brother, he had progressed in his reconstruction of the poem to the sixth verse of the second canto. His rapid progress was due doubtless to the fact that he made very few changes in the introduction which he adapted from the humanitarian version. He revised the final verses of the introduction (vv. 282–293) to fit them to the first verses of the body of the poem, and he added a new passage

(vv. 187–210) as a repudiation of the humanitarian philosophy of the introduction. He may not have copied the introduction, for he could have made these alterations on the original manuscript. When he came to adapt the humanistic *Hyperion* into the body of the poem, however, he met with greater difficulties. On September 21, when he wrote Reynolds, he was striving in vain to remove the Miltonic qualities from the style and he asked Reynolds to help him.

> It may be interesting to you [he said] to pick out some lines from Hyperion and put a mark X to the false beauty proceeding from art, and one | | to the true voice of feeling. Upon my soul 'twas imagination [—] I cannot make the distinction — Every now and then there is a Miltonic intonation — But I cannot make the division properly.

He revised only 55 verses after September 21; for the reconstructed poem (as we have it in Woodhouse's transcript) stops with the sixty-first verse of the second canto. He revised these 55 verses in Hampstead in November and December 1819. Brown's recollections, written down twenty years later, are inexact but they are based undoubtedly upon a grain of fact. Brown said that, in November and December 1819, Keats was composing *The Cap and Bells* in the morning and that "in the evening he was deeply engaged in remodelling the fragment of *Hyperion* into the form of a vision."

In a preceding chapter I have given my reasons for believing that Keats composed the first draft of the introduction to *The Fall of Hyperion, a Dream* in the latter part of September and the first part of October 1818. The period from April 24 to October 24, 1818 was the only period in his life in which he professed humanitarianism and it is, therefore, the only period in which he could have composed this humanitarian introduction. He could not have composed it in the fall of 1819, for in this period he was hostile to humanitarianism. In the second half of August and the first half of September, we have seen, he was cast by adverse circumstances into a mood of painful and irritable defiance in which he cultivated a philosophy of cynical egotism. On September 18, when he recovered suddenly from his defiant and cynical egotism, he regained a healthy and deliberate state of mind and resumed that philosophy of empirical humanism which he had held in Hampstead in April, May, and June and in Shanklin in July and the first half of August.

The causes of Keats's final abandonment of the reconstruction of the poem were, I believe, as much philosophical as stylistic. The humanitarian philosophy of the introduction was as repugnant to him as the Miltonic style of the body of the poem. If his vitality had not been weakened by disease in this period, he might have composed an entirely new version of "Hyperion" which, in accordance with his philosophy of life and poetry, would have been humanistic in theme and natural in style.

Let us consider now the character of this empirical humanism which Keats resumed on September 18 and which he held in the period in which he attempted to combine the two versions of "Hyperion"— the natural and humanitarian vision and the Miltonic and humanistic epic — into *The Fall of Hyperion, a Dream.* The state of mind which he described to his brother on September 21 is the same as that which he had described to Reynolds from Shanklin on July 11.

> From the time you left me, our friends say I have altered completely — am not the same person. . . . Some think I have lost that poetic ardour and fire 'tis said I once had — the fact is perhaps I have: but instead of that I hope I shall substitute a more thoughtful and quiet power. I am more frequently, now, contented to read and think — but now and then, haunted with ambitious thoughts. Qui[e]ter in my pulse, improved in my digestion; exerting myself against vexing speculations — scarcely content to write the best verses for the fever they leave behind. I want to compose without this fever. I hope I one day shall. You would scarcely imagine I could live alone so comfortably "Kepen in solitarinesse."

The feverish, defiant, egotistic mood in which Keats had composed the second part of *Lamia* was dissipated. He was again in the healthy, deliberate, stoical mood in which he had composed the great odes in May, and *Otho the Great* and the first part of *Lamia* in July. His mind was negatively capable and his judgment was suspended.

> I shall beg leave [he wrote Reynolds on September 21] to have a third opinion in the first discussion you have with Woodhouse — just half-way, between both.

The analysis of Dilke's mind which Keats wrote to his brother on September 24 is a fine expression of his negative capability, the fundamental principle of his empirical humanism. It is also an expression of his antipathy to humanitarianism. Dilke was a disciple of William Godwin, the author of *An Enquiry Concerning Political Justice*, from which Wordsworth had derived much of the humanitarianism in *The Excursion.* Eleven months before, we remember, Keats had called Dilke "a Godwin perfectibil[it]y Man."

> Brown [he wrote his brother] complained very much in his letter to me of yesterday of the great alteration the Disposition of Dilke has undergone. He thinks of nothing but "Political Justice" and his Boy. Now the first political duty a Man ought to have a Mind to is the happiness of his friends. I wrote Brown a comment on the subject, wherein I explained what I thought of Dilke's

Character. Which resolved itself into this conclusion. That Dilke was a Man who cannot feel he has a personal identity unless he has made up his Mind about every thing. The only means of strengthening one's intellect is to make up one's mind about nothing — to let the mind be a thoroughfare for all thoughts. Not a select party. The genus is not scarce in population. All the stubborn arguers you meet with are of the same brood. They never begin upon a subject they have not preresolved on. They want to hammer their nail into you and if you turn the point, still they think you wrong. Dilke will never come at a truth as long as he lives; because he is always trying at it. He is a Godwin-methodist.

Keats began to develop this philosophy of negative capability, we have seen, in the fall of 1817. He derived it, with Hazlitt's assistance, from his study of Shakespeare's plays. He defined two types of mind — the negatively capable and imaginative and the egotistic and rational. The negatively capable mind, he said, is satisfied with the isolated fragments of truth which its imagination apprehends; but the egotistic mind, dissatisfied with fragments of truths, attempts to build with its reason an absolute and universal system of truth. In December 1817 he made a contrast between the negatively capable mind of Shakespeare, which was "capable of being in uncertainties, mysteries, doubts, without any irritable reaching after fact and reason," and the egotistic mind of Coleridge, which "would let go by a fine isolated verisimilitude caught from the Penetralium of mystery, from being incapable of remaining content with half-knowledge." In October 1818, when he rejected Wordsworth's humanitarianism and resumed his philosophy of negative capability, he made a contrast between a negatively capable poet such as Shakespeare and an egotistic poet such as Wordsworth. And in March 1819 he made a similar contrast between Shakespeare and Byron. He perceived, as modern humanists perceive, that egotism was the foundation of both Wordsworth's rational and idealistic humanitarianism and Byron's instinctive and cynical materialism.

There is a fine expression of Keat's negative capability also in the contrast which he drew between himself and Byron. He wrote his brother on September 18, 1819:

You speak of Lord Byron and me — There is this great difference between us. He describes what he sees — I describe what I imagine. Mine is the hardest task. You see the immense difference.

Keats made this same distinction between Shakespeare and Wordsworth in October 1818. He meant that Byron, an egotistic poet, describes his own sensations and thoughts and that he himself, a negatively capable poet, describes the sensations and thoughts of other men. His, he believed, is the harder task. Again and again he said that "one mind's imagining into another" is the "highest exertion" of the poetic faculty.

This humanistic philosophy which Keats resumed on September 18 had an influence, as we might expect, upon his reconstruction on September 19, 20, and 21 of the two earlier versions of "Hyperion" into the third version, *The Fall of Hyperion, a Dream.* He used the fragment of the humanitarian vision as the introduction and the incomplete humanistic epic as the body of the third version. He left the humanitarian theme in the introduction, for he could not remove it without recomposing the introduction. He composed and inserted into the introduction, however, a passage of 24 verses (vv. 187–210) in which, speaking as a negatively capable humanist, he denied the humanitarian theme of the introduction.

This passage was omitted from the first edition of *The Fall of Hyperion, a Dream* which was published by Lord Houghton in 1856. It was unknown to editors and critics until the discovery in 1904 of the transcript, made by Woodhouse's clerk and corrected by Woodhouse, from which Lord Houghton had published the poem. It is preserved also in Woodhouse's transcript of the poem in his Book of Transcripts, which was discovered in 1914. Woodhouse cancelled the passage with a pencil and wrote the following note on the first verse: "Keats seems to have intended to erase this and the next twenty-one lines." Woodhouse's judgment was based upon stylistic instead of upon philosophical grounds. Keats had not revised the passage and he had not fitted it smoothly into the context of the introduction, for he abandoned the reconstruction of the poem. When Woodhouse's transcripts were discovered H. B. Forman and Ernest de Sélincourt restored this passage to the poem in their editions; but J. M. Murry [1] omitted the passage in his recent edition because, he said, it is "false to Keats' real train of thought in the context of the poem."

Let us now consider this passage in its context in the introduction. Keats dreamt that he stood in an old sanctuary whose roof was as high as the sky. Looking to the west, he saw an image, huge of feature as a cloud, at the level of whose feet there was an altar with a priestess ministering beside it. Innumerable steps ascended to the altar from the pavement on which he stood. When he approached the image, the veiled priestess said that, if he could not ascend the steps to the altar before the gummed leaves which were burning on it were consumed, he would rot and die on the cold pavement. He climbed the steps to the atar with prodigious toil. A palsied chill

[1] J. M. Murry, *John Keats: Poems and Verses.*

numbed his limbs and threatened to stifle his heart, but, when he reached the top step, warm life poured into his limbs. The old sanctuary, as we have seen, was a ruined temple of Saturn, king of gods and men in the golden, or humanitarian, age of the world. The altar was the altar of humanitarianism and the veiled priestess was Moneta, the goddess of memory. The innumerable steps leading to the altar were the steps of knowledge by means of which humanitarian reformers can expel ignorance, poverty, injustice, and evil from human society and restore the golden age. This is the principle of the perfectibility of human nature and of the progress of society by means of education to a state of happiness — the humanitarian principle which Keats derived from Wordsworth's *Excursion*.

The humanitarian philosophy of poetry is expressed in the dialogue between Moneta and Keats. Moneta defined three types of poets — the thoughtless, the visionary, and the humanitarian. These three types correspond to the three stages of a poet's evolution which Wordsworth defined in *Tintern Abbey* and which Keats adapted in the letter which he wrote to Reynolds on May 3, 1818. Keats compared life to a mansion of many apartments, through two of which he had passed —"the infant or thoughtless Chamber," in which he remained as long as he did not think; and "the Chamber of Maiden-Thought," in which he became aware of the pain, sickness, oppression, and misery of humanity. He could not describe the other chambers, to which dark passages led, because he had not yet entered them. "To this point," he told Reynolds, "was Wordsworth come, as far as I can conceive when he wrote 'Tintern Abbey' and it seems to me that his Genius is explorative of those dark Passages. Now if we live, and go on thinking, we too shall explore them. He is a Genius and superior [to] us, in so far as he can, more than we, make discoveries, and shed a light in them."

Moneta told Keats that if thoughtless poets come by chance into the temple of Saturn they rot on the pavement. "None can usurp this height," she said, "But those to whom the miseries of the world Are misery, and will not let them rest." Then Keats asked:

> Are there not thousands in the world. . . .
> Who feel the giant agony of the world,
> And more, like slaves to poor humanity,
> Labour for mortal good? I sure should see
> Other men here, but I am here alone.

And Moneta replied:

> Those whom thou spak'st of are no visionaries,
> . . . they are no dreamers weak;

They seek no wonder but the human face,
No music but a happy-noted voice —
They come not here, they have no thought to come —
And thou art here, for thou art less than they.

Humanitarian poets, who feel the giant agony of the world and who labor for mortal good, do not need to come into the temple of Saturn. Visionary poets feel the giant agony of the world but, being weak dreamers, they do not labor for mortal good. They need to come into the temple of Saturn to be taught and to be disciplined.

Moneta censured and dismissed Keats as a visionary poet.

What benefit canst thou, or all thy tribe,
Do the great world? Thou art a dreaming thing,
A fever of thyself; think of the earth;
What bliss, even in hope, is there for thee?
What haven? every creature hath its home,
Every sole man hath days of joy and pain,
Whether his labours be sublime or low —
The pain alone, the joy alone, distinct:
Only the dreamer venoms all his days,
Bearing more woe than all his sins deserve.
Therefore, that happiness be somewhat shar'd,
Such things as thou art are admitted oft
Into like gardens thou didst pass erewhile,
And suffer'd in these temples: for that cause
Thou standest safe beneath this statue's knees.

In September 1818, when Keats composed the first draft of this introduction, he accepted this censure without protest and indeed with gratitude.

"That I am favour'd for unworthiness,
By such propitious parley medicin'd
In sickness not ignoble, I rejoice,
Aye, and could weep for love of such award."
So answer'd I, continuing, "If it please,
Majestic shadow, tell me where I am,
Whose altar this, for whom this incense curls;
What image this whose face I cannot see
For the broad marble knees; and who thou art,
Of accent feminine so courteous?" [vv. 182 *et seq.*]

In September 1819, when Keats adapted this humanitarian introduction into *The Fall of Hyperion, a Dream*, very nearly a year had elapsed since he had believed in the rational and idealistic system of humanitarianism. He had lost his faith in the perfectibility of human nature and in the progress of society to a permanent state of happiness. He had resumed his philosophy of negative capability, a humanistic philosophy of individual discipline, and he had established it upon a sound empirical basis. He believed that evil is inherent in the nature of the world; that men, who are a part of nature, cannot escape this evil; and that the only happiness which they can attain is transient and temporary. He believed also that evil is necessary as well as inherent in nature. A world of pains and troubles, in which the hearts of men must feel and suffer in a thousand diverse ways, is necessary, he said, to school the intelligences of men and make them into souls. English writers are the finest writers in the world, he said, because "they have in general been trampled aside into the bye paths of life and seen the festerings of Society." The evil which poets suffer in the world sharpens their negatively capable insight into the hearts and minds of other men.

Believing in this empirical and humanistic philosophy of poetry, Keats could not accept Moneta's humanitarian censure of poets as weak dreamers. He inserted between verses 186 and 187, therefore, the following passage:

> "Majestic shadow, tell me: sure not all
> Those melodies sung into the world's ear
> Are useless: sure a poet is a sage;
> A humanist, physician to all men.
> That I am none I feel, as vultures feel
> They are no birds when eagles are abroad.
> What am I then: thou spakest of my tribe:
> What tribe?" The tall shade veil'd in drooping white
> Then spake, so much more earnest, that the breath
> Moved the thin linen folds that drooping hung
> About a golden censer from the hand
> Pendent —"Art thou not of the dreamer tribe?
> The poet and the dreamer are distinct
> Diverse, sheer opposite, antipodes.
> The one pours out a balm upon the world
> The other vexes it." Then shouted I
> Spite of myself, and with a Pythia's spleen
> "Apollo! faded! O far-flown Apollo!
> Where is thy misty pestilence to creep
> Into the dwellings, through the door crannies
> Of all mock lyrists, large self-worshippers
> And careless Hectorers in proud bad verse?
> Though I breathe death with them it will be life
> To see them sprawl before me into graves.

Keats did not fit this passage smoothly into the text of the introduction. The phrase "Majestic shadow, tell me" (v. 187 and v. 211) and the four verses in which he described "The tall shade veil'd in drooping white" (vv. 184–187 and vv. 216–219) occur both in the inserted passage and in the original text. Needing a description of Moneta in the new passage, he borrowed one which he had already composed and employed, and he forgot afterwards to remove it from its original place in the text.

In the first part of the passage Keats expressed a humanistic theory of the function of the poet in the world. The poet, he said, is a sage, a humanist, a physician to all men, who pours out a balm upon the world. The poet, like Oceanus in *Hyperion*, perceives the naked truths of human life and experience, interprets and expresses these truths to his fellow men, and helps them bear these truths with calm and stoical fortitude. "Receive the truth," he tells them, "and let it be your balm."

In the second part of the passage both Moneta and Keats censured the dreamer, who, in contrast to the humanistic poet, vexes the world. In the year which had elapsed between the composition of the first draft of the introduction and the composition of the new passage, the meaning of "dreamer" had changed in Keats's mind. In the original text the dreamer is the poet who feels the giant agony of the world but who is too weak to labor for mortal good. In this new passage the dreamer is a mock lyrist, a large self-worshipper, a careless hectorer in proud bad verse. In the original text the dreamer is Keats himself, but in the new passage he is Byron, the egotistic poet who expresses his own instinctive passions and who wins the favor and patronage of the public by stimulating their instinctive passions and shocking their moral sensibilities. In the latter part of August 1819, when Keats succumbed to a transient mood of cynical egotism, he imitated Byron because he believed that Byron composed the kind of poetry which the public liked. On September 18, when he resumed his empirical humanism, he explained to his brother the "immense difference" between Byron, an egotistic poet, and himself, a negatively capable poet. In October 1820, when he was voyaging to Italy with Severn, he read the description of the shipwreck in *Don Juan* and cast the book upon the floor in a transport of indignation.

> How horrible an example of human nature [he cried] is this man, who has no pleasure left him but to gloat over and jeer, at the most awful incidents of life. Oh! this is a paltry originality, which consists in making solemn things gay, and gay things solemn, and yet it will fascinate thousands, by the very diabolical outrage of their sympathies.[2]

[2] Lord Houghton, *Life and Letters of John Keats*. H. B. Forman, Variorum Edition, Vol. V, p. 198. See also Sir Sidney Colvin, p. 496.

2

The empirical humanism which Keats resumed on September 18, 1819 manifested itself in his conduct in practical matters as well as in his composition of poetry. The first problem which he had to solve was the necessity of securing money with which to sustain himself and to assist his brother George. On September 10, when he heard of his brother's financial straits, he went to London, as we have seen, to urge Abbey to settle Mrs. Jennings' suit in Chancery and to send money to George Keats. He proposed to Hessey [3] to publish *The Eve of St. Agnes* and *Lamia* immediately, but he was told by Hessey that "it could not answer to do so now."

> I am advised not to publish [he wrote his brother] till it is seen whether the Tragedy will or not succeed. Should it, a few months may see me in the way of acquiring property; should it not it will be a drawback and I shall have to perform a longer literary Pilgrimage.

Keats was too sensible to rely upon the success of either his tragedy or his poems, and he was too independent to live upon the generosity of his friends. He was resolved, he wrote Brown, Dilke, Woodhouse, and his brother, to support himself by contributing to periodicals. He discussed this resolution in the first of the two letters which he wrote Brown on September 23:

> It is quite time I should set myself doing something, and live no longer upon hopes. I have never yet exerted myself. I am getting into an idle-minded, vicious way of life, almost content to live upon others. In no period of my life have I acted with any selfwill but in throwing up the apothecary profession. That I do not repent of. Look at Reynolds, if he was not in the law, he would be acquiring, by his abilities, something towards his support. My occupation is entirely literary: I will do so, too. I will write, on the liberal side of the question, for whoever will pay me. I have not known yet what it is to be diligent. I purpose living in town in a cheap lodging, and endeavouring, for a beginning, to get the theatricals of some paper. When I can afford to compose deliberate poems, I will. . . . While I have some immediate cash, I had better settle myself quietly, and fag on as others do. I shall apply to Hazlitt, who knows the market as well as any one, for something to bring me in a few pounds as soon as possible. I shall not suffer my pride to hinder me. The whisper may go round; I shall not hear it. If I can get an article in the "Edinburgh," I will. One must not be delicate. . .
>
> At the end of another year [he told Brown] you shall applaud me, not for verses, but for conduct.

There is no doubt that Keats could have become a successful reviewer. His letters, which contain acute and profound speculations

[3] Woodhouse's letter to Taylor, September 20, Pierpont Morgan Library.

about poetry and the poetic art, have established him as one of the finest literary critics in English literature. The reviews which he wrote for *The Champion* in December 1817 and in January 1818, while Reynolds was on his vacation, are superior to those which Reynolds wrote for the same periodical. The review of Reynolds' parody on Wordsworth's *Peter Bell*, which he wrote for *The Examiner* for April 25, 1819, is a fine example of tactful reviewing. The ridicule of his Preface to *Endymion* by the Tory reviewers had taught him to be wary of expressing his thoughts naïvely.

> You may say I want tact [he wrote Dilke on September 22] — that is easily acqui[r]ed. You may be up to the slang of a cock pit in three battles. It is fortunate I have not before this been tempted to venture on the common. I should a year or two ago have spoken my mind on every subject with the utmost simplicity. I hope I have learnt a little better and am confident I shall be able to cheat as well as any literary Jew of the Market and shine up an article on any thing without much knowle[d]ge of the subject, aye like an orange.

Keats had come to rely upon Brown for advice in practical matters as he had formerly relied upon his brother George. In this crisis, however, he had to resolve, plan, and act alone; for, a day or two after September 5, Brown had left Winchester to visit Dilke's father and brother-in-law in Chichester and Bedhampton. Keats wrote six letters to Brown, one from London and the others from Winchester; and, when he did not receive a reply from Brown, he was very much perturbed, suspecting that his letters had been opened and withheld in Winchester. Miss Lowell [4] learned from a memoir of Brown by his son, which is in the Day Collection, that Brown, instead of stopping in Chichester and Bedhampton, went on to Ireland and married Abagail Donohue, who had been, it is probable, a servant in his house. The marriage was not legal, it is said, because it was performed by a Catholic priest; but, since Miss Donohue was a Catholic, it was satisfactory to her. Brown returned to England almost immediately after the marriage, arriving in Chichester by September 23, where he found four letters from Keats awaiting him. Three years later he secured possession of his son, who was born in 1820, and took him to Italy, fearing, his son said, that his wife "might appeal to Chancery to give her legal custody of the boy, on the same grounds that Shelley had been deprived of his children." His purpose, it is probable, was to secure a son without the encumbrance of a wife. He had no intention of supporting Miss Donohue as his wife, and he had no consideration for the pain which his conduct might

[4] Amy Lowell, Vol. I, pp. 471–472, Vol. II, p. 311.

cause her. Knowing Keats's ethical code, he shrewdly concealed the marriage from him. The excuse which he gave for his delay in answering Keats's letters was satisfactory to Keats.

> Brown who was at Bedhampton, went thence to Chichester [Keats wrote his brother on September 24], and I still directing my letters Bedhampton — there arose a misunderstand[ing] about them. I began to suspect my Letters had been stopped from curiosity. However yesterday Brown had four Letters from me all in a Lump — and the matter is clear'd up. . . .

When Brown returned to Winchester at the end of September he approved of Keats's plan to support himself by writing articles and reviews for magazines, but he acquiesced unwillingly in Keats's plan to live alone in lodgings in Westminster. Keats did not return to Wentworth Place, Brown's house in Hampstead, because he believed that he would be a trouble and an expense to Brown and because Miss Brawne, whom he had resolved to give up, lived in Dilke's house, which adjoined Brown's. When Brown gave Lord Houghton copies of the letters which Keats had written to him, he omitted passages which he thought persons still living might object to. The meaning of a deleted passage in a letter which Keats wrote to Brown on September 23 is quite clear.

> If you live at Hampstead next winter — I like . . . . . . and I cannot help it. On that account I had better not live there.

On Friday, October 1 Keats wrote Dilke:

> I want you to hire me a couple of rooms (A Sitting Room and bed room for myself alone) in Westminster. Quietness and ch[e]apness are the essentials. . . . I shall with Brown be returned by next Friday. . . .

Dilke, in his brief memoir of Keats, said:

> I then resided in Westminster. I took apartments for him in College S^{t}. His mind at this time was all in a ferment — he now resolved to break off his acquaintance with F. B. at least till he had established himself in some course of life. But it was reason against passion. In two or more days he removed again to Brown's at Hampstead.[5]

Keats arrived in London on Friday, October 8, it is probable, and took possession of the lodgings at 25 College Street, Westminster, which Dilke had engaged for him. On Sunday, October 10 he visited Brown in Hampstead and met Fanny Brawne. His love for her, which he had suppressed for two months, became more vehement than it had ever been before. The next morning, after he had returned to Westminster, he wrote her a letter of ecstatic devotion.

[5] Keats's copy of *Endymion*, Dilke Collection.

My sweet Girl,

I am living today in yesterday: I was in a complete fa[s]cination all day. I feel myself at your mercy. Write me ever so few lines and tell you [me] you will never for ever be less kind to me than yesterday. — You dazzled me. There is nothing in the world so bright and delicate. When Brown came out with that seemingly true story again[s]t me last night, I felt it would be death to me if you had ever believed it — though against any one else I could muster up my obstinacy. Before I knew Brown could disprove it I was for the moment miserable. When shall we pass a day alone? I have had a thousand kisses, for which with my whole soul I thank love — but if you should deny me the thousand and first —'twould put me to the proof how great a misery I could live through. If you should ever carry your threat yesterday into execution — believe me 'tis not my pride, my vanity or any petty passion would torment me — really 'twould hurt my heart — I could not bear it. I have seen Mrs Dilke this morning; she says she will come with me any fine day.

Ever yours

Ah hertê mine! John Keats

Sunday night, after he had passed this ecstatically happy day with Miss Brawne, Keats composed, it is probable, the sonnet *The day is gone*. Neither Keats's manuscript nor Woodhouse's transcript is dated. Lord Houghton dated the sonnet October 1819 without, however, citing his authority. The letter which Keats wrote Miss Brawne on October 11, 1819 does not mention the sonnet, but, as Miss Lowell suggested, it describes the occasion which inspired it. I quote the sonnet from the photograph of the autograph manuscript which H. B. Forman published in *The Bookman* for October 1906:

The day is gone and all its sweets are gone
  Sweet voice, sweet lips soft hand and softer breast
Warm breath, tranc'd whisper, tender semi tone
  Bright eyes, accomplish'd shape, and langrous waist.
Vanish'd unseasonably at shut of eve
  When the dusk Holiday, or Holinight
Of fragrant-curtain'd Love begins to weave
  The ~~texture thick of darkness~~
        woof of darkness thick for hid delight
                all
        and ^ its budded charms
Faded the flower ~~of beuty from my eyes gaze~~
        sight   Beauty   sad eyes
  Faded the ~~voice of Love~~ from my ~~sad ears~~
Faded the shape of Beauty from my arms
  Faded the voice, ~~the whiteness~~
        warmth, whiteness, ~~brilliance~~ paradise
  But as I have read Love's Missal through to day
  He'll let me sleep — seeing I fast and pray.

The evidences of composition indicate that this manuscript was the first draft of the sonnet. Woodhouse transcribed this version into his Book of Transcripts. Lord Houghton printed another version in which the second and third quatrains are transposed. It is possible that Keats made this change, but it is possible also that Lord Houghton tried to improve the sonnet. De Sélincourt observed that the original order of the quatrains work up to a climax in the Shakespearean manner and enhance the total effect. The sonnet is not a good example of Keats's mature style. The first quatrain with its "sweet voice, soft lips, soft hand, and softer breast" is a reversion to the sentimental style of his juvenile sonnets.

Keats's love for Fanny Brawne in October and November 1819 differed in one respect from that which he had felt for her in April, May, June, and July, the four months preceding their estrangement. At that time, we remember, he rebelled against love, complaining that it absorbed him and enslaved him, that it drew him away from his friends, his relatives, and his poetry. When he met Miss Brawne on October 10, after a separation of four months and an estrangement of two months, he surrendered unconditionally to love. From this time to the end of his life he never expressed the slightest rebellion against love, although, as we shall see, he became morbidly jealous of Miss Brawne. On October 13 he wrote a pathetic letter to her, contrasting his present submission to love with his former rebellion against it.

My dearest Girl,

This moment I have set myself to copy some verses out fair. I cannot proceed with any degree of content. I must write you a line or two and see if that will assist me in dismissing you from my Mind for ever so short a time. Upon my Soul I can think of nothing else. The time is passed when I had power to advise and warn you against the unpromising morning of my Life. My love has made me selfish. I cannot exist without you. I am forgetful of everything but seeing you again — my Life seems to stop there — I see no further. You have absorb'd me. I have a sensation at the present moment as though I was dissolving — I should be exquisitely miserable without the hope of soon seeing you. I should be afraid to separate myself far from you. My sweet Fanny, will your heart never change? My love, will it? I have no limit now to my love. . . . You[r] note came in just here. I cannot be happier away from you. 'Tis richer than an Argosy of Pearles. Do not threat me even in jest. I have been astonished that Men could die Martyrs for religion — I have shudder'd at it. I shudder no more — I could be martyr'd for my Religion — Love is my religion — I could die for that. I could die for you. My Creed is Love and you are its only tenet. You have ravish'd me away by a Power I cannot resist; and yet I could resist till I saw you; and even since I have seen you I have endeavoured often "to reason against the reasons of my Love." I can do that no more — the pain would be too great. My love is selfish. I cannot breathe without you.

Yours for ever
John Keats.

Keats was miserable in his lonely lodgings in College Street, Westminster. After his reconciliation with Miss Brawne he was drawn irresistibly to Wentworth Place, Hampstead. On October 16 he visited Brown at Wentworth Place and wrote his sister that he was going to live with him. After stopping three days with Brown he returned to Westminster to give up his lodgings in College Street. On October 19 he wrote Miss Brawne a letter from Dilke's house in Great Smith Street and mailed it in College Street.

My sweet Fanny,

On awakening from my three days dream ("I cry to dream again") I find one and another astonish'd at my idleness and thoughtlessness. I was miserable last night — the morning is always restorative. I must be busy, or try to be so. I have several things to speak to you of tomorrow morning. M[rs] Dilke I should think will tell you that I purpose living at Hampstead. I must impose chains upon myself. I shall be able to do nothing. I sho[u]ld like to cast the die for Love or death. I have no Patience with any thing else — if you ever intend to be cruel to me as you say in jest now but perhaps may sometimes be in earnest, be so now — and I will — my mind is in a tremble, I cannot tell what I am writing.

Ever my love yours
John Keats.

Keats was wondering why he did not seek employment with the magazines, and he knew that his friends were wondering too. He was too ill and too nervous, however, to make a serious effort to do anything. Tuberculosis, which had been attacking his throat intermittently for two years, was now preying upon his lungs. His reconciliation with Miss Brawne made him more desirous of succeeding than ever before; and, at the same time, it aroused his passions, absorbed his declining vitality, and increased his nervousness. His friends Dilke, Brown, and Severn noticed the sudden decline in his health and its consequent effect upon his temperament. "From this period," Dilke[6] said, "his weakness & his sufferings, mental & bodily, increased — his whole mind & heart were in a whirl of contending passions — he saw nothing calmly or dispassionately."

Keats removed to Wentworth Place, Hampstead, it is probable, on October 20. He gave up his plan to earn his living by writing reviews and articles for periodicals and he resumed his reading and

[6] Dilke's Memoir of Keats, Keats's copy of *Endymion*, Dilke Collection.

composing. The story of this final period of his poetry is the tragedy of poetic genius stifled by disease. His mind was teeming with the matter of poetry, and his poetic faculties were coming into the maturity of their power; but he did not have the vitality to endure the exhausting labor of composition, and he was forced to abandon every poem which he began.

The poems which Keats attempted to compose in October and November 1819 indicate the direction in which his poetic genius was evolving. When he resumed his philosophy of negative capability on September 18, he regained as a consequence his ambition to compose plays in the style of Shakespeare's. To prepare himself for reviving the Shakespearean type of drama, he planned to delve into the Italian and English sources of Elizabethan literature. He wrote his brother on September 21 or 22:

> In the course of a few months I shall be as good an Italian Scholar as I am a french one. I am reading Ariosto at present: not managing more than six or eight stanzas at a time. When I have done this language so as to be able to read it tolerably well — I shall set myself to get complete in latin, and there my learning must stop. I do not think of venturing upon Greek. I would not go even so far if I were not persuaded of the power the knowle[d]ge of any language gives one — the fact is I like to be acquainted with foreign languages. It is besides a nice way of filling up intervals, etc. Also the reading of Dante in [is] well worth the while. And in latin there is a fund of curious literature of the middle ages. The Works of many great Men — Aretine and Sanazarius and Machiavell. I shall never become attach'd to a foreign idiom so as to put it into my writings. . . .

When Keats returned to London, he took lodgings in Westminster that he might be near libraries. "I shall live in Westminster," he wrote Woodhouse on September 21, "— from which a walk to the British Museum will be noisy and muddy — but otherwise pleasant enough." On October 3, a few days before he left Winchester, he wrote Haydon:

> Though at this present "I have great dispositions to write" I feel every day more and more content to read. Books are becoming more interesting and valuable to me. I may say I could not live without them. If in the course of a fortnight you can procure me a ticket to the British Museum I will make a better use of it than I did in the first instance.

The decline of his vitality and the nervous and emotional excitement of his reconciliation with Fanny Brawne prevented Keats from reading and studying during the week and a half in which he lived intermittently in College Street, Westminster. After he removed to Wentworth Place, Hampstead, however, he began to read Holinshed's *Chronicles of England, Scotland, and Ireland,* the source from which Shakespeare had derived the matter of his English histories and tragedies. He wrote Taylor on November 17 that he was reading Holinshed's *Elizabeth.* In the latter part of October he attended the *Lectures on the Dramatic Literature of the Age of Elizabeth* which Hazlitt delivered at the Surrey Institution.

> I have been so very lax [he wrote Severn], unemployed, unmeridian'd, and objectless these two months that I even grudge indulding [*sic*] (and that is no great indulgence considering the Lecture is not over till 9 and the lecture room seven miles from Wentworth Place) myself by going to Hazlitt's Lecture. . . . If you should be at the Lecture tomorrow evening I shall see you. . . .

In the first of these lectures Hazlitt discussed the sources of Elizabethan dramatic literature, the very matter into which Keats was delving.

Keats began the composition of *King Stephen,* a chronicle play, in the first part of November; but he abandoned it after he had composed three and one half scenes of the first act.

> As soon as Keats had finished *Otho the Great* [Brown said], I pointed out to him a subject for an English historical tragedy in the death of King Stephen, beginning with his defeat by the Empress Maud, and ending with the death of his son Eustace. He was struck with the variety of events and characters which must necessarily be introduced into it, and I offered to give, as before, their dramatic conduct. The play must open, I began, with the field of battle, when Stephen's forces are retreating — "Stop," he cried, "I have been too long in leading-strings; I will do all this myself." He immediately set about it, and wrote two or three scenes — about 170 lines.
>
> [Manuscript memoir, Houghton-Crewe Collection.] [7]

It is interesting that Coleridge also thought of composing a chronicle play on King Stephen. "In my happier days," Coleridge said, "while I had yet hope and onward-looking thoughts, I planned an historical drama of King Stephen, in the manner of Shakespeare. Indeed it would be desirable that some man of dramatic genius should dramatize all those [kings] omitted by Shakespeare down to Henry VII." [8]

The manuscript of *King Stephen,* which is in the library of the Marquess of Crewe, consists of three quarto leaves in Brown's autograph, containing scene i and 19 verses of scene ii, and five folio leaves in Keats's autograph, containing scene ii, verses 19–54, scene iii, and 58 verses of scene iv. On the recto of the first leaf Brown gave the title, author, and date —

[7] Quoted by Ernest de Sélincourt, p. 555.

[8] Coleridge's *Lectures on Shakespeare,* Everyman Edition, p. 108.

King Stephen.
a fragment
of a tragedy,
by
John Keats
Novr 1819 —

Keats derived or intended to derive the matter of *King Stephen* from Holinshed's *Chronicles*, Selden's *Titles of Honor*, and Shakespeare's chronicle plays. Miss Lowell[9] possessed his copy of Selden's *Titles of Honor*, which (Professor J. L. Lowes suggested) he intended to use as a dictionary of feudal titles and customs. He inscribed his name and the date of purchase on the title page: "John Keats. 1819." On both sides of the flyleaf he began an elaborate alphabetical index, but he made only two entries: "Atheling Page 499," under the letter A, and "Reliefs Page 515," under the letter R. The only markings which he made in the book are in Chapter V, which explains English titles. He had little need to make use of Selden's treatise in the short fragment which he composed. He followed Selden in calling Matilda or Maud by the title of queen, however, instead of Holinshed in calling her by the title of empress.

Keats began his chronicle play with the defeat and capture of King Stephen by Queen Maud in the Battle of Lincoln, which took place on February 2, 1141. He followed very closely Holinshed's story of the battle. The main body of King Stephen's forces, which was composed of footmen, was led, Holinshed said, by the king himself, Baldwin, Earl of Redvers, and other noblemen; a wing of horsemen, by Alain, Duke of Britain, and the earls of Norfolk, Hampton, Mellent, and Warren; and another wing of horsemen, by the Earl of Albemarle and William de Ypres, Earl of Kent. The fore-ward of the queen's forces was led by the Earl of Chester; the middle-ward, by noblemen dispossessed by King Stephen; the rear-ward, by the Earl of Gloucester; and a wing was composed of Welshmen.

Hard it was in the beginning [Holinshed said] to gesse who should haue the better. The wing of the disherited men ouerthrew and bare downe their aduersaries, which were led by the duke of Britain, and the forenamed earles. On the contrarie part, the earle of Albemarle and William de Ypres put the Welshmen to flight, but by the earle of Chester and his retinue, the same earle and William de Ypres were fiercelie assailed afresh, and put out of order. Thus was the kings side put to the worse, namelie his horsemen, who being placed in the forefront, and there ouermatched, fell to galoping. Which thing when the king beheld, he was not yet any whit therewith abashed, but like an hardie captein (as he was no

[9] Amy Lowell, Vol. II, pp. 361–362.

lesse indeed) comforted his footmen whom he had about him, and rushing vpon his enimies, bare them down, and ouerthrew so manie as stood before him, so that with the point of his weapon he made himself waie. His footmen, who were but a few in number to the multitude of his enimies, counteruailed in all points the prowes and manlike dooings of their king and capteine, insomuch that few battels had beene better fought, nor with greater slaughter on both sides, if the kings fore ward (which in manner of the first shranke backe and was disordered, not without some suspicion of treason) had staied the brunt of the enimies a while, as it had beene requisite. At length the king encountring with the earle of Chester, being ouercharged with multitude, was taken prisoner by one William de Cahames.

In the first scene of *King Stephen*, which consists of only 35 verses, the king rallies the fleeing soldiers of Baldwin, Earl of Redvers, and leads them back into the fight. In the second scene messengers report the king's desperate valor to the Earl of Gloucester, the leader of the queen's forces. A messenger, a captain, says:

He sole and lone maintains
A hopeless bustle mid our swarming arms,
And with a nimble savageness attacks,
Escapes, makes fiercer onset, then anew
Eludes death, giving death to most that dare
Trespass within the circuit of his sword!
He must by this have fallen. Baldwin is taken;
And for the Duke of Bretagne, like a stag
He flies, for the Welsh beagles to hunt down.

And another messenger, a knight, exclaims:

. . . I think, my lord, he is no man,
But a fierce demon, 'nointed safe from wounds,
And misbaptized with a Christian name
. . . .
He shames our victory. His valour still
Keeps elbow-room amid our eager swords,
And holds our bladed falchions all aloof —
His gleaming battle-axe being slaughter-sick,
Smote on the morion of a Flemish knight,
Broke short in his hand; upon the which he flung
The heft away with such a vengeful force,
It paunch'd the Earl of Chester's horse, who then
Spleen-hearted came in full career at him.

Keats derived the fact of King Stephen's courage from Holinshed's *Chronicles*, but he drew the manner in which he represented the king's courage from the great fighters in Shakespeare's chronicle plays — Talbot, Faulconbridge, and Richard III. He recalled and employed many of Shakespeare's phrases. For instance, the first messenger said that the king "sole and alone maintains A hopeless bustle mid our swarming arms" and the second messenger described him as "a fierce demon, 'nointed safe from wounds, And misbaptized with a Christian name." This description of King Stephen reminds us of a passage in *King John* (V. iv. 4–5) in which, when the English forces are being defeated by the French, Salisbury says:

> That misbegotten devil, Faulconbridge,
> In spite of spite, alone upholds the day.

In scene i King Stephen, like Richard III, refuses to flee from the battle; and in scene iii he cries for a sword:

> O for a sword!
> I'm faint — a biting sword! a noble sword! —

in terms similar to those in which Richard III cries for a horse:

> A horse! a horse! my kingdom for a horse!

Keats employed the primitive conventions of Shakespeare's chronicle plays without regard to their unsuitability to the modern stage. His battle scenes, which are short and between which there is a change of place, would not be effective unless they were presented on an Elizabethan stage, on which the action is continuous from scene to scene. He represented the battle as the individual combat of the leaders. His warriors are inspired by the virtue of magnanimity, boasting that their heroic deeds will be echoed in the silent pages of their chroniclers. They quote Homer, also, and they swear by the gods of the Greek pantheon.

The chief merit of *King Stephen* is its vivid and authentic representation of the brutal but heroic warfare of twelfth-century England. King Stephen, Queen Maud, the Earl of Gloucester, and the Earl of Chester have strong, individual personalities. Keats's characterization of the Earl of Gloucester gives some indication of the way in which he intended to develop the action of the play. In the second scene the Earl of Gloucester manifests generous admiration for King Stephen's desperate courage. In the fourth scene Queen Maud is incensed by Gloucester's gracious entertainment of King Stephen, his prisoner; and she commands that the king be brought before her for judgment and punishment. In her determination to make the king's imprisonment as rigorous as possible, she is supported by the Earl of Chester. Holinshed, however, represented Queen Maud, the Earl of Gloucester, and the Earl of Chester as of one mind in their harsh treatment of King Stephen. When the Earl of Gloucester was captured by the king's forces in a later battle,

Holinshed said, he was "hardlie handled" because he had dealt harshly with King Stephen.

Keats abandoned *King Stephen* because he did not have the physical vitality to endure the exhausting labor of composing the play. He was not yet convinced that he was suffering from consumption, however, and he thought that his inability to compose the play might be due to his ignorance of dramatic technique. Seeking a subject for another poem, he was drawn between the conflicting attractions of drama and romance. He continued his reading of Holinshed's *Chronicles*; and, when he read the chronicle of Queen Elizabeth, he thought of composing a poem on the Earl of Leicester. He wrote Taylor on November 17:

My dear Taylor,

I have come to a determination not to publish any thing I have now ready written: but for all that to publish a Poem before long and that I hope to make a fine one. As the marvellous is the most enticing, and the surest guarantee of harmonious numbers I have been endeavouring to persuade myself to untether Fancy and let her manage for herself. I and myself cannot agree about this at all. Wonders are no wonders to me. I am more at home amongst men and women. I would rather read Chaucer than Ariosto. The little dramatic skill I may as yet have however badly it might show in a Drama would I think be sufficient for a Poem. I wish to diffuse the colouring of St. Agnes Eve throughout a Poem in which Character and Sentiment would be the figures to such drapery. Two or three such Poems, if God should spare me, written in the course of the next 6 years, wo^{d} be a famous Gradus ad Parnassum altissimum. I mean they would nerve me up to the writing of a few fine plays — my greatest ambition when I do feel ambitious. I am sorry to say that is very seldom. The subject we have once or twice talked of appears a promising one, the Earl of Leicester's history. I am this morning reading Holingshead's Elizabeth. You had some books awhile ago, you promised to send me, illustrative of my Subject. If you can lay hold of them or any others which may be serviceable to me I know you will encourage my low-spirited Muse by sending them — or rather by letting me know when our errand cart Man shall call with my little box. I will endeavour to set my self selfishly at work on this Poem that is to be. —

Your sincere friend
John Keats —

Too languid and nervous to compose a play, his greatest ambition, Keats thought of composing a dramatic romance, a narrative poem, in which he would place vivid, realistic men and women in a sensuous and romantic setting. He would diffuse the coloring of *The Eve of St. Agnes*, he said, throughout a poem in which character and sentiment would be the figures to such drapery. He was no longer content to compose a pure romance, such as *The Eve of St. Agnes*, for he had become more interested in the human affections and passions of drama than in the wonders of romance. In his idea of fusing the poetry of human character with the poetry of romance, he was indebted, as in most matters, to Shakespeare, who combined these two types of poetry in *Romeo and Juliet*, *As You Like It*, *Twelfth Night*, and other plays.

We do not know how far Keats proceeded with his projected dramatic romance of the Earl of Leicester. There is no evidence that he ever composed a single verse. The labor of composing such a poem would have been as great or almost as great as that of composing a chronicle play. After these two failures he realized that he did not have sufficient vitality to compose any serious poem. He believed, however, that he must employ his restless mind in some unexacting kind of composition. So, in a conversation with Brown one day, he conceived the idea of composing a light satirical fairy poem.

> By chance [Brown said] our conversation turned on the idea of a comic faery poem in the Spenser stanza, and I was glad to encourage it. He had not composed many stanzas before he proceeded in it with spirit. It was to be published under the feigned authorship of Lucy Vaughan Lloyd and to bear the title of the *Cap and Bells*, or, which he preferred, the *Jealousies*. This occupied his mornings pleasantly. He wrote it with the greatest facility; in one instance I remember having copied (for I copied as he wrote) as many as twelve stanzas before dinner.
>
> [Brown's Memoir of Keats, Houghton-Crewe Collection.][10]

In the mornings, Brown said, Keats composed stanzas of *The Cap and Bells* and in the evenings he was engaged in remodelling the fragment of *Hyperion* into the form of a vision. At this time, as we have seen, he did not revise more than 55 verses of *Hyperion*. He had found it difficult to revise the poem in September and he found it more difficult now. He could compose stanzas of *The Cap and Bells* with facility, however, for his creative faculties were not excited by it. He composed it *ex tempore* out of matter which was stored in his mind.

> This Poem was written subject to future amendments and omissions [Brown said]: it was begun without a plan, and without any prescribed laws for the supernatural machinery.[11]

The incomplete autograph first draft of the poem, lacking stanzas ix–xvi, xxv–xxvi, xlv–li, and lxxxii–lxxxviii, is in the Pierpont Morgan Library. A fragment of the autograph first draft, containing stanzas xiii-xvi and xlvi–li, is in the Harvard College Library. There is a complete transcript, however, in Woodhouse's Book of Transcripts. Leigh Hunt quoted four stanzas and four verses (xxvi–xxx. 4)

10 Quoted by Ernest de Sélincourt, p. 559.

11 Quoted by H. B. Forman from Lord Houghton's Aldine Edition, Variorum Edition, Vol. III, p. 187.

in an article on *Coaches* in *The Indicator* for August 23, 1820. And Lord Houghton published the poem in 1848. Woodhouse gave the title as follows:

The jealousies
A faery Tale
by
Lucy Vaughan Lloyd
of
Chin a walk, Lambeth

Keats derived the supernatural machinery of the poem from Spenser, Shakespeare, and Drayton. His fairies have the character of those which Shakespeare created in *A Midsummer Night's Dream* by fusing the faeries of romance with the elves of popular tradition. They are dainty, beautiful winged creatures of immaterial substance and exceedingly small size. They live in cities in India and have a monarchical form of government. They fall in love with mortals and steal or exchange human infants. Keats derived Elfinan, the name of the fairy emperor, and Panthea, the name of the city over which Elfinan rules, from the second book of *The Faerie Queene* (II. x. lxx *et seq.*), in which Spenser related the history of the faeries. He derived Hydaspes, the name of the river which flows beside Panthea, and Imaus, the name of the city from which Princess Bellanaine comes, from *Paradise Lost* (III. 431–436). In the first stanza of the poem he described Panthea as follows:

In midmost Ind, beside Hydaspes cool,
There stood, or hover'd, tremulous in the air,
A faery city, 'neath the potent rule
Of Emperor Elfinan. . . .

The description of Panthea as hovering tremulous in the air was suggested to him by the description of the Palace of Oberon in Drayton's *Nymphidia*:

This palace standeth in the air,
By necromancy placed there,
That it no tempests needs to fear,
Which way soe'er it blow it. . . .

Keats took the plot of his poem — the criss-cross loves of fairies and mortals — from *A Midsummer Night's Dream.* As Oberon loves Hippolyta and Titania loves Theseus, so Elfinan loves Bertha Pearl of Canterbury and Bellanaine loves Hubert, a youth of Angle-land. Bertha, like the little Indian boy over whom Oberon and Titania quarrelled, was a fairy changeling. When Elfinan tells Hum, the soothsayer, that he loves Bertha, Hum replies:

> She is a changeling of my management;
> She was born at midnight in an Indian wild. . . .

Hum shows Elfinan as proof of his knowledge of Bertha a sampler which she had made:

> Sire, this is Bertha Pearl's neat handy-work;
> Her *name*, see here, *Midsummer*, *ninety-one*. . . .

This is a reference not only to *A Midsummer Night's Dream* but also to the sampler which Hermia and Helena made.

Keats took a great deal of the matter of this satirical fairy poem from his incomplete serious romance, *The Eve of St. Mark*, which he had composed in February 1819 and revised in September. Bertha Pearl of Canterbury, the mortal maid whom Elfinan loves, is Bertha of *The Eve of St. Mark*, who dwells in the old minster-square. Hum tells Elfinan that, if he will abduct Bertha Pearl, he must be in Kent by twelve o'clock at noon —

> April the twenty-fourth, — this coming day,
> Now breathing its new bloom upon the skies,
> Will end in St. Mark's Eve: — you must away,
> For on that eve alone can you the maid convey.

Hum gives Elfinan "an old And legend-leaved book, mysterious to behold," which is the magic, the potent charm, to cast Bertha Pearl into a fainting fit.

> Lay it on Bertha's table, close beside
> Her work-box, and 'twill help your purpose dearly. . . .

This "legend-leaved book" is the illuminated manuscript in which Bertha reads the legend of St. Mark. Bertha Pearl's sampler,

> Whereon were broider'd tigers with black eyes,
> And long-tail'd pheasants, and a rising sun,
> Plenty of posies, great stags, butterflies
> Bigger than stags, — a moon, — with other mysteries. . . .

corresponds to the winter screen beside which Bertha sits on the Eve of St. Mark,

> On which were many monsters seen,
> Call'd doves of Siam, Lima mice,
> And legless birds of Paradise,
> Macaw, and tender Avadavat,
> And silken-furr'd Angora cat.

An earlier reading of the second verse,

> Call'd Java Pheasants, Doves of Siam,

makes the correspondence closer.

Hum, the soothsayer who aids Elfinan in his love affair with Bertha Pearl, is an alchemist and an astrologer. He has a "furnace-scorched brow" and he can "cast a quiet figure." Keats derived the smattering of mediaeval science with which he builds up the atmosphere around Hum from Chaucer's *Canon's Yeoman's Tale* and Ben Jonson's *Alchemist.* He found a connection, Miss Lowell suggested, between an alchemist and the fairies in Jonson's play, in which Subtle, the alchemist, gulls Dapper by introducing him to his aunt, the Queen of Fairy. Hum's Swiss servant, like the Canon's Yeoman, misuses alchemical and astrological terms such as chalk, aqua vitae, tinder, nitre, grains of paradise (cardamon seeds), and Venus. He adds to his humor by mentioning "*dentes sapientiae* of mice," a reference to the popular "Mouse Cures" of England and Scotland, and "Diddle diddle Dumpling, my son John," a Mother Goose rhyme.

Keats composed *The Cap and Bells* in a parody, or comic imitation, of the style of *Don Juan*, "Lord Byron's last flash poem"; and he intended to publish it under the pseudonym of Lucy Vaughan Lloyd of Chin-a-Walk, Lambeth, who represents doubtless a female admirer of Byron. He knew the Italian medley style in Ariosto's *Orlando Furioso*, which he was reading at this time, as well as in Byron's *Don Juan.* He took a mischievous delight in parodying Byron's style. He recalled the poem which Byron wrote to Lady Byron on March 18, 1816, two months after she had separated from him —

Fare thee well! and if for ever,
Still for ever, fare thee well:
Even though unforgiving, never
'Gainst thee shall my heart rebel. . . .

He parodied these verses in stanza lxviii of *The Cap and Bells*, making Elfinan address Bellanaine, his fiancée, as "Poor Bell," Byron's pet name for Annabel, Lady Byron.

Then Elfinan swift vaulted from the floor,
And lighted graceful on the window-sill;
Under one arm the magic book he bore,
The other he could wave about at will;
Pale was his face, he still look'd very ill:
He bow'd at Bellanaine, and said —"Poor Bell!
Farewell! farewell! and if for ever! still
For ever fare thee well!"— and then he fell
A laughing! — snapp'd his fingers! — shame it is to tell!

Bellanaine is an anagram for Annabel, Lady Byron, and Elfinan, "fam'd ev'rywhere for love of mortal women," is an apt portrait of

Lord Byron. Keats not only parodied Byron's style but he also satirized Byron himself.

The satire, like that in *The Faerie Queene*, is compound rather than simple. The chief object of the satire, as H. B. Forman pointed out, is George Augustus Frederick, Prince of Wales and Prince Regent of England. The Prince Regent was stupid, extravagant, dissolute, and dishonorable. He had an innumerable series of mistresses, the chief of whom were Mrs. Robinson, actress and poetess, Mrs. Fitzherbert, Lady Jersey, Lady Hertford, and Lady Conyngham. The king and the parliament were constantly harassed by the prince's debts and immorality and in 1795, when he was pressed by his creditors, they forced him to marry Caroline, Princess of Brunswick. He detested the princess and in 1796, after she had given birth to a daughter, the Princess Charlotte, he separated from her. His friends and supporters slandered the Princess Caroline, claiming that she had given birth to an illegitimate child; but a commission appointed by the king exonerated her. In 1811, when George III became insane, the prince was made regent of England.

Incidents in *The Cap and Bells* correspond very closely to incidents in the career of the Prince Regent. The embassy which Elfinan was compelled by his parliament to send to Imaus to negotiate a marriage between himself and Princess Bellanaine represents the embassy which George III sent to Brunswick to negotiate a marriage between the Prince of Wales and Caroline, Princess of Brunswick. Crafticant's charge that Bellanaine loved Hubert, a youth of Angleland, represents the charge of adultery which Sir John and Lady Douglas made against Princess Caroline. And the indignation which Elfinan expressed against those statesmen who had forced him to consent to a marriage with Princess Bellanaine represents the Prince Regent's anger at the English statesmen who had compelled him to marry Princess Caroline. In stanzas xvi–xviii Elfinan flung "His limbs upon a sofa, full of spleen, And damn'd his House of Commons, in complete chagrin." "'The square-cut chancellor,'" H. B. Forman [12] explained, "would be Mr. Vansittart, I presume; and 'the tiptoe marquis' might probably be the Marquis of Lansdowne, whose refusal to sit upon the Green Bag Committee was both 'moral' and 'gallant.'" "Esquire Biancopany," Forman said, would be Samuel Whitbread (bianco = white and pane = bread), who defended Princess Caroline in debates in parliament and who, it was said, supplied her with funds for carrying on her case.

Keats worked intermittently on the composition of *The Cap and*

[12] H. B. Forman, Variorum Edition, Vol. III, p. 194.

Bells from about November 20, I believe, to February 3, when he suffered his first hæmorrhage of the lungs. His composition was interrupted in December by increasing illness, it is probable, and in January by the visit of his brother George from America. The hæmorrhage stopped his composition of the poem. On February 23 or 25, 1820 he wrote Reynolds:

> I hope I shall soon be well enough to proceed with my faries [*sic*] and set you about the notes on Sundays and Stray-days.

He had engaged Reynolds, it seems, to write learned notes on the poem as a part of its humor. And in June, 1820 he wrote Brown:

> I shall soon begin upon "Lucy Vaughan Lloyd." I do not begin composition yet, being willing, in case of a relapse, to have nothing to reproach myself with.

Brown had departed from Hampstead on May 7 to go to Scotland.

> It was his [Keats's] choice [Brown said], during my absence, to lodge at Kentish Town, that he might be near his friend, Leigh Hunt, in whose companionship he was ever happy. He went with me in the Scotch smack as far as Gravesend. This was on the 7th of May. I never saw him afterwards. As evidence of his well being I had requested him to send me some new stanzas to his comic faery poem; for, since his illness, he had not dared the exertion of composing. . . . [Manuscript memoir, Houghton-Crewe Collection.][13]

Keats kept resolving to resume the composition of the poem, but there is no record that he did resume it. In August 1820, before he went to Italy with Severn, he wrote Brown that women did not like his poetry because they never see thesmelves dominant in it. He had a tendency, he admitted, to class women with roses and sweetmeats.

> If ever I come to publish "Lucy Vaughan Lloyd" [he said], there will be some delicate picking for squeamish stomachs.

Keats composed two lyric poems in November or December 1819 while he was composing *The Cap and Bells.* There are extant only six letters which he wrote in this period — three to his sister, one to Taylor, one to Severn, and one to Rice. He maintained a brave front in these letters, discussing his prospects in a calm, collected, and hopeful spirit. In reality, however, he was nervous, suspicious, and dejected. His illness prevented him from attaining the objects upon which his happiness depended. It kept him from composing poems and plays by which he hoped to raise his poetic reputation and to acquire funds to support himself and to enable him to marry Fanny Brawne. He could not conceal his desperate unhappiness from Brown and Miss Brawne, with whom he was intimately asso-

[13] Quoted by M. B. Forman, Vol. II, p. 533.

ciated. Brown, after describing Keats's attempt to compose *The Cap and Bells*, said:

He could not resume his employment, and he became dreadfully unhappy. His hopes of fame, and other more tender hopes were blighted. His patrimony, though much consumed in a profession he was compelled to relinquish, might have upheld him through the storm, had he not imprudently lost a part of it in generous loans. . . . All that a friend could say, or offer, or urge was not enough to heal his many wounds. He listened, and, in kindness, or soothed by kindness, showed tranquillity, but nothing from a friend could relieve him, except on a matter of inferior trouble. He was too thoughtful, or too unquiet; and he began to be reckless of health. Among other proofs of recklessness, he was secretly taking, at times, a few drops of laudanum to keep up his spirits. It was discovered by accident, and, without delay, revealed to me. He needed not to be warned of the danger of such a habit; but I rejoiced at his promise never to take another drop without my knowledge; for nothing could induce him to break his word, when once given, — which was a difficulty. Still, at the very moment of my being rejoiced, this was an additional proof of his rooted misery.

[Manuscript memoir, Houghton-Crewe Collection.] [14]

The greater part of the anguish which Keats suffered in this period had its source in his love for Fanny Brawne. He believed that she did not love him as much as he loved her, and he feared that she would love another. He distrusted her desire for social amusements, and he disapproved of her habit of going to town alone to visit Mrs. Dilke. As consumption seized upon him, he became morbidly possessive and jealous. This disease has a tendency, it seems, to stimulate sexual desire and to incite suspicion. In this morbid state of mind he suspected that Brown and Miss Brawne were flirting with each other. Brown's full-blooded joviality, which had amused him a few months before, tortured him now. Knowing Brown's character, he could scarcely endure to see him talk and jest with Miss Brawne. In the same way, Miss Brawne's gay coquetry, which had captivated him, made him distrust her. He was always afraid, he wrote her, that she was a little inclined to the Cressid. In July 1820, when he was living in Kentish Town with Hunt, when Brown was in Scotland, and when Miss Brawne was still in Wentworth Place, Hampstead, he wrote Miss Brawne a letter in which he recalled that jealousy which he had felt when they were neighbors in Wentworth Place in the autumn and winter of 1819.

I cannot forget what has pass'd [he told her]. What? nothing with a man of the world, but to me dreadful. I will get rid of this as much as possible. When you were in the habit of flirting with Brown you would have left off, could your own heart have felt one half of one pang mine did. Brown is a good sort of Man — he did not know he was doing me to death by inches. I feel the effect of every

[14] Quoted by Sir Sidney Colvin, p. 379.

one of those hours in my side now; and for that cause, though he has done me many services, though I know his love and friendship for me, though at this moment I should be without pence were it not for his assistance, I will never see or speak to him until we are both old men, if we are to be. I *will* resent my heart having been made a football. You will call this madness. I have heard you say that it was not unpleasant to wait a few years — you have amusements — your mind is away — you have not brooded over one idea as I have, and how should you? You are to me an object intensely desireable — the air I breathe in a room empty of you is unhealthy. I am not the same to you — no — you can wait — you have a thousand activities — you can be happy without me. Any party, any thing to fill up the day has been enough.

In this state of mind Keats composed a heart-rending sonnet to Miss Brawne, begging her, in an agony of jealousy, to give him all of her love:

I cry your mercy — pity — love! — aye, love!
  Merciful love that tantalises not,
One-thoughted, never-wandering, guileless love,
  Unmask'd, and being seen — without a blot!
O! let me have thee whole, — all — all — be mine!
  That shape, that fairness, that sweet minor zest
Of love, your kiss, — those hands, those eyes divine,
  That warm, white, lucent, million-pleasured breast, —
Yourself — your soul — in pity give me all,
  Withhold no atom's atom or I die,
Or living on, perhaps, your wretched thrall,
  Forget, in the mist of idle misery,
Life's purposes, — the palate of my mind
Losing its gust, and my ambition blind!

There is no contemporary manuscript of this sonnet. The only text that is known is that which Lord Houghton published in 1848. There is no contemporary statement of the date of composition; but the thought of the sonnet has caused all critics to place its date in November or December 1819. Sentimental phrases in the second quatrain —"that shape, that fairness, etc."— connect it with the sonnet, *The Day is gone,* which Keats composed on October 10, 1819. The emotion of the sonnet as a whole, however, is too painful to be sentimental.

Keats expressed the agony of his jealousy also in the blank verse lines, *This living hand,* which he wrote in the manuscript of *The Cap and Bells* between the fifty-first and the fifty-second stanzas. The fragment of the autograph manuscript containing these verses, which is in the Harvard College Library, indicates, as Miss Lowell observed, that he composed these verses before he composed the fifty-second stanza. In the fifty-first stanza he described Bertha

Pearl's sampler, on which was embroidered the motto CUPID I, DO THEE DEFY. This motto reminded him doubtless of the pain which Miss Brawne's conduct had inflicted upon him. "This living hand," he wrote with morbid agony,

> This living hand, now warm and capable
> Of earnest grasping, would, if it were cold
> And in the icy silence of the tomb,
> So haunt thy days and chill thy dreaming nights
> That thou would[st] wish thine own heart dry of blood
> So in my veins red life might stream again,
> And thou be conscience-calm'd — see here it is [—]
> I hold it towards you.

Since the sonnet *I cry your mercy* and the verses *This living hand* were composed in November or December 1819 (in December, I believe), while Keats was in the midst of the composition of *The Cap and Bells*, the final stanzas of *The Cap and Bells* were the last verses of poetry which he composed.

We have come now to the end of the evolution of Keats's poetry. In the last year of his life — from the hæmorrhage of his lungs in Hampstead on February 3, 1820 to his death in Rome on February 23, 1821 — he did not compose any poetry at all. We have already noted the few revisions which he made in his poems in this period. When he became ill on February 3, 1820 he had scarcely begun to revise the texts of the poems which he published at the beginning of the following July, and he permitted his publishers, Woodhouse said, to make a choice between variant readings in different manuscripts. Notes in Woodhouse's books of transcripts show, as we have seen, that Woodhouse had much to do with the selection of the poems to be printed in this volume and with the preparation of the texts of the poems for the press.

The evolution of Keats's poetry was short — from the beginning of 1814 to the beginning of 1820 — but amazingly complex. He was the most myriad-minded English poet since Shakespeare, whom he believed he resembled in the character of his mind. He possessed an unusual combination of highly developed sensuous and emotional with equally highly developed analytical and speculative faculties. He had a negative capability of mind, a suspension of judgment, which enabled him to see both sides of every question and to seek truth without egotistic bias, and an imaginative and objective insight into the minds of other men. He was impelled by his sensuous faculties to express the sensuous beauty of life and by his speculative

51

The Monarch handled o'er and o'er again
These dayschool hieroglyphics with a sigh:
~~With tender~~
Somewhat in sadness but pleas'd in the main
Till this oracular couplet met his eye
Astounded "Cupid I, do thee defy"
It was too much, ~~he fell back on the couch~~ he shrunk back in his Chair
Grew pale as death and fainted very nigh.
Pho, nonsense exclaim'd Hum now don't despair
She does not mean it really - cheer up - hearty - there!

This living hand, now warm and capable
Of earnest grasping, would, if it were cold
And in the icy silence of the tomb,
So haunt thy days and chill thy dreaming nights
That thou would wish thine own heart dry of blood
So in my veins red life might stream again,
And thou be conscience-calm'd - see here it is -
I hold it towards you.

THE VERSES *THIS LIVING HAND, NOW WARM AND CAPABLE, ETC.*, WRITTEN ON A PAGE (CONTAINING STANZA 51) OF THE AUTOGRAPH MANUSCRIPT OF *THE CAP AND BELLS; OR, THE JEALOUSIES*

Reproduced from the original autograph manuscript by permission of the Harvard College Library

faculties to interpret the significance of life for human beings. He was interested both in romantic atmosphere and incident and in the sensations, emotions, and thoughts of real men and women.

There was considerable storm and stress in Keats's mind before he attained a balance and harmony between the different faculties of his mind. The chief problem of his life consisted in his endeavor to develop a philosophy of life and poetry which would satisfy every faculty of his mind in its reaction to the facts of his experience. In the fall of 1816, when he composed *Sleep and Poetry*, he was attracted by Leigh Hunt's superficial and optimistic naturalism, an adaptation of Wordsworth's empirical naturalism. In *Endymion*, in 1817, he formulated a neo-Platonic philosophy of beauty which he learned from his Elizabethan masters, Spenser, Shakespeare, and Drayton, and from his contemporaries, Wordsworth and Shelley. In the fall of 1817 he began to understand the philosophy of negative capability which he developed out of Shakespeare's plays; but in 1818 he was drawn away from this philosophy by the windy humanitarianism which he developed, with Benjamin Bailey's assistance, out of Wordsworth's *Excursion*. In the fall of 1818 he resumed his philosophy of negative capability, and, in the spring of 1819, he established it upon a sound empirical basis. This philosophy, which satisfied every faculty of his mind, ushered in the great creative period of his poetry. It is expressed imperfectly in *Hyperion*, *The Eve of St. Agnes*, and *The Eve of St. Mark* and perfectly in the *Ode to a Nightingale*, the *Ode on Melancholy*, and the *Ode on a Grecian Urn*.

The tragedy of Keats's poetic career consists in the fact that his mind was stifled by disease in the year in which it reached full maturity. He expressed his humanistic and empirical philosophy of negative capability in logical form in his letters and in subjective artistic form in his great odes. He did not attain, however, the goal of his poetic evolution, negatively capable, or dramatic, artistic expression, the composition of plays, in which he represented real and individual men and women in the objective manner of Shakespeare. His letters, in which his friends stand out in vivid and objective form, show that he had the faculty of dramatic characterization. And a few passages in his poems and many passages in his letters show that he had the power of realistic description and the power of both comic and serious satire.

Keats would never have lost, however, his love of sensuous and romantic atmosphere and incident. In November 1819, when he abandoned the composition of the chronicle play *King Stephen*, he thought of composing a poem on the history of the Earl of Leicester, in which he would combine the poetry of romance with the poetry of human character. He wrote Taylor on November 17:

> As the marvellous is the most enticing, and the surest guarantee of harmonious numbers I have been endeavouring to persuade myself to untether Fancy and let her manage for herself. I and myself cannot agree about this at all. Wonders are no wonders to me. I am more at home amongst men and women. I would rather read Chaucer than Ariosto. The little dramatic skill I may as yet have however badly it might show in a Drama would I think be sufficient for a Poem. I wish to diffuse the colouring of St. Agnes Eve throughout a Poem in which Character and Sentiment would be the figures to such drapery. Two or three such Poems, if God should spare me, written in the course of the next 6 years, wo[d] be a famous Gradus ad Parnassum altissimum. I mean they would nerve me up to the writing of a few fine plays — my greatest ambition when I do feel ambitious.

We have in this passage, in my judgment, the truest indication of the direction in which Keats's poetry would have evolved.

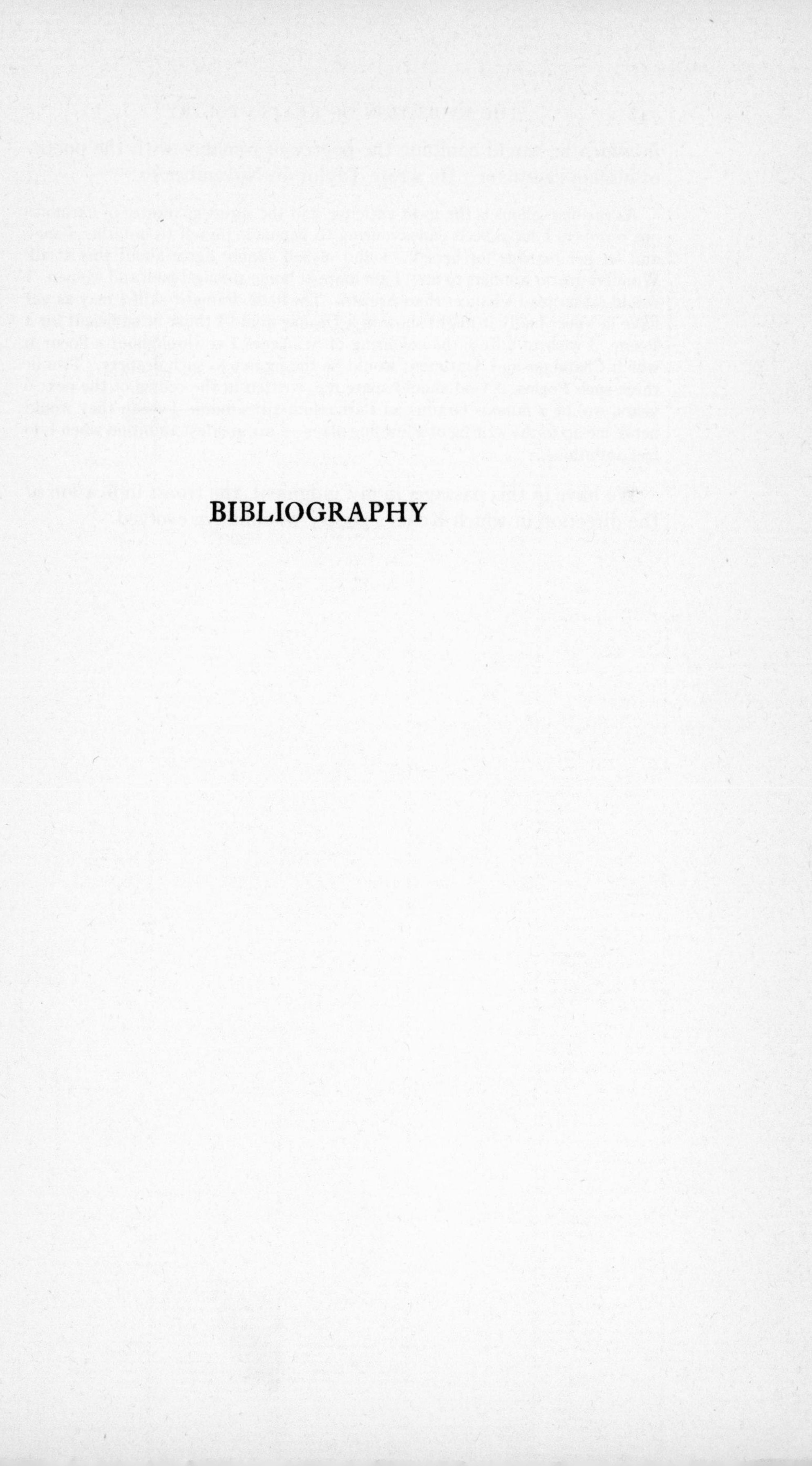

BIBLIOGRAPHY

A BIBLIOGRAPHY OF MANUSCRIPT MATERIAL FOR THE STUDY OF KEATS'S LIFE AND POETRY

In the text of this book I have listed the manuscript material of each poem in the discussion of that poem. In this bibliography, however, I have listed this manuscript material under the collections in which it is kept.

The Pierpont Morgan Library Collection

I

Richard Woodhouse's Scrap-book. A large bound volume of blank pages, in which Woodhouse pasted manuscripts. The manuscripts in the first half of the volume are letters (most of which are transcripts) which were written by Keats's friends and which give much significant information about his life and poetry. There is also a transcript in shorthand of a letter by Keats to John Taylor on June 10, 1817. The manuscripts in the second half of the volume are transcripts of poems by Keats, George Felton Mathew, and others. Most of these transcripts are signed, dated, and annotated. Some of the transcripts of the poems and some of the signatures and notes are in shorthand. At the end of the volume are a manuscript list of Keats's letters to his friends and a manuscript list of the books which Keats owned and of the friends to whom his books were given after his death. The manuscript items in the volume are numbered consecutively.

1. Letter of Richard Woodhouse to John Taylor (latter part of August 1819). Woodhouse promises to copy *The Pot of Basil* for Taylor (the fourth time he has copied it) and to send it to him to Retford, where he was visiting relatives. Woodhouse also mentions John Hamilton Reynolds' *One, Two, Three, Four, Five*, which had just been published.
2. Letter of Richard Woodhouse to his cousin Mary Frogley. Dated merely "Friday Even[g] —" (end of 1818, it is probable). A glowing defense of *Endymion* against the attacks of the reviewers. This letter has been transferred to another volume of manuscripts in the Pierpont Morgan Library.
3. Letter of Richard Woodhouse to John Taylor, dated "Temple Tuesday Ev[g] 31, Aug[t] 1819." A diplomatic defense of the pride which Keats evinced in a letter to Taylor and an offer to lend money to Taylor to lend to Keats.
4. Letter of Richard Woodhouse to John Taylor (August 1820). He mentions *Endymion* and the *Poems* of 1820 and Reynolds' *Fancy*. Dated merely "Friday."
5. Letter of Richard Woodhouse to John Taylor (November 1818). Asks Taylor to have a copy of *Endymion* bound and interleaved for him and requests Taylor to secure a copy of the complimentary sonnet of which they were talking "last night" — the sonnet which the Teignmouth admirer sent to Keats on November 9, 1818.
6. Letter of Richard Woodhouse to Keats, dated "Temple — 10 Dec — 1818." He offers condolence on the death of Tom Keats and says that he is enclosing a letter in which the Misses Jane and Maria Porter express a desire to meet the author of *Endymion*.
7. Letter of Richard Woodhouse to John Taylor, dated "Temple 7 Sept. 1819." He says that he has given money to Hessey to send to Keats in Winchester, and he wishes that he and Taylor and Keats could take a "poetical spree" into France next summer.
8. A memorandum (dated "21 Aug. 1823") by Richard Woodhouse of a conversation with Charles Cowden Clarke about Keats's parents, grandparents, and early poems.

9. A rough draft of a letter by Richard Woodhouse (perhaps a draft of a letter to John Taylor). A discussion of the letter which Keats wrote to Woodhouse on October 27, 1818 about the distinction between the egotistical and negatively capable types of poets. Undated.

10. Letter by Richard Woodhouse to John Taylor. Undated. About the introduction of a friend to the Law Society.

11. Transcript of Richard Woodhouse's letter to Mary Frogley (number 2 above). The margin of the page, together with the words near the margin, is destroyed.

11b. Letter by Richard Woodhouse to John Taylor, dated "Temple 9 Feb[y]/20." About some poem which he and Taylor were reading and evaluating — possibly Keats's *Otho the Great.*

12. Short note by Richard Woodhouse to John Taylor, dated "9 Mar 1819." He says he is enclosing a letter by John Hamilton Reynolds.
Scientific notes on the Basil. On the second half of the preceding manuscript.

13. Notes by Richard Woodhouse on Keats. The following is a complete transcript of these important notes:

"Her feet were sandall'd ready for the way.
The fight at Hampstead.
Loan of money to him at Teignmouth by his lndly [landlady].
If I die you must ruin Lockhart.
Brown, he ought not to have asked me.
I'd rather have died. Wells should have brothers and sicker than I even had [in shorthand].
Thos. K. & Wells"

The fourth, fifth, and sixth notes are the morbid broodings which Keats revealed to Charles Brown in Hampstead at the end of 1819 and the beginning of 1820, when his self-control was finally and completely destroyed by disease. The fourth note refers to John Gibson Lockhart, who wrote the review of *Endymion* in *Blackwood's Edinburgh Magazine.* The fifth note refers to George Keats (or possibly to Benjamin Robert Haydon), who borrowed money from Keats and did not repay him in his hour of need. The sixth note refers to Charles Wells, who played a cruel jest on Tom Keats in the summer of 1818, when he was suffering from the consumption from which he died on December 1, 1818. Wells and an accomplice sent love letters to Tom Keats and signed them "Amena."

14. Transcript by Woodhouse of the inscription on Keats's grave in Rome.

15. Letter by John Taylor to Keats on the eve of his departure to Italy explaining the state of his finances. Dated "Fleet Street 11 Sept 1820." The letter, which has no postmark, was probably not sent to Keats.

16. Letter by John Taylor to Richard Woodhouse (in 1821, after death of Keats). He suggests taking steps to collect from Keats's estate the money which he and others had lent to Keats. Dated merely "Waterloo Place Wednesday."

17. Letter by Taylor and Hessey to Brown, Esq., Poultry, dated "Fleet Street 19 Sept 1820." They promise to honor the bills of Keats in Naples to the amount of £150.

18. Letter by John Taylor to James Augustus Hessey, dated "London 31 August 1820." He relates in detail a visit by Blackwood in his Fleet Street shop in which they discuss the attack on Keats in *Blackwood's Edinburgh Magazine.* A very interesting discussion.

19a. Letter by Charles Brown to John Taylor, dated "Chichester. 5th Sept[r] 1820." Brown tells how he missed seeing Keats when the ship on which Keats sailed for Italy was forced to put into Portsmouth. He gives particulars of Keats's visit with Mr. Snook in Bedhampton.

19b. Letter by James Augustus Hessey to John Taylor, dated "Oct. 6, 1820." He says that Charles Dilke has called with news of Keats.

20. Letter by John Hamilton Reynolds to John Taylor, dated "Exmouth — 21 Sept 1820." He discusses Keats's voyage to Italy.

21. Letter by John Hamilton Reynolds to John Taylor, dated "50 Poland Street 4 July 1820." He alludes to Keats and the *Poems* of 1820.

22. Letter by John Hamilton Reynolds to John Taylor, dated merely "Wednesday Morn[g]." He alludes to Keats. (Probably summer of 1820.)

23. Letter by James Augustus Hessey to John Taylor, dated "Mar. 6. 1818." He says that Keats went off to Teignmouth on the night of the storm on the outside of the coach.

24. Transcript of the letter in defense of Keats which was published in *The Morning Chronicle* on Thursday, October 8, 1818. The article in this transcript is signed "B. B(aily)." The "aily" is added in pencil. The transcript is dated at the end "Temple, Oct. 3 [8?]."

25. Article by Benjamin Bailey relating his conversation with John Gibson Lockhart in July 1818. He wrote this article for insertion in the memoir in Taylor's projected edition of Keats's Literary Remains. Undated.

26. Letter by Benjamin Bailey to John Taylor, dated "Oxford May 20 1818." Bailey discusses *Endymion* and says that he has written an article on the poem for an Oxford newspaper.

27. Letter by Benjamin Bailey to John Taylor (October 1818). Bailey says that he sent an article defending Keats against Blackwood's reviewer to Constable's *Scots and Edinburgh Magazine* and that Constable returned it "without a word."

28. Letter by Benjamin Bailey to John Taylor, dated "Caret Square, Carlisle Oct. 5, 1818." Bailey says that he sent an article in defense of Keats to *Blackwood's Edinburgh Magazine* and that it was returned. "They attack people, but do not leave their columns open to defence." He says that he was introduced to Blackwood, who said that he had seen Taylor in London.

29. Letter by Benjamin Bailey to John Taylor, dated "Oxford, Feb[y] 22 1818." He discusses the second book of *Endymion*. Bailey and Taylor were much disturbed by the moral principles of the romance.

30. Letter by Benjamin Bailey to John Taylor, dated "Oxford, April 9, 1818." He says that he is ready to answer any attack which may be made on *Endymion* or to write a review of the romance.

30a. Letter by Benjamin Bailey to John Taylor, dated "Dallington, July 27 1820." He expresses apprehension that Keats's *Poems* of 1820 will not succeed. He distrusts Keats's moral principles.

30b. Letter by Benjamin Bailey to John Taylor (June 1818). He alludes to his article in defense of Keats in the Oxford newspaper.

31. Letter by Benjamin Bailey to John Taylor, dated "Mt. Fairlawn, Court Square, Carlisle, August 29, 1818." He refers to the expected death of Tom Keats. He describes his conversation with John Gibson Lockhart at the home of Bishop Gleig in Scotland in July, a month before. He expects *Endymion* to be attacked in *Blackwood's Edinburgh Magazine*, although Lockhart had promised that he himself would not attack it. He expresses his disapproval of the principle of love in *Endymion*.

32. Letter by Benjamin Bailey to John Taylor, dated "Dallington, March 26, 1821." He discusses the recent death of Keats. "Reynolds told me, when I was last in London, that poor Keats attributed his approaching end to the poisonous pen of Lockhart. . . ." (See Woodhouse's note in number 13 above.) He asks Taylor to destroy or to return the letters which he had written to Keats.

33. Letter by Benjamin Bailey to John Taylor, dated "Dallington, April 28, 1821." He refers to the notice in the newspapers that Taylor intends to publish the literary

remains of Keats with an account of his life, and he offers to make excerpts from Keats's letters to him and to write an anonymous account of his meeting with Lockhart at Bishop Gleig's. (See number 25 above.)

34. Letter by Benjamin Bailey to John Taylor, dated "Dallington, Feb[y] 16 1821." He discusses the expected death of Keats.

35. Letter by Benjamin Bailey to John Taylor, dated "Dallington, Northampton, Feb[y] 12, 1821." He hopes Keats's health is improving and he discusses the *Poems* of 1820, praising *Hyperion* as the best poem in the volume.

36. Letter by Miss Reynolds (undoubtedly Jane Reynolds) to Richard Woodhouse, dated merely "Thursday morning." She requests Woodhouse to return her album and a letter which Keats had written her. (See number 57 below.)

37. Letter by Mrs. Colonel Green to Richard Woodhouse, dated "Duncan Terrace, Islington, March 29, 1819." She thanks Woodhouse for the perusal of *Endymion* and asks to be remembered to Keats.

38. Letter by Charles Cowden Clarke to Richard Woodhouse, dated "Guildhall 29 Dec[r]/23." He says he is enclosing something (apparently one of Keats's poems) and asks Woodhouse to send him Keats's lines "upon the mystery of the maidenhead."

39. Letter by C. G. Wylie to John Taylor, dated "August 17th 1828." Wylie, in behalf of his sister, Mrs. George Keats, asks Taylor to give an order for the return of bills which have been paid. George Keats repaid the money which Taylor had lent to Keats.

40. Letter by John Hamilton Reynolds to Richard Woodhouse, dated "Esher, April 6 1820." Written by Miss Reynolds from her brother's dictation. He says that he was vexed to hear *Endymion* abused by Mr. Neville and "some ladies who drank tea here."

41. Letter by Charles Brown to John Taylor, dated "Hampstead 8th March" and postmarked "7 o'clock, March 8, 1820." He says that Keats has been taken with violent palpitations of the heart and will be unable to prepare his poems for the press.

42. Letter by Charles Brown to John Taylor, dated "Wentworth Place, 12th Aug[t] Sunday" (1822?). He requests "that the MSS in my handwriting of Keats' poetry may at your earliest convenience be returned."

43. Letter by Charles Brown to John Taylor, dated "Hampstead, Sunday, 18 March" (1821). He announces the news of Keats's death.

44. Letter by Charles Brown to John Taylor, dated "Hampstead Friday 10 March" (1820). He says that Keats is now out of danger. (See number 41 above.)

45. Letter by Charles Brown to John Taylor (March 1820). He says that Keats is recovering, that he desires his poems to be published as soon as convenient, that he desires the volume to begin with *The Eve of St. Agnes*, and that he is revising *Lamia*.

46. Letter by Charles Brown to J. A. Hessey, dated "Hampstead, 24 July 1821." He asks Hessey to remind Taylor to return "the four MSS. books in my handwriting of Mr. Keats's poems."

47. Transcript in shorthand of Keats's letter to John Taylor on "10 June 1817."

48. Transcript of the stanzas "On Some Skulls, in Beauley Abbey, near Inverness."

49. Prefatory title to the transcripts of poems which follow in the volume: "Poems — etc. — by, or relating to, John Keats. All that are not by Keats, have the names of the authors added. — Woodhouse Nov. 1818. Temple."

Transcript of the sonnet "The Poet." No signature and date. Note on opposite page belongs to the song on transcript number 50: "This song was written at the request of some young ladies who were tired of singing the words printed with the air, & desired fresh words to the same tune ab[t] 1815/6 — ."

50. Transcript of the song "Oh! come, my dear Emma, the rose is full blown." No title and date. Signed "J. K" with subscript in shorthand: "from Mary Frogley."

Transcript of a poem beginning "See, the ship in the Bay is riding." No title and date. Signed "J. K." with subscript in shorthand: "from Mary Frogley." (See number 72 below.)

Transcript of a sonnet addressed "To Apollo, written after reading Keats's 'Sleep and Poetry.' —" No signature. Dated "4 March 1818." Probably composed by Woodhouse himself.

51. Prefatory note: "One of Keats's Epistles (p. 53) is addressed to Geo: Felton Matthew, who is very flatteringly hailed as a brother poet. — The verses (p. 29 of Keats's poems) ~~appear~~ I am informed were sent to the Misses Mathew, cousins of the above Gentleman, then at Hastings; & that Mr. M. was then with them. — The next copy of verses (p. 32) — 'On receiving a shell & verses from the same ladies' — appear to be addressed to Mr. Ma~~t~~thew. — I am not aware that Mr. M. has ever published any of his Compositions: — I have obtained the follow [*sic*] copy of verses, which were written by him, & clearly refer to the Copy sent to him by Keats, & published p. 32. — How far Mr. M. is entitled to the poetical character assigned to him by Keats, it would be scarcely fair to judge from this one specimen. — "

Transcript of the poem addressed "To a Poetical Friend. (J. Keats)." Signed "G. F. M." Note on verse 1 of stanza 10: "Alluding to Keats's then profession of a surgeon.—" Note on verse 3 of stanza 11:

"'Mongst boughs pavilion'd, where the Deer's swift leap
Startles the wild bee from the foxglove bell.' —
Keats 7th Son. p. 85."

Postscript: "N. B. Most of the Pieces underwent alteration previously to being published; and it is probable that the allusion to this sonnet, as originally written, was even closer than at present."

Transcript of the poem beginning "Oh - - - -, thou bright beam of joy." Prefatory note: "The following lines, also written by Mr. Mathew, were sent to the young lady, to whom Keats's lines (page 36) were addressed, with a Copy of the Poems of Ossian.— " The transcript is signed and dated "G. F. M. 1814."

52. A transcript of a poem addressed "To a young Lady." Signed "G. F. M." with a subscript in shorthand: "from Mary Frogley."

53. Transcript of the sonnet beginning "Nature withheld Cassandra in the skies." No title and date. Signed "J. Keats."

Transcript of the "Sonnet to Ailsa Rock." Signed "John Keats." Postscript: "Literary Pocket Book for 1819." Transcribed possibly in the handwriting of Charles Cowden Clarke.

54. Transcript of "Sonnet after reading Dante." Signed "John Keats" and dated "April 1819." Transcribed possibly in handwriting of J. A. Hessey.

55. Letter by Richard Woodhouse to John Taylor, dated "Temple 23 Nov 1820." He says that he is returning Reynolds' volume of manuscript poems, and he discusses the third stanza of "In a drear-nighted December" and composes a substitute stanza. A transcript of "In a drear-nighted December" is inserted between the first and second leaves of the letter. The poem is entitled "Song. —."

56. Transcript of the poem beginning "Fill for me a brimming bowl." No title. Signed "J. K." with a subscript in shorthand: "from Mary Frogley." Two phrases in the poem are corrected in shorthand.

57. Transcript of the poem beginning "When I percieve [*sic*] the efforts that combine." Dated "1819." Postscript in shorthand: "Written by Mrs. Reynolds in her daughter's album." "Dear Jane" is addressed in the poem; and this proves that it was Jane's album (instead of Marianne's or Charlotte's) which Woodhouse borrowed and from which he copied several of Keats's poems.

57a. Transcript of the poem beginning "Oh blush not so! Oh blush not so!" No title, signature, and date. One phrase is corrected in shorthand.

58. Transcript of the poem beginning "Unfelt, unheard, unseen." No title. Signed and dated "Keats. 1817."

59. Transcript of the "Sonnet" beginning "Oh! how I love, on a fair Summer's eve." Dated "1816" with a subscript in shorthand: "from Mary Frogley."

Transcript of the "Sonnet" beginning "As from the darkening gloom a silver dove." Dated "1816" with a subscript in shorthand: "from Mary Frogley."

60. Transcript of the sonnet beginning "The day is gone — and all its sweets are gone." No title, signature, and date.

61. Transcript of the "Sonnet" beginning "O Chatterton! how very sad thy fate!" Signed and dated: "J. K. 1815." Note on "amate": "Affright — Spenser." Transcribed possibly in the handwriting of Charles Cowden Clarke.

62. Transcript of the "Song" beginning "O come dearest Emma! The Rose is full bl[own]." No signature and date. Transcribed possibly in the handwriting of George Keats. Earliest extant version.

Transcript of the "Sonnet" beginning "[O So]litude! I must with thee dwell." No signature and date. This sonnet is written on the reverse side of the manuscript of the preceding song. Both poems are transcribed possibly in the handwriting of George Keats.

63. Transcript of a poem which praises Mrs. Reynolds' matronly charms. Prefatory note: "Written in the album of the Countess Dow. [Dowager] of Pembroke." Signed "A. G. S." and dated "8 Oct. 1817."

Transcript in shorthand of a poem, signed "A. G. S." and dated "1 Novr 1817."

64. Transcript of the poem beginning "Hush, hush! tread softly, tread gently, my dear." No title, signature, and date.

65. Transcript of the poem beginning "Over the hill and over the dale." Prefatory note: "From a letter sent by Keats to Rice 25 March 1818. 'I went yesterday to Dawlish fair' —." No title and signature. Dated at the end of the transcript: "25 March 1818."

66. Transcript of the ode beginning "God of the golden Bow!" Title: "Ode to Apollo." No signature and date. Prefatory note:

taking
"As the author & Leigh Hunt were ∧ ~~drinking~~ their wine
after dinner ~~afternoon~~
together, ~~one summer evening~~, at the house of the latter, the
whim to
~~Fancy~~ seised them ~~that they would~~ crown d themselves, ~~as~~
after the fashion of the elder
poets, | with a wreath of laurel.

acquaintances
~~Soon after~~ | they were ~~thus~~ attired, two ∧ ~~friends~~ of Mr. Hunt
while | ~~came in~~
~~happened to pay him a visit:~~ — Just before their entrance
called upon him.
Hunt own
~~that gentleman~~ ∧ removed the crown from his ∧ brows, and
suggested to Keats that he might as well do the same.
K,
The ~~latter~~ however, in the enthusiasm of the moment,
he wo^d not take off
vowed his wreath any human being
~~declared~~ that ∧ for ~~no man alive would he take off~~ his

wreath — and he accordingly wore it without any
explanation, ~~till the gentlemen's departure, to their no~~
~~small surprize.~~ the circum^{ce} after expressing
He mentioned ~~subsequently~~ to one or two of his friends ∧
~~with~~ how foolish he had been
his sense ~~of the impropriety of what he had done;~~ and
his intention of recording it, by some apologetic trifle
suited to the occasion. — He produced shortly afterwards
the following fragment of an
Ode to Apollo."

67. Transcript of the "Song" beginning "The stranger lighted from his steed." Signed "J. K." and dated "1818."

Transcript of the "Daisy's Song" beginning "The Sun with his great eye." Signed "J. K." and dated "1818."

68. Transcript of the valentine beginning "Hadst thou lived in days of old." Prefatory note: "In page 36 of Keats's published poems, are lines 'To xxx.' These have been much altered, prior to publication, from the first copy, which was sent as a valentine on 14 Feby. 1816 to Miss Mary F. — The following is a transcript of the letter sent. — The date is fixed by the post mark. —"

Transcript of a "Sonnet" beginning "Where didst thou find, young Bard, thy sounding lyre?" Prefatory note: "To A. G. S. on reading his admirable verses, written in this (Miss Reynolds' [in shorthand]) album, on either side of the follow^{g} — attempt to pay small tribute thereto." The text and the prefatory note seem to be in different handwritings. I suggest that the sonnet was composed by Woodhouse.

69. Transcript of the song beginning "Think not of it, sweet one, so." No title and signature. Dated "Ab^{t}. 11 Nov. 1817."

Transcript of the "Sonnet. On the Sea" beginning "It keeps eternal whisperings around." Dated "August 1817. Champion." The transcript differs slightly, however, from the version which was published in *The Champion.*

Transcript of the "Sonnet. On Seeing the Elgin Marbles" beginning "My spirit is too weak — Mortality." Postscript: "Examiner." No date and signature.

Transcript of the sonnet "To Haydon. — With a sonnet written on seeing the Elgin Marbles." Postscript: "Examiner." No date and signature.

70. Transcript of the poem beginning "Fill for me a brimming Bowl." No title and signature. Dated "Aug. 1814." Prefatory motto:

> "What wondrous beauty! From this mo[ment I ban]ish
> from my Mind all women. Terence's Eunuch. Act 2, S 4."

This transcript, which is possibly in the handwriting of George Keats, is the earliest extant version of this poem.

71. Transcript of the "— Song. — Tune — Julia to the Wood-Robin." Poem begins "Stay, ruby-breasted warbler, stay." Signed "J. K." with subscript in shorthand: "from Mary Frogley."

Transcript of the epigram "Written on 29 May, the anniversary of the Restoration of Charles the 2^{d}." The epigram begins "Infatuate Britons! will you still proclaim." Signed "J. K." with subscript in shorthand: "from D^{o}. [ditto]" — that is, "from Mary Frogley."

72, 73, 74, and 75. A series of manuscript leaves numbered consecutively 1, 2, 3, 4, 5, 6, 7, 10, 11, and 12, with leaves 8 and 9 missing.

72. MS. p. 1. Prefatory note: "The small pieces marked ~~K~~ F. (10 in number) were copied for my cousin into a volume of M.S. poetry, by Mr. Kirkman, and said to be by Keats.— They appear to be so from internal evidence. They must have been all written before the year 18 . Some of them are perhaps among earliest com-

positions.— They have different degrees of merit.— All are worth preserving: if merely as specimens of his powers at different times, & his Improvement.—"

MS. pp. 1–2. Transcript of the "Song. — Tune — Julia to the wood robin" beginning "Stay, ruby-breasted warbler, stay." No signature and date.

MS. pp. 2–3. Transcript of the song "To Emma" beginning "Oh! come, my dear Emma, the rose is full blown." No signature and date.

MS. p. 3. Transcript of a poem beginning "See! the ship in the bay is riding." No title, signature, and date. Note on opposite page: "This poem K. said had not been written by him. He did not see it; but I repeated the first 4 lines to him."

73. MS. pp. 4–5. Transcript of the valentine beginning "Hadst thou lived in days of old." Dated at end: "14 Feby. 1816." Prefatory note: "In page 36 of Keats's poems published in 1817 are lines, addressed 'to xxx' (Mary). — The published lines were much altered from those originally sent, which were written at the request of Geo: Keats & sent as a valentine to the Lady in question — The following is a copy of the original valentine which is now in the lady's custody — The post-brand bears date the 14 February 1816. — This was one of 3 poetical valentines written by him at the same time." There are two notes on the page opposite the second page of the transcript. Note "(a)" refers to verse 27: "This line I have corrected from the printed poem — In the original it is written 'From the which four milky plumes' & without a verb.— The mistake was probably made by G. K. in copying it out." This note proves that Miss Frogley's copy of the valentine was in George Keats's handwriting. Note "(b)" refers to verse 32: "'his trusty sword the *servant* of his might.' Spenser. f. q."

74. MS. pp. 6–7. Transcript of the poem beginning "Fill for me a brimming bowl." No title and signature. Dated at end: "Aug. 1814." Note on opposite page: "See p. 28 — where a sonnet is addressed (I believe) to the same lady who is here alluded to." Second note written under the first note: "Feby. 1819 K. this day said they both related to the same person. And see p. 64." Woodhouse refers to the sonnets *Time's sea* and *When I have fears*, which he transcribed on pages 28 and 64 of his Book of Transcripts (Houghton-Crewe Collection).

MS. p. 7. Transcript of the sonnet "On Peace" beginning "O Peace! and dost thou with thy presence bless." No signature and date.

MSS. 8 and 9 are missing; but on the reverse side of MS. 7 are two notes which refer to the sonnet which had been transcribed on MS. 8. The first note is in longhand: "This sonnet would seem to have been written on the death of some person — & probably a female — ." The second note, written under the first, is in shorthand: "Inquired of K whether it was not so/and he said he had written it on the death of his grandmother/about Feb. 2 it was [or about Feb. 27?]/but that he had never told any one before (not even his brother) the occasion upon which it was written//He said he was tenderly attached to her/ Feby 1819." I have identified and discussed this sonnet in the text. A photograph of the shorthand note is printed in the text.

74. MS. p. 10, and 75. MS. pp. 11–12. Transcript of the "Ode. To Apollo.—" beginning "In thy western Halls of gold." No signature. Dated at end: "Feby. 1815."

On the reverse side of MS. 10 there is the following note on "laurel'd peers" in stanza 4:

"(a) This expression occurs in Sonnet 1, p. 79 of the published poems.— & has there the same meaning as here.

'Many the wonders I this day have seen:
'The Sun, when first he kist away the tears
'That fill'd the eyes of Morn; — the *laurel'd peers*
'Who from the feathery gold of Evening lean; ' etc.

"The expression in the last of the above lines, has some similarity, also, to the last line but one of this ode.— 'And charm the ear of evening fair.'— Perhaps one of the two pieces was written soon after the other (the ode first) & the author, after using the expression 'laurel'd peers' in a place, where its import was easily understood, used it in another place, where it was not so clearly intelligible — & was the ode sent by him from the seaside to his Brother George, along with the Sonnet?

"There is a great degree of reality about all that Keats writes: and there must be many allusions to particular circumstances, in his poems: which would add to their beauty & interest, if properly understood — To arrest some few of these circumstances, & bring them to view in connexion with the poetic notice of them, is one of the objects of this collection — and of the observations — as it is of the notes in the interleaved copies of his published works. How valuable would such notes be to Shakespeare's Sonnets, which teem with allusions to his life, & its circumstances, his age, his loves, his patrons, etc. R. W."

On a manuscript p. 16 facing MS. p. 11 there is a transcript of the stanza which Woodhouse composed as a substitute for the third stanza of Keats's poem "In a drear-nighted December." (See number 55 above.)

MS. p. 12. Transcript of the epigram "—Lines—Written on 29 May.—the anniversary of Charles's Restoration.—on hearing the Bells ringing.—" The epigram begins "Infatuate Britons, will you still proclaim." No signature. Note on opposite page: "(a) written probably when much in company with Leigh Hunt—."

76. Transcript of a poem "To Woman.— (from the Greek)" beginning "Oh thou! by Heaven ordained to be." No signature and date. I do not believe that this poem was written by Keats.

77. Notes by Woodhouse on the sources of Keats's words and phrases.

78. Transcript of the *Grippus* fragment, which is apparently a fragment of a comedy. It is possible, as Miss Lowell argued, that this fragment was composed by Keats. Printed by Miss Lowell, Vol. II, pp. 535-544.

79. Transcript of the poem beginning "There is a joy in footing slow across a silent plain." Note at end: "Extract from J K's letter to B B dated Inverary 18 July 1818." Transcript of this extract which introduces the poem in the letter. Postscript: "K's own punctuation is adhered to."

80. First draft of the Advertisement which the publishers prefixed to the *Poems* of 1820. This indicates that Woodhouse wrote the Advertisement.

81. Transcript in shorthand of "Isabella or The Pot of Basil." This is a transcript of the autograph manuscript which is now in George Keats's Book of Autographs and Transcripts (Egerton MS. 2780, British Museum).

82. Draft of a letter by Richard Woodhouse to John Taylor (April or May of 1820). Woodhouse suggests an alteration for a passage in *Lamia* to which Taylor had objected. Keats was too ill at this time to revise his manuscripts for the press.

83. Woodhouse's list of Keats's letters to his friends.

84. "List of Mr. John Keats's Books." Apparently in the handwriting of Charles Brown. Also a list of the persons to whom Keats's books were given by Charles Brown after Keats's death.

II

A thin bound volume in which the following manuscripts are pasted:

Letter by Richard Woodhouse to his cousin Mary Frogley. Dated merely "Friday Even[g]—" (end of 1818, it is probable). A glowing defense of Keats's *Endymion* against the attacks of the reviewers. This letter has been transferred to this volume from Woodhouse's Scrap-Book.

Letter by Richard Woodhouse to John Taylor, dated "Weymouth Monday 20 Sept. 1819." Woodhouse says that he was with Keats in London on Sunday, September 12; that they argued about the sentimentality of *The Pot of Basil*, Keats censuring it and Woodhouse defending it; that Keats read *Lamia,* which he had just completed in Winchester; and that Keats read and explained alterations which he had made in *The Eve of St. Agnes.*

Page 4. Letter by John Hamilton Reynolds to John Taylor.

Page 4. An autograph manuscript of the sonnet beginning "Much have I travell'd in the Realms of gold." No title, date, and signature. Inscribed "To Mariane Reynolds—" in the handwriting of her brother John Hamilton Reynolds. Keats probably gave the manuscript to Reynolds and Reynolds gave it to his sister.

Page 5. Autograph manuscript of the sonnet beginning "As late I wander d in the happy fields." No title, signature, and date.

Page 8. Lock of Keats's hair. Note by Woodhouse: "A lock of the hair of John Keats, which I cut off at Gravesend on Sunday the Septbr 1820 on board the Maria Crowther just prior to leaving him — He was to sail for Naples for the benefit of his health on the following day —

Rd Woodhouse."

The envelope is dated "18 Sept. 1820."

Page 9. Autograph manuscript of the letter by Keats to Benjamin Robert Haydon, dated "Thursday Morning" (February 5, 1818).

Pages 13–24. A fragment of the original autograph manuscript of *The Cap and Bells.*

Page	13.	Manuscript	containing	stanzas	I–II, and XXIV and XXVII.
"	14.	"	"	"	III–IV and XXX–XXXI.
"	15.	"	"	"	V–VI and XXVIII–XXIX.
"	16.	"	"	"	VII–VIII and XXXIII–XXXVI.
"	17.	"	"	"	XVII (2) and XVIII–XXVI.
"	18.	"	"	"	XXXII and XXXVI–XXXVII.
"	19.	"	"	"	XXXVII–XLIV.
"	20.	"	"	"	LII–LIX.
"	21.	"	"	"	LX–LXIV.
"	22.	"	"	"	LXV–LXIX.
"	23.	"	"	"	LXX–LXXXI.

Page 25. Manuscript (possibly autograph) of the first draft of the song "Think not of it, sweet one, so." No title, signature, and date.

Page 26. Transcript of a sonnet beginning "The House of Mourning written by Mr Scott, —" No title, signature, and date. I have quoted and discussed this unpublished sonnet in the text. A photograph of the transcript is printed in the text of this book.

Page 27. Transcript by Richard Woodhouse of Charles Brown's "List of Mr John Keats's Books."

III

Autograph manuscripts of the following letters by Keats:

To John Taylor, January 30, 1818.

To John Taylor, February 27, 1818.

To John Taylor, April 24, 1818.

To Fanny Keats, July 2, 1818.

To George and Georgiana Keats, September 17, 1819.

To John Taylor, August 14, 1820.

To John Taylor, August 14, 1820. Second letter to Taylor on this date.

To an unknown correspondent, September 1820.

Collection of the Marquess of Crewe

(*Houghton-Crewe Collection*)

I

Original autograph manuscript of the "Ode to the Nightingale." The manuscript consists of two half sheets of note-paper: on the recto of leaf 1 are the first and second stanzas and six verses of the third stanza; on the verso of leaf 1, the sixth and seventh stanzas; on the recto of leaf 2, four verses of the third stanza and the fourth and fifth stanzas and on the verso of leaf 2, the eighth stanza. This manuscript was reproduced in photograph by Sir Sidney Colvin in *The Monthly Review* for March 1903 and in *The John Keats Memorial Volume*, 1921.

Fragment of an autograph manuscript of the first part of *Lamia*, consisting of two leaves.

The manuscript of *King Stephen*, consisting of five folio leaves in Keats's handwriting and three quarto leaves in Charles Brown's handwriting.

Fragment of the autograph manuscript of the first ode *To Fanny*, containing stanzas 2, 3, 5, 6, and 7. No date.

Autograph manuscript of *Lines written in the Highlands after a Visit to Burns's Country*. Apparently a first draft.

Transcript by Charles Brown of the sonnet *Bright star!*. Dated "1819."

Transcript of *The Fall of Hyperion, a Dream*. This transcript was made by two of Richard Woodhouse's clerks in 1833–34 (probably from Woodhouse's own transcript in his Book of Transcripts); and it was twice corrected by Woodhouse, once in pencil and once in ink. It is probably the manuscript from which Lord Houghton published the poem in 1856. It was published by Ernest de Sélincourt in 1905 together with a facsimile of the autograph manuscript of *Hyperion*.

Autograph manuscript of a letter by Keats to Benjamin Bailey, October 1817.

Autograph manuscript of a letter by Keats to Thomas Keats, July 23, 1818.

Autograph manuscript of a letter by Keats to George and Georgiana Keats, October 1818.

Autograph manuscript of the greater part of the letter by Keats to George and Georgiana Keats, February, March, and April 1819. The autograph manuscript of another part of this letter is in the Harvard College Library.

Autograph manuscript of the letter by Keats to George and Georgiana Keats, December 1818.

II

A volume "in which the late Lord Houghton bound up a quantity of the materials he had used in the preparation of the *Life and Letters*, as well as of correspondence concerning Keats addressed to him both before and after the publication of his book. The chief contents are the manuscript memoir of Keats by Charles Brown . . . ; transcripts by the same hand of a few of Keats's poems; reminiscences or brief memoirs of the poet by his friends Charles Cowden Clarke, Henry Stephens, George Felton Mathew, [Caroline Mathew], Joseph Severn, and Benjamin Bailey; together with letters from all the above, from John Hamilton Reynolds, and several others." (Sir Sidney Colvin's description of the volume.)

III

Richard Woodhouse's Commonplace Book. A commonplace book, published by Taylor and Hessey in 1811, in which Woodhouse in the midsummer of 1819 transcribed the greater part of Keats's unpublished poems. There are many corrections in the transcriptions, most in Woodhouse's handwriting but some in Taylor's and some in Keats's. The first eleven pages of the volume are missing; apparently they were cut out by Woodhouse himself, for he altered several cross references to poems on these pages. The following is a list of the transcripts in the order in which they appear in the volume.

The last thirteen verses of the song "Hence, Burgundy, Claret and Port." The fragment begins with verse 29 "As doth a Mother wild." Dated at end: "Feb. 1818."

"To J. H. R. In answer to his Robin Hood Sonnets," beginning "No, those days are gone away." Dated at end: "3 Feby. 1819" (really "1818"). Postscript: "The Sonnets in reply to which the above lines were written are on the next page."

Two sonnets by John Hamilton Reynolds on Robin Hood, the first beginning "The trees in Sherwood forest are old and good" and the second beginning "With coat of Lincoln green and mantle too." Dated "Yellow Dwarf 21 Feby. 1818."

"Lines on the Mermaid Tavern," beginning "Souls of poets dead and gone." No date.

"Sonnet written by J. H. Reynolds in a collection of M. S. poetry," beginning "Sweet poets of the gentle antique line." Dated "Feby. 1818." Postscript: "Upon this sonnet being shewn to Keats, he denied the position maintained in the 2 last lines & entered his protest against it on the opposite blank page."

The valentine beginning "Hadst thou lived in days of old." Dated at end: "14 Feby. 1816." Prefatory note: "The lines at p. 36 of Keats's printed poems are altered from a copy of verses written by K. at the request of his brother George, and by the latter sent as a valentine to the Lady.— The following is a copy of the lines as orig^{y}. written."

"To ——," beginning "Think not of it, sweet one, so." Signed "J. K." and dated "ab^{t}. 11 Nov. 1817 from K's M.S."

The sonnet beginning "Oh! how I love, on a fair Summer's eve." Signed "J. K." and dated "1816."

The sonnet beginning "As from the darkening gloom a silver dove." Signed "J. K." and dated "1816."

The sonnet beginning "After dark Vapors have oppressed our plain." Signed and dated "J. Keats Jan: 31, 1817."

"Sonnet — written on a blank space at the end of Chaucer's tale 'The flowre & the lefe'—." Signed and dated "J. K. Feby. 1817."

"Sonnet — To Keats. On reading his sonnet written in Chaucer." Signed "J. H. Reynolds" and dated "27 Feb. 1817."

"Sonnet — To a young Lady who sent me a laurel crown." Signed "J. Keats." No date.

"Sonnet — On Mrs. Reynolds' Cat." Signed "J. Keats" and dated "16 Jany. 1818."

"On sitting down to read King Lear once again." Signed "J. Keats." No date.

The sonnet beginning "Time's sea hath been five years at its slow ebb." Signed "J. Keats" and dated "4 Feby. 1818." Postscript: "See lines p. 3 probably written to the same person." I overlooked the date when I took notes on this volume, but the date has been recorded by H. B. Forman.

"Lines written upon reading a sonnet by J. H. Reynolds which will be found on p. 17." These lines (a sonnet) begin "Blue: tis the Life of Heaven — the domain." Signed and dated "J. K. 8 Feby. 1818." Reynolds' sonnet begins "Sweet poets of the gentle antique line."

"To the Nile." A sonnet. Dated and signed "Feb: 6. 1818. J. K."

"On the sea" beginning "It keeps eternal whisperings around." Signed "J. K." and dated "Champion 17 Augt. 1817."

"Lines Rhymed in a letter received (by J. H. R.) from Oxford" beginning "The Gothic looks solemn." Signed "J. K." No date.

"Song" beginning "In a drear-nighted December." Signed "J. Keats." I did not notice a date on this transcript, but H. B. Forman said that Woodhouse dated it "about October or December 1818."

"Fragment of an Ode to Apollo" beginning "God of the golden Bow." Signed "J. Keats." No date.

"Hyperion." This transcript was made by one of Woodhouse's clerks and corrected by Woodhouse in pencil. It was the manuscript, as H. B. Forman pointed out, from which the epic was printed in the *Poems* of 1820. There are stains of printer's ink in the volume, and there are remains of sealing-wax before and after the transcript of the epic, indicating that the rest of the volume was sealed up while it was at the press.

"Saint Agnes Eve." After stanza iii there is a stanza which was omitted in the printed version in the *Poems* of 1820. No date.

"Lines on visiting Staffa" beginning "Not aladdin magian." No date.

The ode beginning "Bards of passion and of mirth." Dated "26 Mar. 1819."

The sonnet beginning "When I have fears that I may cease to be." Dated "Feby. 1818."

"— Sonnet. To Homer —" beginning "Standing aloof in giant ignorance." Dated "1818."

"La belle Dame Sans Mercy" beginning "O what can ail thee, knight-at-arms." Dated "1819." Marginal note in pencil: "Vide Album for alterations."

The poem beginning "Welcome joy and welcome sorrow." Dated "1818." Prefatory inscription and motto:

"Fragment from Milton —
Under the play
Of each his faction, they to battle bring
Their embryon atoms."

"Lines on the Mermaid Tavern." No date.

The sonnet beginning "As Hermes once took to his feathers light." No date.

"Sonnet To Sleep (Irregular)" beginning "O soft embalmer, etc." Dated "1819."

"—D^{o} — on the Sonnet. — (Irregular)" beginning "If by dull rhymes, etc." Dated "1819."

"Sonnet — on Fame" beginning "Fame, like a wayward Girl, will still be coy." Dated "1819."

"Lines on seeing a lock of Milton's hair" beginning "Chief of organic numbers." Dated "21 Jany. 1818."

"Ode — To the Nightingale." Dated "May 1819."

"Isabella or The Pot of Basil." Signed "J. K." Note: "Written at Teignmouth in the spring of 1818 at the suggestion of J. H. R." Note on opposite page: "The story is taken from Boccace's Decameron. Day 4. Novel 5."

IV

Richard Woodhouse's Book of Transcripts of Keats's Poems. A large bound volume of blank pages into which Woodhouse transcribed a great number of Keats's poems. There are many notes on the poems, some of them being in shorthand; and there are corrections in pencil and in red ink. On the back of the front cover there is the following inscription: "Richd Woodhouse. Temple. Nov. 1818." The following are the contents of the volume in the order in which they appear:

"Sonnet" beginning "As from the darkening gloom a silver dove." Dated "1816."

"Sonnet" beginning "Oh! how I love, on a fair Summer's eve." Dated "1816."

"Ode — to Apollo" beginning "God of the golden Bow." No date. Note at end: "from a M. S. in Keats's writing." Note on opposite page: "As Keats & Leigh Hunt were taking their wine together after dinner at the house of the latter, the whim seized them (probably at Hunt's instigation) to crown themselves with laurel after the fashion of the elder Bards — While they were thus attired, two of Hunt's friends happened to call upon him — Just before their entrance H. removed the wreath from his own brows, and suggested to K. that he might as well do the same. K. however in his mad enthusiastic way, vowed that he would not take off his crown for any human being: and he accordingly wore it, without any explanation as long as the visit lasted —

"He mentioned the circumstance afterwards to one of his friends along with his sense of the folly (and I believe presumption) of his conduct — and he said he was determined to record it by an apologetic ode to Apollo on the occasion — He shortly after wrote this fragment."

"Song" beginning "In a drear-nighted December." Note: "from J. H. Reynolds." Dated "Dec. 1817" with subscript in shorthand: "The date from Reynolds' album."

"To——" beginning "Think not of it, sweet one, so." Dated "Ab^{t}. 11 Nov. 1817." Note: "from J. K.'s M. S."

"Sonnet" beginning "After dark vapours have oppressed our plain." Dated "31 Jany. 1817." Note: "from J. H. R." In another note, referring to the last phrase in the sonnet "a Poet's death," Woodhouse cites the death of Pope "as related in Spence & in *Edn. Rev.*, May 1820, p. 330."

"Sonnet. To a young Lady who sent me a laurel crown." No date. Note: "from J. K.'s — M. S."

"Sonnet. Written on the blank space of a leaf at the end of Chaucer's tale of 'The flowre and the lefe.'" Dated "Feby. 1817."

"Sonnet — to Keats. On reading his sonnet written in Chaucer —." Signed "J. H. Reynolds" and dated "27 Feb: 1817."

"Sonnet. On seeing the Elgin Marbles. 1st" beginning "My spirit is too weak! Mortality." No date. Note on opposite page: "This sonnet was written at the Instigation of B. R. Haydon, the painter, who accompanied K. to see them — and who was one of the first to discover, & who was indefatigable in proclaiming, their unrivalled excellence.— etc."

"Sonnet To B. R. Haydon — with the foregoing Sonnet on the Elgin Marbles" beginning "Haydon! forgive, etc." No date.

"Sonnet" beginning "Sweet poets of the gentle antique line." Signed "J. H. R." and dated "Feby. 1818."

"Answer. J. Keats." Sonnet beginning "Blue: tis the Life of Heaven — the domain." Dated "8 Feby. 1818."

"Sonnet on Mrs. Reynolds' Cat." Dated "16 Jany. 1818."

"Sonnet. On sitting down to read 'King Lear' once again." Dated in red ink: "22 Jany. 1818. C. B."

"Sonnet on the Sea" beginning "It keeps eternal whisperings, etc." Dated "Aug. 1817 Champion."

"Sonnet To the Nile." Dated "Feb: 6. 1818." Note: "from J. K.'s M. S."

"To ——." A sonnet beginning "Time's sea hath, etc." Dated "Feby. 1818." Note on opposite page: "See p. ~~6~~ 222 — where lines are inserted alluding to the same lady to whom this is addressed. See also p. 64." The lines on page 222 are "Fill for me a brimming bowl" and the poem on page 64 is the sonnet "When I have fears." This sonnet "Time's sea" is on page 28 of this volume of transcripts.

"Lines —— Rhymed in a letter to J. H. R. from Oxford" beginning "The Gothic looks solemn." Dated in pencil: "Mid. 1818."

"The Pot of Basil." Note at end of transcript: "Written at Teignmouth in the Spring of 1818 on the suggestion of J. H. R." Note on opposite page: "The old translation from which Keats took the Poem will be found at page 191." See below.

The poem beginning "Hence Burgundy Claret & Port." Dated "Feby. 1818."

"To John H. Reynolds In answer to his Robin Hood Sonnets" beginning "No, those days are gone away." Dated in red ink: "3 Feby. 1818." Quotation from Keats's letter to Reynolds: "I hope you will like them, they are at least written in the spirit of outlawry."

"Lines on the Mermaid Tavern." No date.

"Lines on visiting Staffa" beginning "Not Aladdin magian." No date.

The sonnet beginning "When I have fears that I may cease to be." Dated "From J. K.'s letter to W. H. R. [*sic*] 31 Jany. 1818." Page 64 of this volume of transcripts.

"To J. H. Reynolds Esq." The poetic epistle beginning "Dear Reynolds, as last night I lay in bed." In the prose part of the epistle Woodhouse transcribed one sentence, the next to the last, in shorthand. Signed "John Keats" and dated "Teignmouth 25 Mar. 1818."

"Ode" beginning "Bards of passion and of mirth." Note at end: "from J. H. R. 26 Mar. 1819."

Sonnet beginning "As Hermes once took to his feathers light." Dated "April 1819." On the opposite page Woodhouse quotes the source in Cary's *Dante*.

"Ode. To Psyche" beginning "O Goddess! hear these tuneless numbers, wrung." Note at end: "Given by J. K. to J. H. R. 4 May 1819."

The *ex tempore* lines beginning "And what is Love? — It is a doll dress'd up." Signed "J. K." and dated "C. B. 1819."

"La belle dame sans Mercy." Signed "J. K." and dated "C. B. 1819." On the opposite page Woodhouse wrote a note on Chaucer's translation of a French poem which has the same title.

"Sonnet. To Homer" beginning "Standing aloof, etc." Signed "J. K." and dated "C. B. 1818."

"Hyperion." Note at end: "The copy from which I took the above was the original & only copy. The alterations are noted in the margin — With the exception of them, it was completed and written down at once as it now stands." Note: "Copied 20 Ap^{l}. 1819 from J. K.'s manuscript written in 1818/9."

"Saint Agnes' Eve." Signed "J. K." Note: "Copied from J. K.'s rough M. S. 20 Ap. 1819. Written about the latter end of 1818 & the beginning of 1819." Note on opposite page: "This copy was taken from K's original M. S. He afterwards altered it for publication, & added some stanzas & omitted others. His alterations are noticed here. The published copy differs from both in a few particulars. K. left it to his Publishers to adopt which they pleased & to revise the whole." After stanza three in this transcript there is a stanza which was omitted in the published version.

"The Eve of Saint Mark.—" After the verses "Exalt amid the tapers shine At Venice x x x x" there is a space, and then there are 16 verses in Middle English beginning "Gif ye wol stonden, hardie wight." Note on opposite page: "Copied from J. K.'s M. S." Dated "Written 13/17 Feby. 1819. R. W."

"Song" beginning "Hush, hush! tread softly, etc." Dated "1818." Note: "from C.B."

"Ode to May — Fragment" beginning "Mother of Hermes, etc." Dated "1 May 1818."

The poem beginning "Welcome Joy, and welcome sorrow." Signed "J. K." and dated "C. B. 1818." Prefatory inscription:

"Fragment from Milton —
Under the play
Of each his faction, they to battle bring
Their embryon atoms."

"Fragment of *Castle-builder*." Signed "J. K." and dated "C. B. 1818."

"Extract — from an opera.—" beginning "O were I one of the Olympian twelve." No date.

"Daisy's Song." No date.

"Extracts from an opera continued —." Signed "J. K." and dated "C. B. 1818."

The sonnet beginning "Nature withheld Cassandra in the skies." Dated "Sept/Dec 1818." On the opposite page Woodhouse copied Ronsard's sonnet of which Keats's is a free translation. This transcript of Keats's sonnet, like all other transcripts, ends with the twelfth verse.

"To Autumn." Note at end of the transcript of the ode: "The alterations in C. B.'s copy are mark'd in red ink."

The sonnet beginning "Spenser, a jealous honourer of thine." Signed and dated "J. K. Feb: 5." Note: "fr.[om] J. K.'s M. S."

"Ode — on Melancholy —." Dated "1819." Note: "from C. B."

"Ode — on Indolence —." Dated "1819." Note: "from C. B."

"Character of C. B. 1819 —" beginning "He is to weet a melancholy carle." Signed "J. K." and dated "1819. C. B."

"Sonnet. To Sleep." Signed "J. K." and dated "C. B. 1819." Note: "The word 'lulling' is in K.'s handwriting. The correction was made when He borrowed this book to select a small poem to write in an album, intended to consist of original poetry, for a lady." "Lulling" is substituted for "dewy."

"Sonnet on Fame" beginning "Fame, like a wayward girl, etc." Signed "J. K." and dated "C. B. 1819."

"Sonnet. To Fame" beginning "How fever'd is the man, etc." Signed "J. K." and dated "C. B. 1819."

"Sonnet.— (Irregular)" beginning "If by dull rhymes, etc." Signed "J. K." and dated "C. B. 1819."

"On seeing a lock of Milton's hair." Signed "J. K." and dated "21 Jany. 1818. C. B."

"Ode. To a Nightingale —." Signed "J. K." and dated "C. B. May 1819."

"Song of four Fairies." Signed "J. K." and dated "C. B. 1819." Note: "Corrected by Keats's copy for the press."

"The Fall of Hyperion — A Dream —." No date. This transcript by Woodhouse is the authoritative text of the poem, since the autograph manuscript is lost and since the other transcripts were made by two of Woodhouse's clerks (probably from Woodhouse's transcript).

"Ode. To Fancy." Dated "1818." Note: "from C. B."

"Song" beginning "I had a Dove, etc." Dated "1818." Note: "from C. B."

"Fragment" beginning "Where's the Poet? etc." Dated "1818." Note: "from C. B."

"Ode. On a Grecian Urn." Dated "1819." Note: "from C. B."

Page 190 of this volume of transcripts. Note: "The following is the translation of Boccaccio's tale of Isabella, from which Keats took his poem (p. 30). It is extracted from 'The Novels & Plays of the renowned John Boccaccio, the first refiner of Italian Prose: containing a hundred curious novels by 7 honorable ladies & 3 noble gentlemen etc. The 5th edn. London. Printed for Awnsham Churchill, at the Black Swan at Amen Corner. MDCLXXXIV.'" On pages 190–191 Woodhouse transcribed passages from this translation of Boccaccio's *Pot of Basil*.

"On a Leander, which a young lady (Miss Reynolds [in shorthand]) gave the author." Signed "J. K." and dated "Mar. 1816." Note: "I believe it was once Keats's intention to write a series of M. S. sonnets & short poems on some of Tassie's gems."

"Apollo to the Graces." Subtitle: "Written to the tune of the air in Don Giovanni." Note: "From the orig^l. in Miss Reynolds' possession."

"Stanzas" beginning "You say you love; but with a voice." Note in shorthand: "from Miss Reynolds and Mrs. Jones."

"The jealousies / A faery Tale / by / Lucy Vaughan Lloyd / of / Chin a walk, Lambeth." No date.

The sonnet beginning "The day is gone, and all its sweets are gone." No date.

The poem beginning "There is a joy in footing slow across a silent plain." Note: "Copied from K's letter: — I have adhered to his own punctuation throughout." On the opposite page Woodhouse copied that part of Keats's letter to Benjamin Bailey (Inverary, July 18, 1818) which introduces the poem.

The sonnet beginning "Four Seasons fill the Measure of the year." Note with date: "Sept. 1818 — transcribed from K's letter to B. B."

"Sonnet. To Chatterton." Signed "J. K." and dated "1815."

"Sonnet. To Lord Byron." Dated "Decr. 1814."

" To J. R." The sonnet begins "O that a week could be an age, and we." No date.

"— Song — Tune Julia to the Wood-Robin" beginning "Stay, ruby breasted warbler, stay." No signature and date.

"To *Emma* (Mathews [in shorthand])." The song begins "O come my dear Emma, etc." The letter " F " is written at the foot of the transcript. Note on opposite page: "This Song was written off in a few minutes at the request of some ladies who wished for words to sing to this tune — the Misses Reynolds [in shorthand]."

"On Peace." The sonnet begins "O Peace! and dost thou with thy presence bless." The letter "F" is written on the lower left corner of the page. We learn from Woodhouse's Scrap-book that the letter "F" means that he obtained the poem from Mary Frogley.

"Ode. To Apollo.—" beginning "In thy western halls of gold." Dated "Feby. 1815." The letter " F " is written at the foot of the transcript. Note on "laurel'd peers" in stanza 4: "The expression occurs in Sonnet 1, of the Poems of K. publ^d. by Olliers. It has there the same meaning as here. — Keats told me so, when I enquired of him what he intended, long before I had seen this ode.

'Many the wonders I this day have seen:—
The sun, when first he kiss'd away the tears
That fill'd the eyes of morn: the *laurel'd peers*
Who from the feathery gold of Evening lean, etc.'

"The expression in this last line has also some similarity to the last but one of this ode, 'And charm the ear of evening fair'— The two pieces were probably written near about the same time — and the ode first. And the author, after using the expression in a place where its import was plain, used it afterwards, as a known term, in a place where its meaning was scarcely intelligible."

The poem beginning "Fill for me a brimming bowl." Dated "August 1814." The letter "F" is written on the lower left corner of the page. Note: "At p. 28 will be found a sonnet alluding to the same lady — Keats mentioned the circumstances of obtaining a casual sight of her at Vauxhall, in answer to my inquiry — Feby. 1819. See also p. 64." The sonnet on page 28 is "Time's sea" and the sonnet on page 64 is "When I have fears." This poem "Fill for me a brimming bowl" is on page 222, to which it had been transferred from page 6.

"To x x x x" beginning "Hadst thou liv'd in days of old." Dated "14 Feby. 1816." The letter "F" is written at the foot of the transcript. Note: "These lines were written by K. at his Brother George's request & sent as a valentine to a lady (Miss Frogley [in shorthand]) from whose copy I have transcribed them. They were afterwards altered for Publication — and will be found with the variations at p. 36 of the first volume of Poems he published. There were three valentines written by him on that same occasion." There are two notes on the text. Note "(a)" refers to verse 27: "I have corrected this line from the printed Copy— It is miscopied in the original, 'O'er the which four milky plumes' — without any verb —." Note "(b)" refers to verse 32: " 'His trusty sword the *servant* of his might.' Spenser. f. q."

"Contents of this volume." A table of contents.

Textual notes on "Endymion." Woodhouse compares the original autograph manuscript with the printed text, giving copious variant readings from the manuscript.

V

Richard Woodhouse's Book of Transcripts of Keats's Letters. A bound volume into which Woodhouse transcribed a number of letters written by Keats to John Taylor, John Hamilton Reynolds and his sisters, James Rice, Benjamin Bailey, and Richard Woodhouse. The original manuscripts of many of these letters are in a volume in the Harvard College Library. The original manuscripts of some of the letters are lost, and these letters are known only in Woodhouse's transcripts.

Transcripts by John Jeffrey (Georgiana Keats's second husband) of letters written by Keats to George and Georgiana Keats in Kentucky. These transcripts are very imperfect, with many omissions and alterations. Most of the original manuscripts have been discovered, but a few are still missing.

Harvard College Library Collection

Comprising the Collection of the late Miss Amy Lowell

I

The original autograph manuscript of *The Eve of St. Agnes*, consisting of five leaves (8 x 10½ inches) of very thin paper. "I took down [to Bedhampton and Chichester]," Keats wrote his brother George on February 14, 1819, "some thin paper and wrote on it a little poem call'd St. Agnes' Eve. . . ." The stanzas are written in double columns on both sides of the leaves. The first seven stanzas, which are missing in the manuscript, are supplied in another hand on heavier paper. The manuscript has numerous alterations and corrections. There is a signed attestation of the manuscript by Joseph Severn. The signature of Frederick Locker-Lampson, dated 1881, is written on the first leaf. And there is a typewritten note by Miss Lowell concerning the manuscript.

An autograph manuscript (either first or second draft) of the sonnet "On the first looking into Chapman's Homer." The manuscript is a single leaf (small quarto). The rhymes of the two quatrains of the sonnet are connected by marginal lines. On the verso of the leaf is another manuscript: "Burns's Letters." At the bottom of the page is the signature of Frederick Locker dated 1841.

Original autograph manuscript of the ode "To Autumn." The manuscript, which consists of two quarto leaves, has many alterations and corrections. Note in the manuscript: "Presented to Miss A. Barker by the author's Brother, Sun. Nov. 15, 1839. Given to my Granddaughter Elizabeth Ward, May 14th, '96. Anna H. B. Ward." (The note is in Mrs. Ward's handwriting.)

Original autograph manuscript of the poetic *Epistle to my Brother George.* It was sent as a letter to George Keats and dated "Margate Aug^{t}. . . ." A corner of the manuscript has been torn off and with it the precise date and one or two words of the introductory prose.

A fragment of the original autograph manuscript of the poem beginning "I stood tip-toe upon a little hill," containing verses 38–48 on one side of the sheet and verses 53–64 on the other side. This fragment was given by Charles Cowden Clarke to James T. Fields, the Boston publisher.

An autograph manuscript of verses 97–182 of the poem beginning "I stood tip-toe upon a little hill." Note by Benjamin Robert Haydon: "Given me by my Dear Friend Keats. B. R. Haydon. Original manuscript of part of his first volume." The signature of Frederick Locker is at the foot of page 2 of the manuscript.

A fragment of an autograph manuscript of *Isabella; or, The Pot of Basil.* The manuscript is a quarto leaf of two pages. With a manuscript of one page of blue paper containing an essay on "John Keats" by Algernon Charles Swinburne, with Swinburne's name at the end in pencil in another handwriting.

A fragment (consisting of six pages) of the original autograph manuscript of *The Cap and Bells*, containing stanzas 13–16 and 46–51. Eight blank verses, beginning "This living hand, now warm and capable," are written upside down on the page after stanza 51. A typewritten transcript of these verses is laid in. A larger fragment of the original autograph manuscript of *The Cap and Bells* is in the Pierpont Morgan Library.

Leigh Hunt's Note-book, containing the original autograph manuscript of the first seventeen verses of the *Lines on seeing a Lock of Milton's Hair.* These verses are written on two pages in the note-book between pages containing Hunt's poem *Hero and Leander*.

A fragment of an autograph manuscript of *Otho the Great.* The fragment is an oblong quarto page containing 11 verses. Mounted for framing. On the verso is Frederick Locker's endorsement, dated June 1881.

An autograph manuscript of the "Chorus of Fairies."

II

A volume of autograph manuscripts of letters written by John Keats to John Taylor, Benjamin Bailey, Miss Reynolds, James Augustus Hessey, James Rice, and Richard Woodhouse. With John Taylor's memorandum of Richard Abbey's recollections of the Keats family. The title, half-title, and contents of the volume are printed. The collection was bequeathed by Richard Woodhouse to John Taylor, and on Taylor's death it passed into the possession of his niece, who sold it at auction; it was bought by a London bookseller, from whom Miss Lowell purchased it.

Autograph manuscript of John Taylor's memorandum of Richard Abbey's recollections of the Keats family. Dated "Waterloo Place 20 April 1827" and addressed with letter to "Richd Woodhouse Esq. King's Bench Walk Temple." Postscript dated "April 23 1827," and postmark dated "Noon 24 Ap 1827." The manuscript consists of 13 pages.

Autograph manuscripts of the following letters by Keats:

To George Keats, August 1816. This letter, which contains the poetic epistle to George Keats, is also listed above.

To Charles Cowden Clarke, December 17, 1816.

To Taylor and Hessey, April 1817.

To Taylor and Hessey, May 16, 1817.

To Taylor and Hessey, June 10, 1817.

To Jane Reynolds, September 14, 1817.

To Benjamin Bailey, October 8, 1817.

To Benjamin Bailey, November 5, 1817. Only the second half of this letter. The first half is in the possession of Mrs. James B. Murphy of New York.

To Benjamin Bailey, November 22, 1817.

To Benjamin Bailey, January 23, 1818.

To John Taylor, February 5, 1818.

To Benjamin Bailey, March 13, 1818.

To James Rice, March 24, 1818.

To Benjamin Bailey, May 28, 1818.

To Benjamin Bailey, June 10, 1818.

To John Taylor, June 21, 1818.

To George Keats, June 27, 1818.

To Benjamin Bailey, July 18, 1818.

To Jane Reynolds, September 1, 1818.

To Richard Woodhouse, October 27, 1818.

To James Rice, November 24, 1818.

To Richard Woodhouse, December 18, 1818.

To John Taylor, December 24, 1818.

To Joseph Severn, March 29, 1819.

To Fanny Keats, April 17, 1819.

To George and Georgiana Keats in February, March, and April 1819 (two pages). This fragment begins at (March) "17 — Wednesday —" and ends with "but as I am." The greater part of the autograph manuscript is in the possession of the Marquess of Crewe.

To Benjamin Bailey, August 14, 1819.

To Fanny Brawne, August 16, 1819.

To John Taylor, August 24, 1819.

To John Taylor, September 1, 1819.

To James Augustus Hessey, September 5, 1819.

To John Taylor, September 5, 1819.

To Richard Woodhouse, September 21, 1819.

To Joseph Severn, October 1819.

To Joseph Severn, December 6, 1819.

To James Rice, December 1819.

To Fanny Brawne, May 1820.

To John Taylor, June 11, 1820.

To Fanny Brawne, July 1820.

To Charles Brown, September 28, 1820.

Autograph manuscript of the notice written by Keats for John Taylor as an excuse to callers for absence.

III

Autograph manuscript of the letter by Percy Bysshe Shelley to Keats, "Pisa 27 July, 1820."

Autograph manuscript of Richard Woodhouse's notes on Keats's method of composing poetry. Manuscript consists of two sheets of paper.

Autograph manuscript of a letter by Benjamin Robert Haydon to an unnamed correspondent, "London Nov 29th 1845," telling the story of his introduction of Keats to Wordsworth. The unnamed correspondent, I believe, was Edward Moxon, publisher of *The Life, Letters and Literary Remains of John Keats*, the author of which was Richard Monckton Milnes (Lord Houghton). See the two letters by Haydon to Moxon in the Bemis Collection below.

Autograph manuscript of a letter by Tom Keats to John Taylor, June 1818.

Autograph manuscript of a letter by Tom Keats to John Taylor, June 30, 1818.

Autograph manuscript of a letter by George Keats to Keats, June 18, 1820.

Transcript of a letter by George Keats to Keats at Teignmouth in 1818.

Autograph manuscript of a letter by George Keats to John Taylor, June 1818. Written from 29 Brunswick Square.

Autograph manuscript of letter by George Keats to Charles Wentworth Dilke, 1824.

Autograph manuscript of a letter by George Keats to Charles Wentworth Dilke, 1825.

Autograph manuscript of a letter by George Keats to Charles Wentworth Dilke, April 29, 1825.

Autograph manuscript of a letter by George Keats to Charles Wentworth Dilke, April 1828.

Autograph manuscript of a letter by George Keats to Charles Wentworth Dilke, 1830.

Autograph manuscript of a letter by Richard Woodhouse to Keats, October 21, 1818.

Autograph manuscript of a letter by Richard Woodhouse to Keats, September 16, 1820.

Autograph manuscript of a letter by Charles Brown to Richard Woodhouse, December 1, 1818.

Autograph manuscript of a letter by John Taylor to Richard Woodhouse, September 25, 1819.

Autograph manuscript of a letter by John Taylor to Michael Drury, February 19, 1821.

Autograph manuscript of a letter by John Taylor to George Keats, February 17, 1821.

Contemporary transcript of a letter by Joseph Severn to William Haslam, September 17, 1820.

Contemporary transcript of a letter by Joseph Severn to Mrs. Brawne, January 11, 1821.

Contemporary transcript of a letter by Joseph Severn to William Haslam, January 15, 1821.

Autograph manuscript of a letter by Joseph Severn to John Taylor, January 25, 1821.

Autograph manuscript of a letter by Joseph Severn to John Taylor, written shortly after Keats's death.

Contemporary transcript of a letter by Joseph Severn to Charles Brown, December 14, 1820.

Autograph manuscript of a letter by Dr. James Clark to a Mr. Gray, January 13, 1821. Dr. Clark was Keats's physician in Rome.

Contemporary transcript of an "Extract of a letter from Dr. Clark," dated "Rome Nov. 27 1820."

Contemporary transcript of an "Extract of a letter from Dr. Clark," dated "Rome, Jan. 3," 1821.

Autograph manuscript of a letter by John Aitkin to Keats.

IV

A copy of the *Poems* of 1817, presented by Keats to the Misses Reynolds.

A copy of the *Poems* of 1817, presented by Keats to George Keats.

A copy of the *Poems* of 1820, presented by Keats to Fanny Brawne. Inscribed "F. B. from J. K."

A copy of the *Poems* of 1820, presented by Keats to B. Davenport, Esq. This copy has Keats's famous denial of the Advertisement. The page of the Advertisement is reproduced in photograph by Miss Lowell, Vol. II, between pages 424 and 425.

V

A copy of Leigh Hunt's *Foliage*, presented by Hunt to Keats. Given by Keats to Fanny Brawne.

Keats's copy of the first volume of *The Works of Mr. Edmund Spenser*, in six volumes, published by Mr. Hughes. London: Printed for Jacob Tonson. 1715. This volume, which contains the first canto of *The Faerie Queene*, is copiously marked and underscored by Keats.

Keats's copy of William Hazlitt's *Characters of Shakespear's Plays*. Published by C. and J. Ollier. London, 1817. This volume is marked and annotated by Keats.

Keats's copy of Z. Jackson's *Shakespeare's Genius Justified: Being Restorations and Illustrations of Seven Hundred Passages in Shakespeare's Plays*. London, 1819. A few markings and annotations by Keats.

Keats's copy of John Selden's *Titles of Honor*. The third Edition Carefully Corrected. London, 1672. On the title page, in Keats's handwriting, is the inscription: "John Keats. 1819." Keats began but did not complete an index of titles on the flyleaf.

A silver medal won by Keats in the Clarke School in 1810.

British Museum Collection

I

The autograph manuscript of *Hyperion*. Twenty-seven sheets of paper ($15\frac{3}{4}$ x $9\frac{1}{8}$ inches). The verses are written on the recto side of the sheets with a few revised passages written on the reverse sides. The manuscript, owned in succession by Leigh Hunt, Thornton Hunt, and Miss Bird, was acquired by the British Museum in 1904. It was published in photograph by Ernest de Sélincourt in 1905.

The Poetical Works of Geoffrey Chaucer. Edinburgh, 1782. Fourteen volumes bound in 7. Volume XII contains the autograph of the sonnet beginning "This pleasant Tale is like a little copse," written on a blank space at the end of "The Floure and the Leafe." The sonnet is signed and dated: "J. K. Feby 1817.—"

II

George Keats's Book of Autographs and transcripts of Keats's Poems (MS. Eg. 2780). At the top of the first page of the manuscripts is the signature and date: "George Keats 1820." H. B. Forman suggested that in January 1820, when George Keats was visiting Keats in London, he got together all he could of Keats's unpublished poems, taking such autograph manuscripts as were available and making transcripts of other manuscripts; and that, on his return to Kentucky, he had these autographs and transcripts bound together in a binding of strong brown leather. The following is a list of the contents in the order in which they are bound in the volume.

Autograph manuscript. "The Pot of Basil. 1818." The date, written after the title, is in the handwriting of George Keats.

Autograph manuscript. "Ode. 1818." Poem begins "Souls of Poets, dead and gone."

Transcript. "Song. 1818." The first sixteen verses of the poem beginning "Hence Burgundy, Claret, and Port."

Transcript. "Saint Agnes Eve. 1819." The first four stanzas.

Autograph manuscript. "The Eve of Saint Mark. 1819." The date, written after the title, is in the handwriting of George Keats.

Transcript. The remaining stanzas of "Saint Agnes Eve," stanzas 5 to the end.

Transcript. "Ode on Melancholy. 1819."

Transcript. "Ode to the Nightingale. 1819."

Transcript. "Ode on a Grecian Urn. 1819."

Newspaper clipping. "Sonnet, on the Death of the Poet Keats."

Transcript. "Fragment. 1818." Poem begins "Welcome joy and welcome sorrow."

Transcript. "Fragment. 1818." Poem begins "Where's the Poet? Show him! show him!"

Transcript. "To Autumn. 1819."

Transcript. "To John Reynolds in answer to his Sonnets on Robin Hood. 1818." Poem begins "No, those days are gone away."

Transcript. "Lines on seeing a Portrait of Keats. By the author of L'Improvisatrice. L. E. L. 1824."

Transcript. The first three stanzas of Shelley's *Adonais*.

Transcript. "Sonnet by Mrs. Norton 1840."

Transcript. "Lines written in the Scotch Highlands."

"To Miss Keats of Louisville Ky." A poem composed by an "unknown Bard."

III

Autograph manuscripts of the following letters by Keats:

To Fanny Keats, September 10, 1817.
To Benjamin Robert Haydon, January 23, 1818.
To Fanny Keats, August 18, 1818.
To Fanny Keats, August 25, 1818.
To Fanny Keats, October 9, 1818.
To Fanny Keats, October 16, 1818.
To Fanny Keats, October 26, 1818.
To Fanny Keats, November 5, 1818.
To Fanny Keats, December 1, 1818.
To Fanny Keats, December 31, 1818.
To Fanny Keats, January 1819.
To Fanny Keats, February 1819.
To Fanny Keats, February 27, 1819.
To Fanny Keats, March 13, 1819.
To Fanny Keats, March 24, 1819.
To Fanny Keats, April 13, 1819.
To Fanny Keats, May 13, 1819.
To Fanny Keats, May 26, 1819.
To Fanny Keats, June 9, 1819.
To James Elmes, June 12, 1819.
To Fanny Keats, June 14, 1819.
To Fanny Keats, June 16, 1819.

To Fanny Keats, July 6, 1819.
To Fanny Keats, August 28, 1819.
To Fanny Keats, October 16, 1819.
To Fanny Keats, November 17, 1819.
To Fanny Keats, December 20, 1819.
To Fanny Keats, December 22, 1819.
To Fanny Keats, February 7, 1820.
To Fanny Keats, February 11, 1820.
To Fanny Keats, February 14, 1820.
To Fanny Keats, February 19, 1820.
To Fanny Keats, February 24, 1820.
To Fanny Keats, March 20, 1820.
To Fanny Keats, April 1820.
To Fanny Keats, April 1, 1820.
To Fanny Keats, April 12, 1820.
To Fanny Keats, April 21, 1820.
To Fanny Keats, May 4, 1820.
To Fanny Keats, June 23, 1820.
To Fanny Keats, July 6, 1820.
To Fanny Keats, July 22, 1820.
To Fanny Keats, August 14, 1820.
To Fanny Keats, August 23, 1820.

Dilke Collection

In the Keats Memorial House and in the Hampstead Public Library

I

Keats's copy of the facsimile reprint (in 1808) of the First Folio Edition of Shakespeare's Works. The title page has the autograph signature of Keats dated 1817; and underneath the signature is the inscription "to F. B." Keats gave the volume, it is probable, to Fanny Brawne when he was preparing to go to Italy. There are very interesting annotations in Keats's handwriting: one on *A Midsummer Night's Dream,* five on *Troylus and Cressida,* and three on *King Lear.* The markings and underlinings are confined to five plays. There are two poems in the volume written in Keats's handwriting: the ode *On seeing a Lock of Milton's Hair* and the sonnet *On sitting down to read King Lear once again.* The sonnet, which has no signature, is dated "Jan^{y} — 22 — 1818."

Keats's copy of *The Poetical Works of William Shakespeare,* royal octavo, 1806. An inscription on the title page says that the volume was presented to Keats by John Hamilton Reynolds in 1819; and a note on the fly-leaf facing the title indicates that the volume was given by Keats to Joseph Severn in 1820. There is an autograph of the sonnet "Bright Star, would I were stedfast as thou art" on a blank page opposite *The Lover's Complaint.* There is also an autograph of Reynolds' sonnet "I have no chill despondence that I am" (the *Farewell to the Muses*), signed "J H R" and dated "14 Feby. 1818." At the end of the volume is the autograph of the sonnet "I fear'd to gaze upon her in the day," signed with Severn's initials.

Keats's copy of Milton's *Paradise Lost,* 2 vols. Edinburgh, 1807. Inscription on the title page: "Mrs. Dilke, from her sincere friend J. Keats." There are numerous markings, underscorings, and annotations in Keats's handwriting. On the fly-leaf of Volume II is the autograph first draft of the sonnet *To Sleep.*

Keats's copy of *The Literary Pocket-Book* for 1819, edited by Leigh Hunt and published by C. and J. Ollier. Inscription on the fly-leaf: "John Keats, from his friend Leigh Hunt." Above the inscription, "F. B." is written in pencil. On the first two pages of the diary there is the autograph of the "Song" beginning "Hush, hush, tread softly, hush, hush, my dear." In the diary, also, are entries of birthdays, notably those of Fanny Brawne, Tom Keats, Handel, and Haydn.

Keats's copy of Volumes II, III, and IV of *The Dramatic Works* of Ben Jonson and Beaumont and Fletcher, 1811. Inscription on the title-page of Volume II: "George Keats to his affectionate brother John." On the blank page facing the comedy by Beaumont and Fletcher, *The Fair Maid of the Inn*, there is the autograph first draft of the ode "Bards of passion and of mirth."

A photograph of an autograph manuscript of a poem beginning "Yes! I shall live — the breath of Fame." Undated. The poem was an *ex tempore* trifle, written by Keats evidently in the album or commonplace book of a lady.

II

A copy of *Endymion*, having a number of blank pages bound in at the end of the volume, on which are transcribed seventeen lyric poems which Keats composed in 1818 and 1819. On a blank page at the beginning of the volume is the inscription: "Keats' own copy, with his shorter poems in his own hand. Charles W. Dilke." On a blank page opposite the "Lines on seeing a lock of Milton's hair" is a note in Dilke's handwriting: "It should be remember'd that Keats was wholly innocent of spelling." After the transcripts of the lyric poems there is a short memoir of Keats in Dilke's handwriting. Most scholars, including Sir Sidney Colvin and H. B. Forman, have expressed their belief that these lyric poems are not transcribed in Keats's handwriting. The following is a list of the lyric poems:

"Sonnet" beginning "When I have fears, etc." Dated at end "1817.—"

"Sonnet.— To Homer" beginning "Standing aloof in giant ignorance." Dated "1818."

"Sonnet" beginning "If by dull rhymes our English must be chain'd." Dated "1819."

"Sonnet. On a Dream" beginning "As Hermes once took to his feathers light." Dated "1819."

"Sonnet. To Sleep" beginning "O soft embalmer of the still midnight." Dated "1819.—"

"Sonnet. On sitting down to read King Lear once again" beginning "O golden tongued Romance, with serene Lute!" Dated "22 Jany 1818. —"

"Sonnet. On Fame" beginning "Fame, like a wayward Girl, will still be coy." Dated "1819.—"

"Sonnet. On Fame" beginning "How fever'd is the Man, who cannot look." Dated "1819."

"Sonnet. To the Nile" beginning "Son of the old moon-mountains African!" Dated "1818.—"

"Lines on seeing a lock of Milton's hair." Dated "21 Jany 1818."

Poem beginning "Souls of Poets dead and gone." Dated "1818."

"Lines written in the Highlands after a visit to Burns' country. — 1818."

Poem beginning "Ever let the fancy roam." Dated "1818."

"Ode to the Nightingale." Dated "May 1819."

"Ode on a Grecian Urn." Dated "1819.—"

"To John Reynolds, in answer to his Robin Hood sonnets" beginning "No those days are gone away." Dated "1818."

"Song" beginning "Hush, hush! tread softly! etc." No date.

Dilke's short memoir of Keats, written on the pages after the transcripts of the lyric poems.

III

Autograph manuscripts of the following letters by Keats:

To C. W. Dilke, November 1817.
To Tom Keats, July 17, 1818.
To C. W. Dilke, September 21, 1818.
To C. W. Dilke, January 24, 1819.
To C. W. Dilke, July 31, 1819.
To C. W. Dilke, September 22, 1819.
To C. W. Dilke, October 1, 1819.
To C. W. Dilke, March 4, 1820.
To C. W. Dilke, May 1820.
To Fanny Brawne, May 1820.
To Mrs. Brawne, October 24, 1820.

IV

Autograph manuscript of letter by Tom Keats to C. W. Dilke, "Tuesday morning" (probably in June or July 1818).

Autograph manuscript of letter by C. and J. Ollier to George Keats, April 29, 1817. The publishers say that they regret that they published Keats's poems.

Autograph manuscript of letter by Charles Brown to C. W. Dilke, from Inverness, August 17, 1818.

Autograph manuscript of letter by Bryan Waller Procter to Keats. Undated (probably February 1820).

Fragment of an autograph manuscript of a letter by Leigh Hunt to Keats, addressed from Mortimer Terrace. Undated (but about August 1820).

Autograph manuscript of letter by Charles Brown to Fanny Brawne, Florence, December 17, 1829.

Autograph manuscript of letter by Georgiana Keats to Mrs. C. W. Dilke. From Louisville, Kentucky. Undated.

Transcript of part of letter by George Keats to H. B. Wylie. Dated Louisville, November 26, 1836.

Autograph manuscript of letter by Henry R. Wylie to C. W. Dilke (enclosing the transcript above), February 15, 1837.

Autograph manuscript of letter by Joseph Severn to C. W. Dilke, February 3, 1859.

Fragment of an autograph manuscript of letter by Major C. Brown of Taranaki, New Zealand, to Sir C. W. Dilke, Bart., M.P.

V

Keats's copy of Ovid's *Metamorphosis*. Publii Ovidii Nasonis Metamorphoseon Libri xv. Interpretatione et notis Illustravit Daniel Crispinus Helvetius ad usum Serenissimi Delphini. London, 1806. On the front cover is the signature with date: "John Keats emer: 1812." The signature is not in Keats's handwriting.

Keats's copy of Bacon's *Advancement of Learning*. The volume has many annotations (of no importance) in Keats's handwriting, made when he was a boy in the Clarke School.

Keats's French Grammar. Inscribed on back of front cover: "Jno. Keats May 19th 1807."

Keats's copy of Lempriere's *Classical Dictionary*. Sixth Edition, Corrected. 1806. There are no autograph or identification marks; but Sir Charles Dilke wrote on the end-paper that "Family tradition states that this was Keats's."

Note-book kept by Keats as a medical student.

Keats's copy of Livy's Roman History. On the title page is the signature "B. Bailey" and on the fly-leaf is the inscription "B. Bailey, Magdalen Hall, Oxon., presents this volume to his friend John Keats, July, 1818."

Keats's copy of the second volume of Burton's *Anatomy of Melancholy*, 2 vols., 11th Edition, Corrected. 1813. This volume was presented to Keats by Charles Brown. It has underlinings and annotations in Keats's handwriting.

Dilke's copy of *The Poetical Works of John Milton*. 1 vol. London, 1811. The volume is marked and annotated. At the beginning of the fourth book of *Paradise Lost* there is an annotation by Dilke, to which Keats refers in an annotation upon this book in his copy of *Paradise Lost*, the copy (listed above) which he gave to Mrs. Dilke.

Charles Cowden Clarke's copy of *The Works of Thomas Chatterton*, containing his Life by G. Gregory, D. D. and Miscellaneous Poems. London, 1803. It has been suggested that a copy of this edition may have been the one used by Keats.

VI

Facsimile of a page of Benjamin Robert Haydon's Journals, being a sketch for the portrait of Keats, introduced by the painter into his picture *Christ's Entry into Jerusalem*.

Facsimile of another page from Benjamin Robert Haydon's Journals, reproducing a sketch made by Keats.

Draft of "An Elegy on the Death of the Poet Keats" by "Barry Cornwall" (Bryan Waller Procter) in the handwriting of the author.

Locket containing a lock of Keats's hair, cut from the poet's head after his death, probably by Severn.

Plaster mask of Keats, probably made by Benjamin Robert Haydon during Keats's life.

Plaster bust of Keats, published by P. MacDowell, September 9, 1828. Done under the supervision of Fanny Brawne and Fanny Keats.

Reproduction in photogravure of a miniature portrait of Keats by Joseph Severn.

Collection of Frank B. Bemis, Esq., Boston, Mass.[1]

An autograph manuscript of *Lamia*, the fair copy prepared and revised for the press.

An autograph manuscript of the sonnet beginning "Come hither all sweet maidens soberly." Dated "March 181–," the last figure of the year being indecipherable.

Autograph manuscript of letter by Keats to Fanny Brawne, October 13, 1819.

Autograph manuscript of letter by Keats to Fanny Brawne, February 10, 1820.

Autograph manuscript of letter by Keats to Fanny Brawne, February 1820.

[1] I have compiled the items in this and the following private collections, which I have not had an opportunity to examine, from lists and descriptions in the following books: Miss Amy Lowell's *John Keats*; M. B. Forman's *The Letters of John Keats*; H. B. Forman's *The Complete Works of John Keats* (Variorum Edition); Miss C. F. E. Spurgeon's *Keats's Shakespeare*; and the *Catalogue of a Loan Exhibition Commemorating the Anniversary of the Death of John Keats (1821–1921). Held at the Public Library of the City of Boston February 21 to March 14 1921*. I cannot therefore vouch for the accuracy or the completeness of the items in these collections.

Autograph manuscript of letter by Keats to James Rice, February 16, 1820.

Autograph manuscript of letter by Keats to Benjamin Robert Haydon. Undated. Probably August 1820.

Autograph manuscript of letter by Tom Keats to Mary Anne Jeffrey, May [17], 1818.

Autograph manuscript of letter by Benjamin Robert Haydon to Edward Moxon, London, November 28, 1845. It contains copies of Keats's (Elgin Marbles) sonnets. Haydon says that he thinks that John Hamilton Reynolds went with him and Keats to see the Elgin Marbles.

Autograph manuscript of letter by Benjamin Robert Haydon to Edward Moxon, London, November 30, 1845. Haydon sends letters by Keats to himself for Richard Monckton Milnes's inspection.

Autograph manuscript of letter by Launcelot Archer to A. Forbes Sievekin (referring to Marianne Jeffrey).

A copy of *Endymion*, presented by Keats to Shelley.

A copy of the *Poems* of 1817, presented by Keats to Joseph Severn. Inscribed: "The Author consigns this copy to the Severn with all his heart."

A copy of the *Poems* of 1817, presented by Keats to Charles Wells. Inscribed: "From J. K. to his young friend Wells."

A copy of *Endymion*, owned by Charles Wells.

A copy of *Endymion*, owned by Benjamin Robert Haydon.

A copy of *Lamia, Isabella, etc.* (*Poems* of 1820), presented by Keats to Charles Lamb. Inscribed: "To Charles Lamb Esqr., with the Author's respeful comps."

Other copies of the three volumes of poems published by Keats.

Collection of Fred Holland Day, Esq., Norwood, Mass.

Transcript of letter by Keats to Charles Cowden Clarke, November 1816.

Autograph manuscript of letter by Keats to Fanny Brawne, February 4, 1820.

Autograph manuscript of letter by Keats to Fanny Brawne, February 24, 1820.

Transcript of letter by Keats to Mrs. Wylie, February 1820.

Tom Keats's Copy-book. This volume was given by Tom Keats to John Scott. It has been examined and described by H. B. Forman and Miss Lowell. It contains, among other things, transcripts by Tom Keats of several of Keats's early poems: "Specimen of an Induction to a Poem"; "Calidore"; "On receiving a curious shell"; "Imitation of Spenser"; "Sonnet to my Brother George"; "Sonnet to Solitude"; sonnet "Written to his brother Tom on his Birthday," dated "Nov. 18, 1816"; sonnet "Had I a man's fair form"; "Sonnet to a Lady [G. A. W.]," dated "Dec. 1816"; sonnet "Written in disgust of Vulgar Superstition," dated "Sunday Evening, Dec. 24, 1816"; sonnet "To Charles Wells on receiving a bunch of roses"; sonnet "On looking into Chapman's Homer," dated "1816"; and "Sonnet" beginning "Great Spirits now on earth are sojourning," dated "1816."

Autograph manuscript of letter by George Keats to Keats, January 30, 1820.

A manuscript memoir of Charles Brown by his son C. A. Brown.

Autograph manuscript of letter by Joseph Ritchie to Rev. Richard Garnett (referring to Keats).

A lock of hair cut from Keats's head by Fanny Brawne a short time before he left England for Italy.

A copy of the *Poems* of 1817, presented by Keats to Wordsworth. Inscribed: "To W. Wordsworth with the Author's sincere Reverence."

A copy of *Lamia, Isabella, etc.* (*Poems* of 1820), presented by Keats to William Hazlitt. Inscribed: "To Wm Hazlitt Esqre with the Author's sincere respects."

Other copies of the three volumes of poems published by Keats.

Autograph manuscript of letter by Charles Cowden Clarke to William Potter, November 18, 1851. Two pages. Answer to a request for Keats manuscripts.

Autograph manuscript of letter by Benjamin Robert Haydon to James Elmes. Four pages. About a new poem by Wordsworth and other literary matters.

Autograph manuscript of letter by John Taylor to John Nicholls. Sun Office, August 21, 1820. One page.

Collection of W. Van R. Whitall, Esq., New York

Richard Woodhouse's interleaved and annotated copy of *Endymion*.

Collection of James Freeman Clarke, Esq., Boston, Mass.

Autograph manuscript of the "Ode to Apollo" beginning "God of the Golden bow." At the bottom of the sheet is the inscription in the handwriting of George Keats: "Original manuscript of John Keats presented to Jas. Clarke, Esqr. G. Keats." The following note by the Rev. James Freeman Clarke refers to the manuscript: "John Keats. Original MSS. of his Ode to Apollo. Given to me by his brother, George Keats, in Louisville, Ky. This Ode was first printed by Monckton Milnes (Lord Houghton) from a copy made by me from this MSS. and sent to him." The Rev. James Freeman Clarke was a Unitarian minister in Louisville and Associate Editor of *The Western Messenger*, a monthly magazine "devoted to Religion and Literature." He published the "Ode to Apollo" in the magazine for May 1836 (Volume 1, p. 736).

Autograph manuscript of the letter by Keats to Thomas Keats, "Auchencairn, July 3d" (1818). The letter contains the song "Meg Merrilies" (66 verses). It is endorsed by Tom Keats: "Received 13 July. Answered 13 July, from John."

Collection of Mrs. Roland Gage Hopkins, Brookline, Mass.

Autograph manuscript of letter by Keats to Joseph Severn, postmarked "6 June, 1818."

Autograph manuscript of letter by Keats to Jane Reynolds, second half of September 1817. Printed by Miss Lowell, Volume I, pp. 493–494. It is not in M. B. Forman's edition of Keats's letters.

Collection of Dr. Roderick Terry, Newport, R. I.

Autograph manuscript of the poem "Hither, hither, love —."

Collection of Dr. E. Horner, London

A copy of the *Poems* of 1817, presented by Keats to Reynolds. Inscribed: "To J. H. Reynolds from his friend J. Keats." This volume was purchased in Leipzig by Dr. Horner's father from an English gentleman (it is believed a clergyman) in or about the year 1875. The volume contains two sonnets "On receiving a laurel crown from Leigh Hunt" and "To the Ladies who saw me crown'd" in Keats's handwriting on the blank page which immediately precedes the Sonnets. It contains also in Keats's handwriting the two sonnets "On Seeing the Elgin Marbles" and "To Haydon with a Sonnet on Seeing the Elgin Marbles" on the blank page at the end following *Sleep and Poetry*. The two laurel crown sonnets have been published in photograph in *The Times* for May 18, 1914, pp. 9–10. See also *The Times Literary Supplement* for May 21, 1914.

COLLECTION OF THOMAS J. WISE, ESQ., LONDON

Fragment of an autograph manuscript of *Otho the Great*, containing the first three acts and the first scene of the fourth act.

Autograph manuscript of letter by Keats to Leigh Hunt, May 10, 1817.

Autograph manuscript of letter by Keats to Fanny Keats, February 8, 1820.

COLLECTION OF MITCHELL KENNERLEY, ESQ., NEW YORK

Autograph manuscript of letter by Keats to Jane Reynolds, October 31, 1817.

COLLECTION OF MRS. JAMES B. MURPHY, NEW YORK

Fragment of the autograph manuscript of letter by Keats to Benjamin Bailey, November 5, 1817. The other half of the letter is in the Harvard College Library.

COLLECTION OF CARL H. PFORZHEIMER, ESQ., NEW YORK

Autograph manuscript of letter by Keats to George and Tom Keats, January 5, 1818.

COLLECTION IN THE VICTORIA AND ALBERT MUSEUM

Autograph manuscript of letter by Keats to Taylor and Hessey, February or March 1818.

Autograph manuscript of letter by Keats to Taylor and Hessey, March 23, 1818.

COLLECTION OF GEORGE ARMOUR, ESQ., PRINCETON, N. J.

Keats's copy of *The Dramatic Works of William Shakespeare*. Printed by C. Whittingham, Chiswick, 1814. Seven volumes. Inscribed in both of the first two volumes: "John Keats, April 1817." Markings and a few annotations.

COLLECTION OF DR. ROSENBACH, NEW YORK

Autograph manuscript of letter by Keats to Miss Jeffrey, May 31, 1819.

Fragment of the autograph manuscript of letter by Keats to Georgiana Keats, January 13, 1820.

COLLECTION OF A. EDWARD NEWTON, ESQ., PHILADELPHIA

Autograph manuscript of letter by Keats to Fanny Brawne, September 13, 1819.

Autograph manuscript of letter by Keats to Fanny Brawne, March 1820.

WATSON COLLECTION OF MSS., SCOTTISH NATIONAL PORTRAIT GALLERY

Autograph manuscript of letter by Keats to Charles Cowden Clarke, March 26, 1817.

COLLECTION OF MRS. C. QUARITCH WRENTMORE

Autograph manuscript of letter by Keats to Horace Smith, February 19, 1818.

COLLECTION OF PROFESSOR EDWARD BURGESS, NEW YORK UNIVERSITY

Autograph manuscript of letter by George Keats to Marianne and Sarah Jeffrey, March 1818.

Transcript of a letter by John Hamilton Reynolds to Keats, October 14, 1818.

Collection of W. A. White, Esq., Brooklyn, N. Y.

A copy of the proof sheets of *Lamia*, corrected by Richard Woodhouse.

Collection of Lucius Wilmerding, Esq., New York

A copy of the *Poems* of 1817, presented by Keats and his brother George to Georgiana Augusta Wylie.

A copy of *Palmerin of England*, 5 vols. London, 1817. Marked by Keats.

Collection of William M. Elkins, Esq., Philadelphia

A copy of the *Poems* of 1817, presented by Keats to Thomas Richards. Inscribed: "From the author to his Friend, Thos. Richards." This copy contains transcripts of the two sonnets by Leigh Hunt "On receiving a Crown of Ivy from John Keats," and a sonnet addressed to Keats and probably composed by Charles Ollier.

Collection in the Authors' Club, New York

A copy of *The Rogve: or, The Life of Guzman de Alfarache.* Written in Spanish by Matheo Aleman. The Third Edition Corrected. London, 1634. At the top of the page of dedication is the inscription in James Rice's handwriting: "Purchased by me A. D. 1819 — and given to John Keats and upon his death 1821 — returned to me. Rice." On the top margin of the first page of the book proper is the inscription in Rice's handwriting: "John Keats From his Friend J^s Rxxx 20th April 1818."

Collection of Oliver R. Barrett, Esq., Chicago

Keats's passport to Italy.

Miscellaneous Manuscripts

These manuscripts have been examined and described by H. B. Forman, Sir Sidney Colvin, Ernest de Sélincourt, and other scholars. They are now in the possession of unknown private collectors.

Autograph manuscript of *Endymion*, containing the revised first draft of the first book and a fair copy of the second, third, and fourth books. This manuscript remained in the possession of the Taylor family until 1897, when it was sold at auction. The first draft of the last three books of the romance was examined by Richard Woodhouse, but it has not been reported by any later scholar. (H. B. Forman.)

The manuscript of the rejected Preface to *Endymion*, attached to the rejected title page and dedication (the whole consisting of six quarto leaves evidently detached from the manuscript of *Endymion* above), was formerly in the collection of Dr. John Webster, M.P. for Aberdeen. (H. B. Forman.)

Autograph manuscript of the *Ode to Psyche*. Formerly owned by Townley Green. (H. B. Forman.)

Autograph manuscript of the lines "Unfelt, unheard, unseen" and the *Ode to Apollo* ("God of the golden bow"). Formerly owned by Townley Green. (H. B. Forman.)

A fragment of the original autograph manuscript of *The Pot of Basil*, containing stanzas XXX to XL, exclusive of stanza XXXII, was formerly possessed by a Mr. R. A. Potts. (H. B. Forman.)

Keats's copy of Cary's translation of Dante's *Divine Comedy*, 3 vols. Printed for Taylor and Hessey. London, 1814. It contains the autograph of the sonnet *As Hermes once* and Fanny Brawne's transcript of the sonnet *Bright star!* This copy was given by Keats to Fanny Brawne. Owned and described by H. B. Forman.

Autograph manuscript of *In drear-nighted December*, once possessed by a Mr. Charles Law. (H. B. Forman.)

Autograph manuscript of verses 1–96 of *I stood tip-toe upon a little hill.* (H. B. Forman.)

Autograph manuscript of the last twelve verses of *I stood tip-toe upon a little hill.* The manuscript is dated "Dec. 18," thus giving the exact date on which Keats completed the poem. The manuscript is listed and printed in the catalogue of John Grant, bookseller, Edinburgh, for May 1933. Marginal inscription: "John Keats MS. Charles Cowden Clarke."

Autograph manuscript of the sonnet *On leaving some Friends at an early Hour.* (H. B. Forman.)

A scrap-book containing autograph manuscripts of three of Keats's poems. It was lent to H. B. Forman by a Mr. Sabin of 118 Shaftesbury Avenue, London.

1. Autograph manuscript of the sonnet *The day is gone.* Reproduced in photograph by H. B. Forman in *The Bookman* for October 1906.
2. Autograph manuscript of the sonnet *To Spenser.* Reproduced in photograph by H. B. Forman in *The Bookman* for October 1906.
3. A leaf of an autograph manuscript of *The Eve of St. Mark.* It contains 16 verses in Middle English which are not in the autograph manuscript in George Keats's Book of Autographs and Transcripts (British Museum Collection) but which are in Woodhouse's transcript in his Book of Transcripts (Houghton-Crewe Collection). Reproduced in photograph by H. B. Forman in *The Bookman* for October 1906.

A few leaves torn from a pocket note-book (preserved by Joseph Severn), containing the autograph first draft of the sonnet *To my Brother George* and an autograph draft of two quatrains of the sonnet *To my Brothers.*

Autograph manuscript of *Robin Hood* together with a manuscript of Shelley's sonnet *To the Nile.* Discovered by S. R. Townshend Mayer among Leigh Hunt's manuscripts. Examined and described by H. B. Forman.

Autograph manuscript of the sonnet *Blue! 'Tis the life of heaven — the domain.* Published in photograph in *The Century Guild Hobby Horse* for July 1886. The manuscript was given to Oscar Wilde by Mrs. Speed, daughter of George Keats.

Richard Woodhouse's interleaved and annotated copy of the *Poems* of 1817. Examined by Ernest de Sélincourt when it was in the possession of a Mr. Bourdillon.

George Keats's Scrap-book. Formerly owned and described by H. B. Forman as follows: "A curious volume originally used for writing fair copies of poems in — poems from various hands. At a later stage it was converted into a scrap-book — newspaper cuttings and other curiosities being stuck over pages of George Keats's writing; and in one part several of George's copies from John's poems are inserted, having at their head the autograph manuscript of the sonnet to Mrs. George Keats (when Miss Wylie), whom I suppose to have been the owner of the book, seeing that it contains among its curiosities the original parchment commission of James Wylie, as adjutant of the Fifeshire Regiment of Fencible Infantry, signed by George III. in 1794."

Henry Stephens' Copy-book. It contains transcripts, made by Stephens in 1828, of all the poems which Keats published in his *Poems* of 1817 and eight unpublished poems, including the sonnet *Before he went to feed with owls and bats* and the *Sonnet Written in Disgust of Vulgar Superstition* (with note: "written by J. K. in 15 minutes"). (H. B. Forman.)

A copy of the *Poems* of 1817, containing a manuscript sonnet addressed to Keats and probably composed by Charles Ollier. (H. B. Forman.)

A number of Keats's letters, especially those to Fanny Brawne, were transcribed by H. B. Forman from autograph manuscripts which are now dispersed in unknown private collections.

Autograph manuscript of Benjamin Robert Haydon's Journals. Examined by H. B. Forman, who transcribed two or three of Keats's letters from autograph manuscripts and a few passages of Haydon's recollections of Keats. The Journals were edited by Tom Taylor with omissions and alterations and published in 1853. The original manuscript of the Journals is now lost.

Autograph manuscripts of letters by Keats:
1. To Mrs. Jeffrey, May 1818; 2. To the Misses M. and S. Jeffrey, June 4, 1818; and 3. To Miss Jeffrey, June 9, 1819. Formerly in the possession of A. Forbes Sieveking, Esq. Published in *The Fortnightly Review* for December 1893. (M. B. Forman.)

Autograph manuscript of letter by Keats to his sister Fanny Keats, written on the second page of a letter by Mrs. Dilke to Fanny Keats, dated from Wentworth Place on December 18, 1818. Described and printed by M. B. Forman in *The Times Literary Supplement* for Thursday, October 4, 1934.

Autograph manuscript of letter by Keats to his sister Fanny Keats, Wednesday, March 31, 1819. Keats gave his sister answers to questions which the parson had asked her. This letter shows that Keats had been well instructed in the Anglican Catechism. Described and printed by M. B. Forman in *The Times Literary Supplement* for Thursday, October 4, 1934.

Manuscript of letter by Keats to his sister Fanny Keats, Monday, September 11, 1820. This letter was written by Fanny Brawne from Keats's dictation. Described and printed in *The Times Literary Supplement* for Thursday, October 4, 1934.

LIST OF BOOKS REFERRED TO IN THE TEXT

I

John Keats. *Poems*. London: Printed for C. & J. Ollier, 3 Welbeck Street, Cavendish Square. 1817. Republished in exact facsimile by Noel Douglas, 38 Great Ormond Street, London, W. C. 1927.

John Keats. *Endymion*. A Poetic Romance. London: Printed for Taylor and Hessey, 93 Fleet Street. 1818. Republished in type facsimile, with introduction and notes by H. C. Notcutt. London: Humphrey Milford. 1927.

John Keats. *Lamia, Isabella, The Eve of St. Agnes, and other Poems*. London: Printed for Taylor and Hessey, Fleet Street. 1820. Republished in exact facsimile by Noel Douglas, 38 Great Ormond Street, London, W. C. 1927.

Richard Monckton Milnes. *Life, Letters, and Literary Remains of John Keats*. In Two Volumes. London: Edward Moxon, Dover Street. 1848.

Bibliographical and Historical Miscellanies of the Philobiblon Society (1856–57). Richard Monckton Milnes contributed "Hyperion, a Vision" or "Another Version of Keats's 'Hyperion' " to the third volume of these *Miscellanies*. A few copies of the poem were also printed in pamphlet form apart from the *Miscellanies*.

Lord Houghton (Richard Monckton Milnes). *The Life and Letters of John Keats*. A New Edition. In One Volume. London: Moxon & Co., Dover Street. 1867. An appendix contains "Hyperion, a Vision."

Lord Houghton. *The Poetical Works of John Keats*. Chronologically arranged and edited, with memoir. London: George Bell and Sons. 1876. Aldine Edition.

Harry Buxton Forman. *The Poetical Works and other Writings of John Keats*. Now first brought together, including poems and numerous letters not before published.

Edited, with notes and appendices. Four Volumes. London: Reeves & Turner. 1883. Reissued in 1889. Library Edition.

Harry Buxton Forman. *The Complete Works of John Keats.* Five Volumes. Glasgow: Gowans & Gray. 1900–01. Variorum Edition.

Harry Buxton Forman. *The Poetical Works of John Keats.* With an Introduction and Textual Notes. Oxford: At the Clarendon Press. MCMVI. "Oxford Keats."

W. T. Arnold. *The Poetical Works of John Keats.* London: Kegan Paul, Trench, & Co. MDCCCLXXXIIII.

G. Thorn Drury. *Poems of John Keats.* With an Introduction by Robert Bridges. Two Volumes. London: Lawrence & Bullen. 1896. New York: Charles Scribner's Sons. 1896. Muses' Library Edition.

Sidney Colvin. *Letters of John Keats to his Family and Friends.* London: Macmillan & Co. 1891.

Sidney Colvin. *The Poems of John Keats in Chronological Order.* Two Volumes. London: The Florence Press, Chatto & Windus. 1917. New York: Brentano's. 1917.

Ernest de Sélincourt. *The Poems of John Keats.* London: Methuen & Co., Ltd. 1905. Fourth Edition, Revised, 1921. Fifth Edition, 1926.

Ernest de Sélincourt. *Hyperion.* A Facsimile of Keats's Autograph Manuscript. With a Transliteration of the Manuscript of *The Fall of Hyperion, a Dream.* With Introductions and Notes. Oxford: At the Clarendon Press. 1905.

J. Middleton Murry. *John Keats: Poems and Verses.* Edited and Arranged in Chronological Order. Two Volumes. London: The King's Printers. 1930. New York: Viking Press. 1930.

The Keats Letters Papers and other Relics forming the Dilke Bequest in the Hampstead Public Library. Reproduced in fifty-eight collotype facsimiles, edited with full transcriptions and notes, and an account of the portraits of Keats, by George C. Williamson, Litt. D., together with forewords by Theodore Watts-Dunton, an Introduction by H. Buxton Forman, C. B., and fourteen portraits of Keats. London: John Lane, The Bodley Head. MCMXIV.

Maurice Buxton Forman. *The Letters of John Keats.* A New Edition, with Additional Letters. Two Volumes. Oxford: University Press. 1931.

II

Charles Cowden Clarke. "Recollections of Keats," *Atlantic Monthly* for January 1861.

Charles Cowden Clarke. "Recollections of Keats," *Gentleman's Magazine* for February 1874.

Charles and Mary Clarke. *Recollections of Writers.* London: Sampson Low. 1878.

Benjamin Ward Richardson. "An Esculapian Poet—John Keats." *The Asclepiad,* A Book of Original Research and Observation. Published quarterly. London. April 1884.

Walter Cooper Dendy. *The Philosophy of Mystery.* London: Longmans. 1841.

William Sharp. *The Life and Letters of Joseph Severn.* London: Sampson Low. 1892.

Leigh Hunt. *Lord Byron and Some of his Contemporaries.* With Recollections of the Author's Life, and of his Visit to Italy. London: Colburn. 1828. Second Edition. In Two Volumes. London: Colburn. 1828.

Leigh Hunt. *Imagination and Fancy.* Or Selections from the English Poets. Illustrative of these First Requisites of their Art; with Markings of the best Passages, Critical Notices of the Writings, and an Essay in Answer to the Question, "What is Poetry?" London: Smith Elder and Co. 1844. Third Edition. 1852.

Leigh Hunt. *Autobiography.* With Reminiscences of Friends and Contemporaries. In Three Volumes. London: Smith, Elder and Co. 1850. New York: Harper & Brothers. 1850.

The Correspondence of Leigh Hunt. Edited by his Eldest Son. In Two Volumes. London: Smith, Elder & Co. MDCCCLXII.

Tom Taylor. *Life of Benjamin Robert Haydon, Historical Painter, from his Autobiography and Journals.* In Three Volumes. London: Longmans. 1853. Second Edition. 1853.

Frederick Wordsworth Haydon. *Benjamin Robert Haydon: Correspondence and Table-Talk.* With a Memoir by his Son. With Facsimiles and Illustrations from his Journals. In Two Volumes. London: Chatto and Windus. 1876.

The Papers of a Critic. Selected from the Writings of the Late Charles Wentworth Dilke. With a Biographical Sketch by his Grandson, Sir Charles Wentworth Dilke, Bart., M.P. In Two Volumes. London: Murray. 1875.

Matthew Arnold. *On the Study of Celtic Literature.* London: Smith, Elder and Co. 1867.

Matthew Arnold. "John Keats." Ward's English Poets, Volume IV, pp. 427–437. London: Macmillan and Co. 1880. Republished in *Essays in Criticism,* Second Series. London: Macmillan and Co. 1893.

Sidney Colvin. *Keats.* London: Macmillan and Co. 1887. "English Men of Letters" Series.

Sidney Colvin. *John Keats, His Life and Poetry, His Friends, Critics, and After-Fame.* London: Macmillan & Co. 1917. New York: Charles Scribner's Sons. 1917.

Robert Bridges. *John Keats, A Critical Essay.* London: Privately Printed. 1895.

Johannes Hoops. *Keats' Jugend und Jugendgedichte.* Sonderabdruck aus Englische Studien XXI. Band, 2. Heft 1895.

Johannes Hoops. *Keats' Hyperion.* Heidelberg: No date. Introduction, dated London, 1898.

W. T. Read. *Keats and Spenser.* Heidelberg: Printed by E. Geisendörfer. 1897.

The John Keats Memorial Volume. Edited by G. C. Williamson. London and New York: John Lane. 1921. Contents:
- E. de Sélincourt: "The Warton Lecture on Keats."
- Lascelles Abercrombie: "The Second Version of *Hyperion.*"
- Frederick S. Boas: "On first looking into Chapman's *Homer.*"
- A. C. Bradley: "Keats and 'Philosophy.'"
- A. Clutton-Brock: "Keats and Shelley — A Contrast."
- Sidney Colvin: "A Morning's Work in a Hampstead Garden."
- Beatrice Harraden: "The Manuscript of Keats's *Hyperion.*"
- Amy Lowell: "The Lost Letter of Keats, September 22nd, 1819."
- Arthur Lynch: "John Keats."
- T. Fairman Ordish: "The Fulfilment of Keats."
- George C. Williamson: "The Keats Letters, Papers, and other Relics forming the Dilke Bequest at Hampstead."
- Thomas Wise: "A Bibliography of the Writings of John Keats."

Raymond D. Havens. *The Influence of Milton on English Poetry.* Cambridge (Mass.): Harvard University Press. 1922.

Amy Lowell. *John Keats.* With Illustrations. Two Volumes. Boston and New York: Houghton Mifflin Co. 1925.

J. Middleton Murry. *Keats and Shakespeare.* A Study of Keats's Life from 1816–1820. Oxford: University Press. 1925.

J. Middleton Murry. *Studies in Keats.* Oxford. 1930.

H. W. Garrod. *Keats.* Oxford: At the Clarendon Press. 1926.

Clarence Dewitt Thorpe. *The Mind of John Keats.* New York: Oxford University Press. 1926.

Caroline F. E. Spurgeon. *Keats's Shakespeare.* A Descriptive Study Based on New Material. Oxford: University Press. 1928.

Floyd Dell. "Keats's Debt to Robert Burton." *The Bookman* (New York), Vol. LXVII (1928), pp. 13–17.

Earle Vonard Weller. *Keats and Mary Tighe*. The poems of Mary Tighe with parallel passages from the work of John Keats. New York: The Century Co. for the Modern Language Association of America. MCMXXVIII.

A. W. Crawford. *The Genius of Keats*. An Interpretation. London: Arthur H. Stockwell, Ltd., 29 Ludgate Hill, E. C. 4. 1932.

Roberta D. Cornelius. "Two Early Reviews of Keats's First Volume." *Publications of The Modern Language Association*. Vol. XL (March 1925), pp. 193–210.

Arthur Beatty. *William Wordsworth. His Doctrine and Art in their Historical Relations*. University of Wisconsin Studies in Language and Literature. Number 24. Second Edition. Madison. 1927.

H. M. MacCracken. "The Source of Keats's *Eve of St. Agnes*." *Modern Philology*. Vol. V.

Edmund Blunden. *Leigh Hunt, A Biography*. London. 1930.

Edmund Blunden. *Leigh Hunt's "Examiner" Examined*. Comprising some account of that celebrated newspaper's contents, etc., 1805–25, and selections by or concerning Leigh Hunt, Lamb, Keats, Shelley, and Byron, illustrating the literary history of that time, for the most part previously unprinted. London: Cobden-Sanderson. 1928.

Grace Warren Landrum. "More concerning Chapman's Homer and Keats." *Publications of the Modern Language Association*. Vol. XLII (December 1927), pp. 986–1009.

George L. Marsh and Newman I. White. "Keats and the Periodicals of His Time." *Modern Philology*. Vol. XXXII, pp. 37–53.

John L. Lowes. "*La Belle Dame sans Merci* and Dante." *London Times Literary Supplement*, for May 3, 1934, p. 322.

John H. Birss and Louis A. Holman. "Unlocated Letters of John Keats." *Notes and Queries*. Vol. CLXVI, p. 7.

John H. Birss. "A new Fragment of a Keats Letter." *Notes and Queries*. Vol. CLXVI, pp. 257–258.

Maurice Buxton Forman. "New Keats Letters." *London Times Literary Supplement* for October 4, 1934, p. 670. Three letters: 1. A letter by Keats to his sister Fanny Keats on the second page of a letter by Mrs. Dilke to Fanny Keats on December 18, 1818. 2. A letter by Keats to his sister Fanny Keats on March 31, 1819. 3. A letter by Keats to his sister Fanny Keats on September 11, 1820. The letter was written by Fanny Brawne from Keats's dictation.

Douglas Bush. "Notes on Keats's Reading." *Publications of the Modern Language Association*. Vol. L (September 1935), pp. 785–806.

H. W. Garrod. "Keats and 'Miss Mary F—'." *The Times Literary Supplement* for September 5, 1935. This article was published after the text of this book was already set up in page form, and so I could only refer to it in a footnote. I made the discovery announced in this article six years ago and wrote it up in this book as a new discovery. I am indebted to Mr. Garrod however for the interpretation of the shorthand inscription after the title of the song "To Emma" in Woodhouse's Book of Transcripts.

INDEX

INDEX